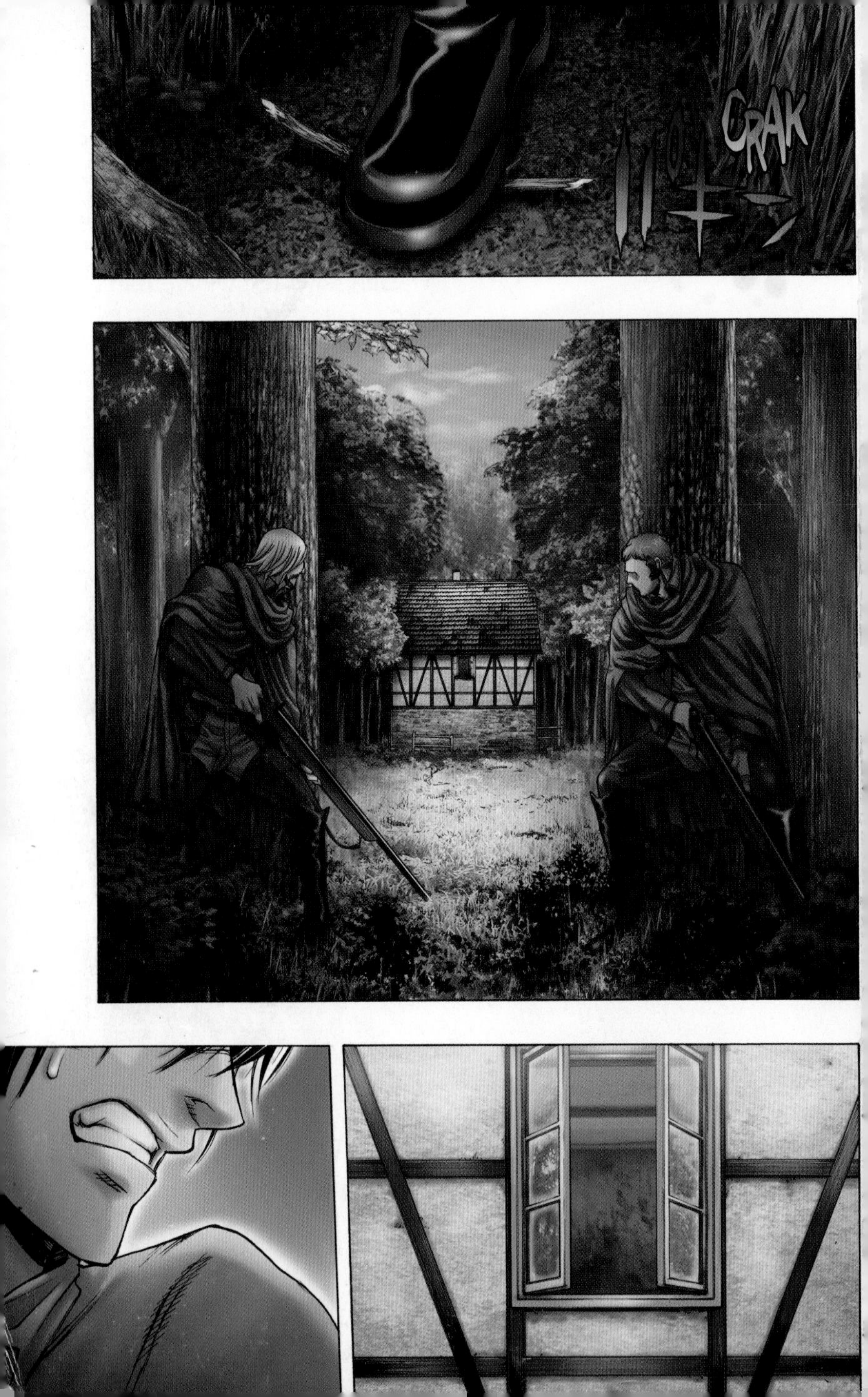
CRAK

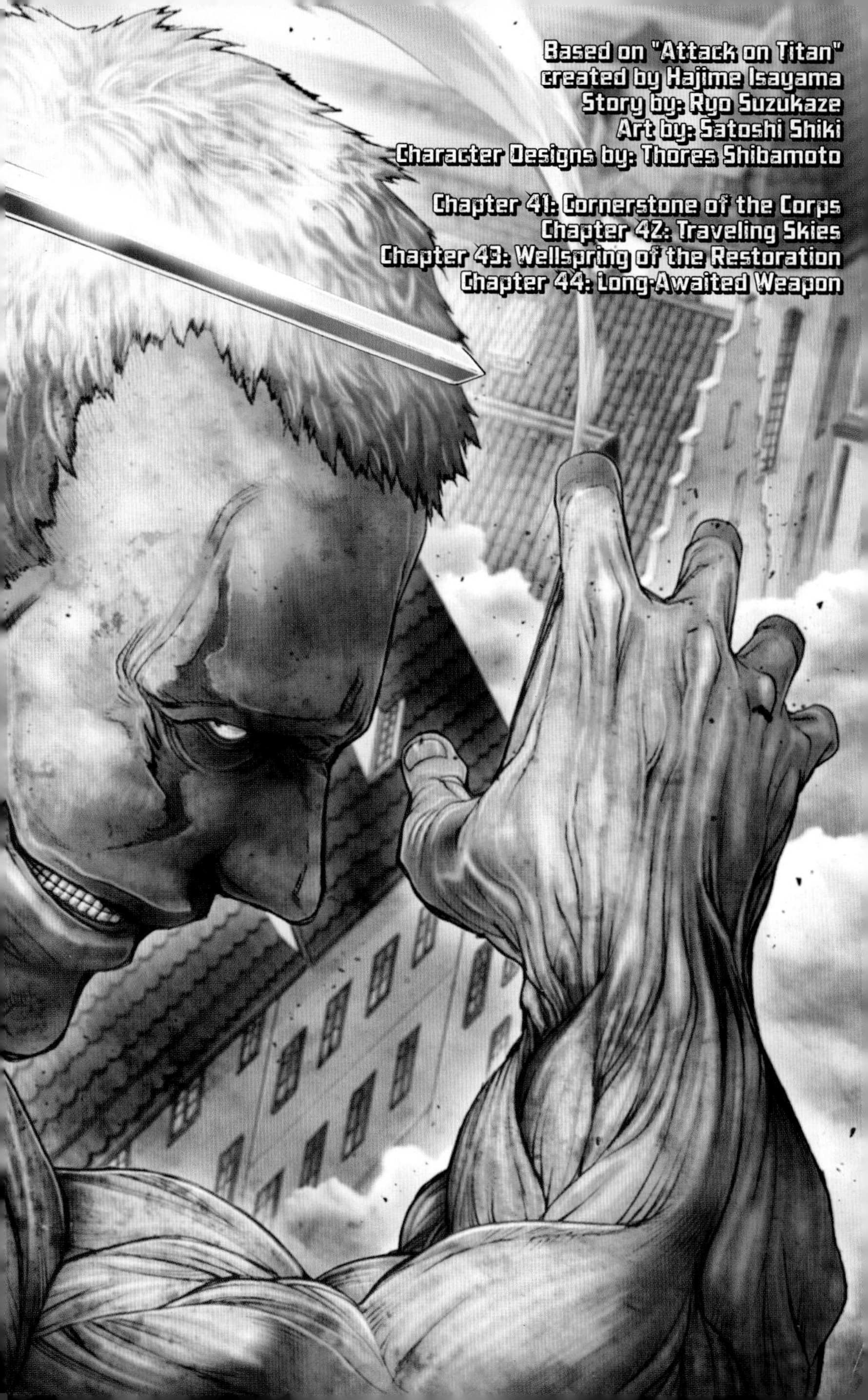
Based on "Attack on Titan"
created by Hajime Isayama
Story by: Ryo Suzukaze
Art by: Satoshi Shiki
Character Designs by: Thores Shibamoto
Chapter 41: Cornerstone of the Corps
Chapter 42: Traveling Skies
Chapter 43: Wellspring of the Restoration
Chapter 44: Long-Awaited Weapon

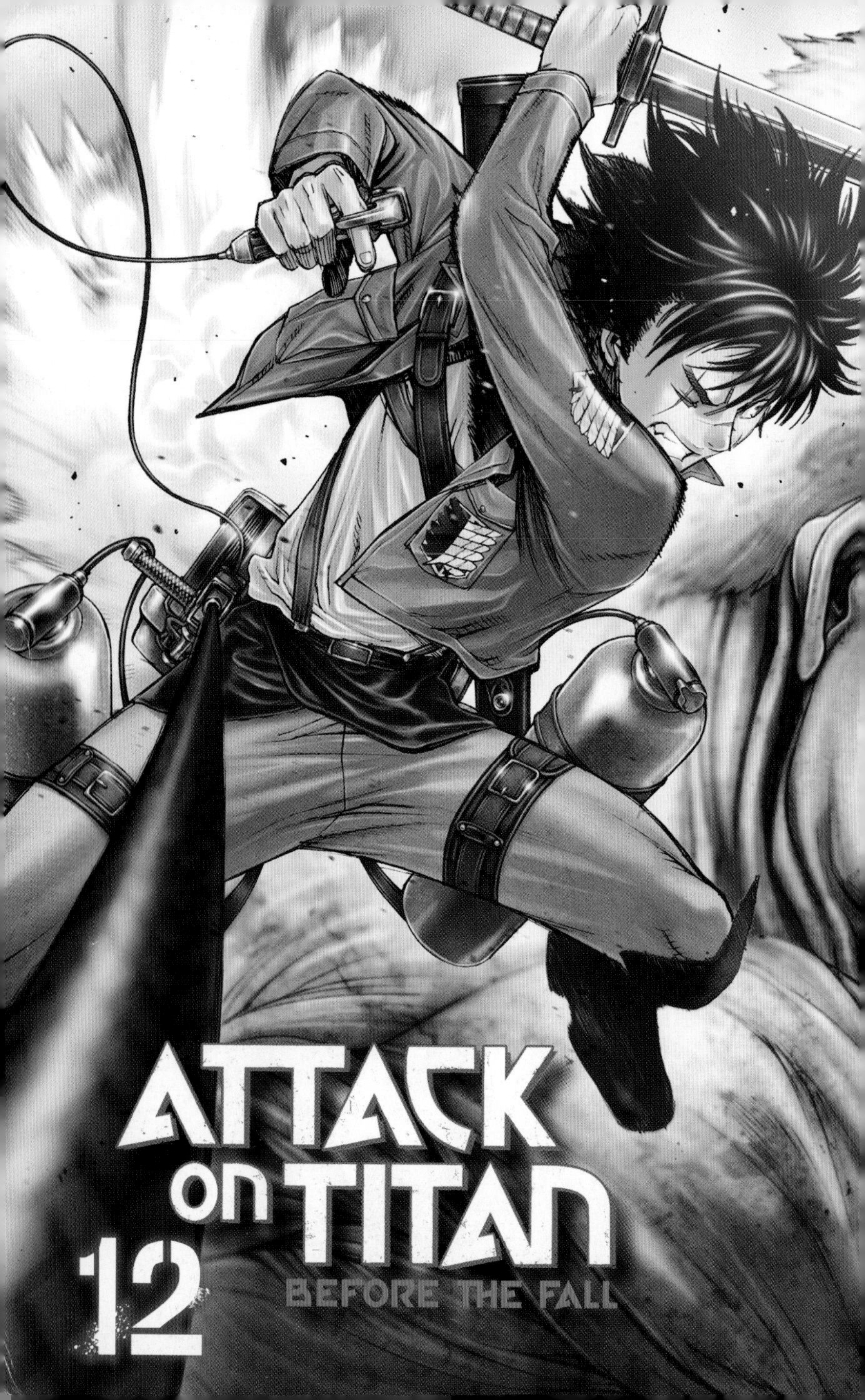
ATTACK
on TITAN
12
BEFORE THE FALL

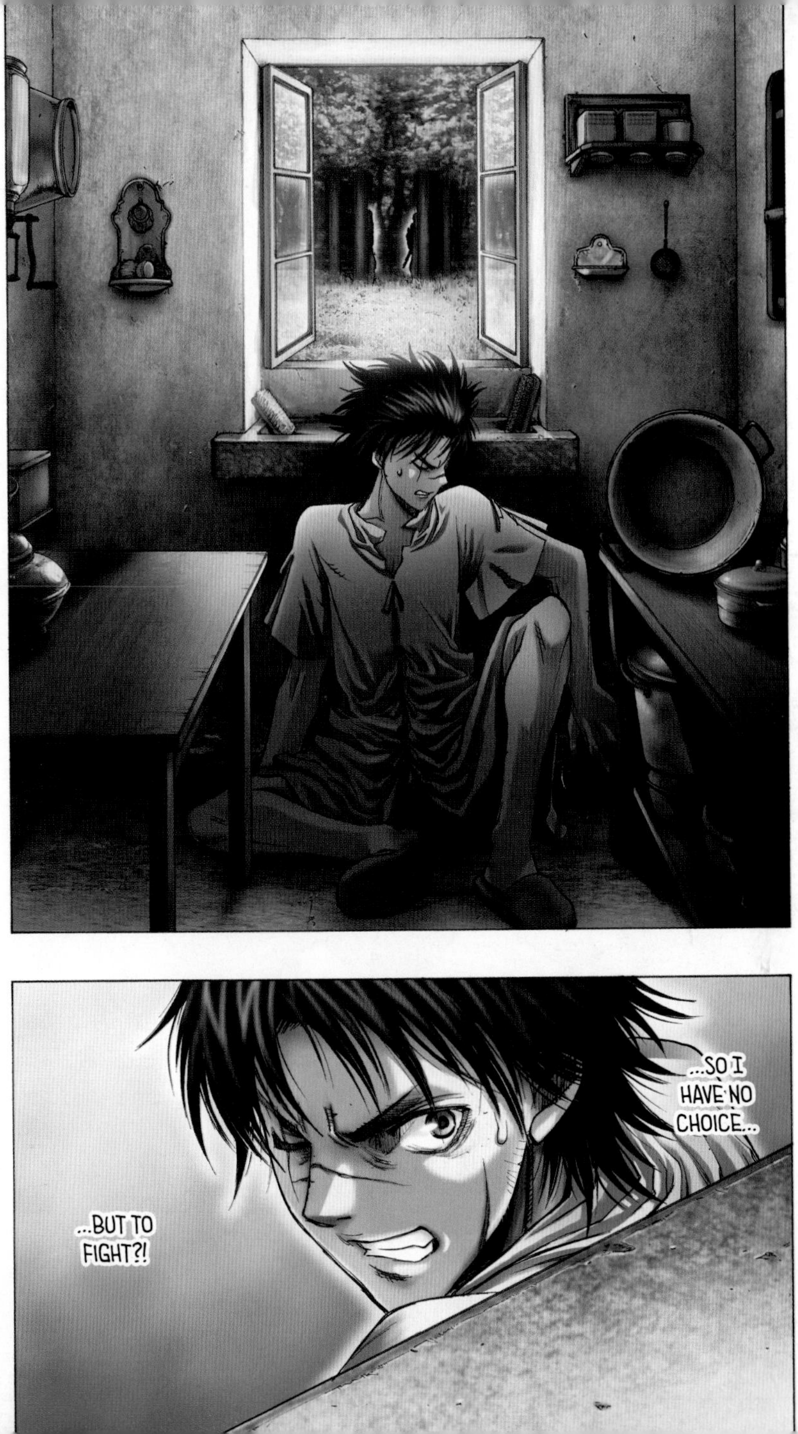
...SO I HAVE NO CHOICE...
...BUT TO FIGHT?!

Before the Fall Character Profiles

Kuklo

A 15-year-old boy born from a dead body packed into the vomit of a Titan, which earned him the moniker, "Titan's Son." He is fascinated with the Device as a means to defeat the Titans. Xavi defeated him in battle and left him for dead, until Rosa's group found and rescued him.

Sharle Inocencio

First daughter of the Inocencios, a rich merchant family within Wall Sheena. When she realized that Kuklo was a human, she taught him to speak and learn. She escaped her family home and went into the underground ward in search of Angel, inventor of the Device.

Cardina Baumeister

Kuklo's first friend in the outside world, and his companion in developing the Device.

Carlo Pikale

Jorge's son and current captain of the Survey Corps. After they battled Titans together, he has great respect for Kuklo.

Jorge Pikale

Training Corps instructor. A former Survey Corps captain who was hailed as a hero for defeating a Titan.

Xavi Inocencio

Head of the Inocencio family and Sharle's brother. Member of the Military Police in Shiganshina District.

Rosa Carlstead

The daughter of Maria and Sorum, Angel's longtime friends. She's in training now, hoping to enter the Survey Corps.

Angel Aaltonen

A former inventor who developed a tool to fight the Titans 15 years ago, known simply as "The Device."

When a Titan terrorized Shiganshina District and left behind a pile of vomit, a baby boy was miraculously born of a pregnant corpse. This boy was named Kuklo, the "Titan's Son," and treated as a sideshow freak. Eventually the wealthy merchant Dario Inocencio bought Kuklo to serve as a punching bag for his son, Xavi. On the other hand, when she learned he was human and not the son of a Titan, Xavi's sister Sharle decided to teach him the words and knowledge of humanity instead. Two years later, Kuklo escaped from the mansion along with Sharle, who was being forced into a marriage she did not desire.

In Shiganshina District, the Survey Corps was preparing for its first expedition outside of the wall in 15 years. Kuklo snuck into the expedition's cargo wagon, but the Titan they ran across was far worse of a monster than he expected. He helped the Survey Corps survive, but inside the walls he was greeted by the Military Police, who wanted the "Titan's Son" on charges of murdering Dario. In prison, he met Cardina, a young man jailed over political squabbles. They hoped to escape to safety when exiled beyond the Wall, but found themselves surrounded by a pack of Titans. It was through the help of Jorge, former Survey Corps Captain and first human to defeat a Titan, that the two boys escaped with their lives. The equipment that Jorge used was the very "Device" that was the key to defeating the Titan those 15 years ago. Kuklo and Cardina escaped the notice of the MPs by hiding in the Industrial City, where they found Sharle. It is there that the three youngsters learned the truth of the ill-fated Titan-capturing expedition 15 years earlier, and swore to uphold the will of Angel, the inventor of the Device.

Next, Kuklo and Cardina headed back to Shiganshina to test out a new model of the Device developed by Xenophon, Angel's friend and rival, but while they were gone, a rebellion by anti-establishment dissidents broke out in the Industrial City. Kuklo was able to slip through the chaos to rescue Sharle from the dissidents. But just as they started to celebrate their reunion, Sharle's brother Xavi arrived, and turned his sword on Kuklo. Xavi won the battle by inflicting a grievous blow on Kuklo, who fell into the river and washed up downstream, where Rosa and her companions found him. Sharle was taken back to the Inocencio mansion, but following her belief that Kuklo was still alive, she escaped and headed underground to find Angel, whom she convinced to help improve the Device. Meanwhile, the Military Police were closing in on Kuklo's hideout in the woods, looking for remnants of the dissident movement.

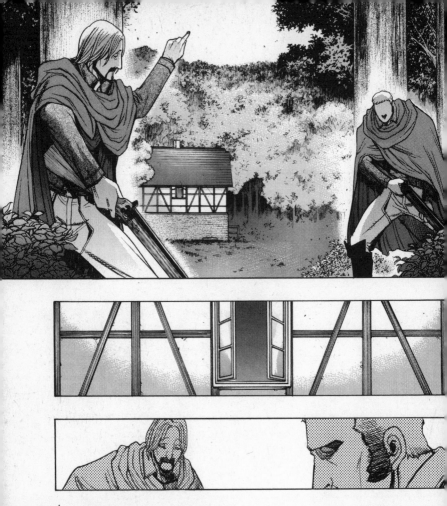

HEY!
WHAT ARE
YOU GUYS
DOING OVER
THERE?!

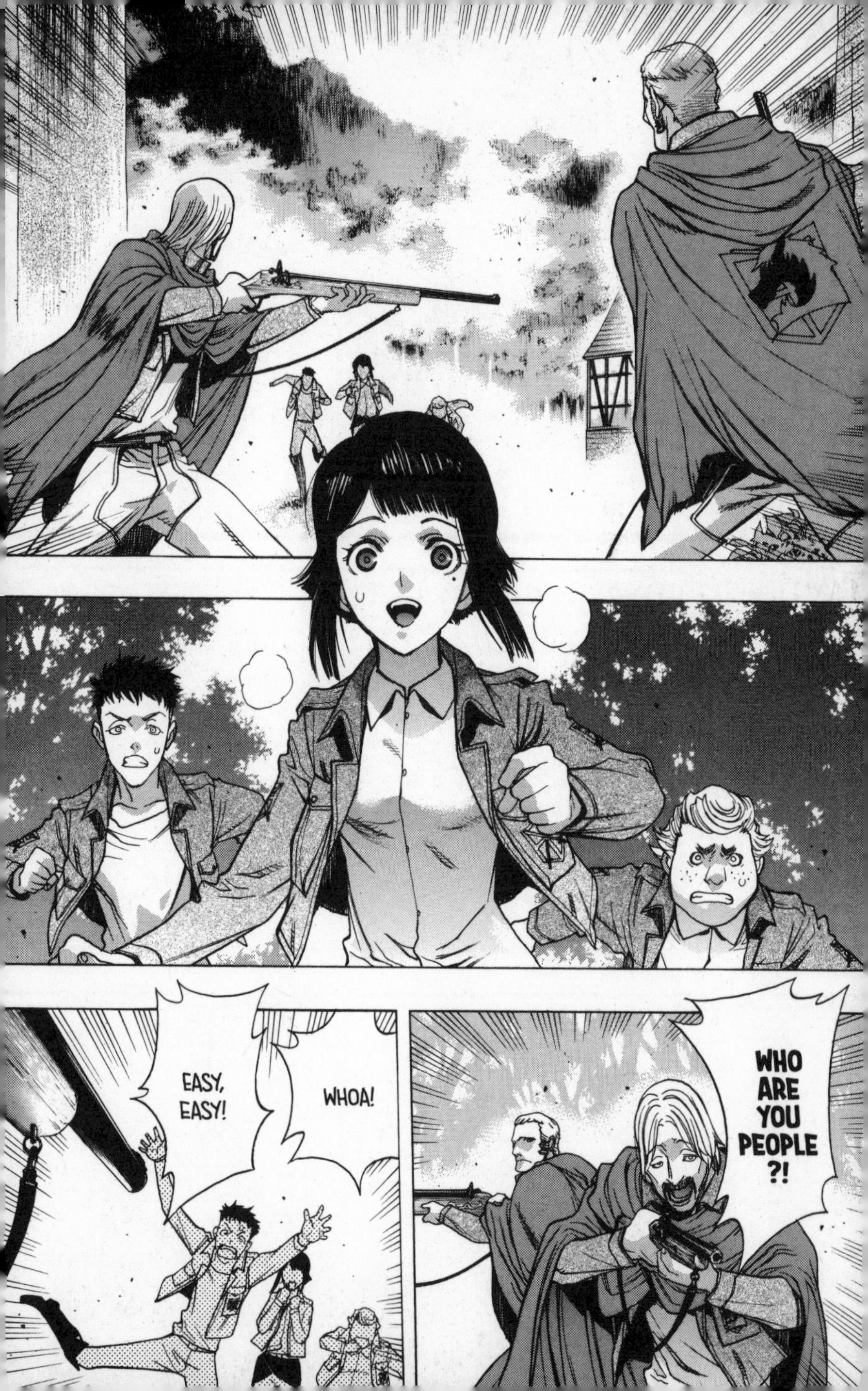
WHO ARE YOU PEOPLE?!
WHOA!
EASY, EASY!

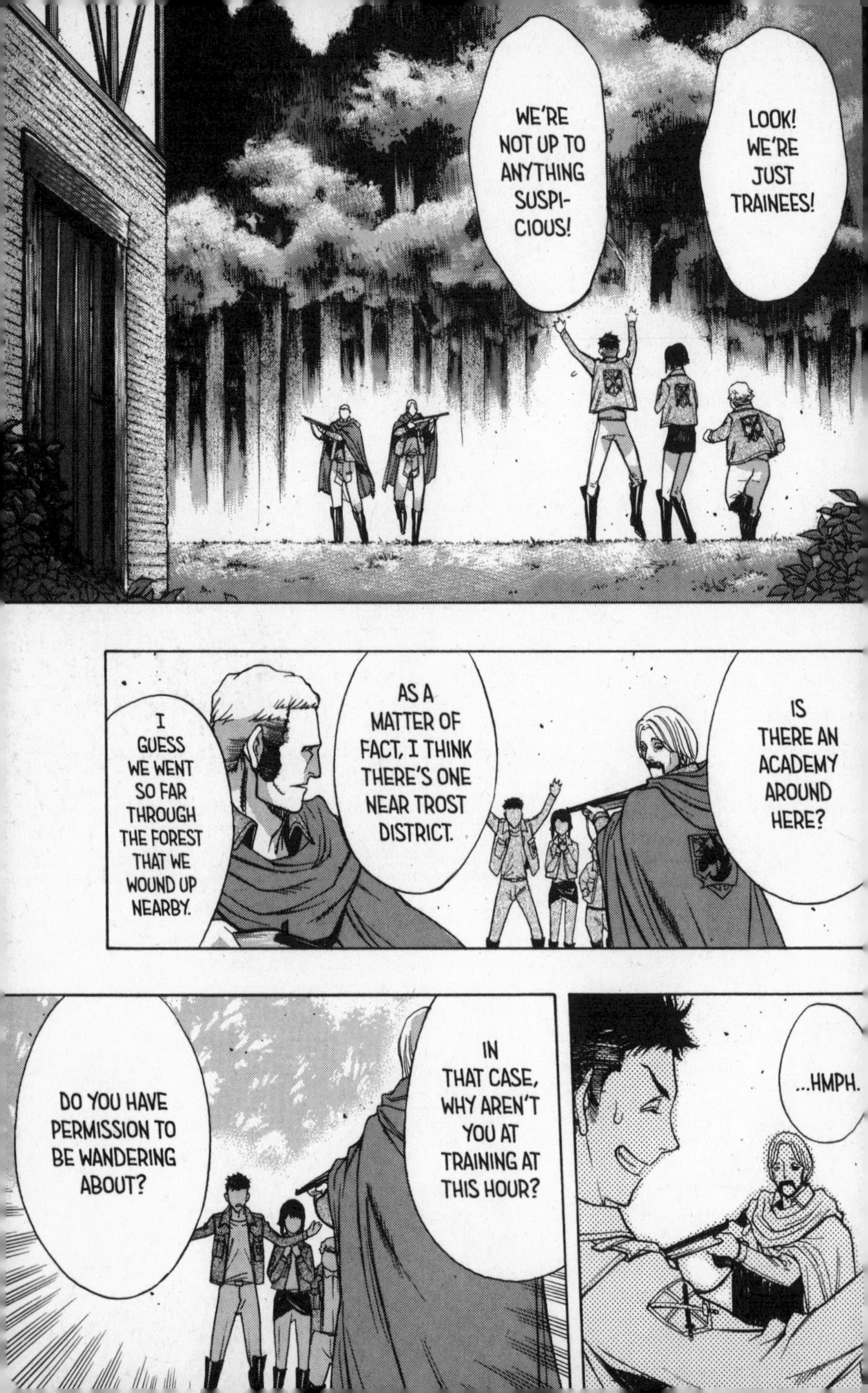
LOOK! WE'RE JUST TRAINEES!
WE'RE NOT UP TO ANYTHING SUSPICIOUS!
IS THERE AN ACADEMY AROUND HERE?
AS A MATTER OF FACT, I THINK THERE'S ONE NEAR TROST DISTRICT.
I GUESS WE WENT SO FAR THROUGH THE FOREST THAT WE WOUND UP NEARBY.
...HMPH.
IN THAT CASE, WHY AREN'T YOU AT TRAINING AT THIS HOUR?
DO YOU HAVE PERMISSION TO BE WANDERING ABOUT?

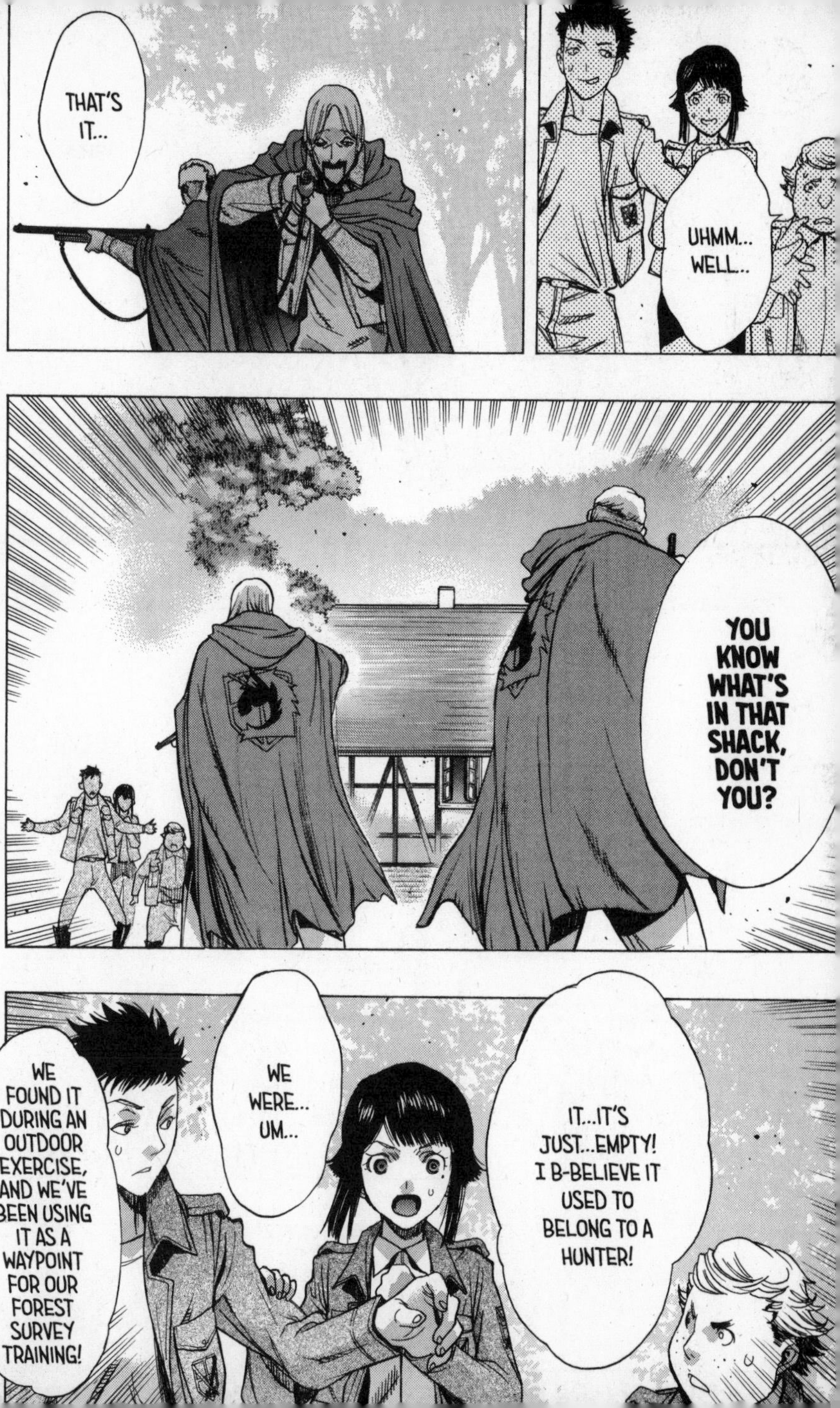
UHMM... WELL...
THAT'S IT...
YOU KNOW WHAT'S IN THAT SHACK, DON'T YOU?
IT...IT'S JUST...EMPTY! I B-BELIEVE IT USED TO BELONG TO A HUNTER!
WE WERE... UM...
WE FOUND IT DURING AN OUTDOOR EXERCISE, AND WE'VE BEEN USING IT AS A WAYPOINT FOR OUR FOREST SURVEY TRAINING!

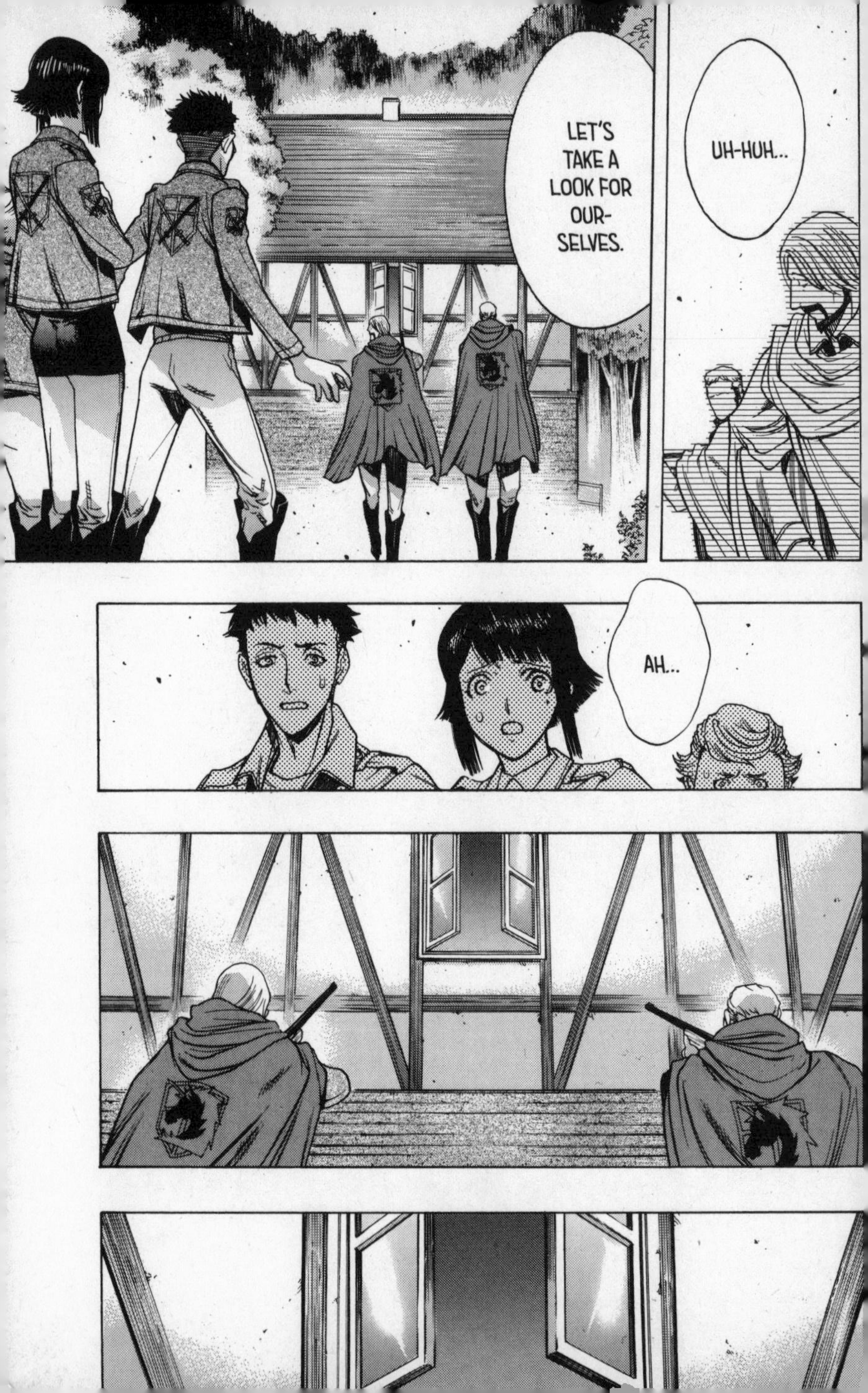
UH-HUH...
LET'S TAKE A LOOK FOR OUR-SELVES.
AH...

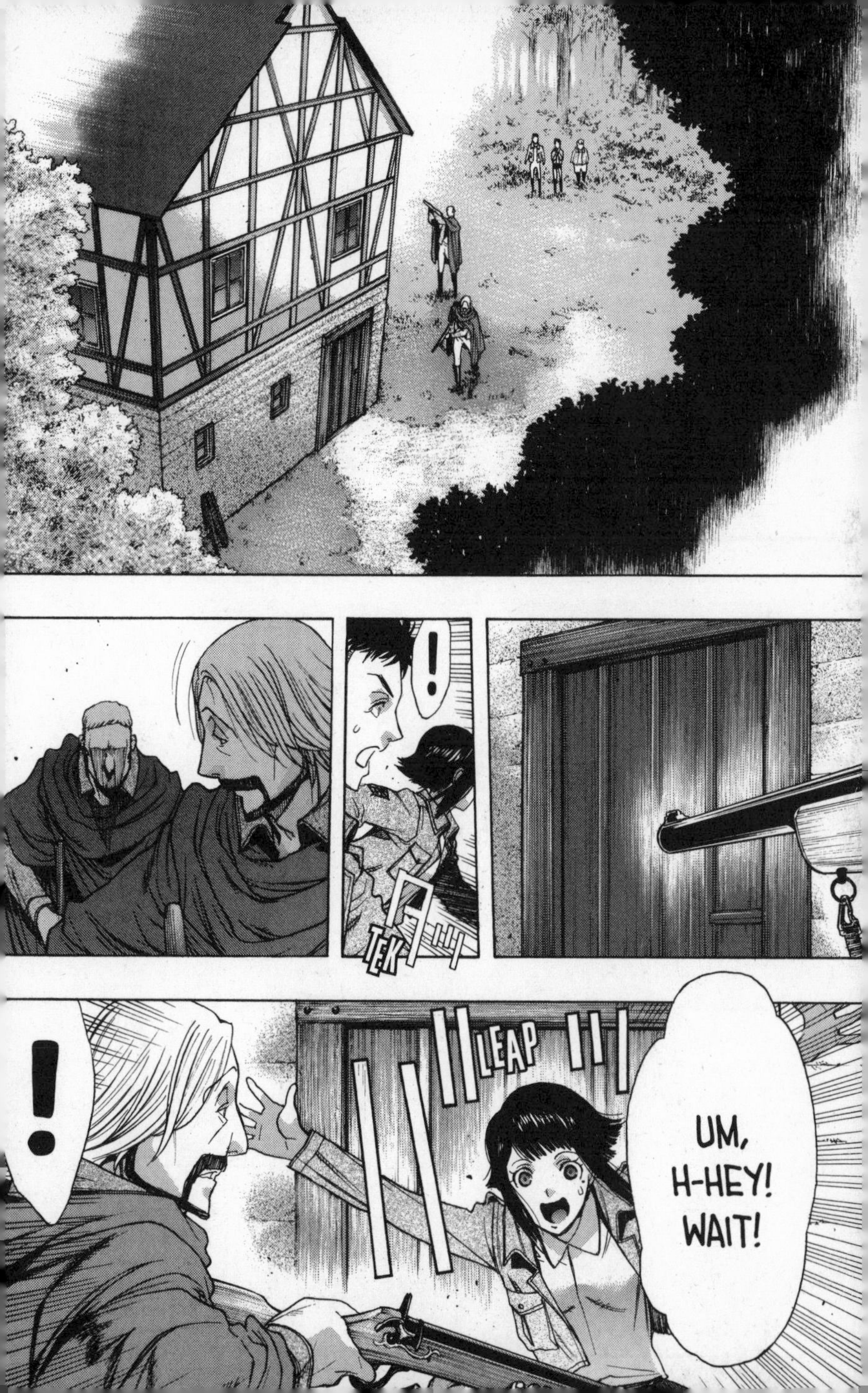
!
TEK
UM, H-HEY! WAIT!
LEAP
!

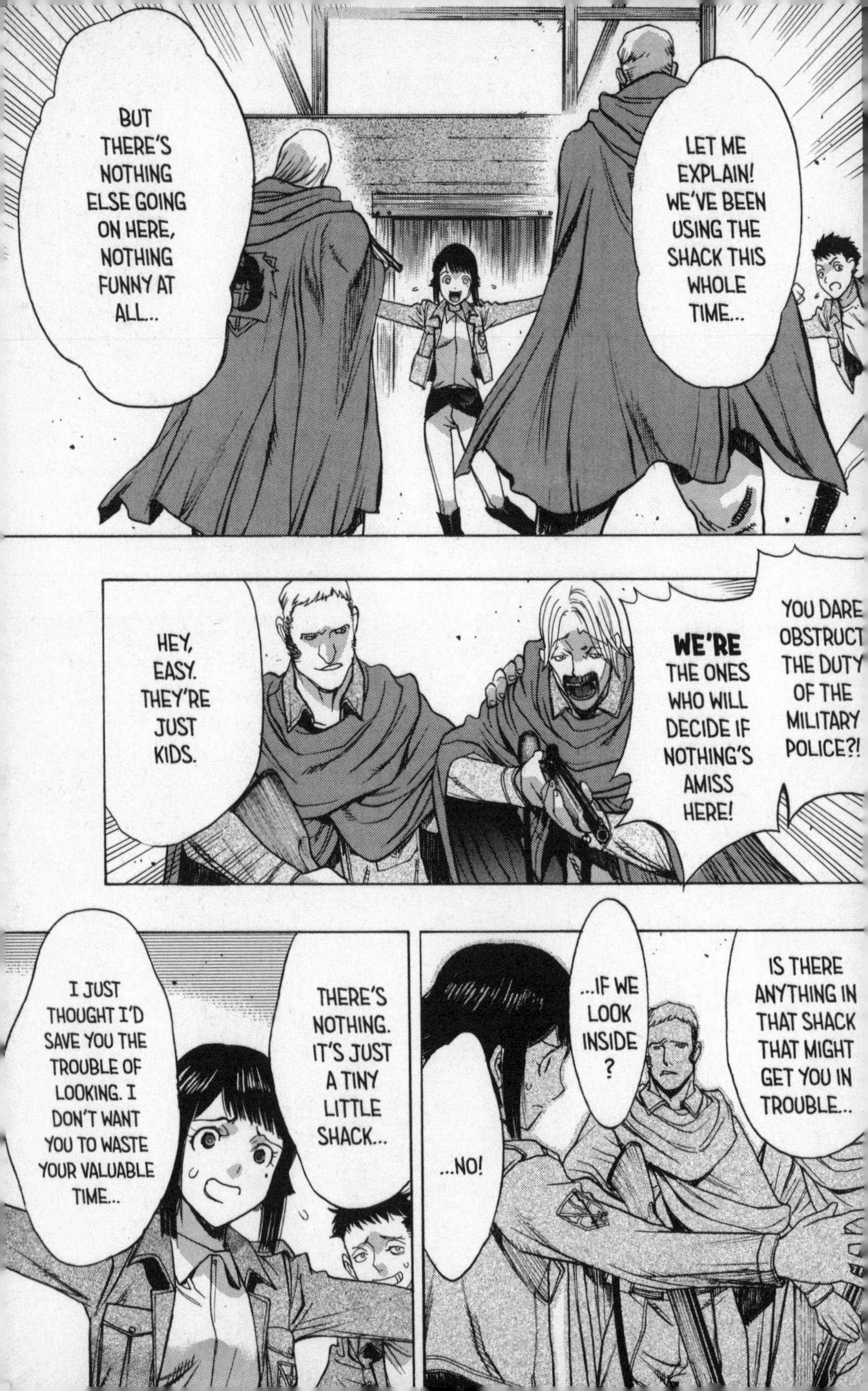
LET ME EXPLAIN! WE'VE BEEN USING THE SHACK THIS WHOLE TIME...
BUT THERE'S NOTHING ELSE GOING ON HERE, NOTHING FUNNY AT ALL...
YOU DARE OBSTRUCT THE DUTY OF THE MILITARY POLICE?!
WE'RE THE ONES WHO WILL DECIDE IF NOTHING'S AMISS HERE!
HEY, EASY. THEY'RE JUST KIDS.
IS THERE ANYTHING IN THAT SHACK THAT MIGHT GET YOU IN TROUBLE...
...IF WE LOOK INSIDE?
...NO!
THERE'S NOTHING. IT'S JUST A TINY LITTLE SHACK...
I JUST THOUGHT I'D SAVE YOU THE TROUBLE OF LOOKING. I DON'T WANT YOU TO WASTE YOUR VALUABLE TIME...

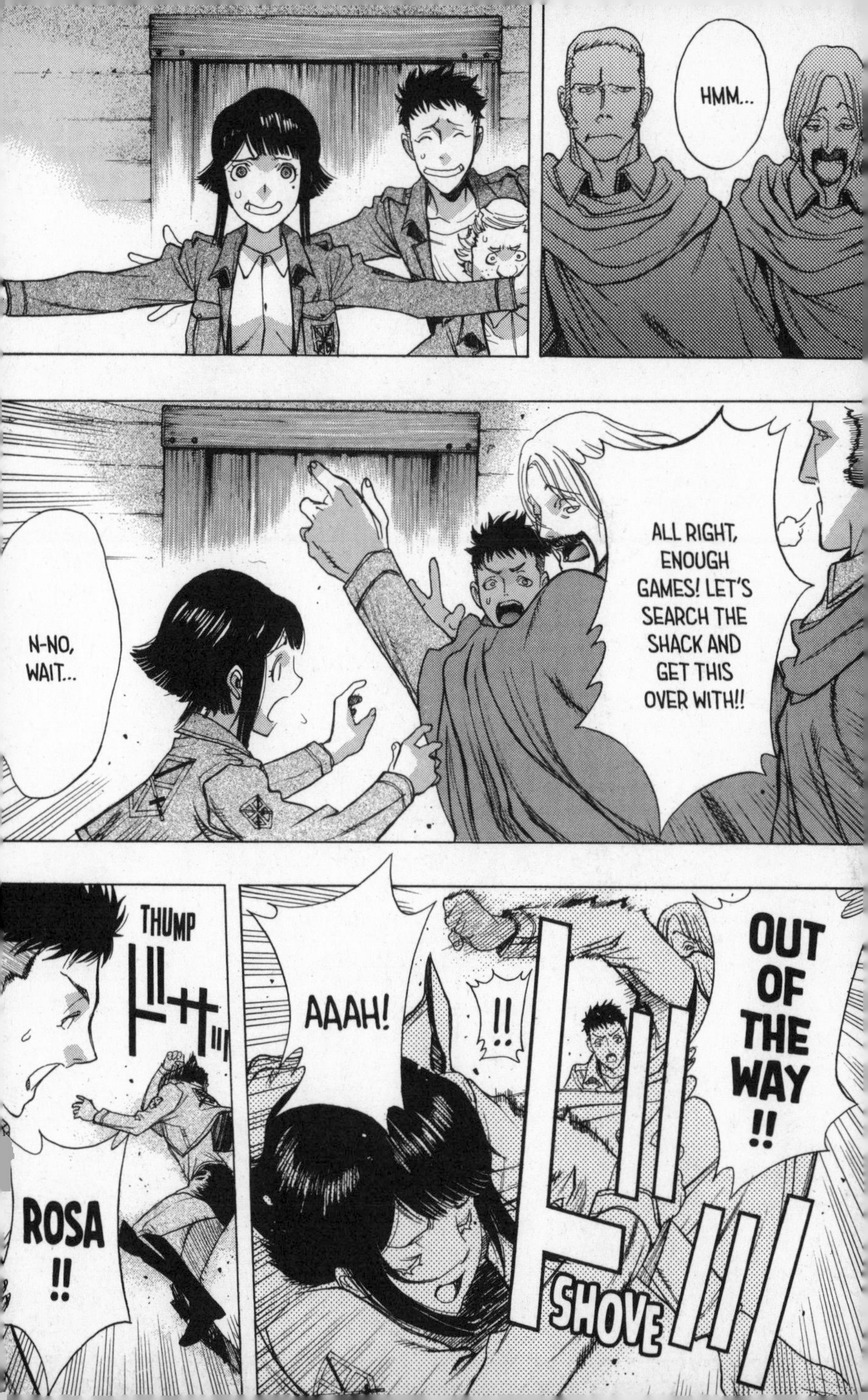
HMM...
ALL RIGHT, ENOUGH GAMES! LET'S SEARCH THE SHACK AND GET THIS OVER WITH!!
N-NO, WAIT...
OUT OF THE WAY!!
!!
AAAH!
SHOVE
THUMP
ROSA!!

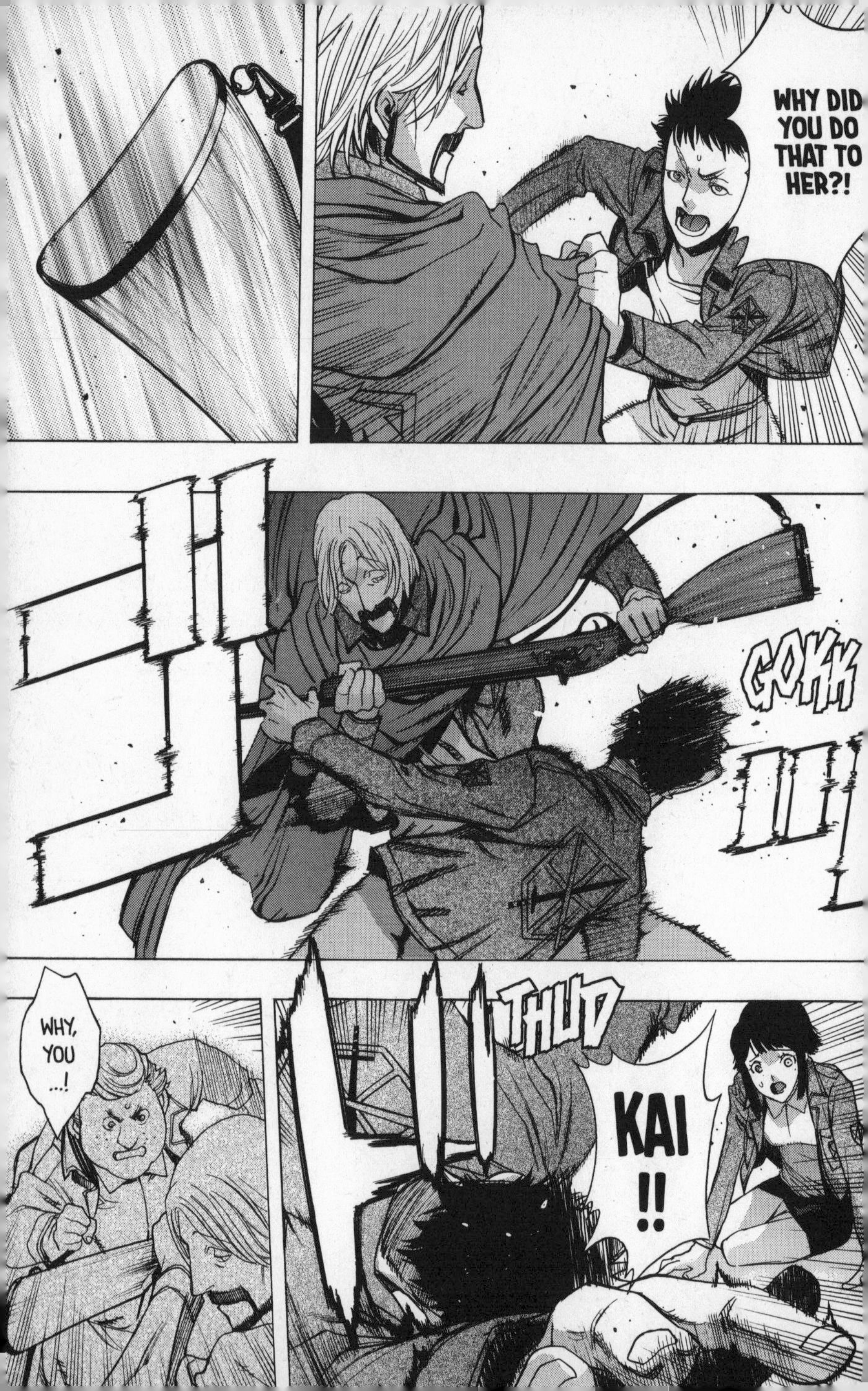
WHY DID YOU DO THAT TO HER?!
GOKK
KAI !!
THUD
WHY, YOU ...!

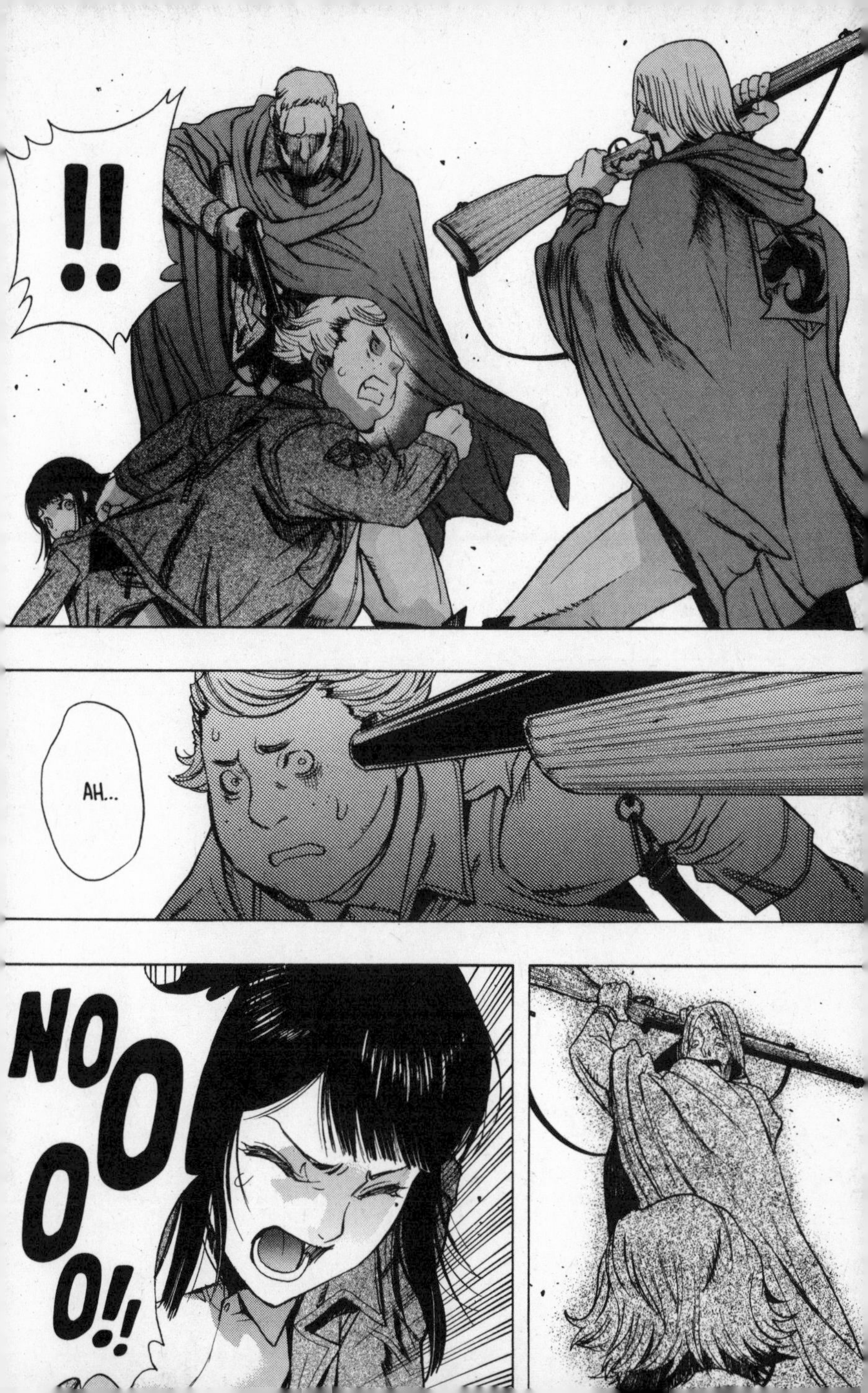
!!
AH...
NOOOO!!

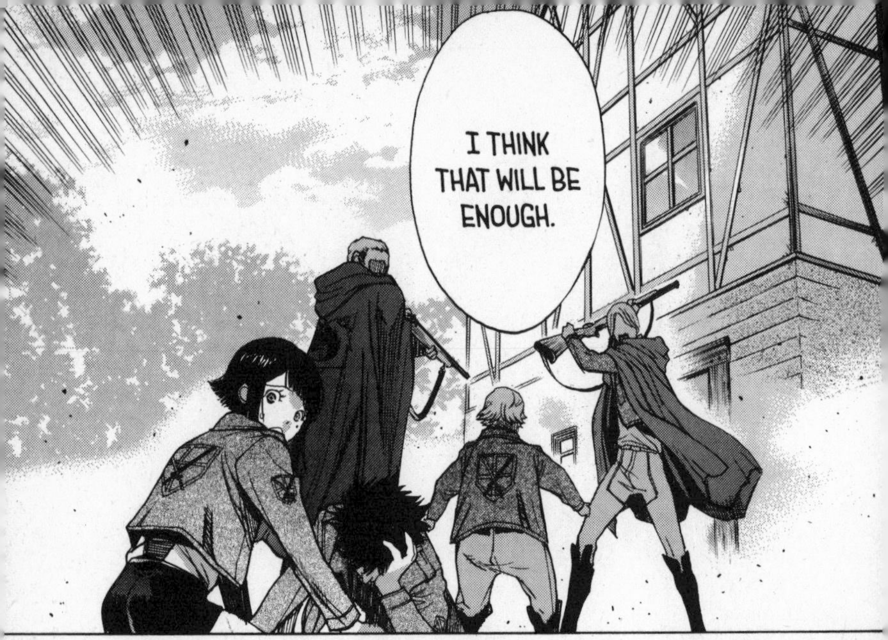
I THINK THAT WILL BE ENOUGH.
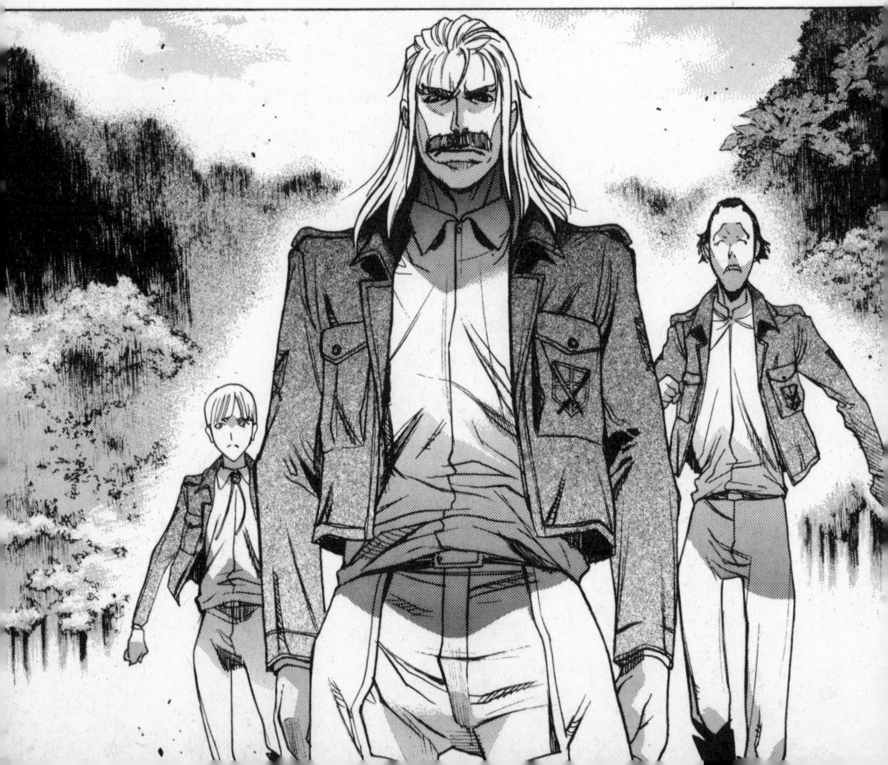

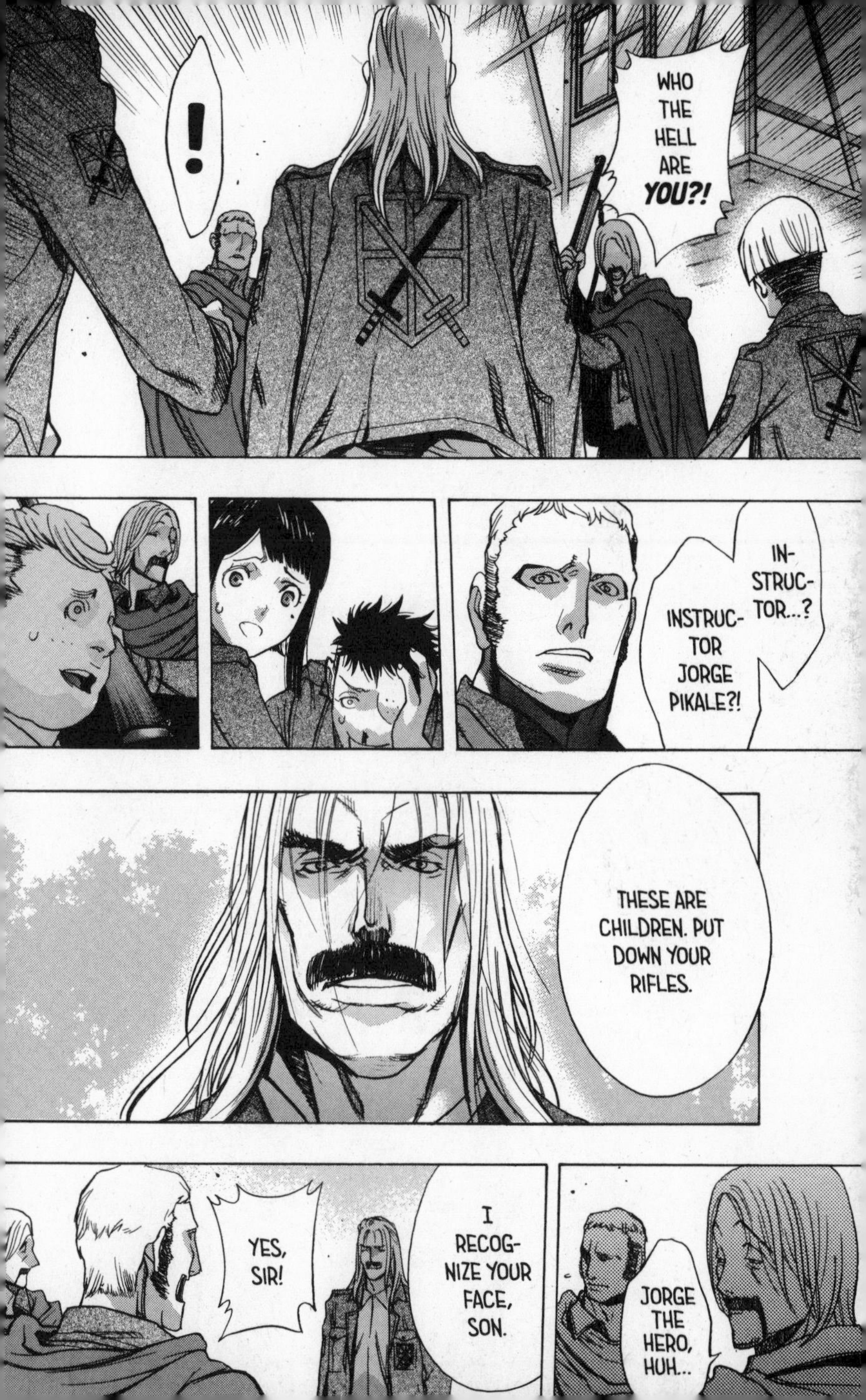
WHO THE HELL ARE YOU?!
!
IN-STRUCTOR...?
INSTRUCTOR JORGE PIKALE?!
THESE ARE CHILDREN. PUT DOWN YOUR RIFLES.
JORGE THE HERO, HUH...
I RECOGNIZE YOUR FACE, SON.
YES, SIR!

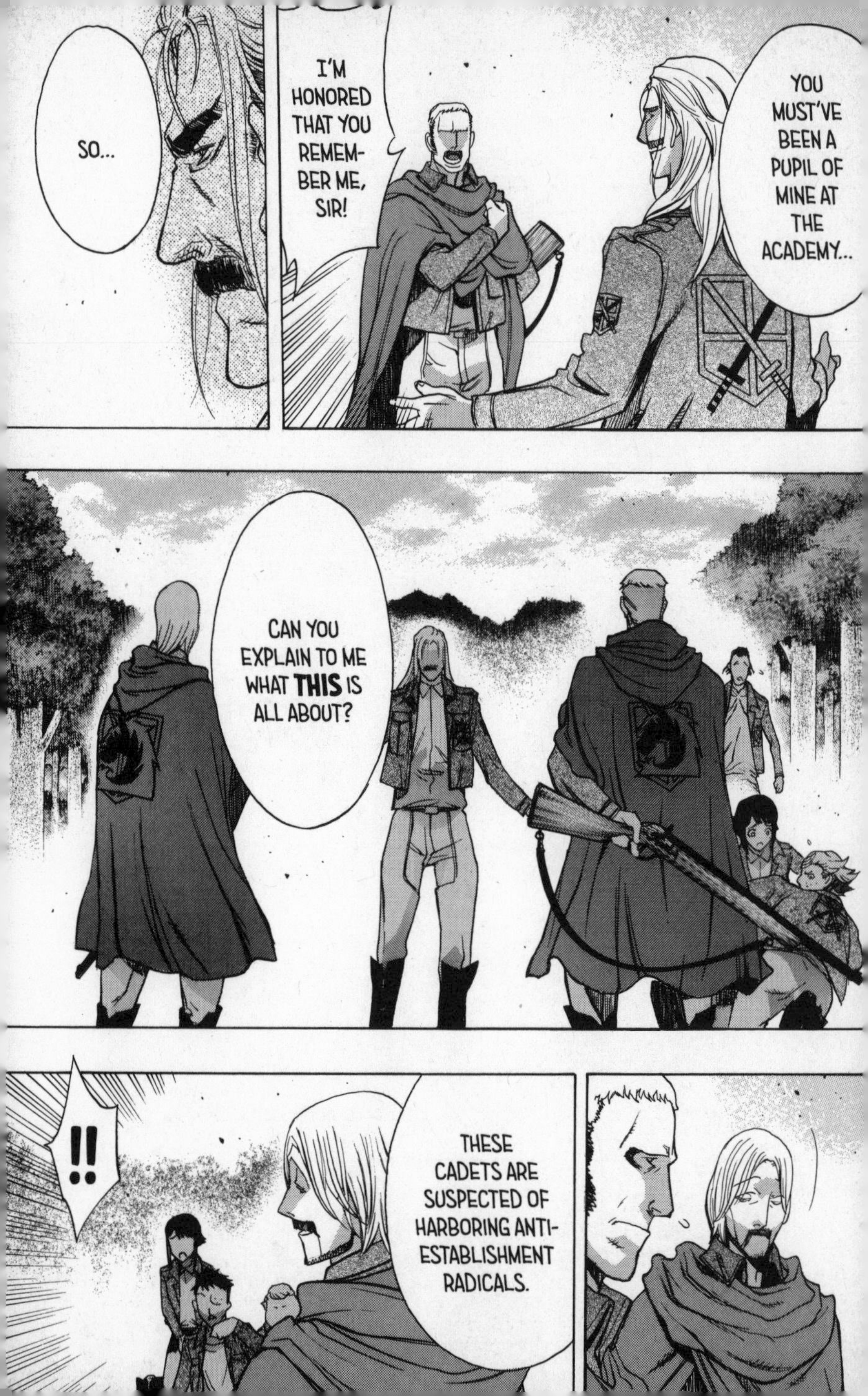
YOU MUST'VE BEEN A PUPIL OF MINE AT THE ACADEMY...
I'M HONORED THAT YOU REMEMBER ME, SIR!
SO...
CAN YOU EXPLAIN TO ME WHAT **THIS** IS ALL ABOUT?
THESE CADETS ARE SUSPECTED OF HARBORING ANTI-ESTABLISHMENT RADICALS.
!!

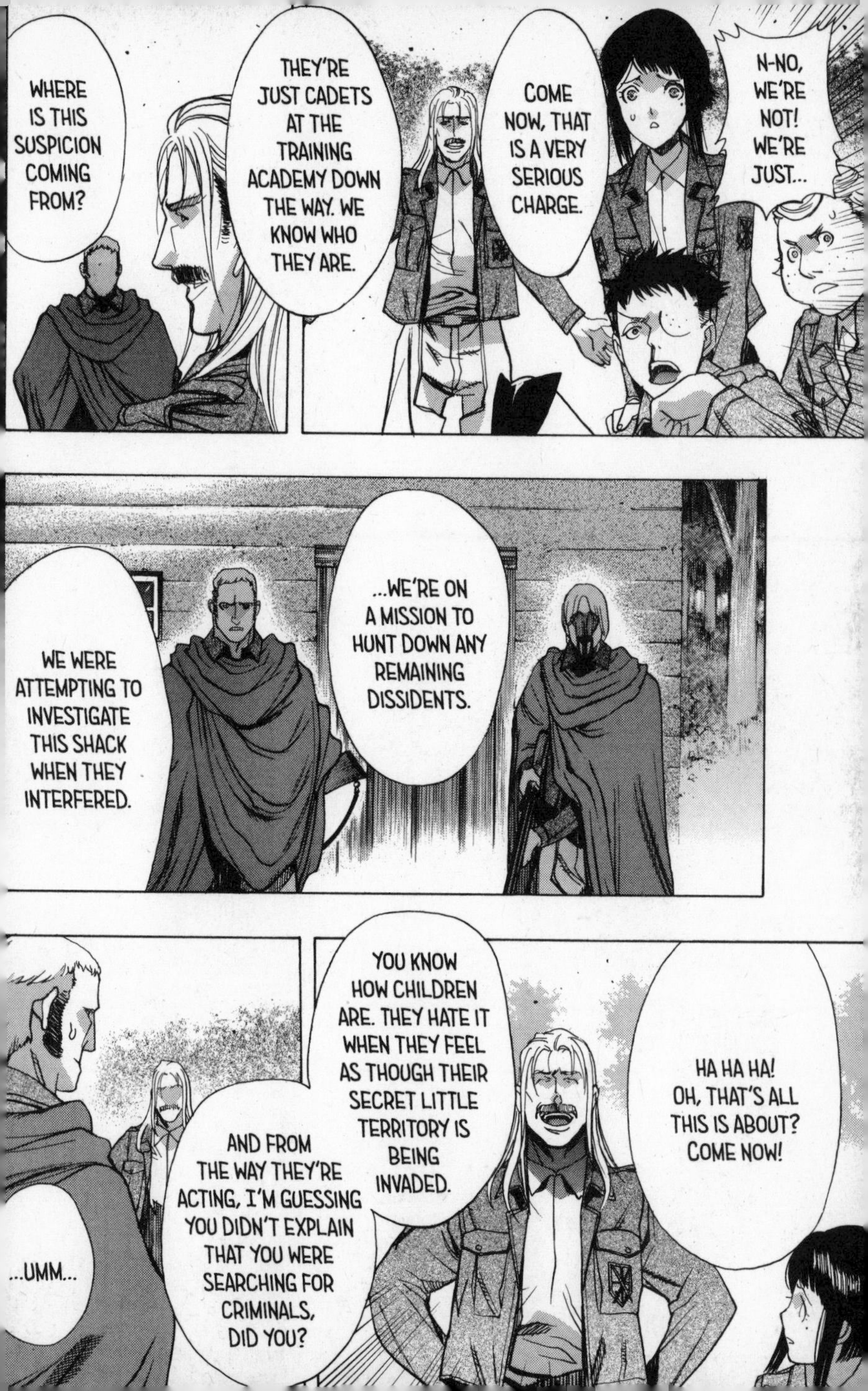
N-NO, WE'RE NOT! WE'RE JUST...
COME NOW, THAT IS A VERY SERIOUS CHARGE.
THEY'RE JUST CADETS AT THE TRAINING ACADEMY DOWN THE WAY. WE KNOW WHO THEY ARE.
WHERE IS THIS SUSPICION COMING FROM?
...WE'RE ON A MISSION TO HUNT DOWN ANY REMAINING DISSIDENTS.
WE WERE ATTEMPTING TO INVESTIGATE THIS SHACK WHEN THEY INTERFERED.
HA HA HA! OH, THAT'S ALL THIS IS ABOUT? COME NOW!
YOU KNOW HOW CHILDREN ARE. THEY HATE IT WHEN THEY FEEL AS THOUGH THEIR SECRET LITTLE TERRITORY IS BEING INVADED.
AND FROM THE WAY THEY'RE ACTING, I'M GUESSING YOU DIDN'T EXPLAIN THAT YOU WERE SEARCHING FOR CRIMINALS, DID YOU?
...UMM...

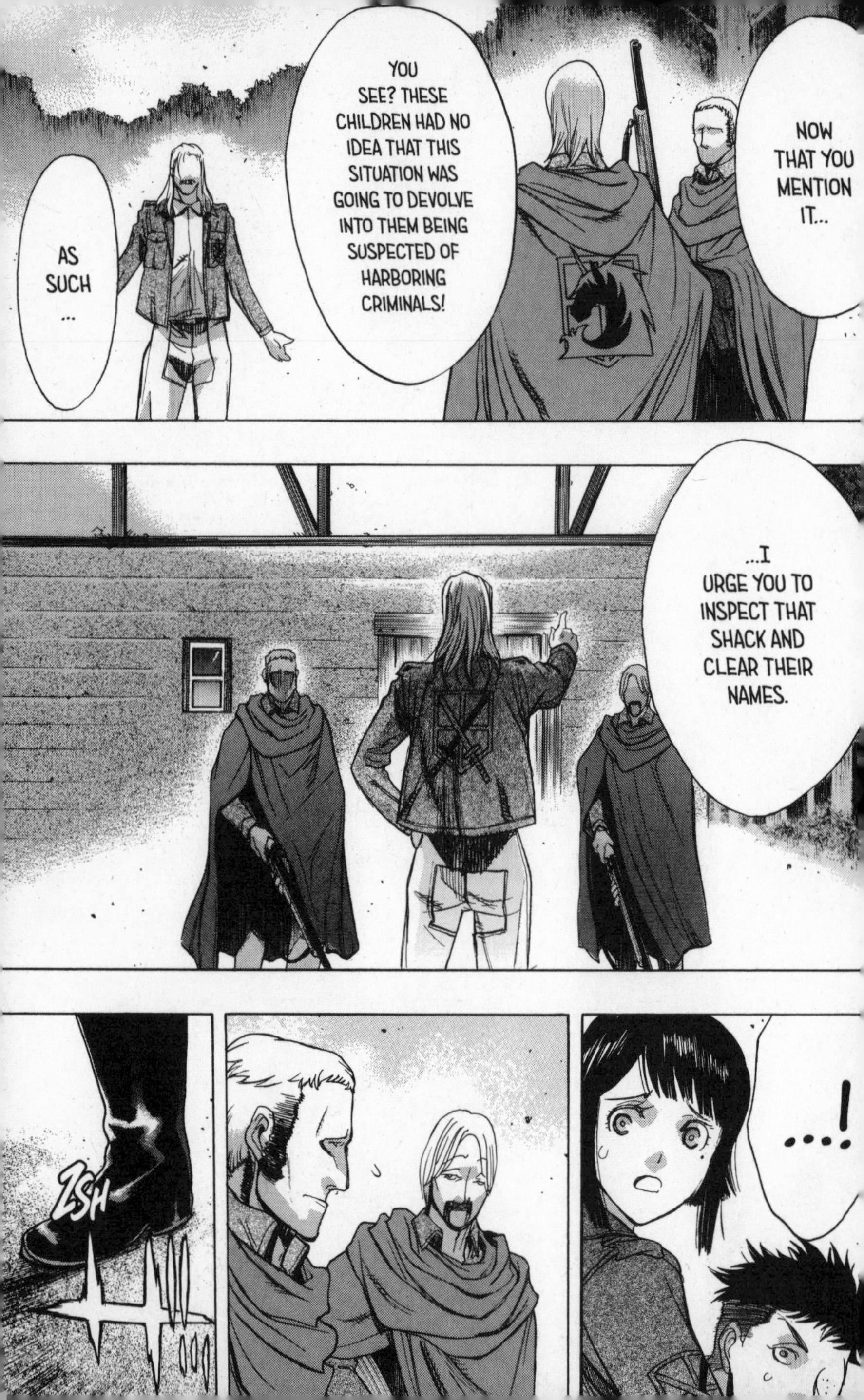
NOW THAT YOU MENTION IT...
YOU SEE? THESE CHILDREN HAD NO IDEA THAT THIS SITUATION WAS GOING TO DEVOLVE INTO THEM BEING SUSPECTED OF HARBORING CRIMINALS!
AS SUCH ...
...I URGE YOU TO INSPECT THAT SHACK AND CLEAR THEIR NAMES.
...!
ZSH

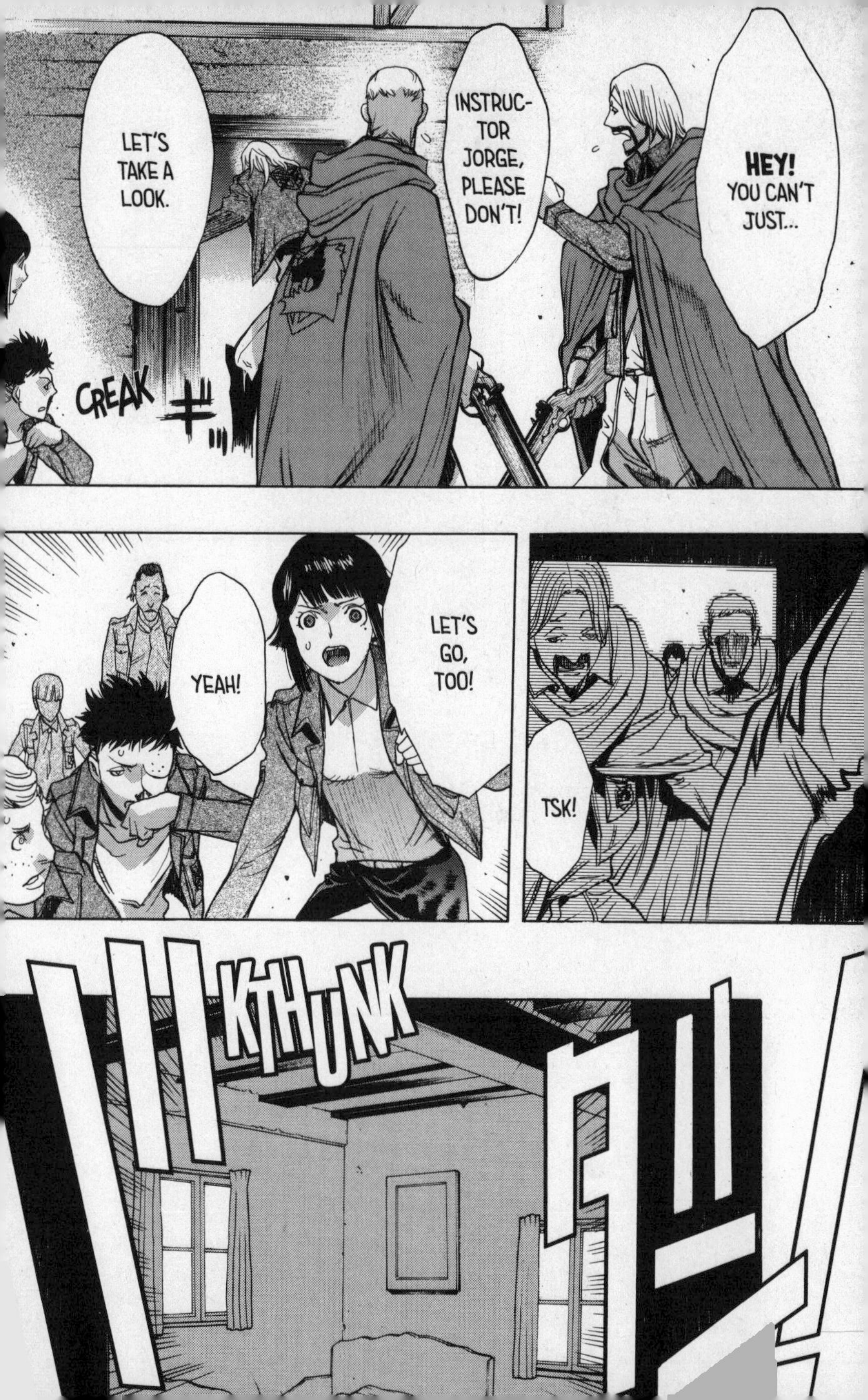
HEY! YOU CAN'T JUST...
INSTRUCTOR JORGE, PLEASE DON'T!
LET'S TAKE A LOOK.
CREAK
TSK!
LET'S GO, TOO!
YEAH!
KTHUNK

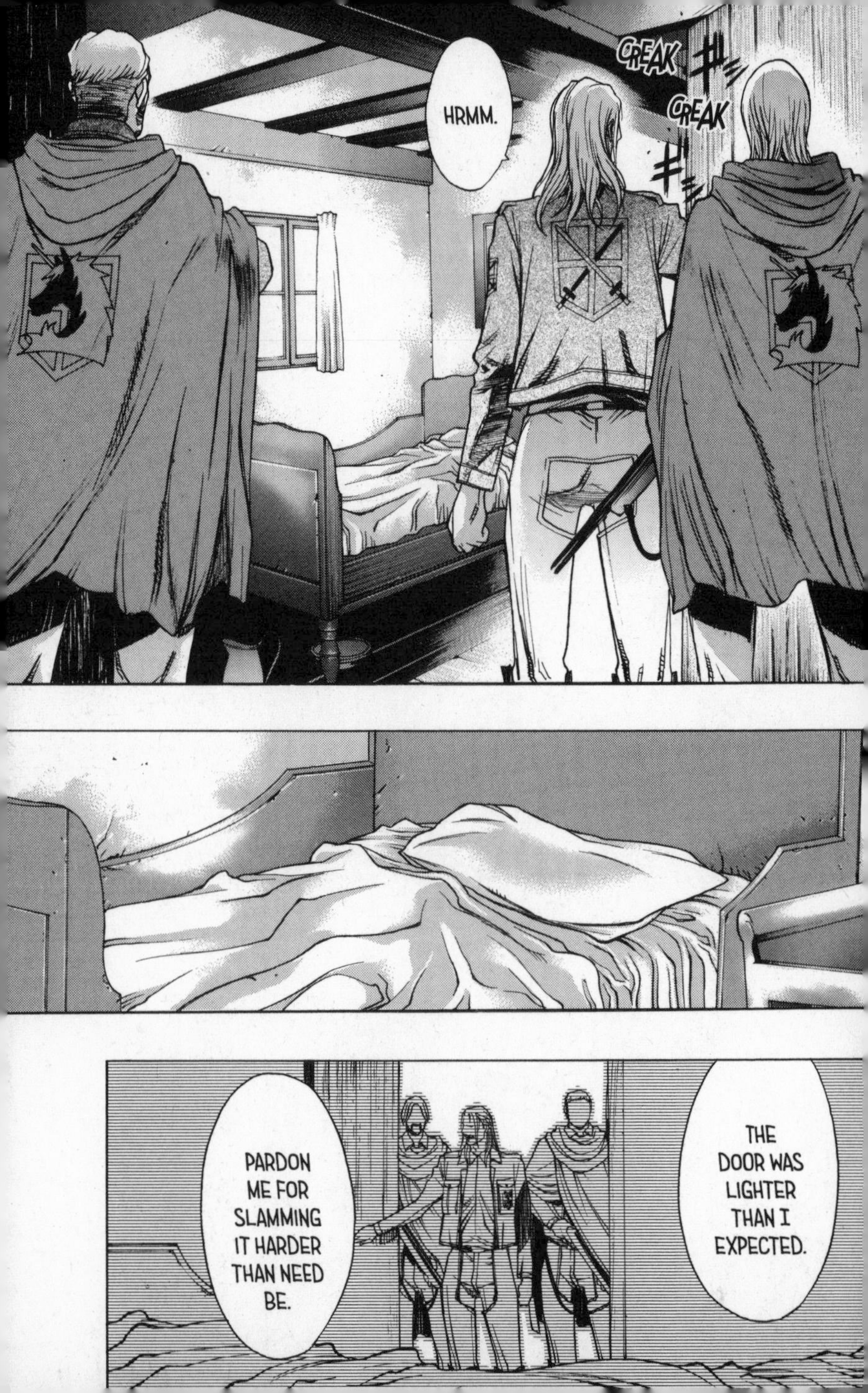
CREAK
CREAK
HRMM.
THE DOOR WAS LIGHTER THAN I EXPECTED.
PARDON ME FOR SLAMMING IT HARDER THAN NEED BE.

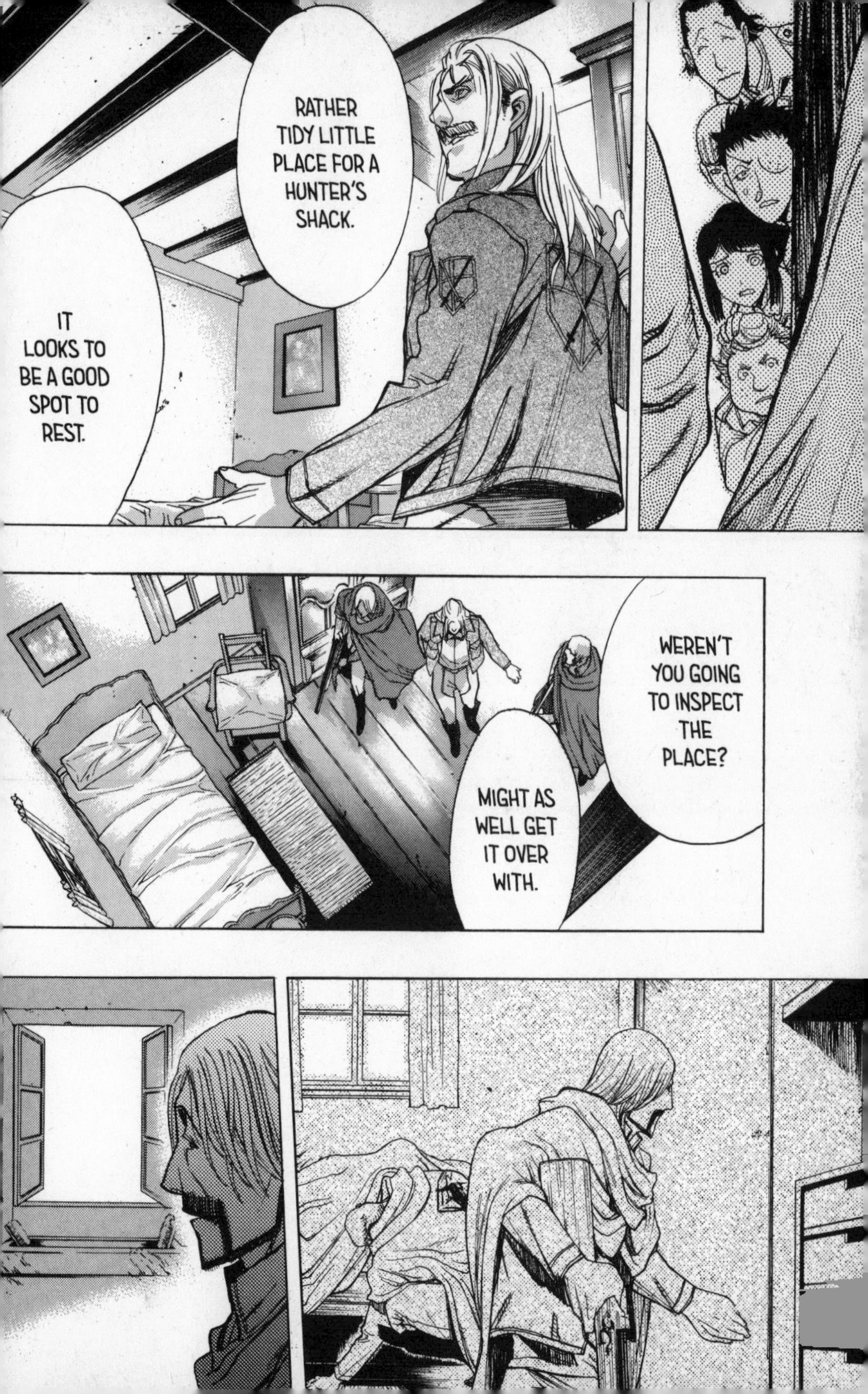
RATHER TIDY LITTLE PLACE FOR A HUNTER'S SHACK.
IT LOOKS TO BE A GOOD SPOT TO REST.
WEREN'T YOU GOING TO INSPECT THE PLACE?
MIGHT AS WELL GET IT OVER WITH.

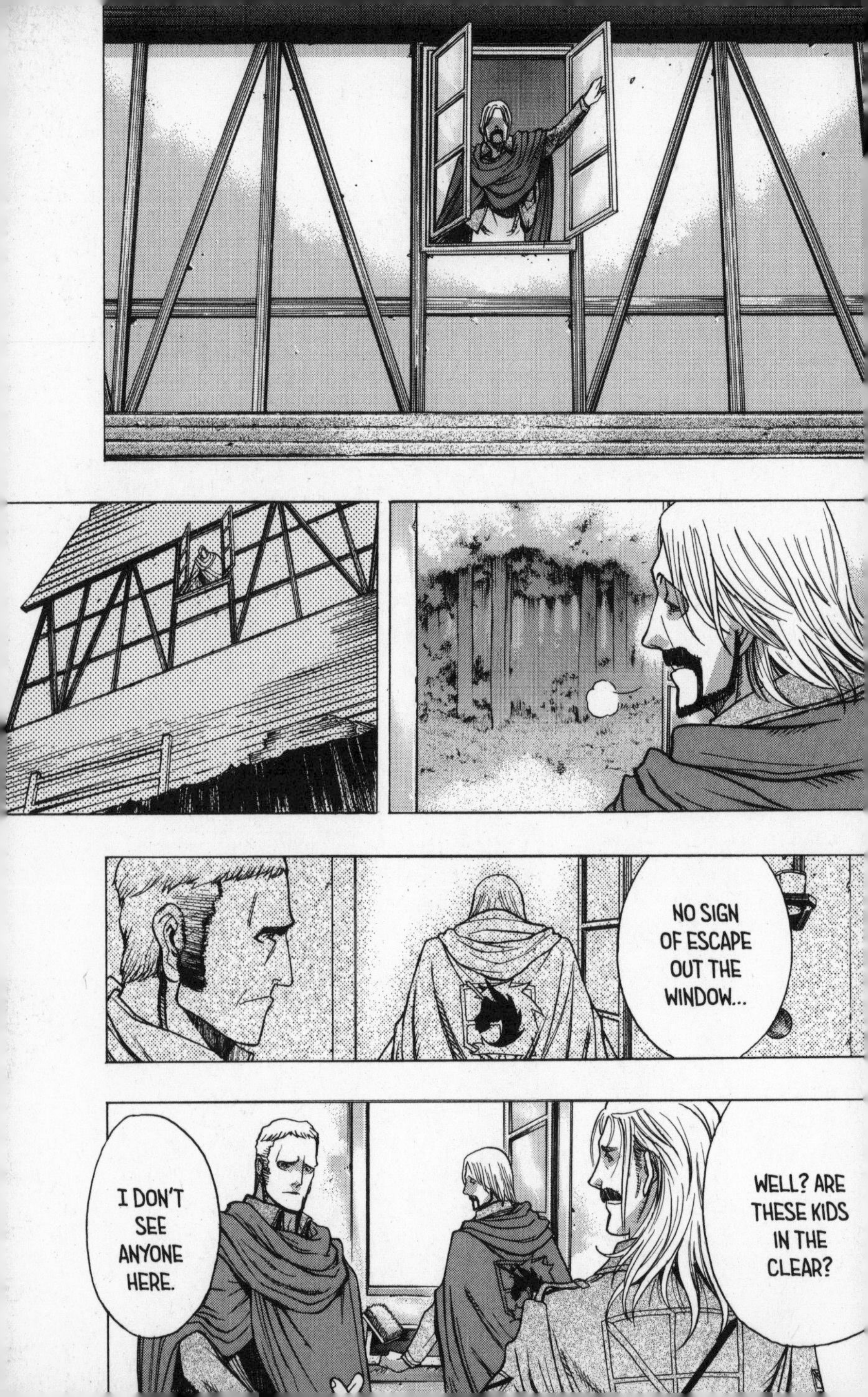
NO SIGN OF ESCAPE OUT THE WINDOW...
WELL? ARE THESE KIDS IN THE CLEAR?
I DON'T SEE ANYONE HERE.

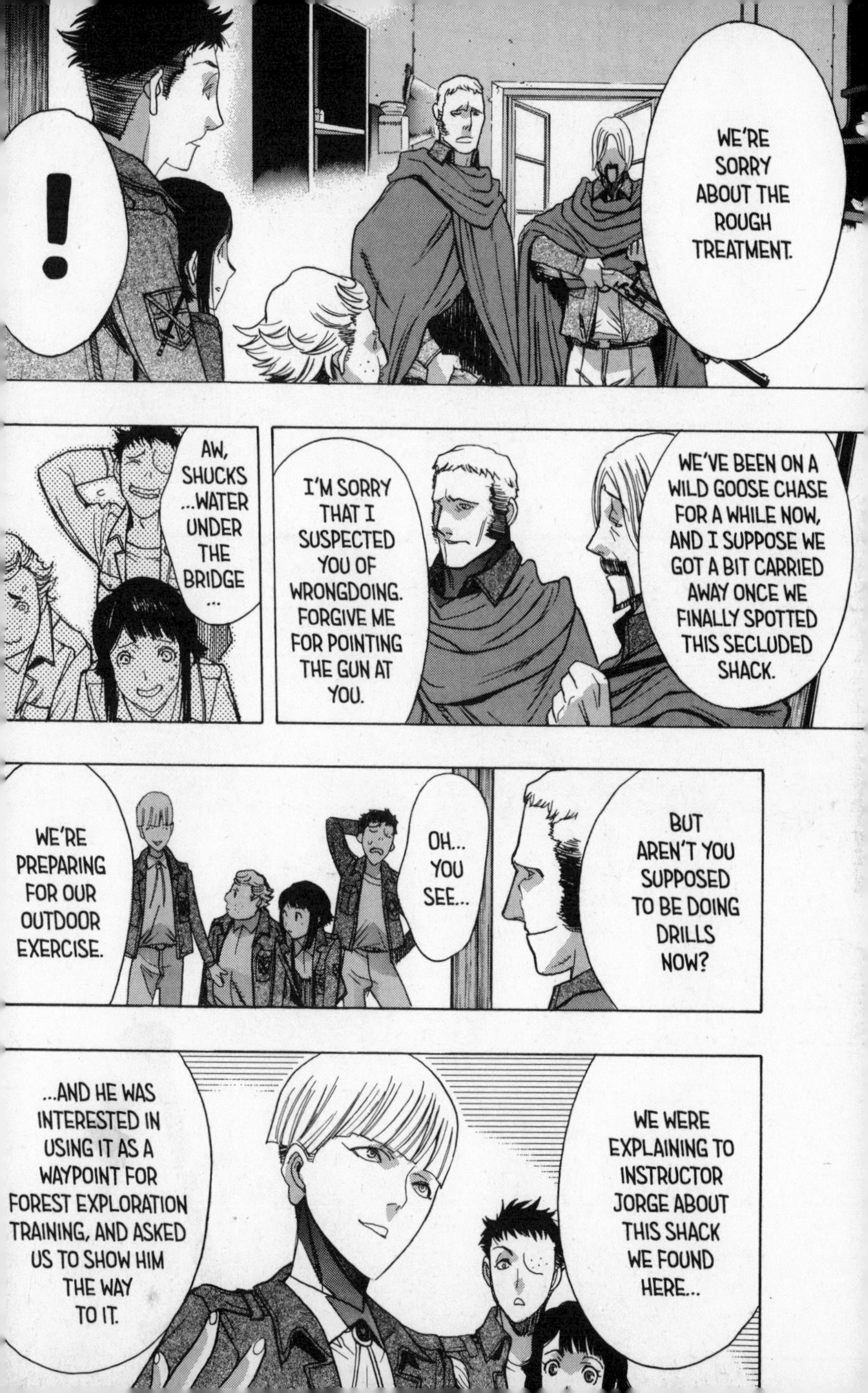
WE'RE SORRY ABOUT THE ROUGH TREATMENT.
!
WE'VE BEEN ON A WILD GOOSE CHASE FOR A WHILE NOW, AND I SUPPOSE WE GOT A BIT CARRIED AWAY ONCE WE FINALLY SPOTTED THIS SECLUDED SHACK.
I'M SORRY THAT I SUSPECTED YOU OF WRONGDOING. FORGIVE ME FOR POINTING THE GUN AT YOU.
AW, SHUCKS ...WATER UNDER THE BRIDGE ...
BUT AREN'T YOU SUPPOSED TO BE DOING DRILLS NOW?
OH... YOU SEE...
WE'RE PREPARING FOR OUR OUTDOOR EXERCISE.
WE WERE EXPLAINING TO INSTRUCTOR JORGE ABOUT THIS SHACK WE FOUND HERE...
...AND HE WAS INTERESTED IN USING IT AS A WAYPOINT FOR FOREST EXPLORATION TRAINING, AND ASKED US TO SHOW HIM THE WAY TO IT.

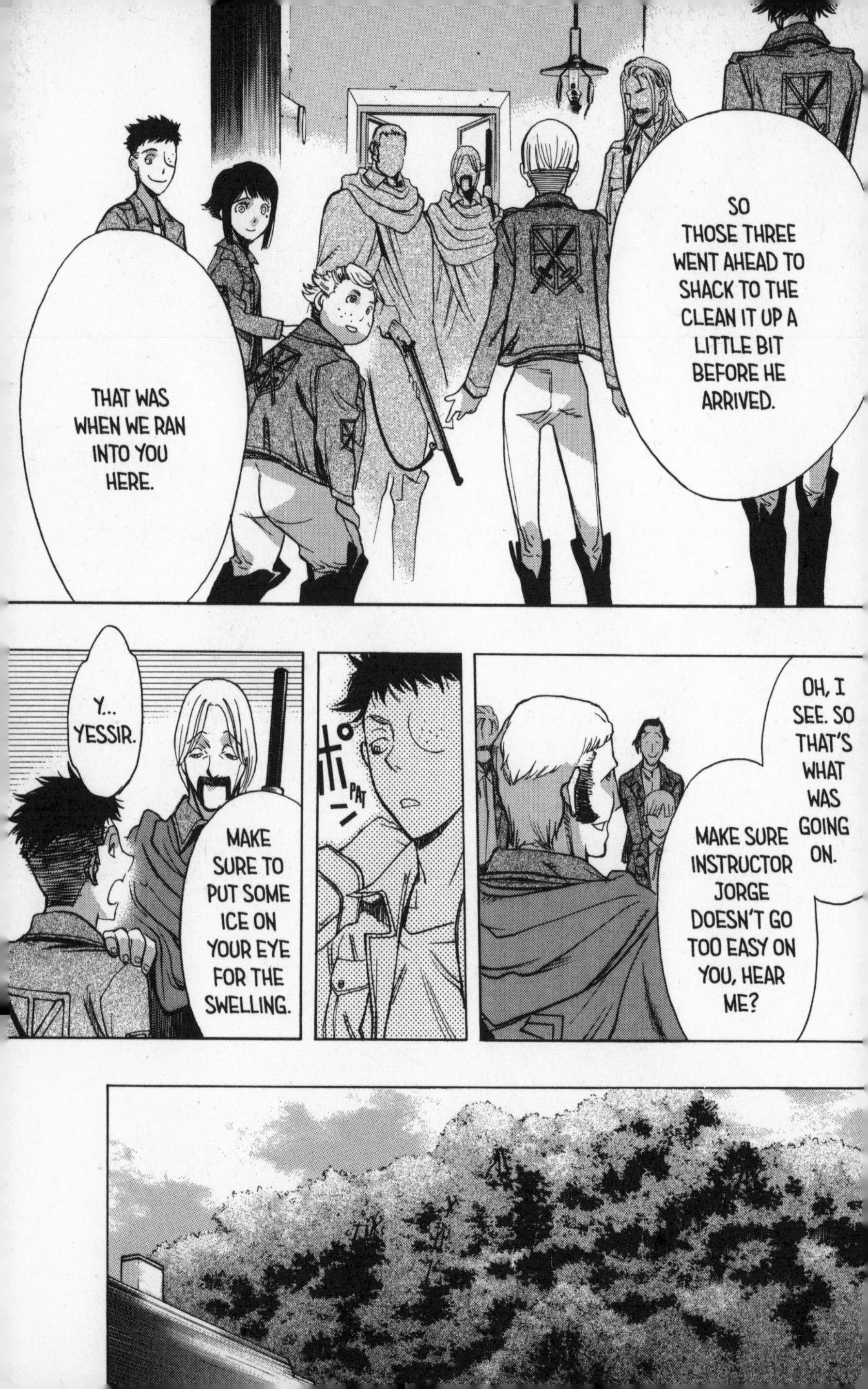
SO THOSE THREE WENT AHEAD TO SHACK TO THE CLEAN IT UP A LITTLE BIT BEFORE HE ARRIVED.
THAT WAS WHEN WE RAN INTO YOU HERE.
OH, I SEE. SO THAT'S WHAT WAS GOING ON.
MAKE SURE INSTRUCTOR JORGE DOESN'T GO TOO EASY ON YOU, HEAR ME?
PAT
MAKE SURE TO PUT SOME ICE ON YOUR EYE FOR THE SWELLING.
Y... YESSIR.

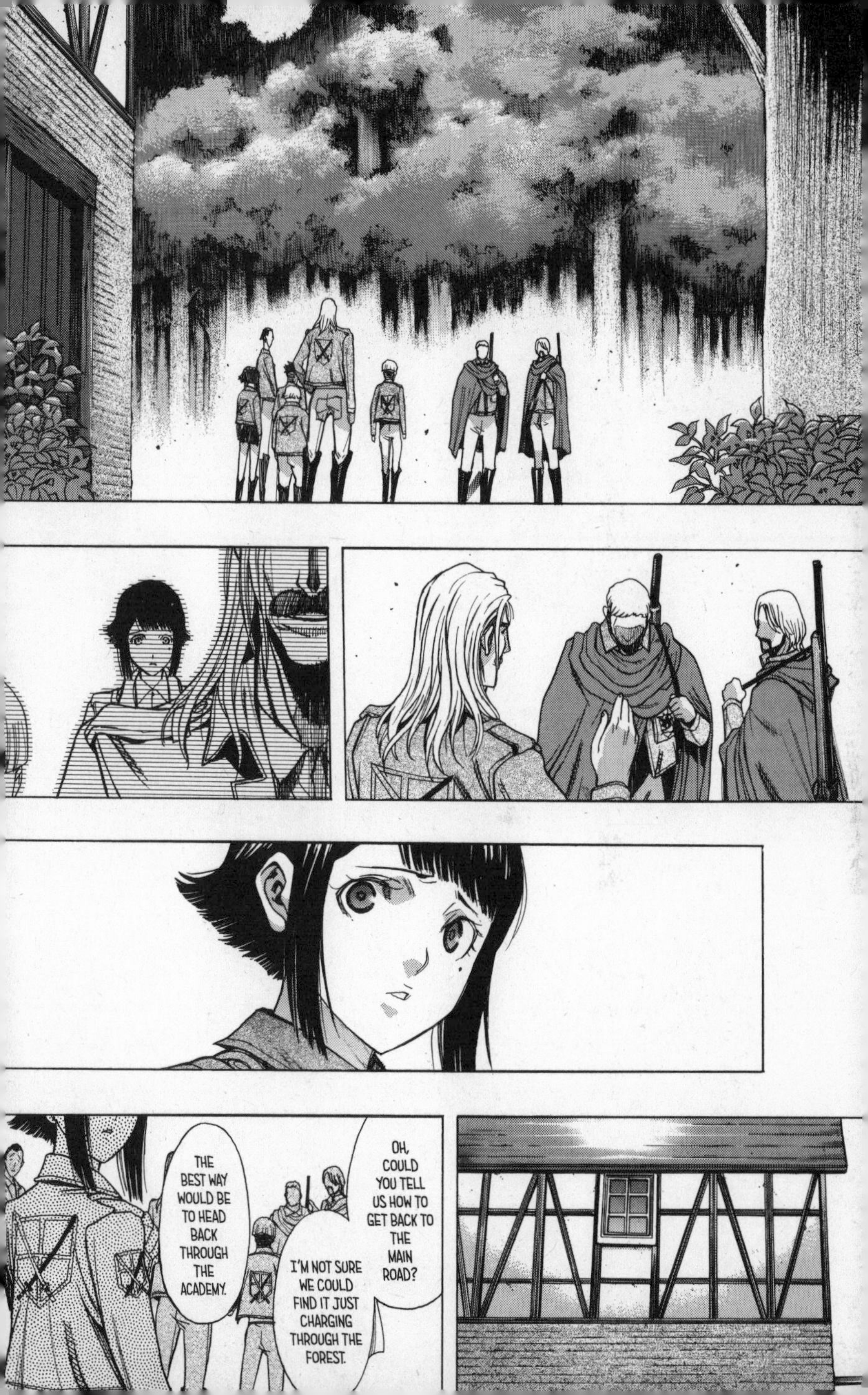
OH, COULD YOU TELL US HOW TO GET BACK TO THE MAIN ROAD?
I'M NOT SURE WE COULD FIND IT JUST CHARGING THROUGH THE FOREST.
THE BEST WAY WOULD BE TO HEAD BACK THROUGH THE ACADEMY.

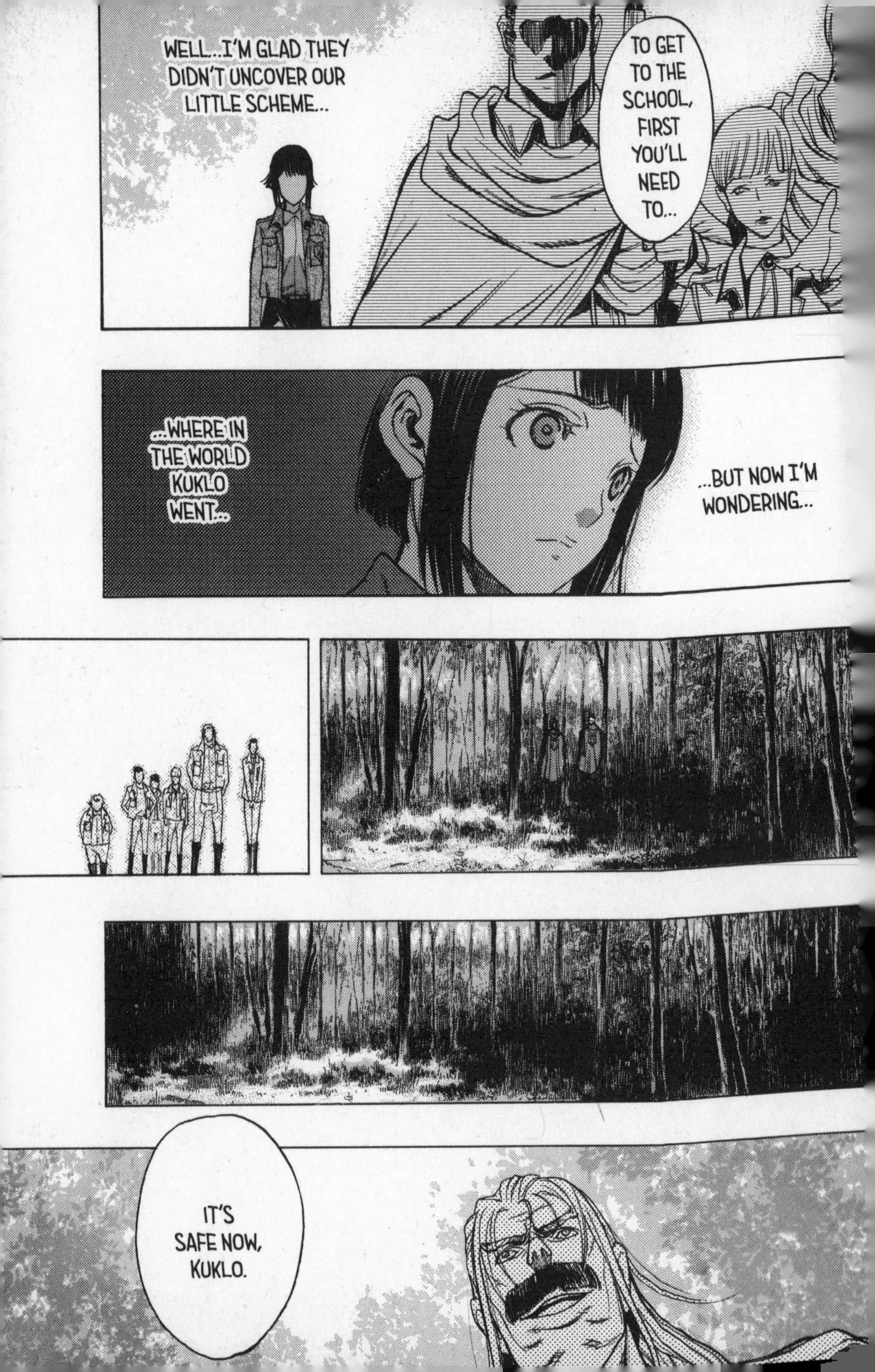
TO GET TO THE SCHOOL, FIRST YOU'LL NEED TO...
WELL...I'M GLAD THEY DIDN'T UNCOVER OUR LITTLE SCHEME...
...BUT NOW I'M WONDERING...
...WHERE IN THE WORLD KUKLO WENT...
IT'S SAFE NOW, KUKLO.

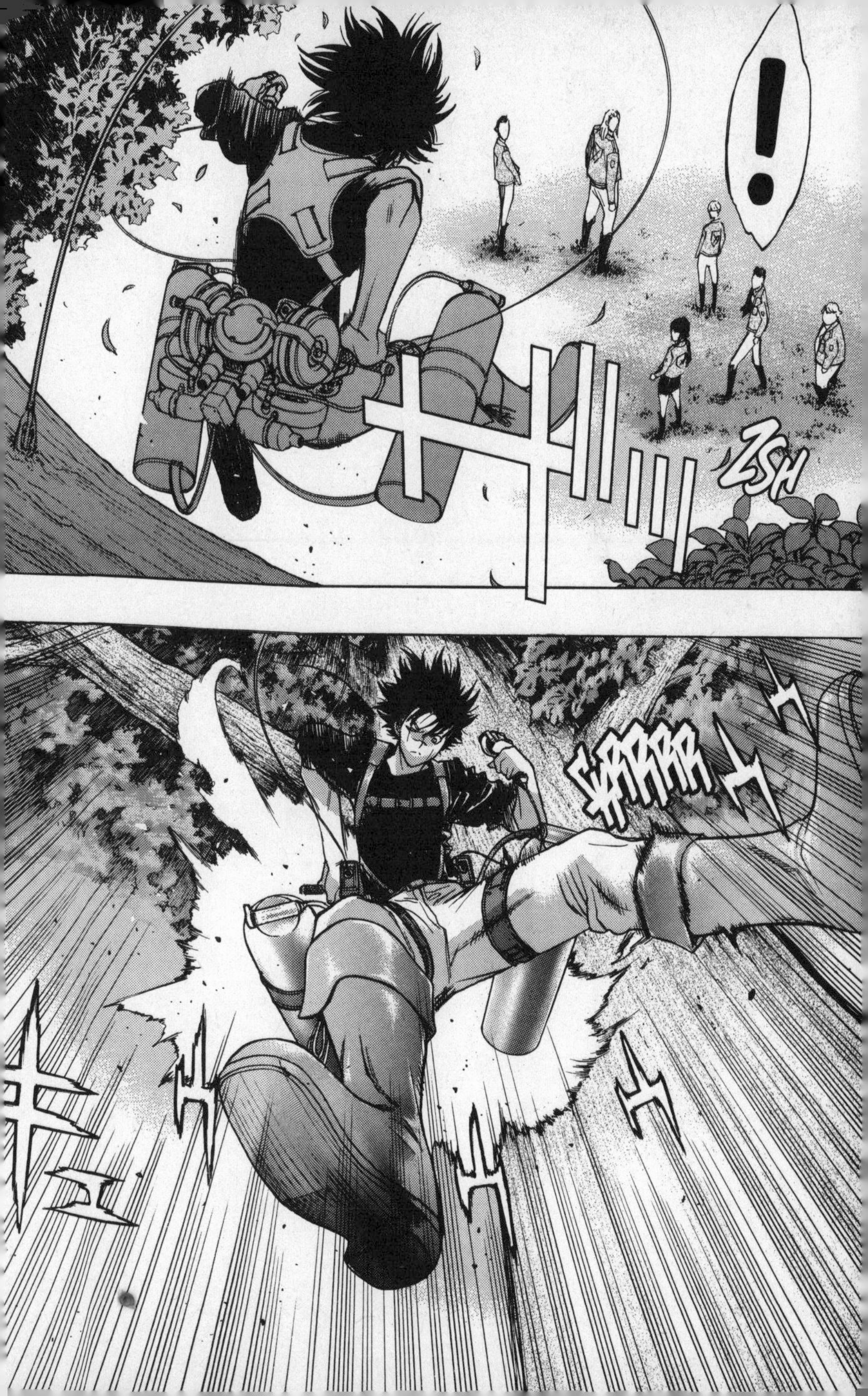
!
ZSH
SHRRRR

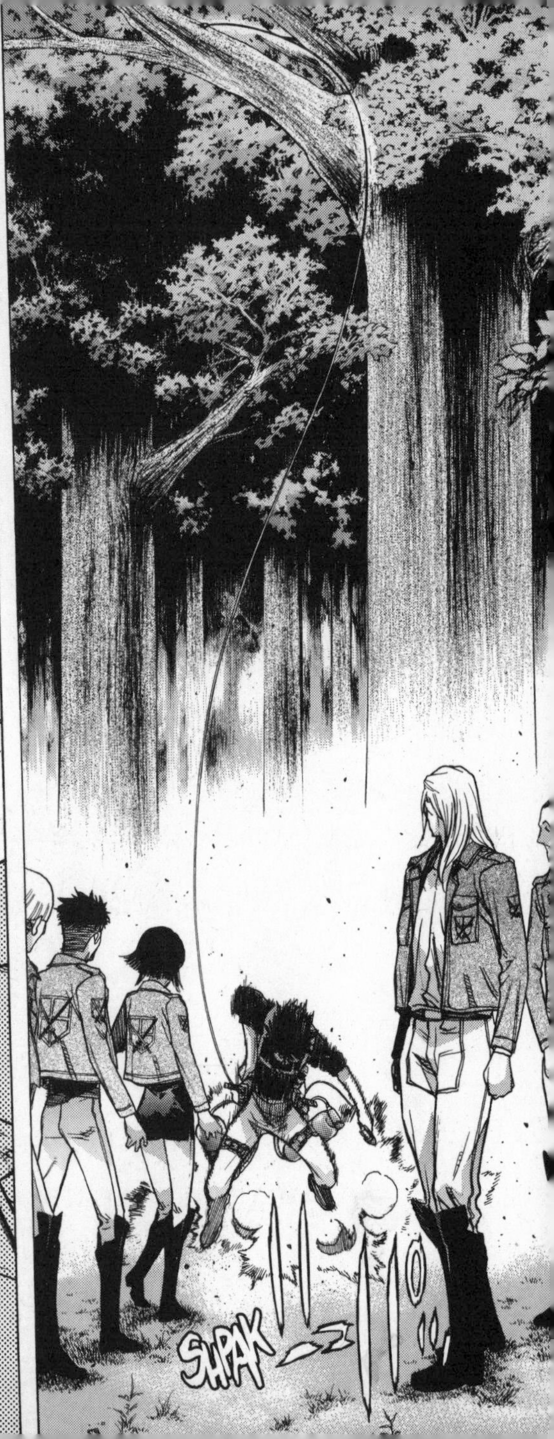
SHPAK
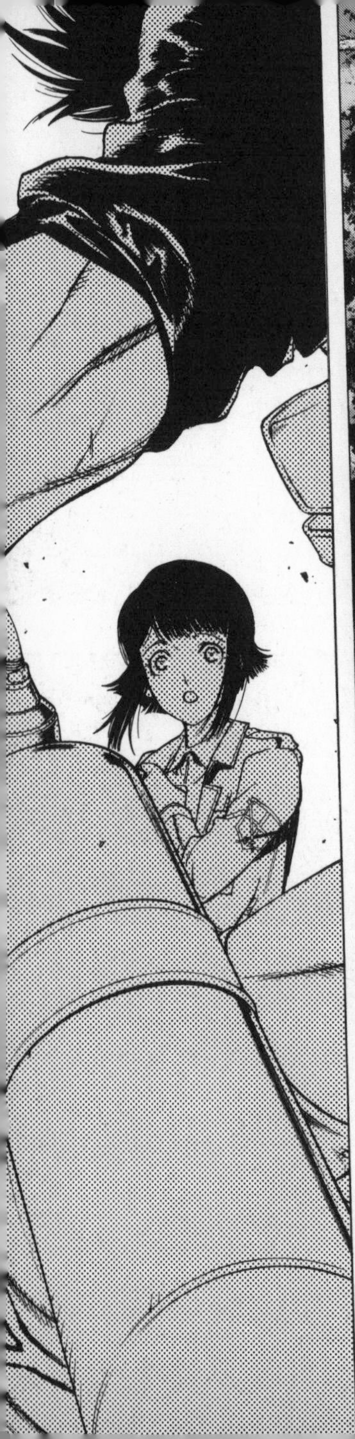

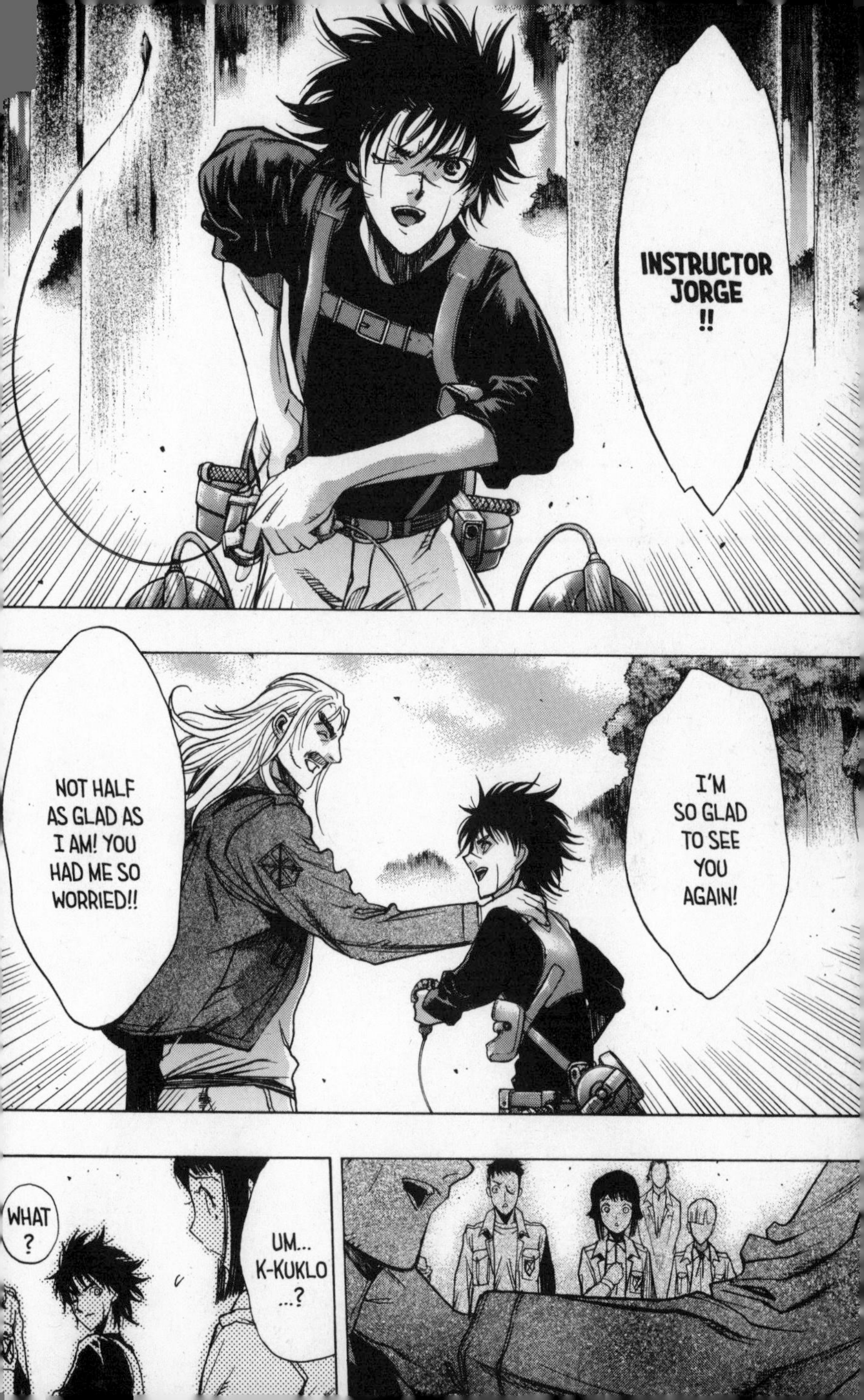
INSTRUCTOR JORGE!!
I'M SO GLAD TO SEE YOU AGAIN!
NOT HALF AS GLAD AS I AM! YOU HAD ME SO WORRIED!!
UM... K-KUKLO...?
WHAT?

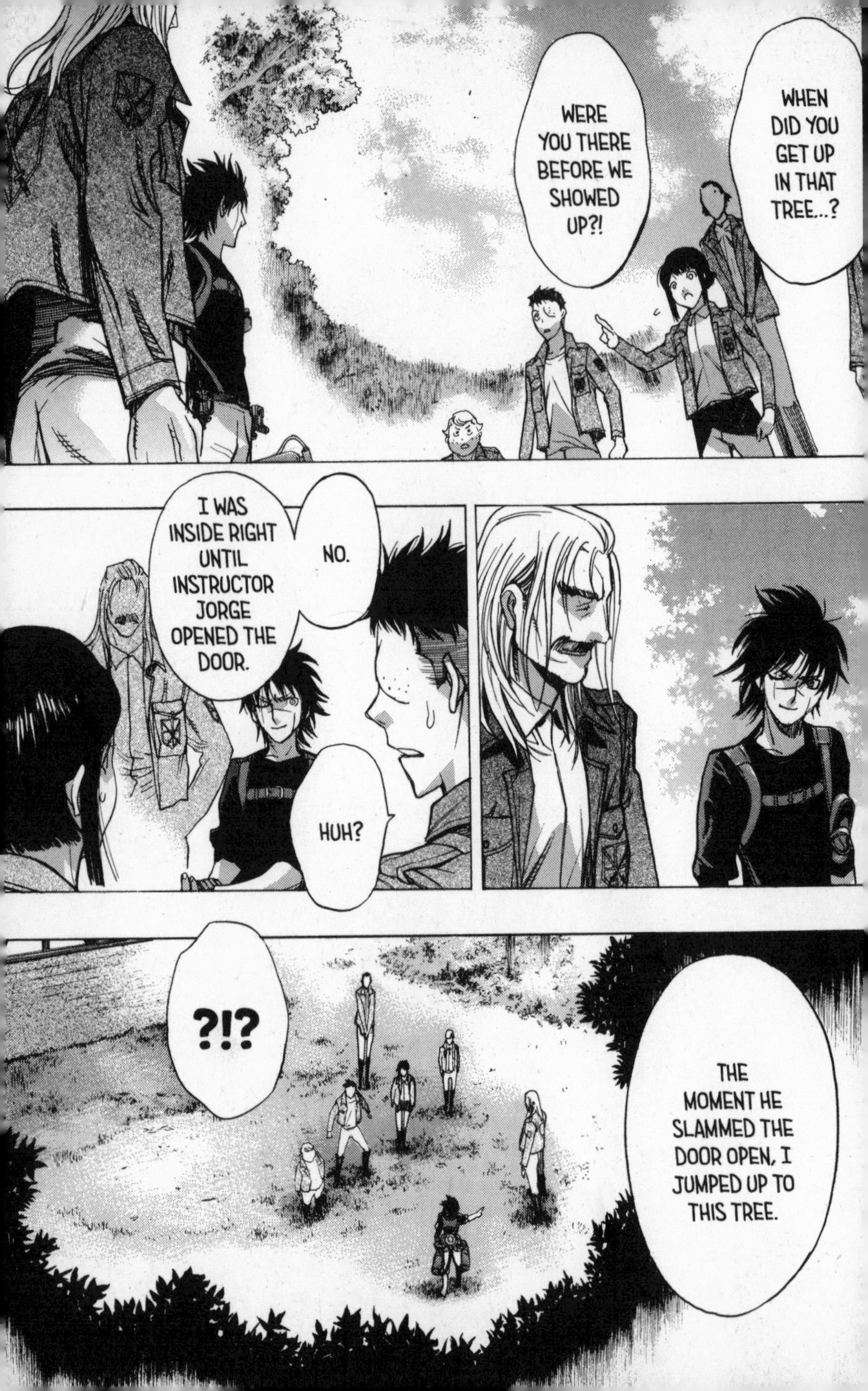
WHEN DID YOU GET UP IN THAT TREE...?
WERE YOU THERE BEFORE WE SHOWED UP?!
NO.
I WAS INSIDE RIGHT UNTIL INSTRUCTOR JORGE OPENED THE DOOR.
HUH?
THE MOMENT HE SLAMMED THE DOOR OPEN, I JUMPED UP TO THIS TREE.
?!?

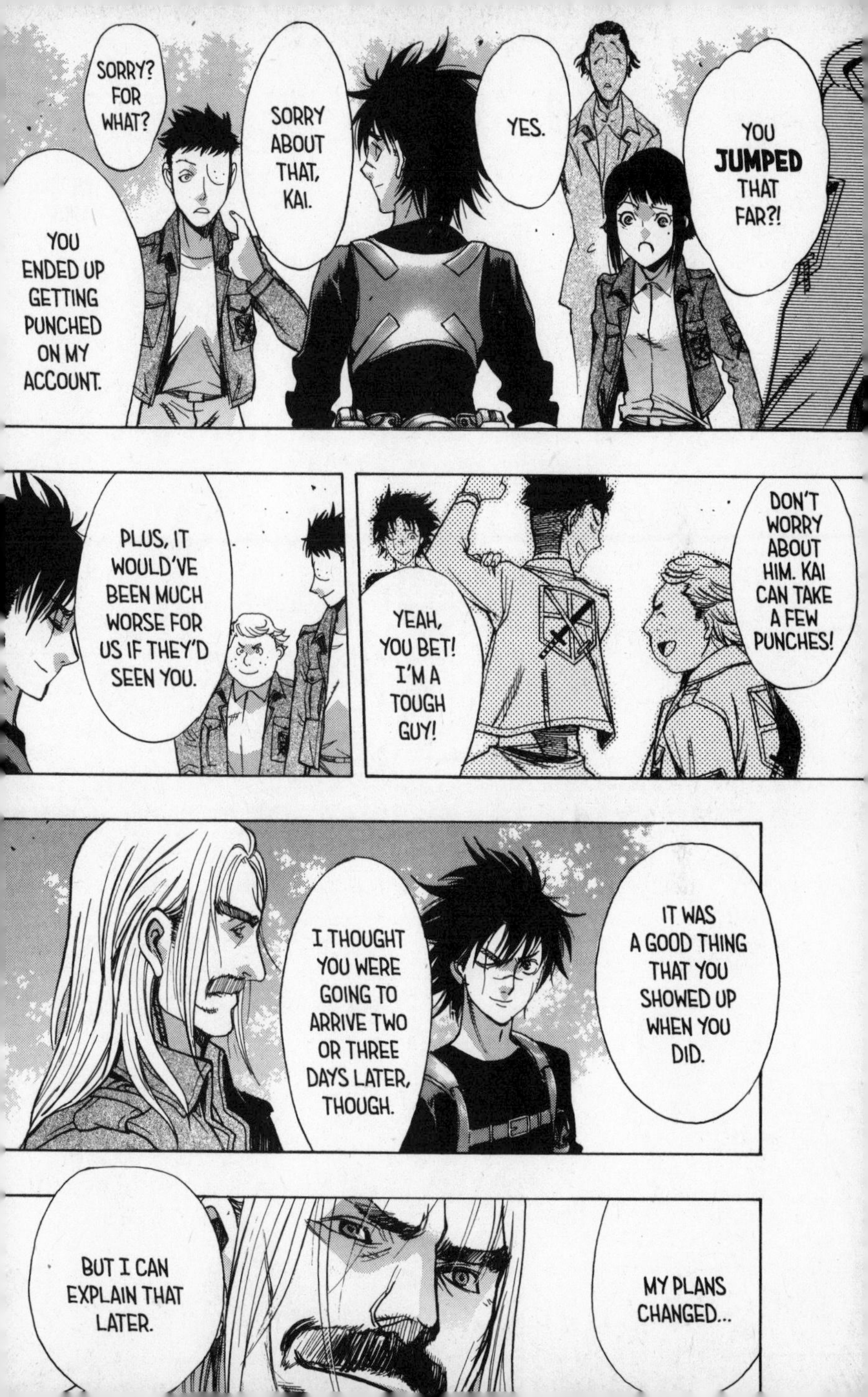
YOU JUMPED THAT FAR?!
YES.
SORRY ABOUT THAT, KAI.
SORRY? FOR WHAT?
YOU ENDED UP GETTING PUNCHED ON MY ACCOUNT.
DON'T WORRY ABOUT HIM. KAI CAN TAKE A FEW PUNCHES!
YEAH, YOU BET! I'M A TOUGH GUY!
PLUS, IT WOULD'VE BEEN MUCH WORSE FOR US IF THEY'D SEEN YOU.
IT WAS A GOOD THING THAT YOU SHOWED UP WHEN YOU DID.
I THOUGHT YOU WERE GOING TO ARRIVE TWO OR THREE DAYS LATER, THOUGH.
MY PLANS CHANGED...
BUT I CAN EXPLAIN THAT LATER.

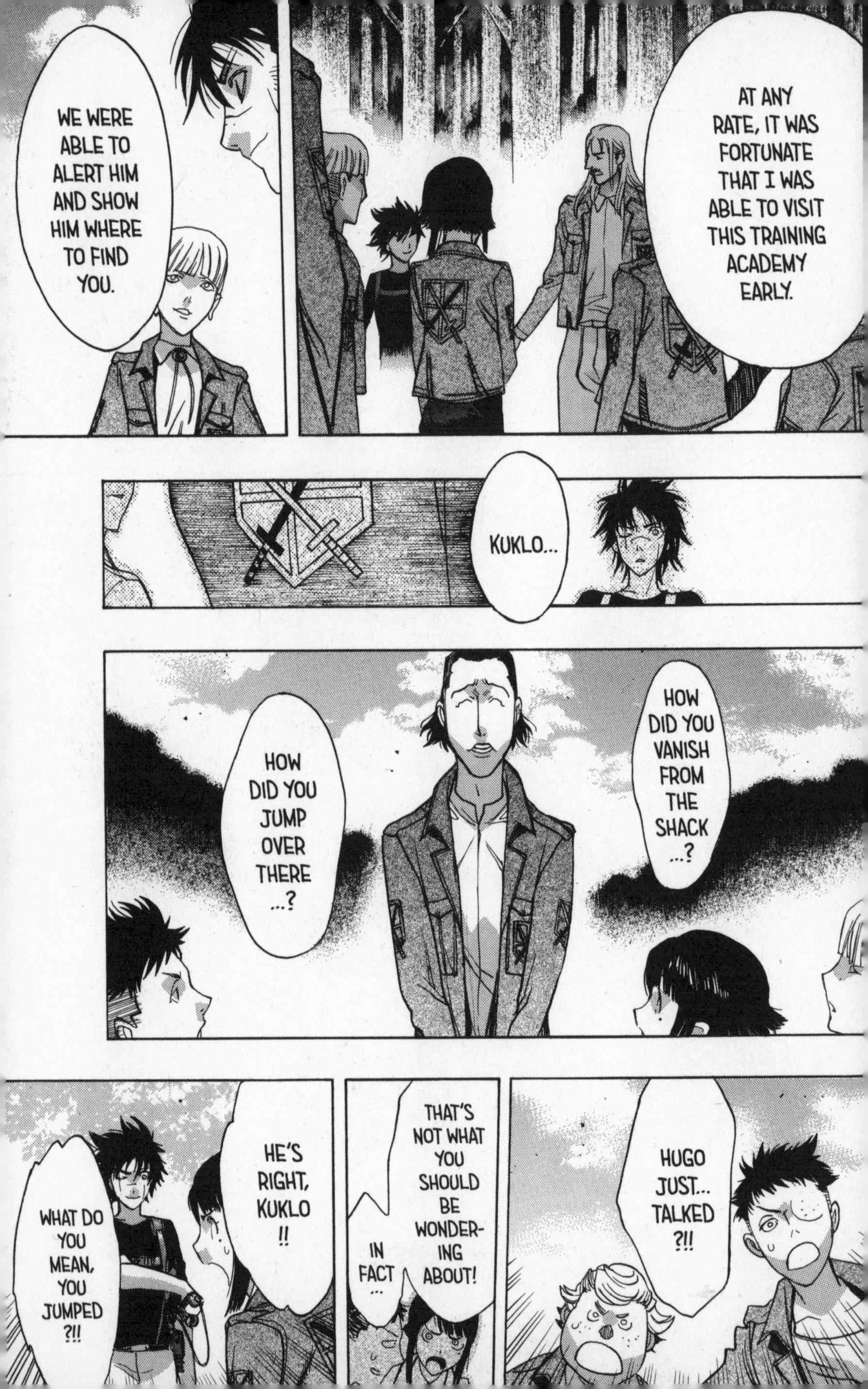
AT ANY RATE, IT WAS FORTUNATE THAT I WAS ABLE TO VISIT THIS TRAINING ACADEMY EARLY.
WE WERE ABLE TO ALERT HIM AND SHOW HIM WHERE TO FIND YOU.
KUKLO...
HOW DID YOU VANISH FROM THE SHACK ...?
HOW DID YOU JUMP OVER THERE ...?
HUGO JUST... TALKED ?!!
THAT'S NOT WHAT YOU SHOULD BE WONDER-ING ABOUT!
IN FACT ...
HE'S RIGHT, KUKLO !!
WHAT DO YOU MEAN, YOU JUMPED ?!!

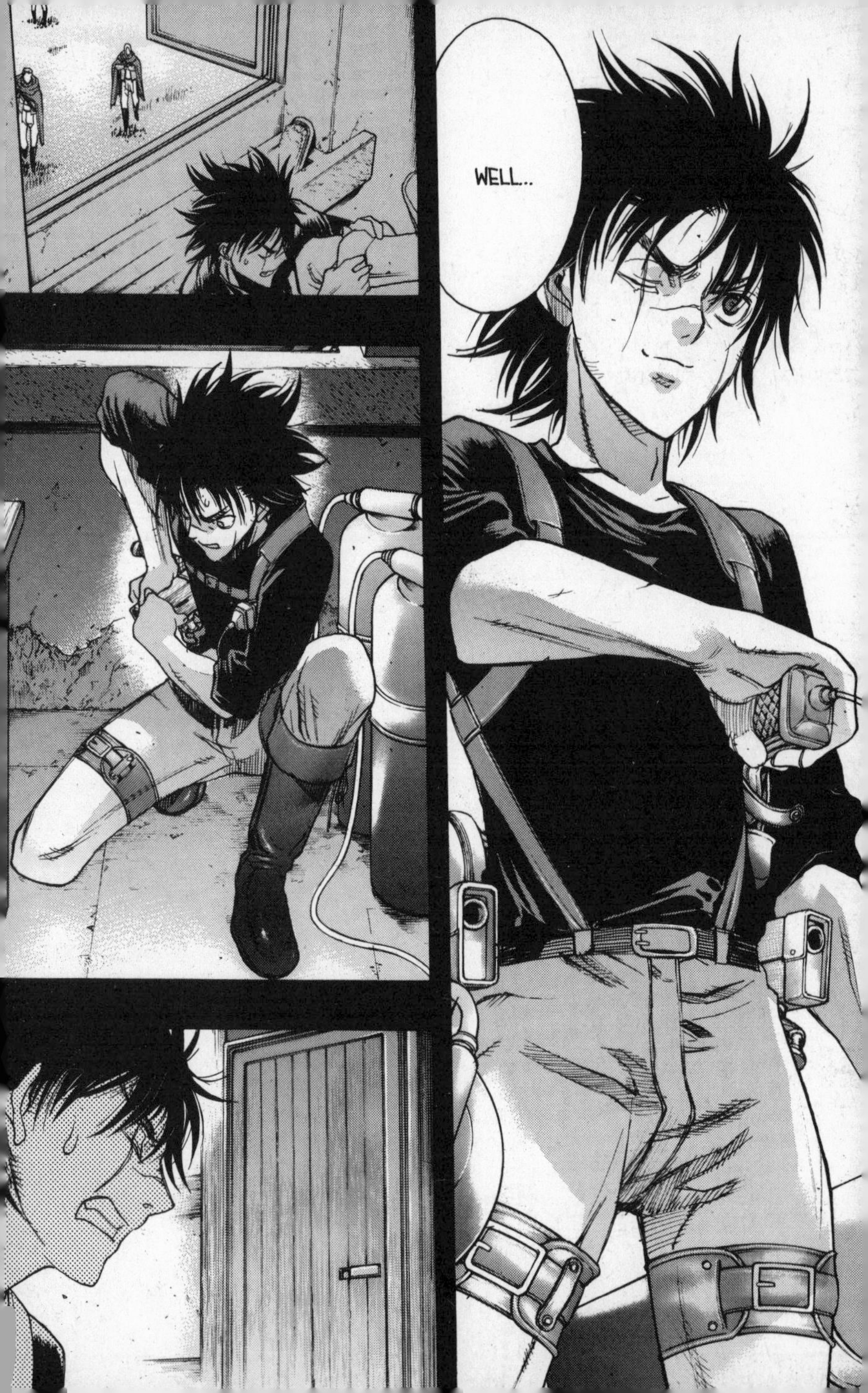
WELL...

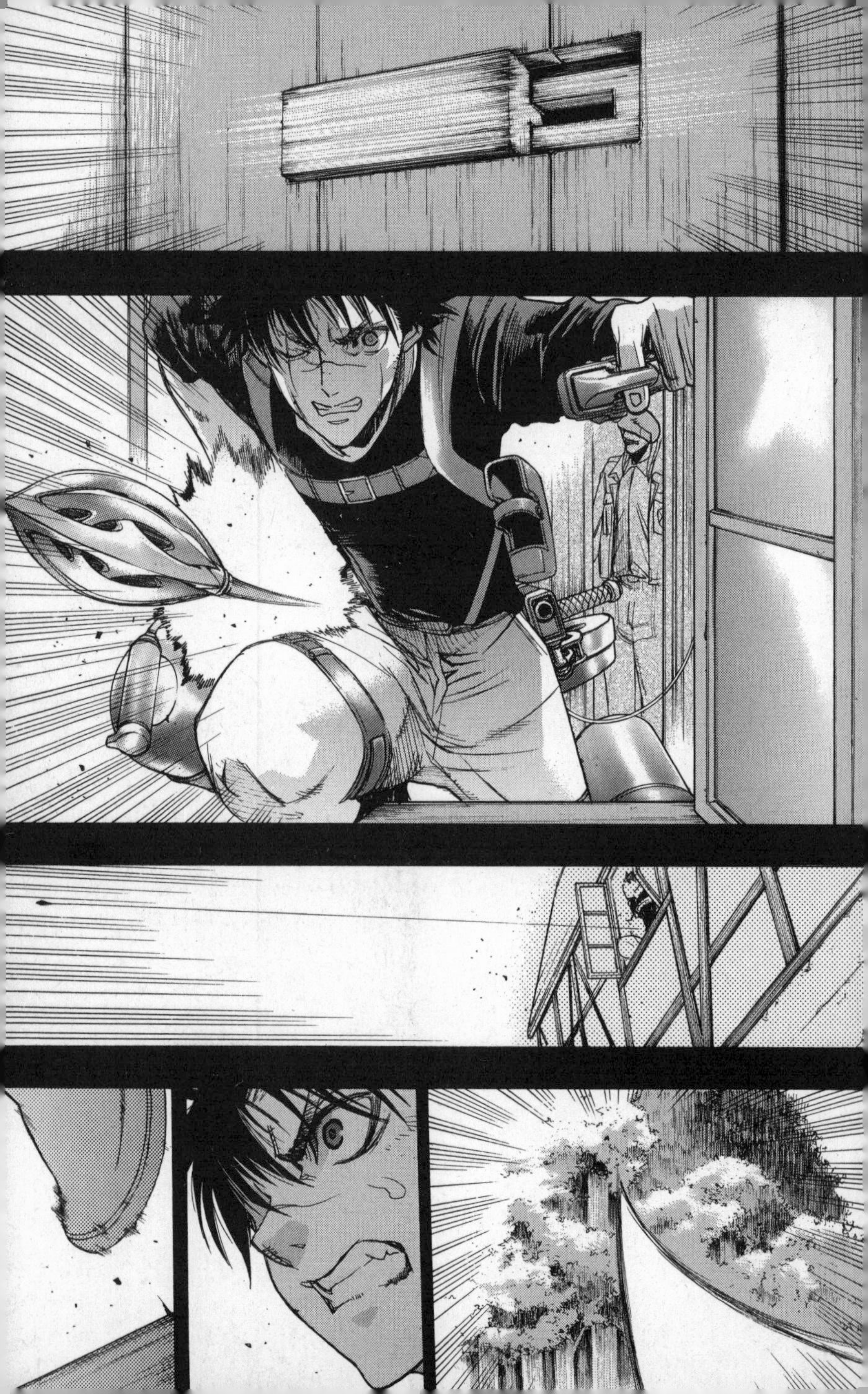

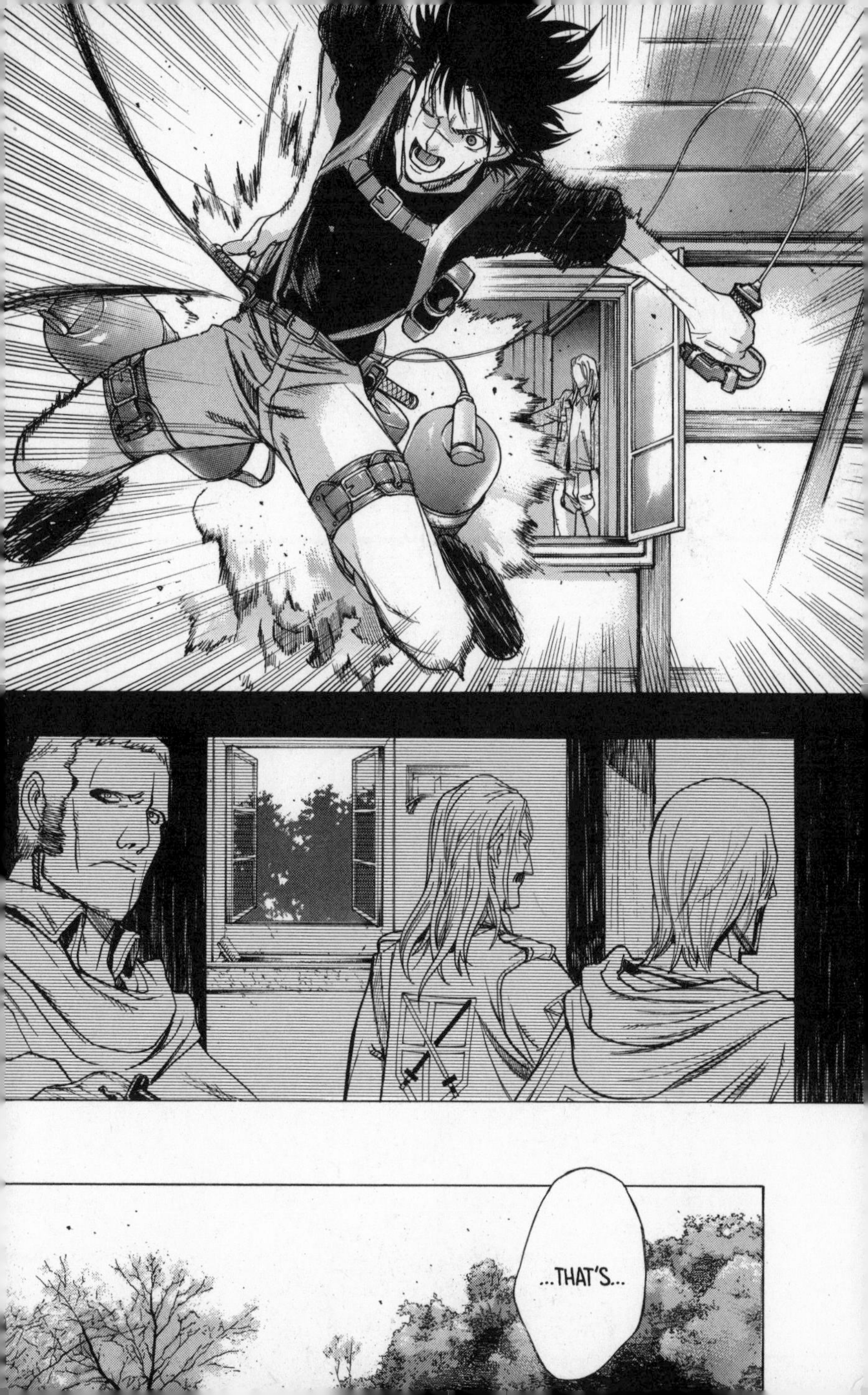
...THAT'S...

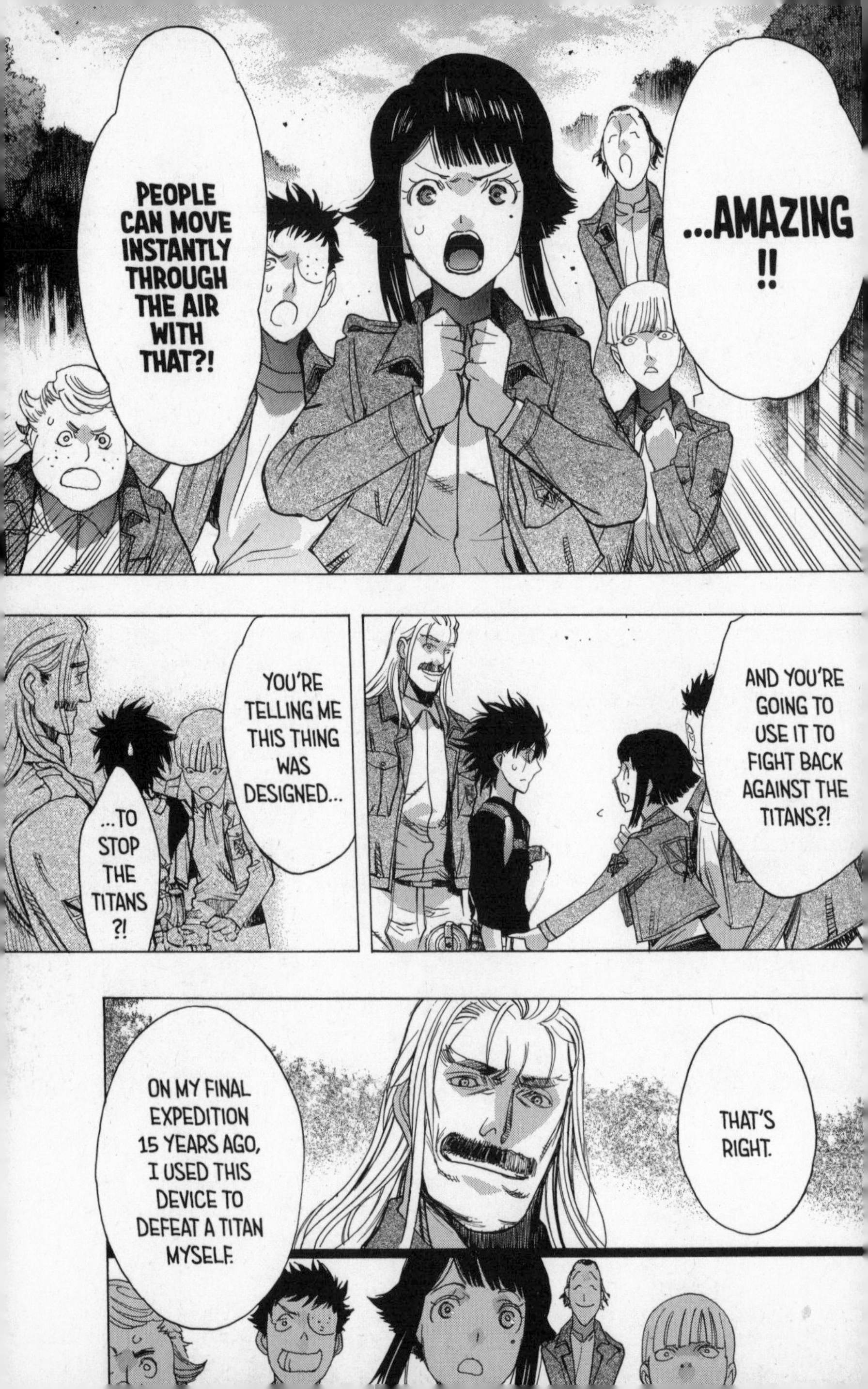
...AMAZING !!
PEOPLE CAN MOVE INSTANTLY THROUGH THE AIR WITH THAT?!
AND YOU'RE GOING TO USE IT TO FIGHT BACK AGAINST THE TITANS?!
YOU'RE TELLING ME THIS THING WAS DESIGNED...
...TO STOP THE TITANS?!
THAT'S RIGHT.
ON MY FINAL EXPEDITION 15 YEARS AGO, I USED THIS DEVICE TO DEFEAT A TITAN MYSELF.

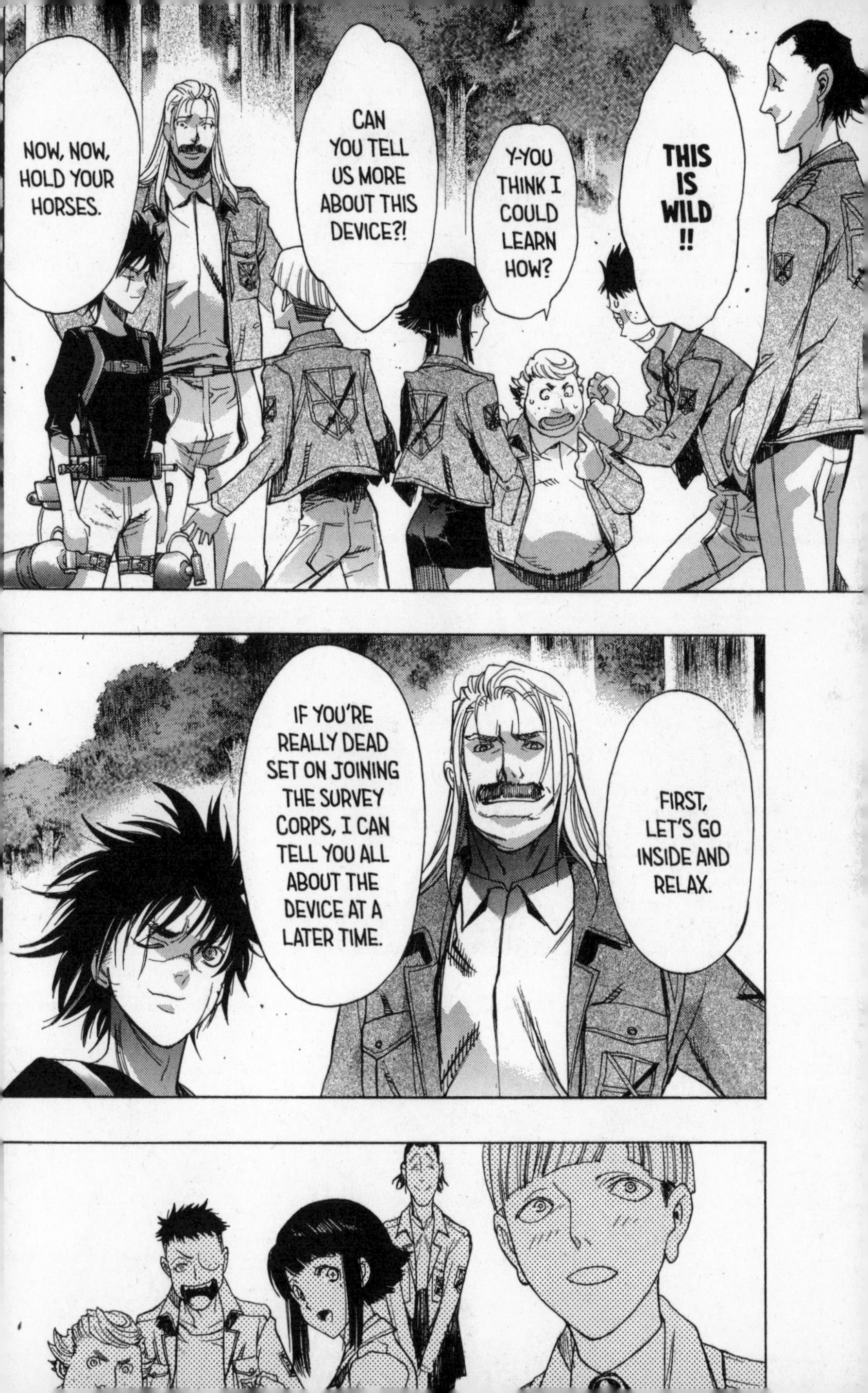
THIS IS WILD!!
Y-YOU THINK I COULD LEARN HOW?
CAN YOU TELL US MORE ABOUT THIS DEVICE?!
NOW, NOW, HOLD YOUR HORSES.
FIRST, LET'S GO INSIDE AND RELAX.
IF YOU'RE REALLY DEAD SET ON JOINING THE SURVEY CORPS, I CAN TELL YOU ALL ABOUT THE DEVICE AT A LATER TIME.

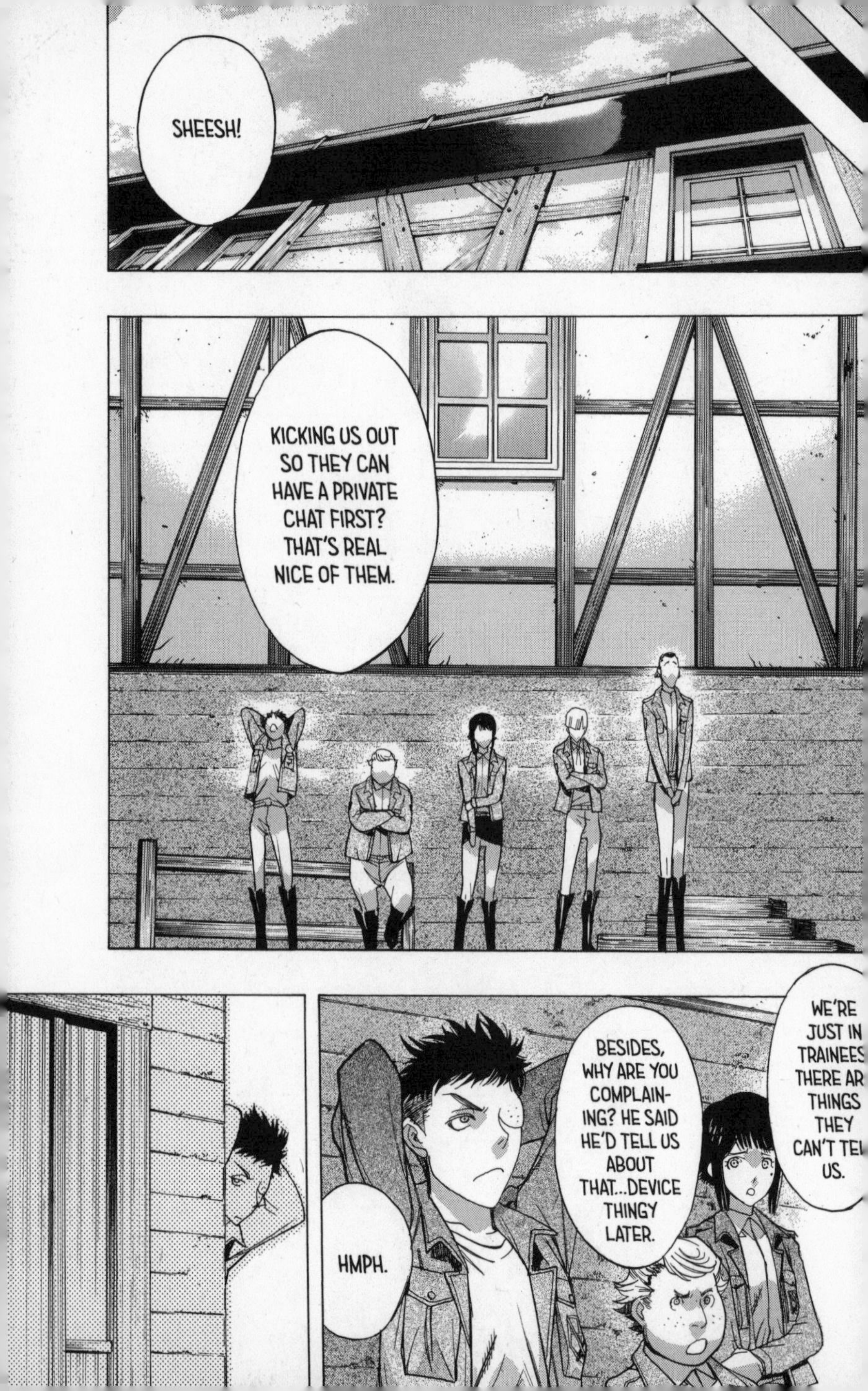
SHEESH!
KICKING US OUT SO THEY CAN HAVE A PRIVATE CHAT FIRST? THAT'S REAL NICE OF THEM.
WE'RE JUST IN TRAINEES THERE AR THINGS THEY CAN'T TEL US.
BESIDES, WHY ARE YOU COMPLAIN-ING? HE SAID HE'D TELL US ABOUT THAT...DEVICE THINGY LATER.
HMPH.

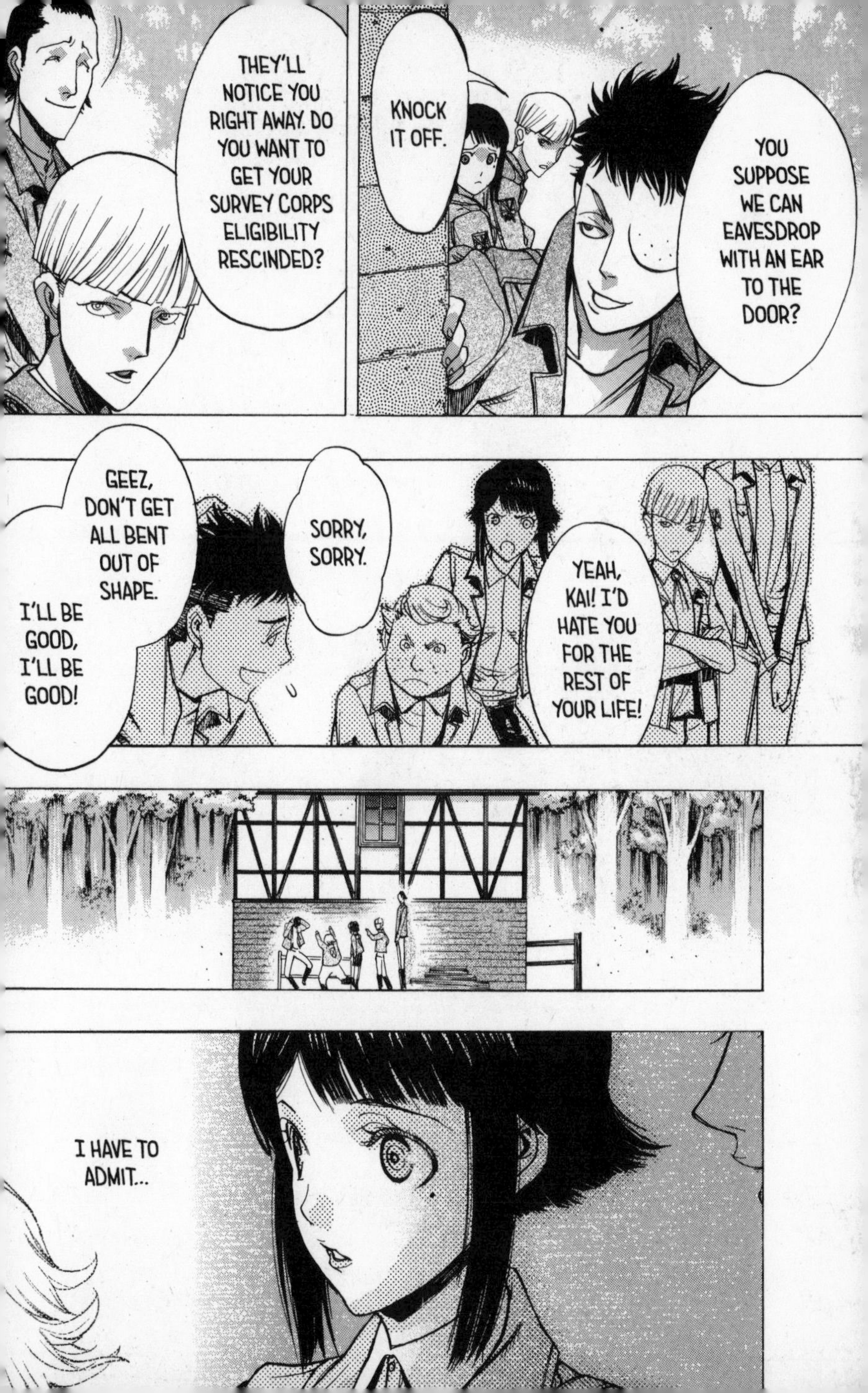
YOU SUPPOSE WE CAN EAVESDROP WITH AN EAR TO THE DOOR?
KNOCK IT OFF.
THEY'LL NOTICE YOU RIGHT AWAY. DO YOU WANT TO GET YOUR SURVEY CORPS ELIGIBILITY RESCINDED?
YEAH, KAI! I'D HATE YOU FOR THE REST OF YOUR LIFE!
SORRY, SORRY.
GEEZ, DON'T GET ALL BENT OUT OF SHAPE.
I'LL BE GOOD, I'LL BE GOOD!
I HAVE TO ADMIT...

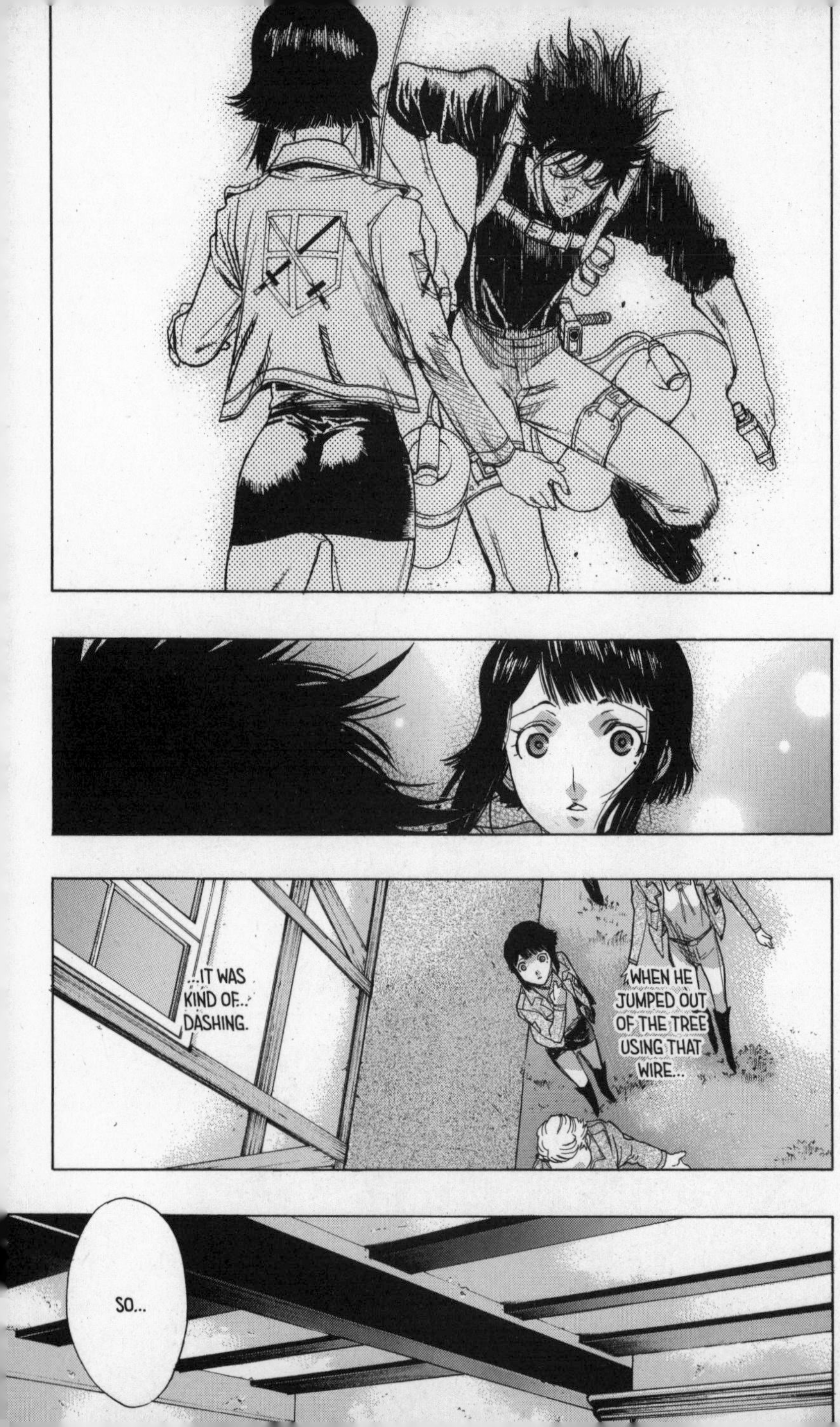
WHEN HE JUMPED OUT OF THE TREE USING THAT WIRE...
...IT WAS KIND OF... DASHING.
SO...

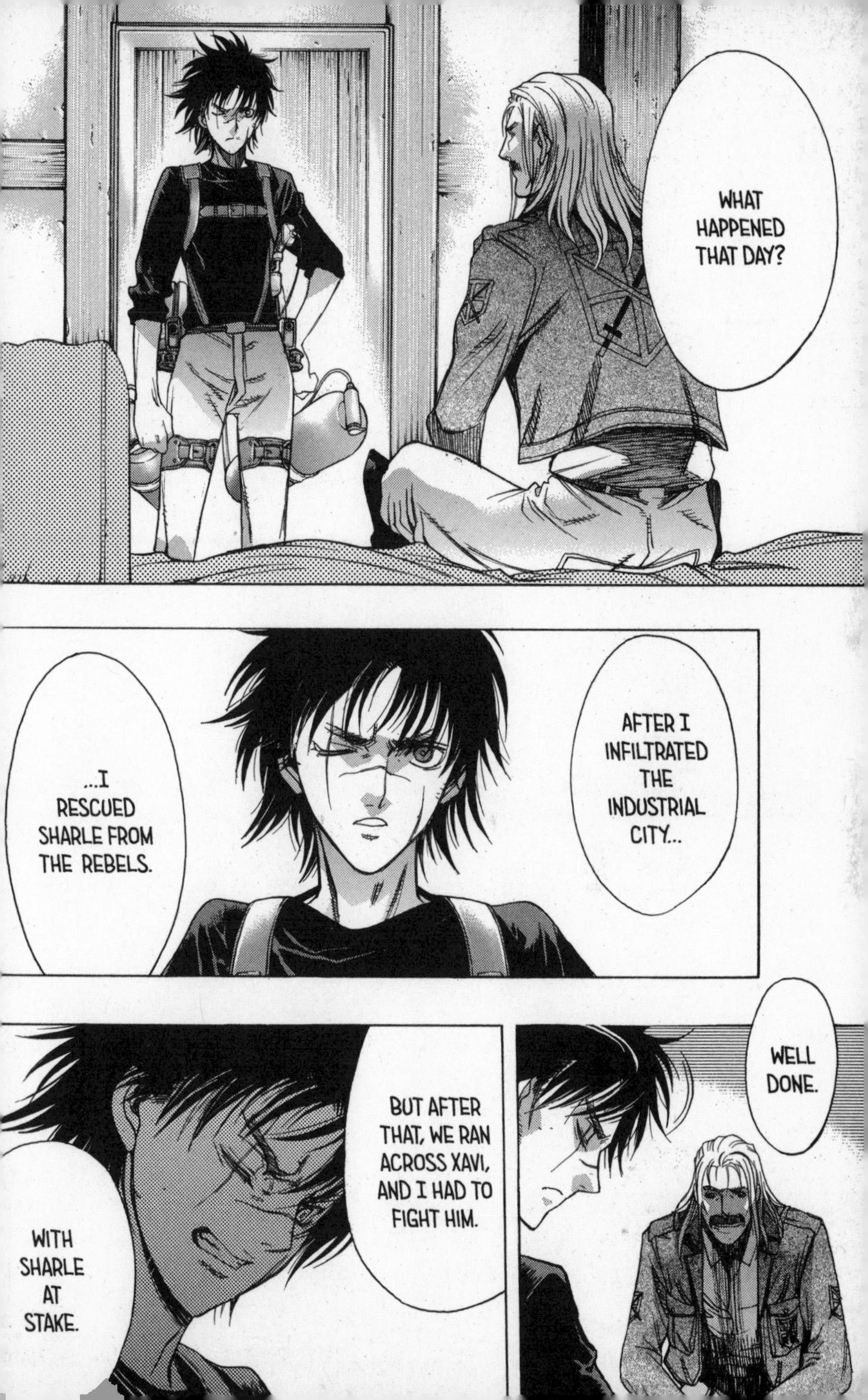
WHAT HAPPENED THAT DAY?
AFTER I INFILTRATED THE INDUSTRIAL CITY...
...I RESCUED SHARLE FROM THE REBELS.
WELL DONE.
BUT AFTER THAT, WE RAN ACROSS XAVI, AND I HAD TO FIGHT HIM.
WITH SHARLE AT STAKE.

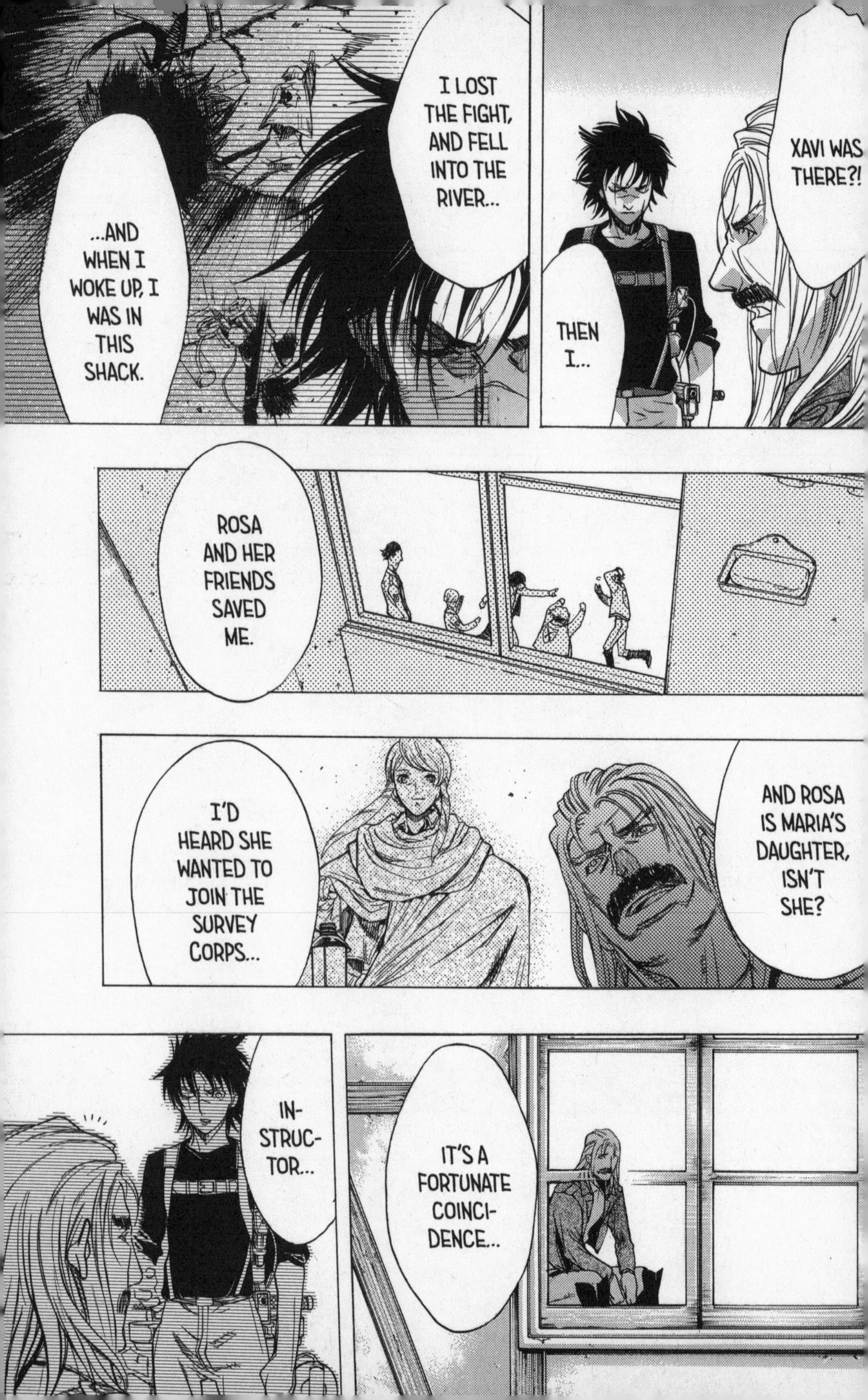
XAVI WAS THERE?!
THEN I...
I LOST THE FIGHT, AND FELL INTO THE RIVER...
...AND WHEN I WOKE UP, I WAS IN THIS SHACK.
ROSA AND HER FRIENDS SAVED ME.
AND ROSA IS MARIA'S DAUGHTER, ISN'T SHE?
I'D HEARD SHE WANTED TO JOIN THE SURVEY CORPS...
IT'S A FORTUNATE COINCI-DENCE...
IN-STRUC-TOR...

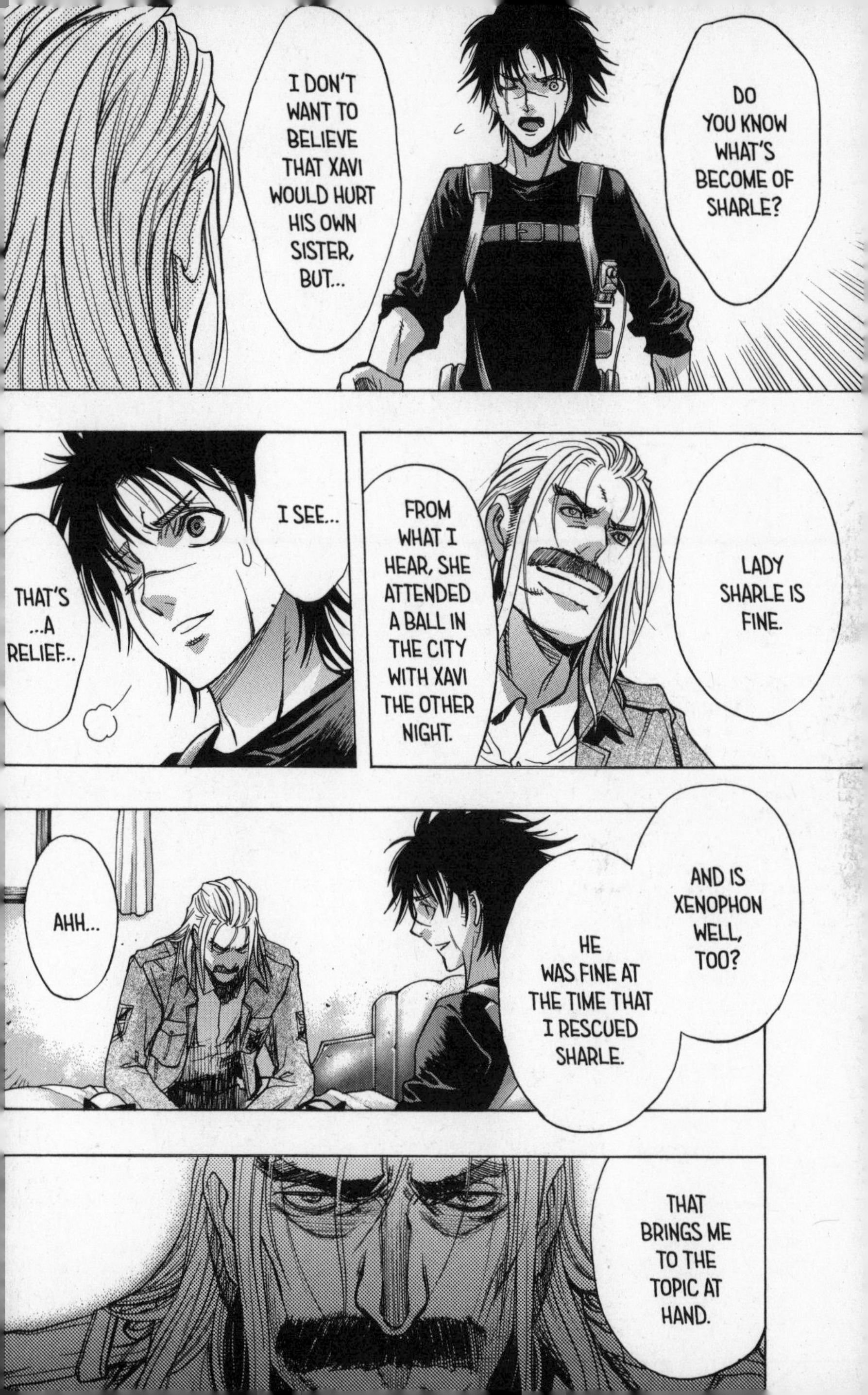
DO YOU KNOW WHAT'S BECOME OF SHARLE?
I DON'T WANT TO BELIEVE THAT XAVI WOULD HURT HIS OWN SISTER, BUT...
LADY SHARLE IS FINE.
FROM WHAT I HEAR, SHE ATTENDED A BALL IN THE CITY WITH XAVI THE OTHER NIGHT.
I SEE...
THAT'S ...A RELIEF...
AND IS XENOPHON WELL, TOO?
HE WAS FINE AT THE TIME THAT I RESCUED SHARLE.
AHH...
THAT BRINGS ME TO THE TOPIC AT HAND.

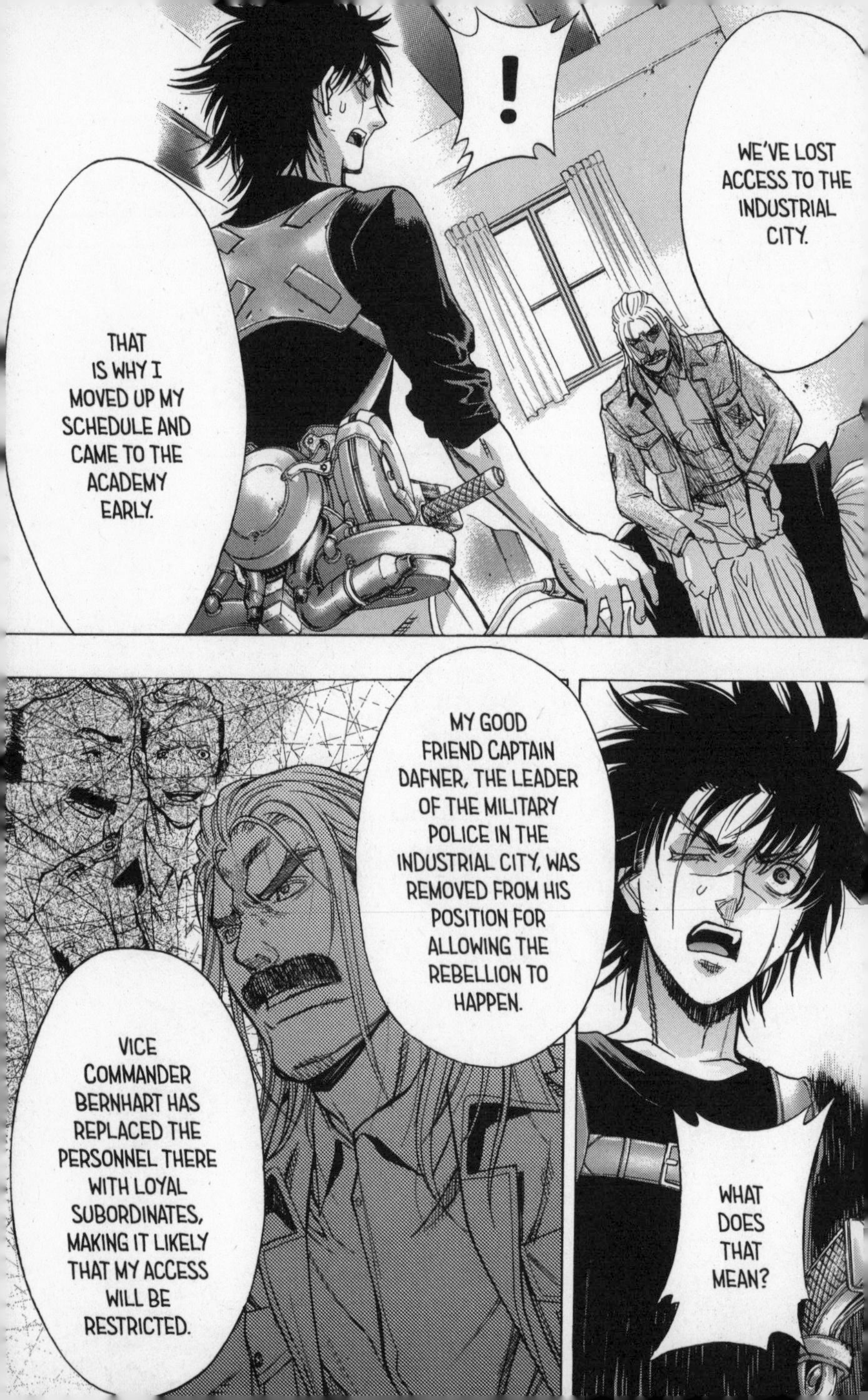
WE'VE LOST ACCESS TO THE INDUSTRIAL CITY.
!
THAT IS WHY I MOVED UP MY SCHEDULE AND CAME TO THE ACADEMY EARLY.
WHAT DOES THAT MEAN?
MY GOOD FRIEND CAPTAIN DAFNER, THE LEADER OF THE MILITARY POLICE IN THE INDUSTRIAL CITY, WAS REMOVED FROM HIS POSITION FOR ALLOWING THE REBELLION TO HAPPEN.
VICE COMMANDER BERNHART HAS REPLACED THE PERSONNEL THERE WITH LOYAL SUBORDINATES, MAKING IT LIKELY THAT MY ACCESS WILL BE RESTRICTED.

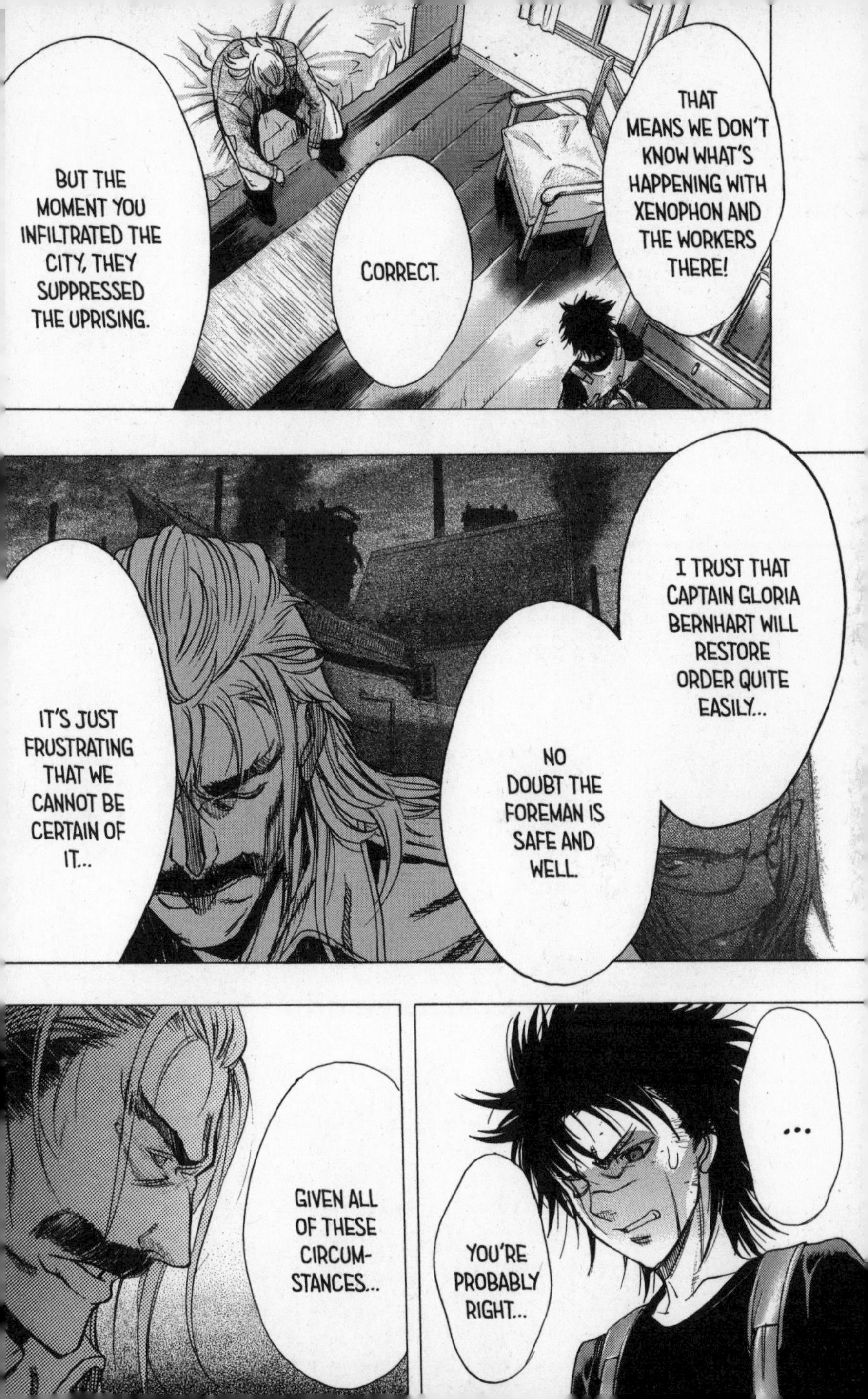
THAT MEANS WE DON'T KNOW WHAT'S HAPPENING WITH XENOPHON AND THE WORKERS THERE!
CORRECT.
BUT THE MOMENT YOU INFILTRATED THE CITY, THEY SUPPRESSED THE UPRISING.
I TRUST THAT CAPTAIN GLORIA BERNHART WILL RESTORE ORDER QUITE EASILY...
NO DOUBT THE FOREMAN IS SAFE AND WELL.
IT'S JUST FRUSTRATING THAT WE CANNOT BE CERTAIN OF IT...
...
YOU'RE PROBABLY RIGHT...
GIVEN ALL OF THESE CIRCUM-STANCES...

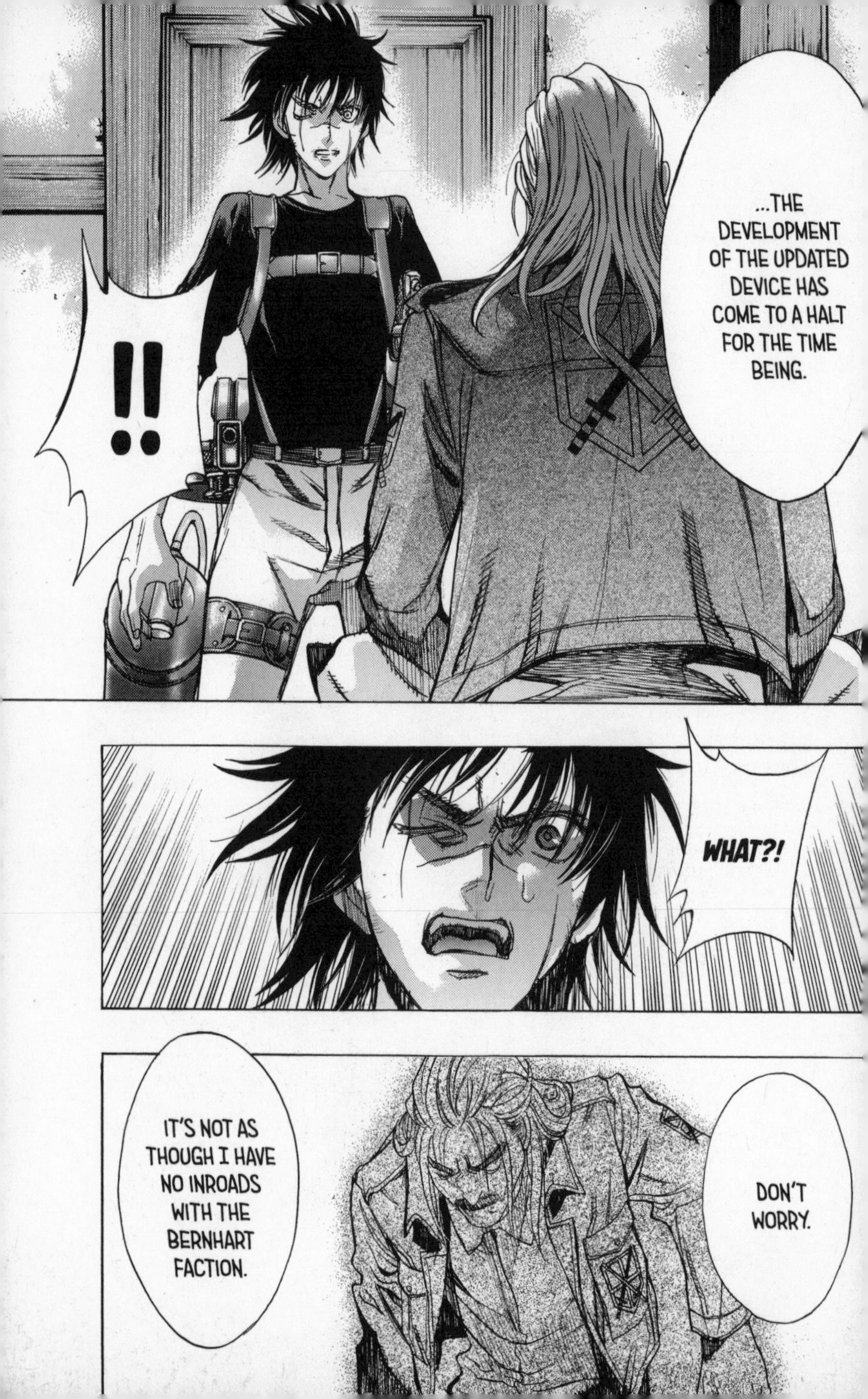
...THE DEVELOPMENT OF THE UPDATED DEVICE HAS COME TO A HALT FOR THE TIME BEING.
!!
WHAT?!
DON'T WORRY.
IT'S NOT AS THOUGH I HAVE NO INROADS WITH THE BERNHART FACTION.

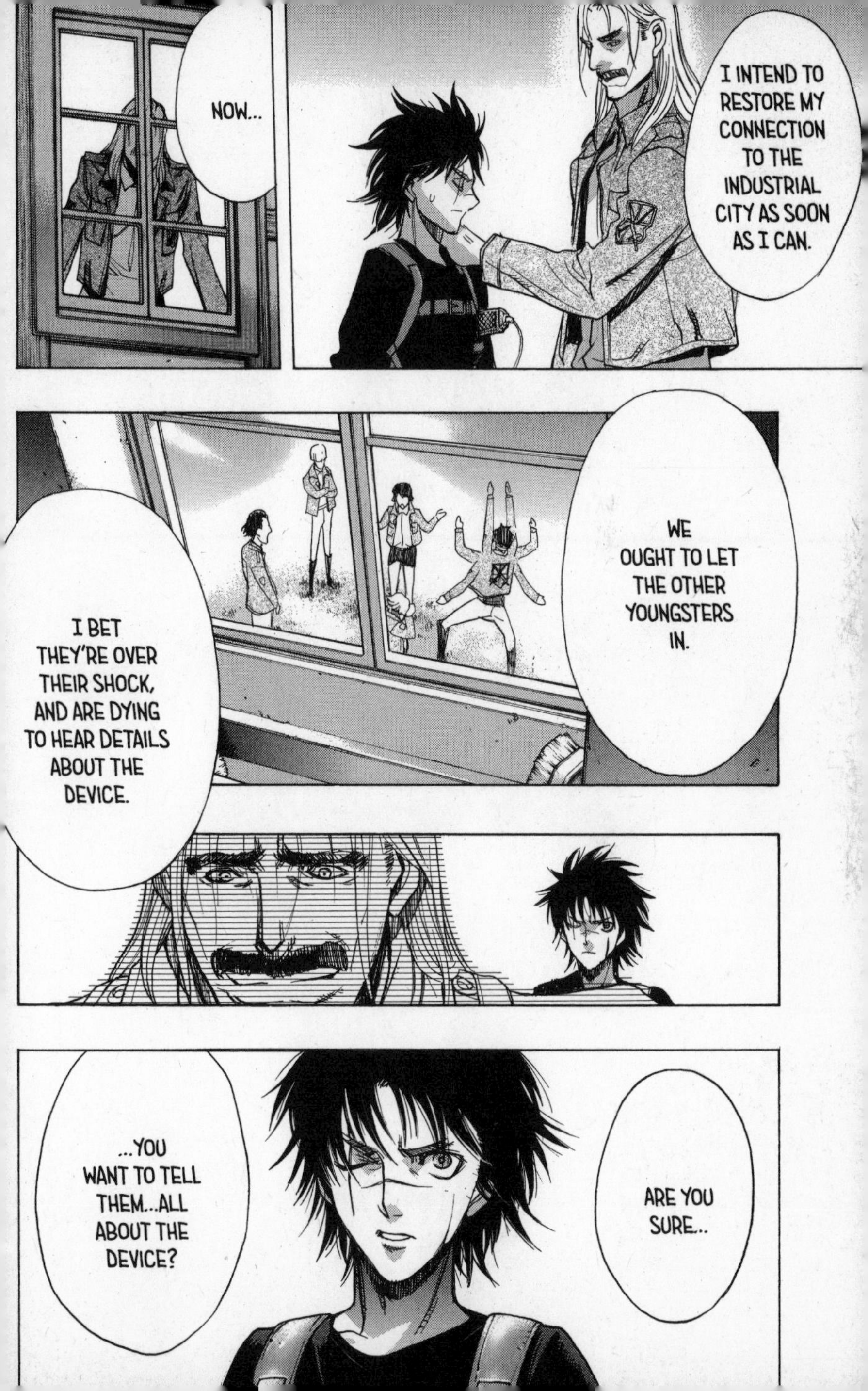
I INTEND TO RESTORE MY CONNECTION TO THE INDUSTRIAL CITY AS SOON AS I CAN.
NOW...
WE OUGHT TO LET THE OTHER YOUNGSTERS IN.
I BET THEY'RE OVER THEIR SHOCK, AND ARE DYING TO HEAR DETAILS ABOUT THE DEVICE.
ARE YOU SURE...
...YOU WANT TO TELL THEM...ALL ABOUT THE DEVICE?

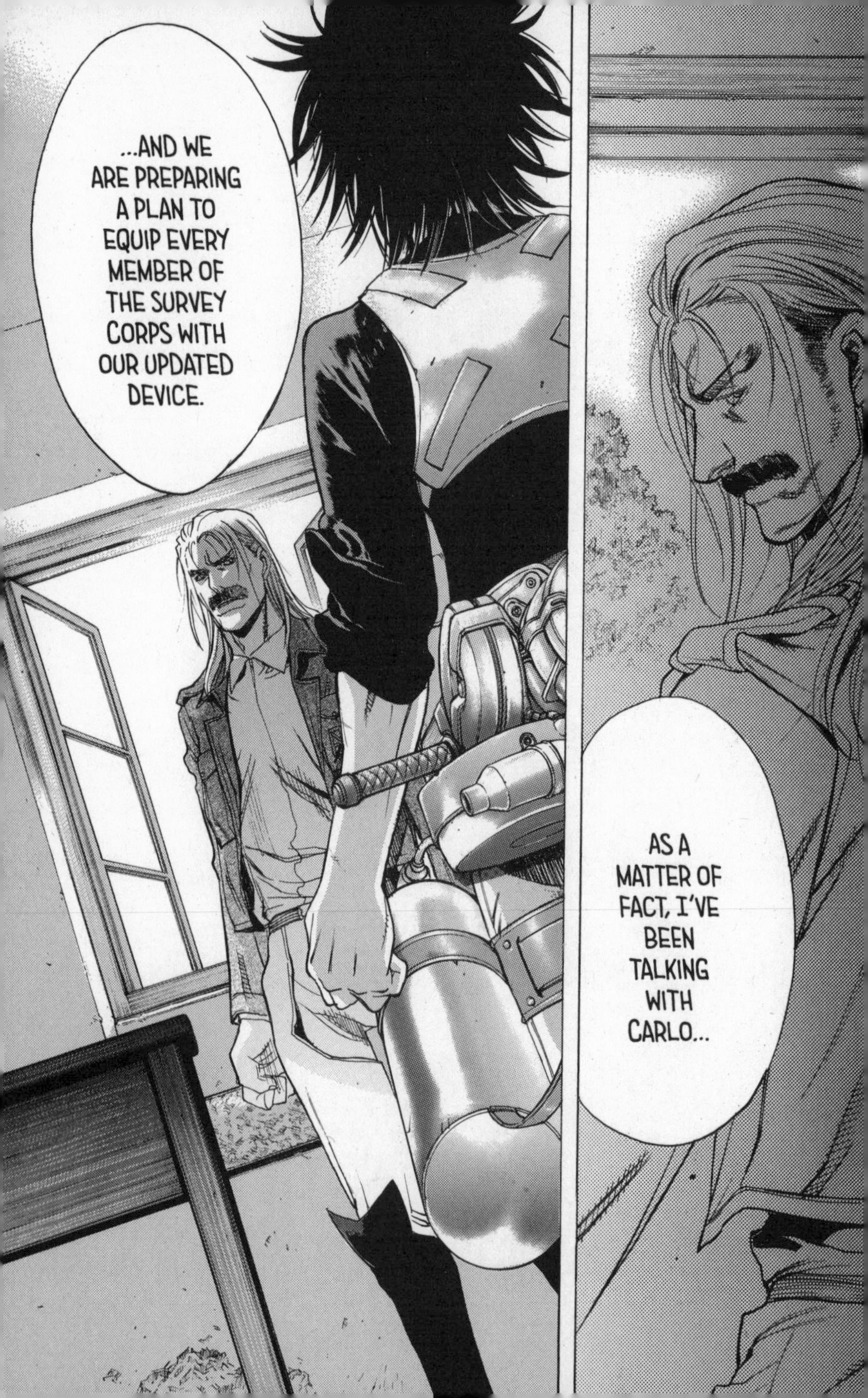
AS A MATTER OF FACT, I'VE BEEN TALKING WITH CARLO...
...AND WE ARE PREPARING A PLAN TO EQUIP EVERY MEMBER OF THE SURVEY CORPS WITH OUR UPDATED DEVICE.

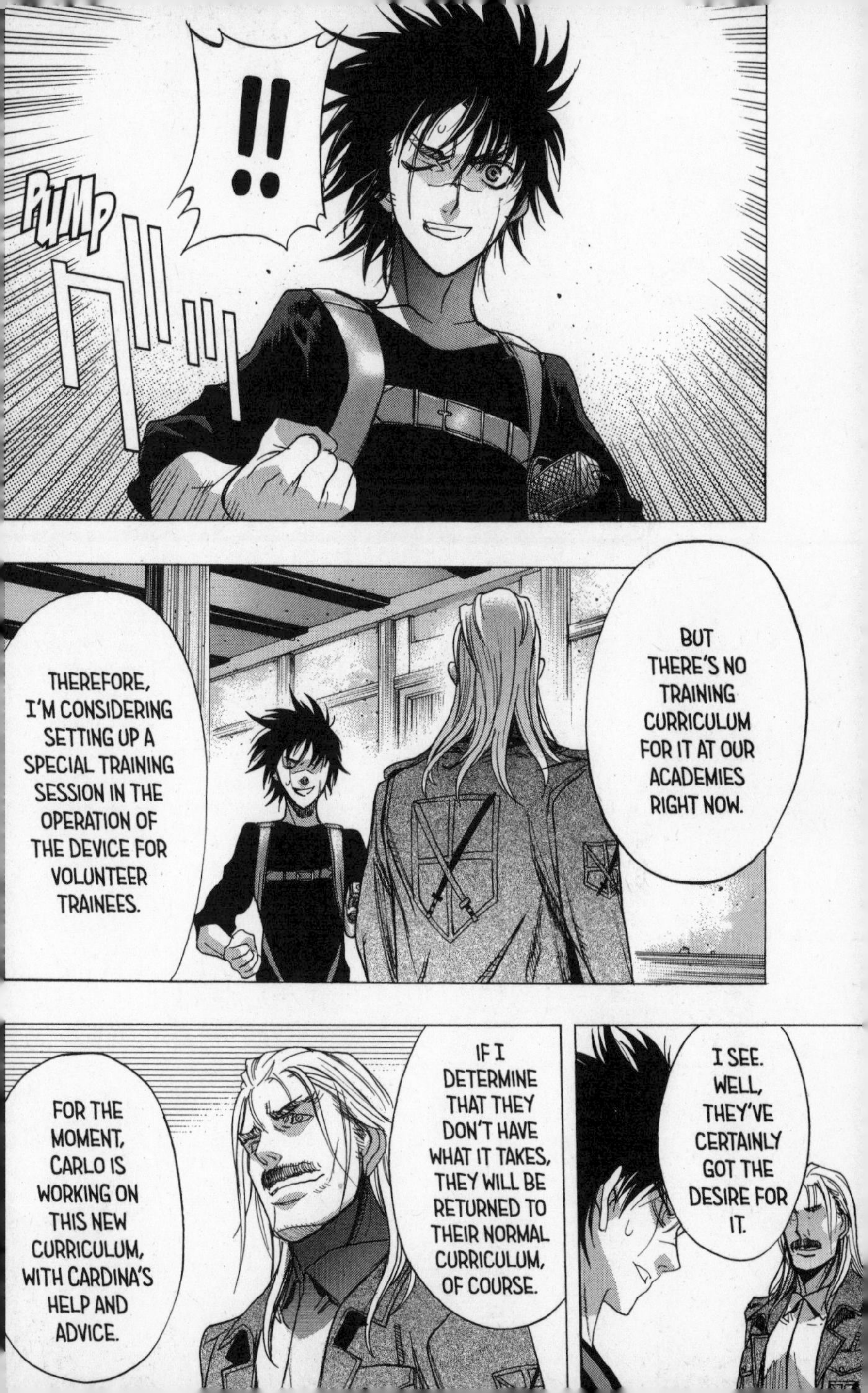
!!
PUMP
BUT THERE'S NO TRAINING CURRICULUM FOR IT AT OUR ACADEMIES RIGHT NOW.
THEREFORE, I'M CONSIDERING SETTING UP A SPECIAL TRAINING SESSION IN THE OPERATION OF THE DEVICE FOR VOLUNTEER TRAINEES.
I SEE. WELL, THEY'VE CERTAINLY GOT THE DESIRE FOR IT.
IF I DETERMINE THAT THEY DON'T HAVE WHAT IT TAKES, THEY WILL BE RETURNED TO THEIR NORMAL CURRICULUM, OF COURSE.
FOR THE MOMENT, CARLO IS WORKING ON THIS NEW CURRICULUM, WITH CARDINA'S HELP AND ADVICE.

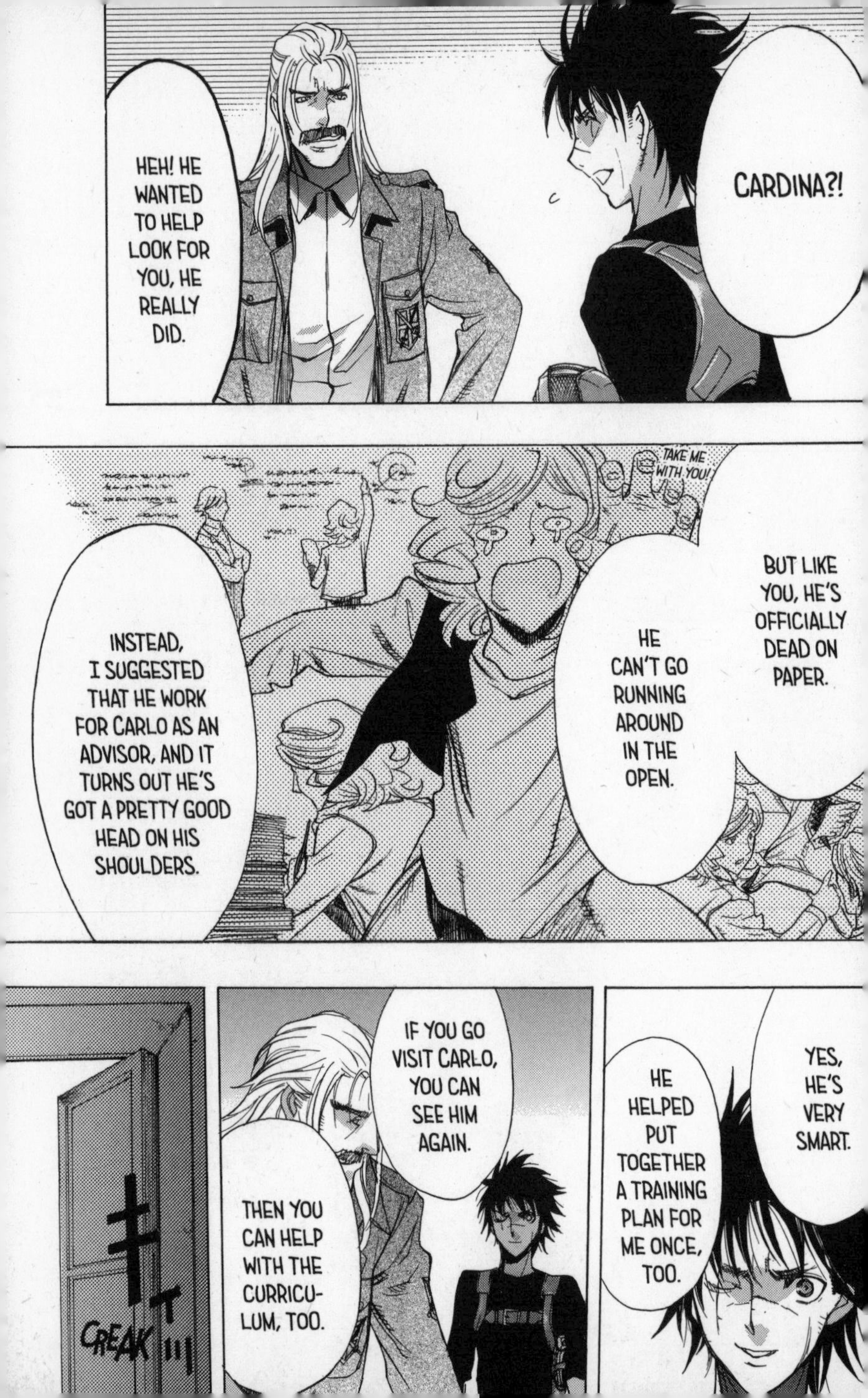
CARDINA?!
HEH! HE WANTED TO HELP LOOK FOR YOU, HE REALLY DID.
TAKE ME WITH YOU!
BUT LIKE YOU, HE'S OFFICIALLY DEAD ON PAPER.
HE CAN'T GO RUNNING AROUND IN THE OPEN.
INSTEAD, I SUGGESTED THAT HE WORK FOR CARLO AS AN ADVISOR, AND IT TURNS OUT HE'S GOT A PRETTY GOOD HEAD ON HIS SHOULDERS.
YES, HE'S VERY SMART.
HE HELPED PUT TOGETHER A TRAINING PLAN FOR ME ONCE, TOO.
IF YOU GO VISIT CARLO, YOU CAN SEE HIM AGAIN.
THEN YOU CAN HELP WITH THE CURRICU-LUM, TOO.
CREAK

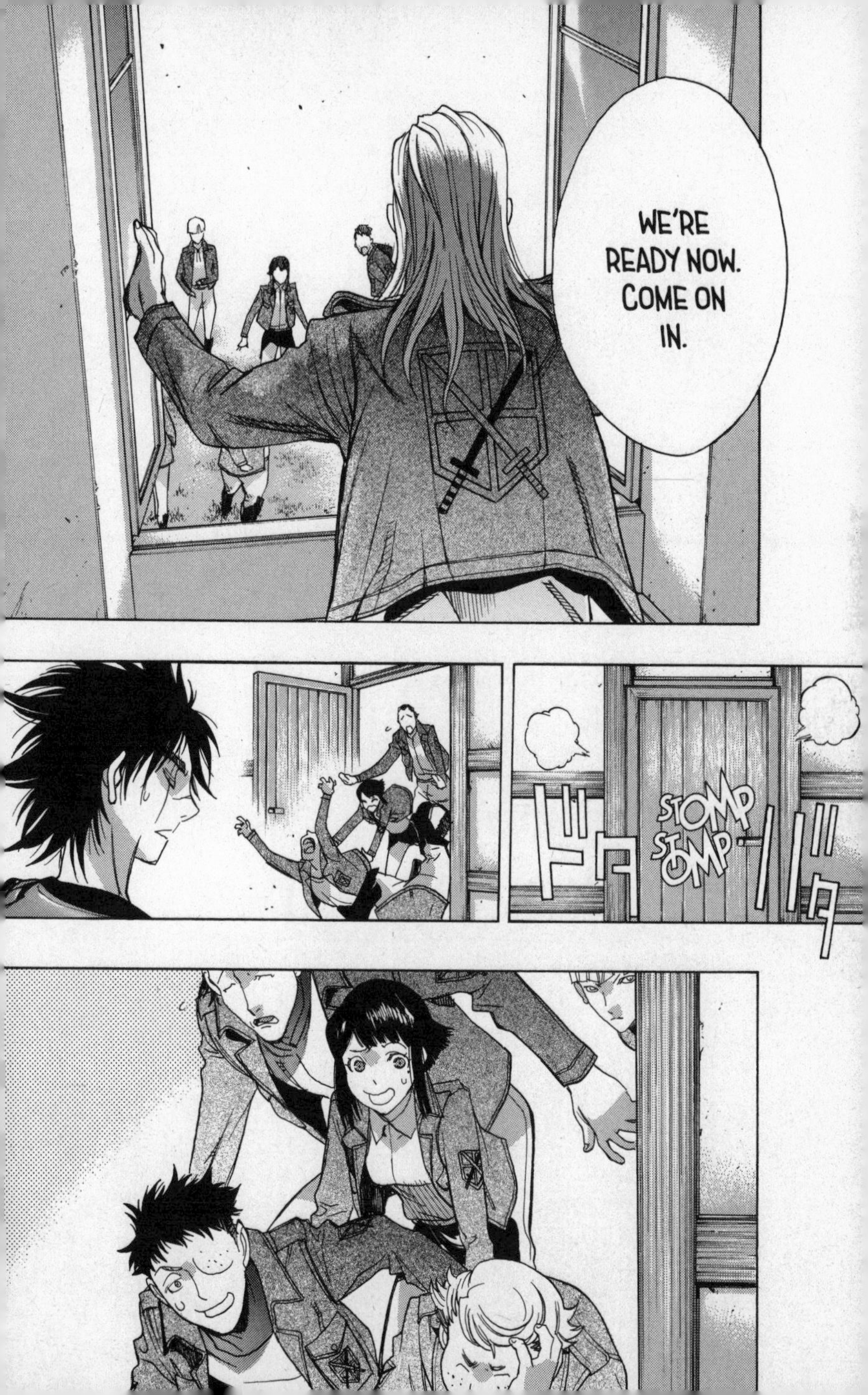
WE'RE READY NOW. COME ON IN.
STOMP STOMP

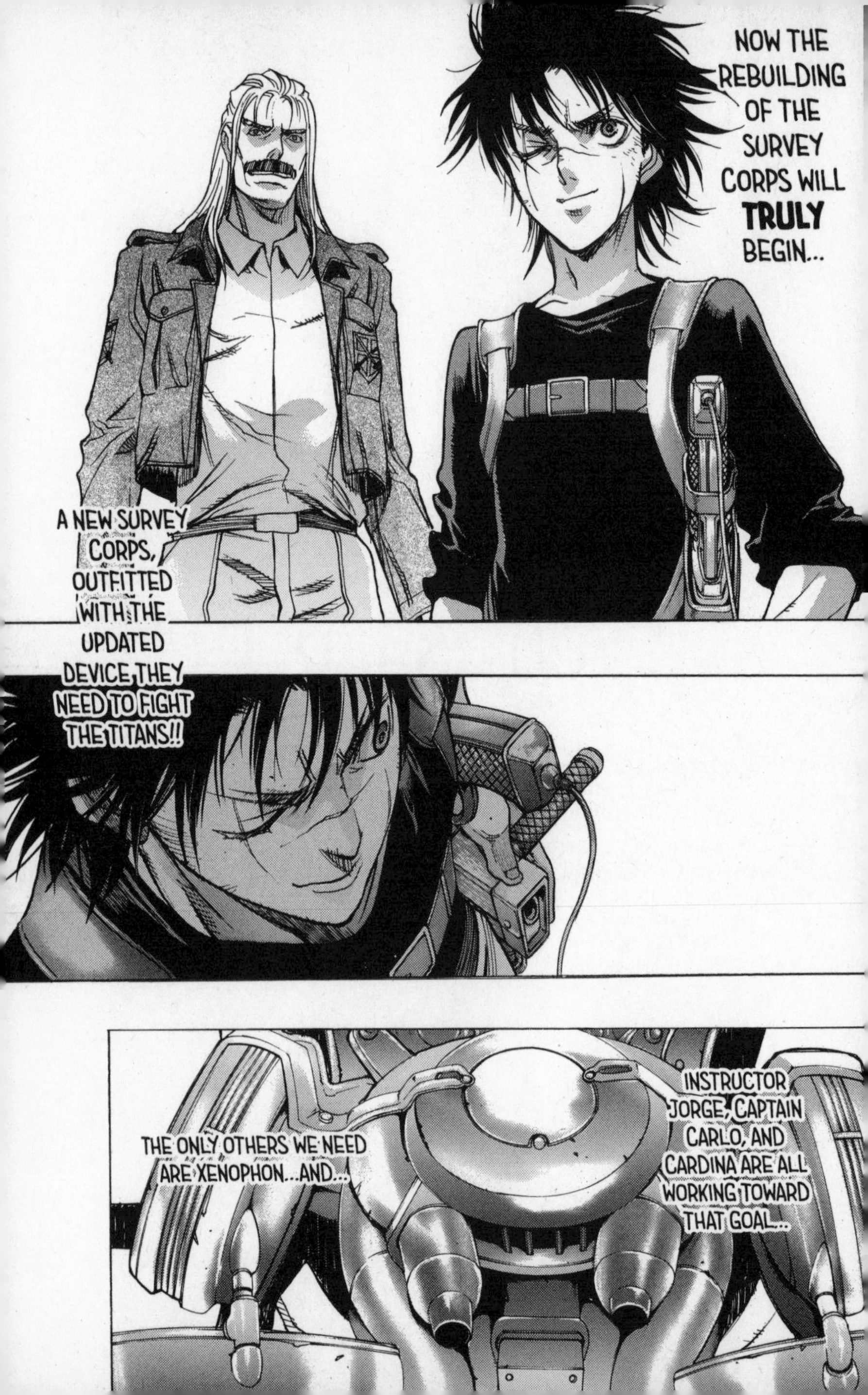
NOW THE REBUILDING OF THE SURVEY CORPS WILL **TRULY** BEGIN...
A NEW SURVEY CORPS, OUTFITTED WITH THE UPDATED DEVICE THEY NEED TO FIGHT THE TITANS!!
INSTRUCTOR JORGE, CAPTAIN CARLO, AND CARDINA ARE ALL WORKING TOWARD THAT GOAL...
THE ONLY OTHERS WE NEED ARE XENOPHON...AND...

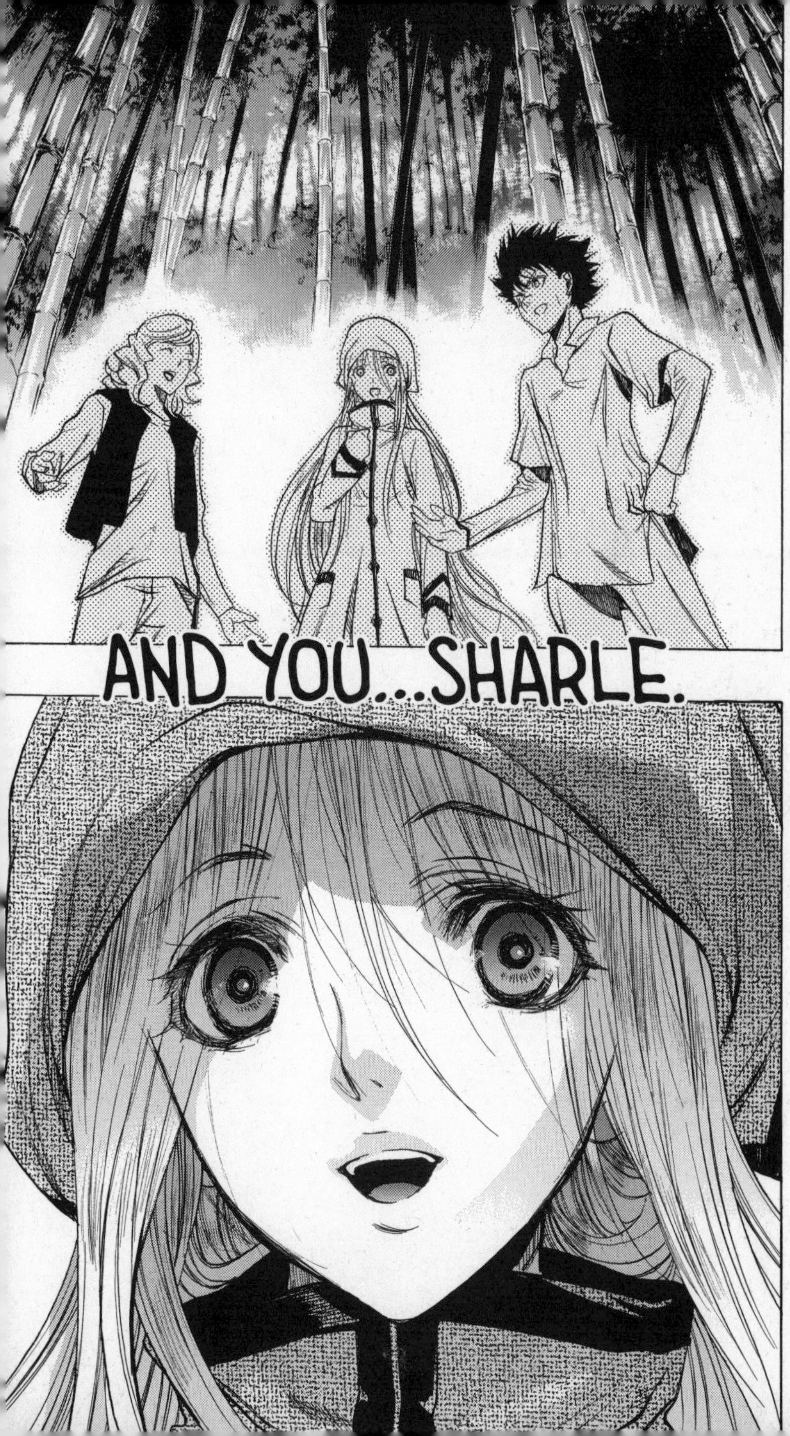
AND YOU...SHARLE.

Chapter 41: Cornerstone of the Corps · End

ATTACK on TITAN

BEFORE THE FALL

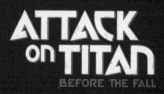

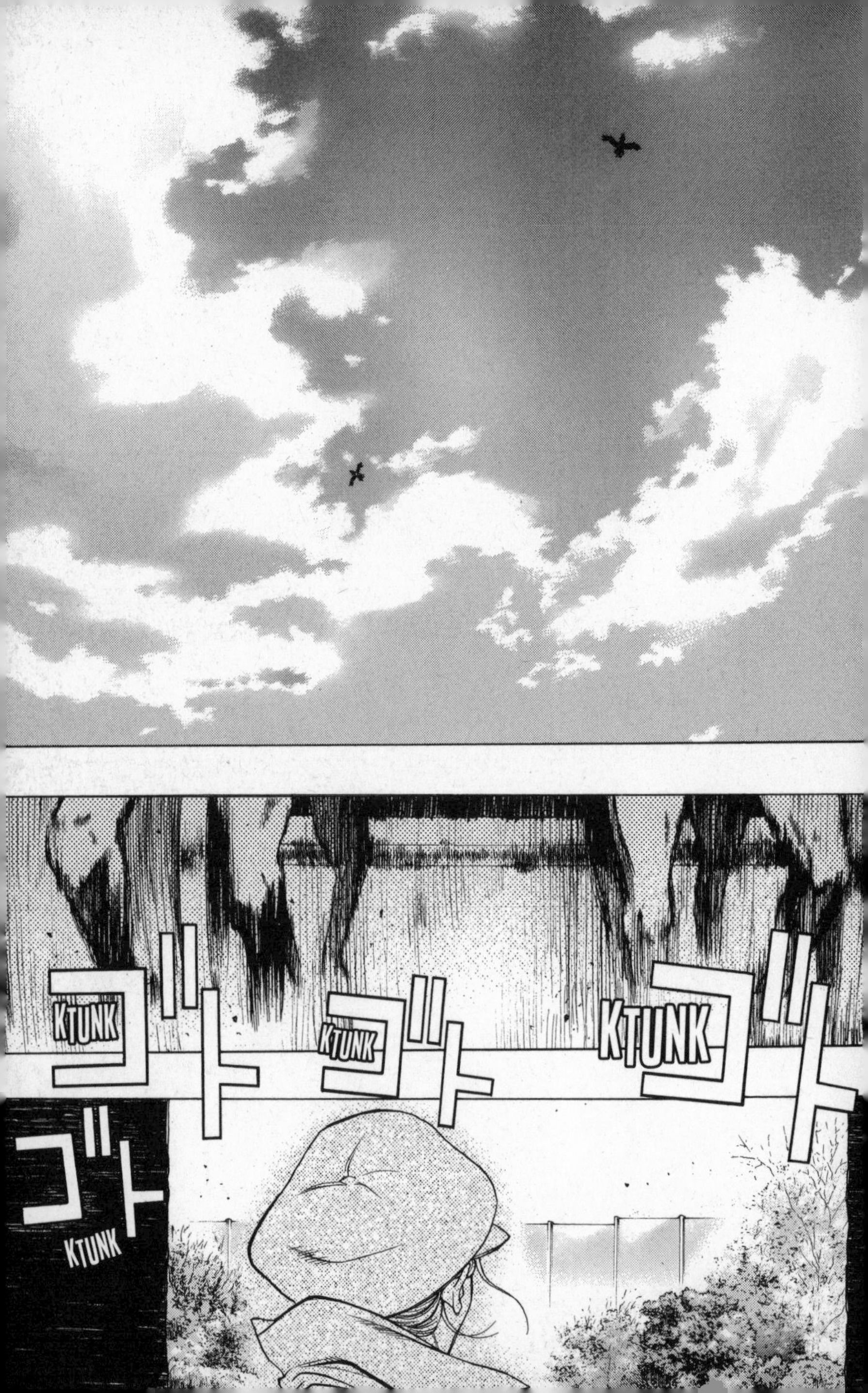

ゴト
KTUNK
ゴト
KTUNK
ゴト
KTUNK
ゴト
KTUNK

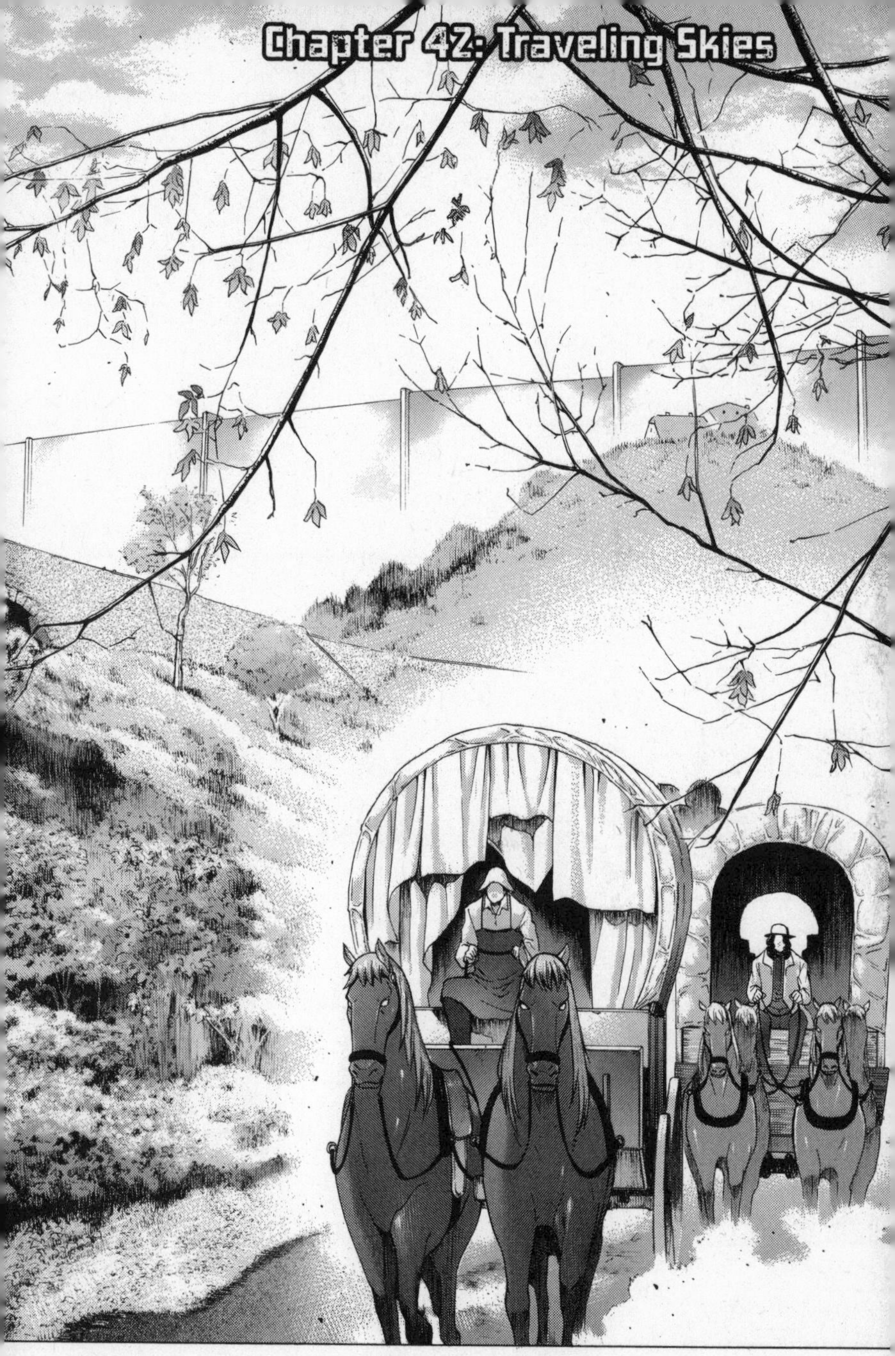
Chapter 42: Traveling Skies

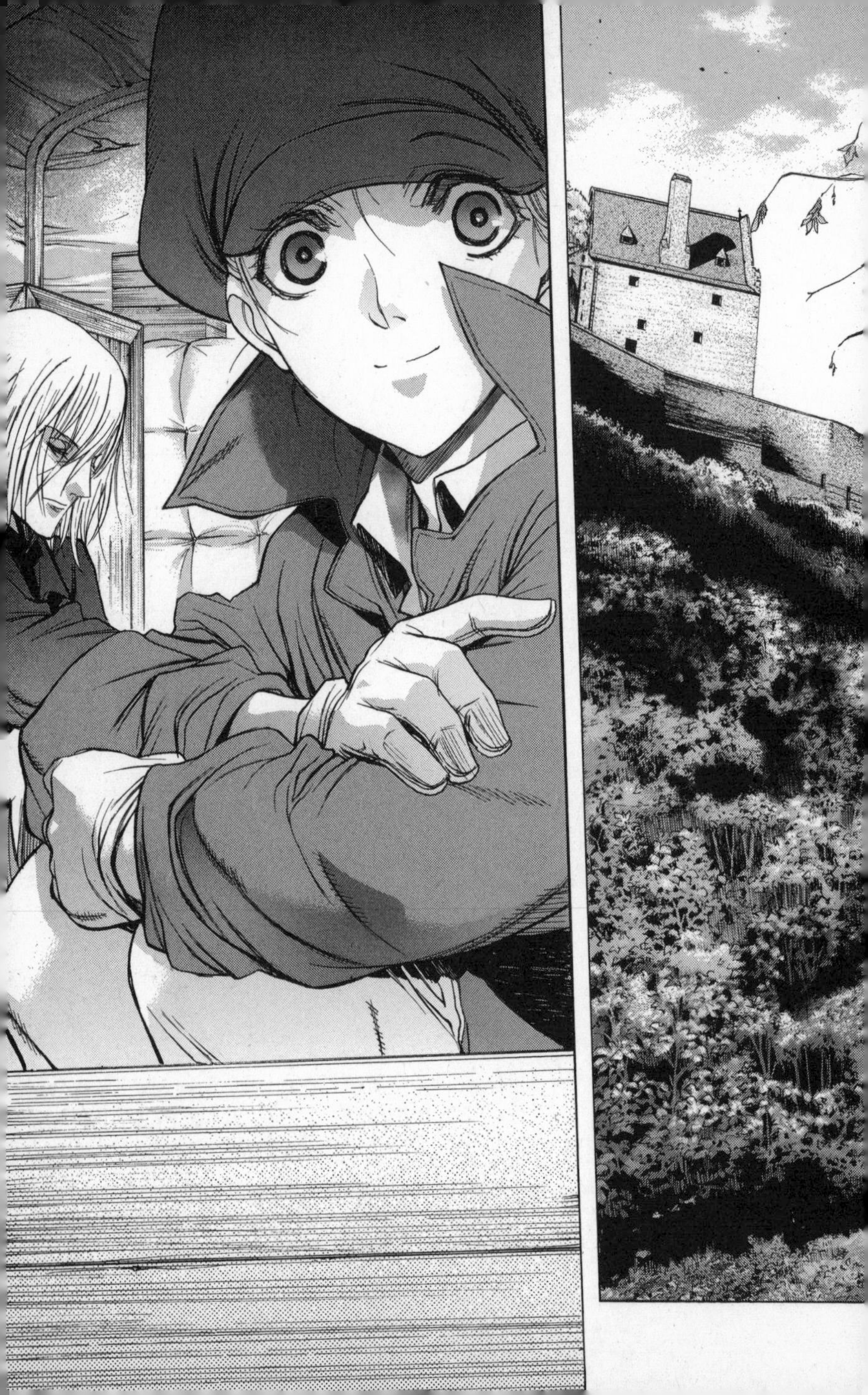

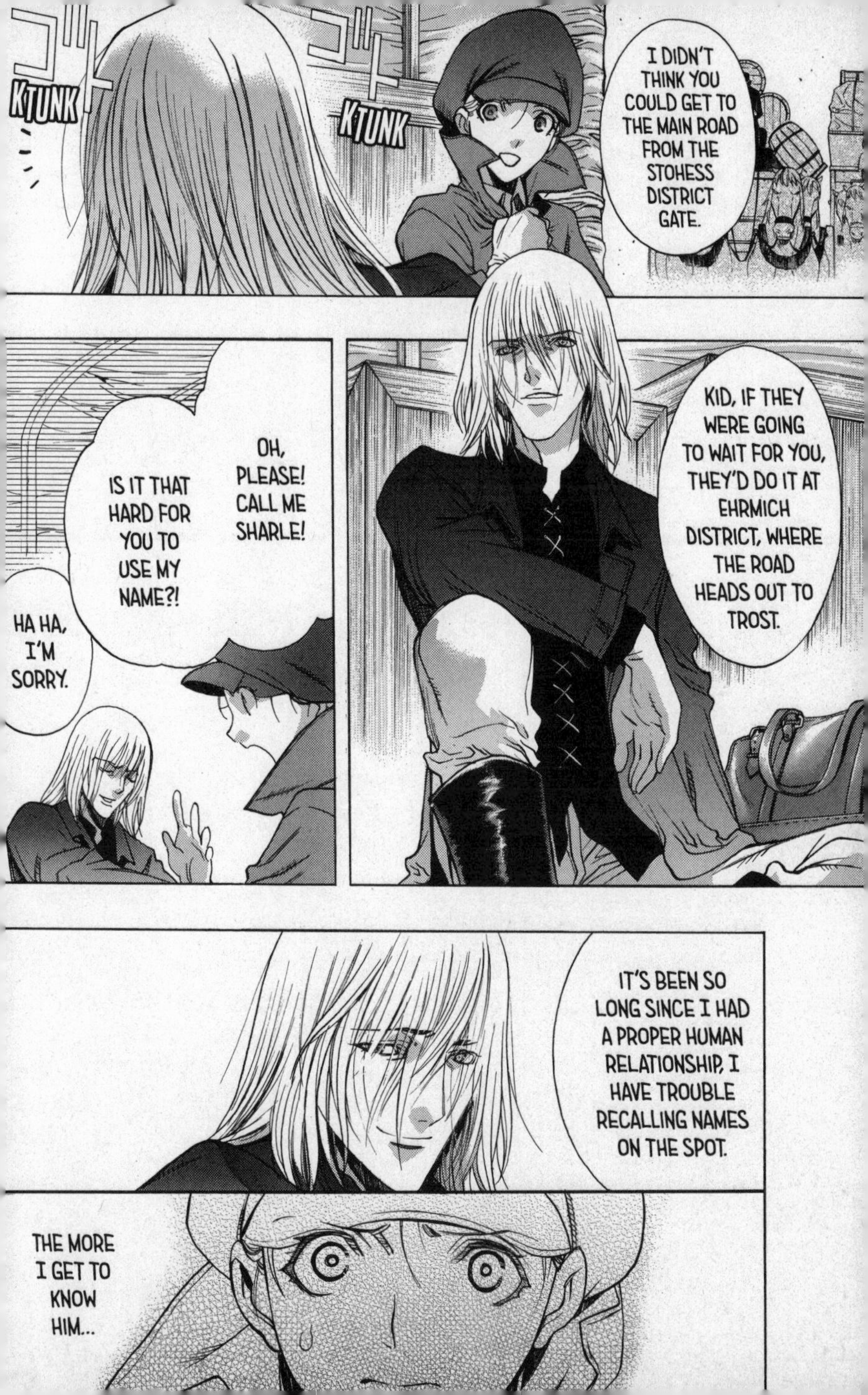
I DIDN'T THINK YOU COULD GET TO THE MAIN ROAD FROM THE STOHESS DISTRICT GATE.
KTUNK
KTUNK
KID, IF THEY WERE GOING TO WAIT FOR YOU, THEY'D DO IT AT EHRMICH DISTRICT, WHERE THE ROAD HEADS OUT TO TROST.
OH, PLEASE! CALL ME SHARLE!
IS IT THAT HARD FOR YOU TO USE MY NAME?!
HA HA, I'M SORRY.
IT'S BEEN SO LONG SINCE I HAD A PROPER HUMAN RELATIONSHIP, I HAVE TROUBLE RECALLING NAMES ON THE SPOT.
THE MORE I GET TO KNOW HIM...

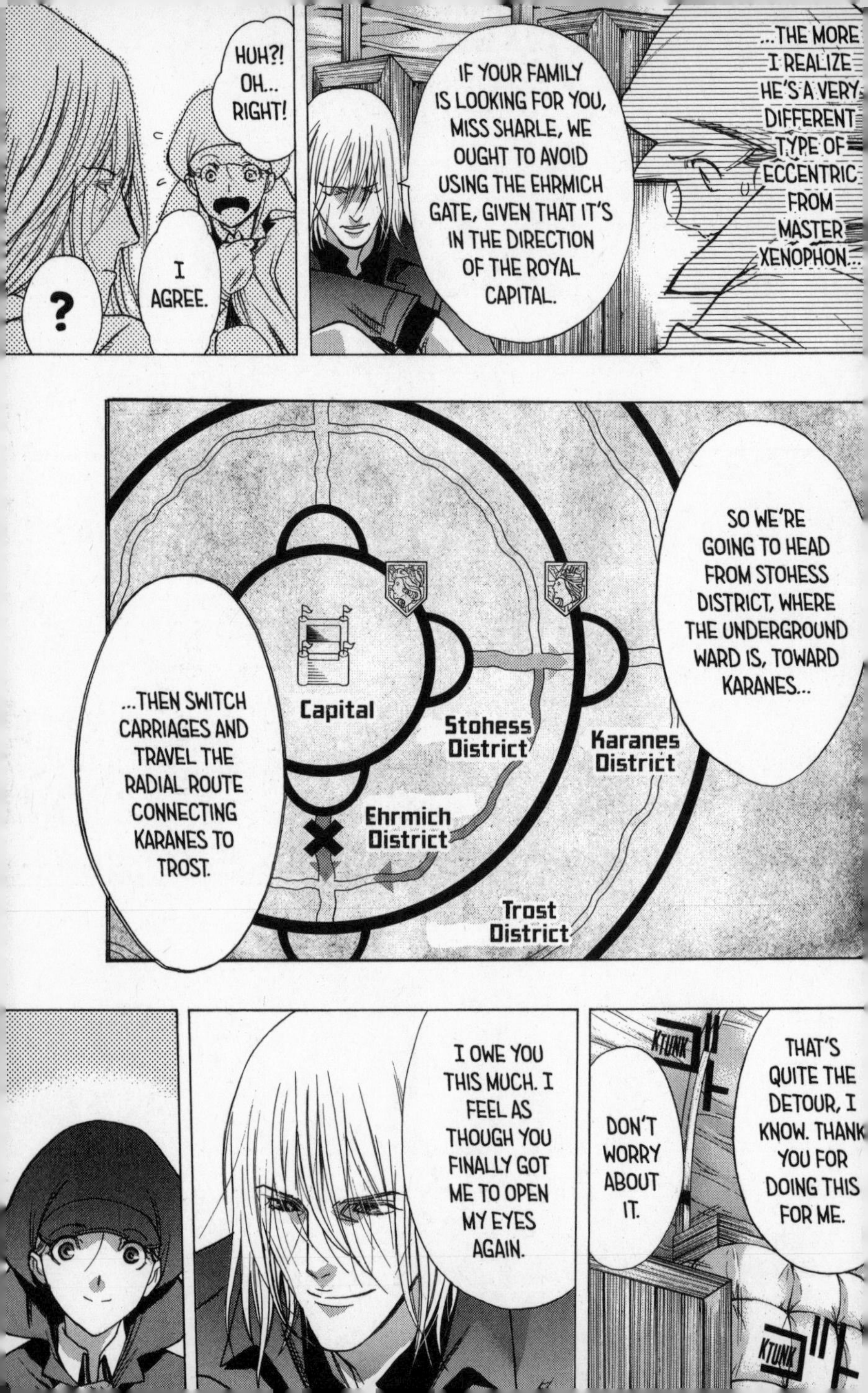

...THE MORE I REALIZE HE'S A VERY DIFFERENT TYPE OF ECCENTRIC FROM MASTER XENOPHON...
IF YOUR FAMILY IS LOOKING FOR YOU, MISS SHARLE, WE OUGHT TO AVOID USING THE EHRMICH GATE, GIVEN THAT IT'S IN THE DIRECTION OF THE ROYAL CAPITAL.
HUH?! OH... RIGHT!
I AGREE.
?
SO WE'RE GOING TO HEAD FROM STOHESS DISTRICT, WHERE THE UNDERGROUND WARD IS, TOWARD KARANES...
Capital
Stohess District
Karanes District
Ehrmich District
Trost District
...THEN SWITCH CARRIAGES AND TRAVEL THE RADIAL ROUTE CONNECTING KARANES TO TROST.
THAT'S QUITE THE DETOUR, I KNOW. THANK YOU FOR DOING THIS FOR ME.
KTUNK
DON'T WORRY ABOUT IT.
KTUNK
I OWE YOU THIS MUCH. I FEEL AS THOUGH YOU FINALLY GOT ME TO OPEN MY EYES AGAIN.

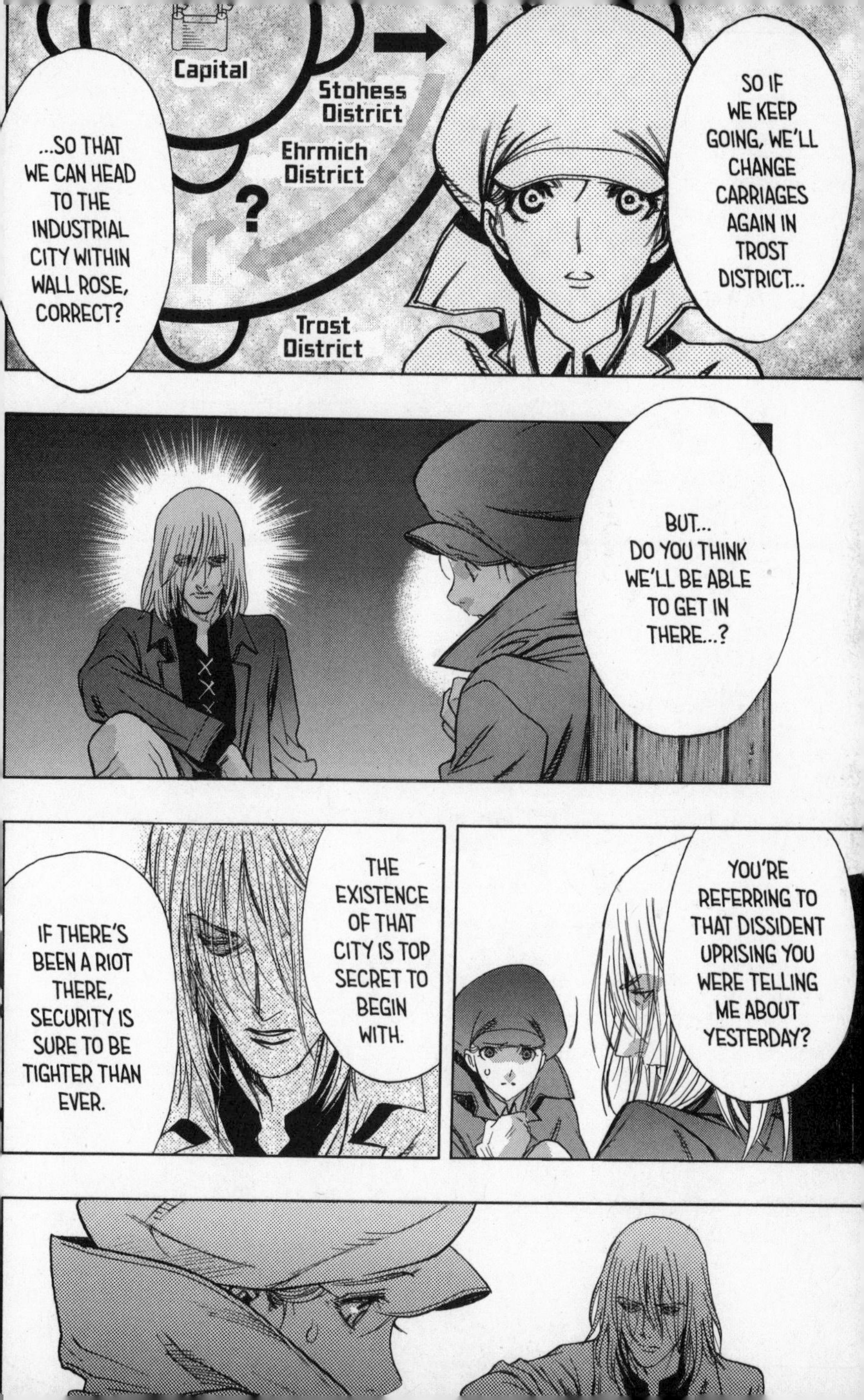
SO IF WE KEEP GOING, WE'LL CHANGE CARRIAGES AGAIN IN TROST DISTRICT...
Capital
Stohess District
Ehrmich District
?
Trost District
...SO THAT WE CAN HEAD TO THE INDUSTRIAL CITY WITHIN WALL ROSE, CORRECT?
BUT... DO YOU THINK WE'LL BE ABLE TO GET IN THERE...?
YOU'RE REFERRING TO THAT DISSIDENT UPRISING YOU WERE TELLING ME ABOUT YESTERDAY?
THE EXISTENCE OF THAT CITY IS TOP SECRET TO BEGIN WITH.
IF THERE'S BEEN A RIOT THERE, SECURITY IS SURE TO BE TIGHTER THAN EVER.

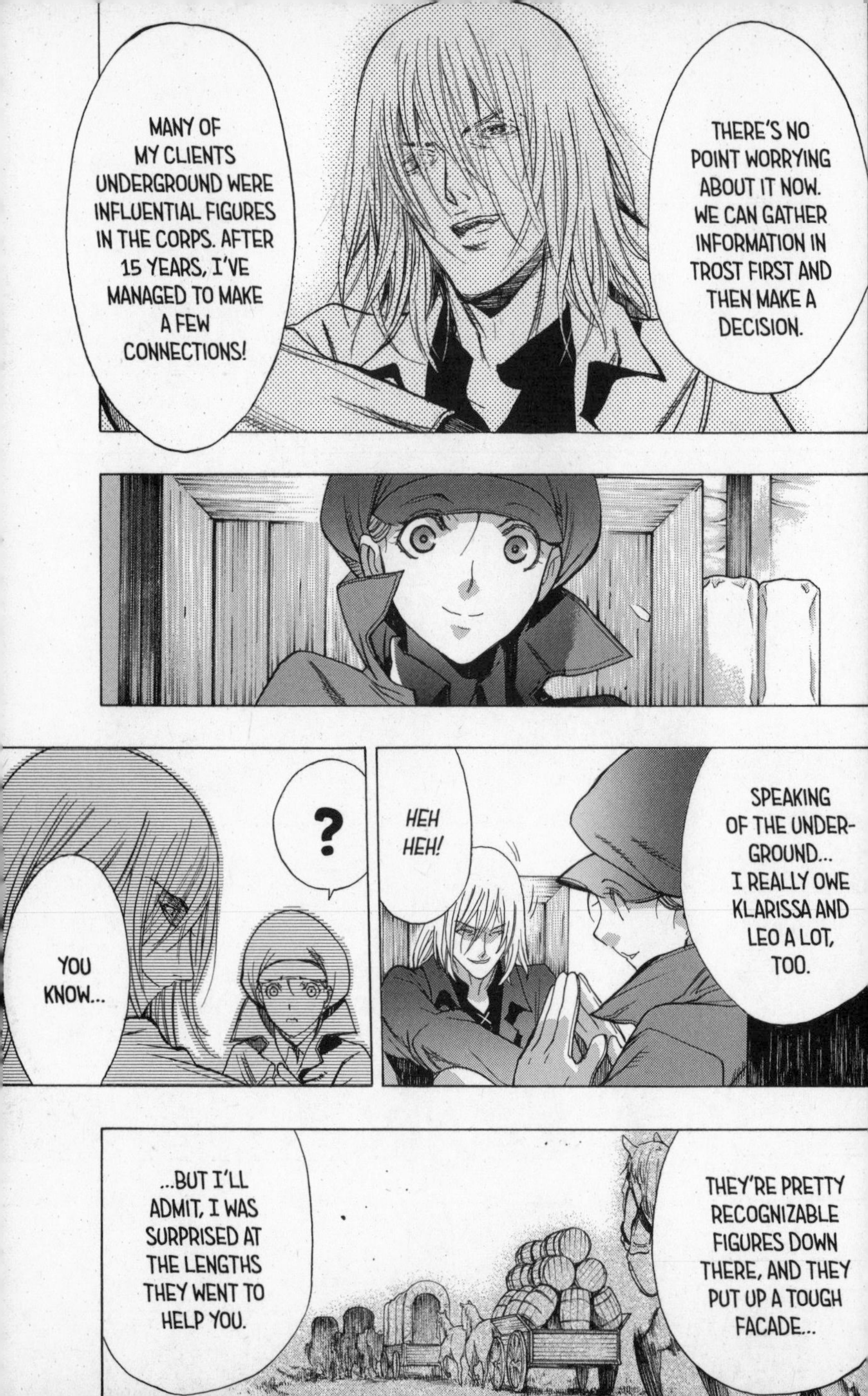
THERE'S NO POINT WORRYING ABOUT IT NOW. WE CAN GATHER INFORMATION IN TROST FIRST AND THEN MAKE A DECISION.
MANY OF MY CLIENTS UNDERGROUND WERE INFLUENTIAL FIGURES IN THE CORPS. AFTER 15 YEARS, I'VE MANAGED TO MAKE A FEW CONNECTIONS!
SPEAKING OF THE UNDERGROUND... I REALLY OWE KLARISSA AND LEO A LOT, TOO.
HEH HEH!
?
YOU KNOW...
THEY'RE PRETTY RECOGNIZABLE FIGURES DOWN THERE, AND THEY PUT UP A TOUGH FACADE...
...BUT I'LL ADMIT, I WAS SURPRISED AT THE LENGTHS THEY WENT TO HELP YOU.

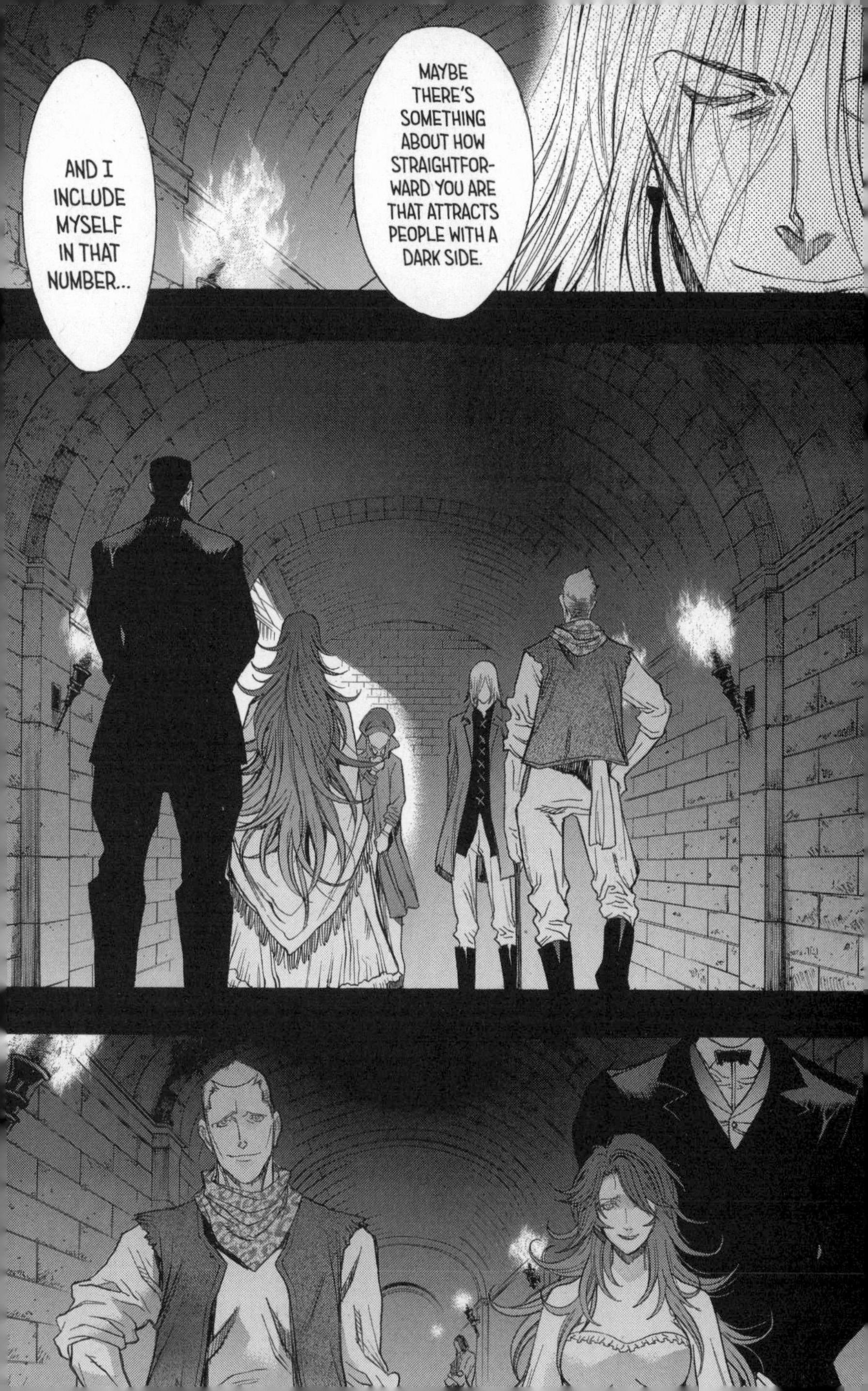
MAYBE THERE'S SOMETHING ABOUT HOW STRAIGHTFOR-WARD YOU ARE THAT ATTRACTS PEOPLE WITH A DARK SIDE.
AND I INCLUDE MYSELF IN THAT NUMBER...

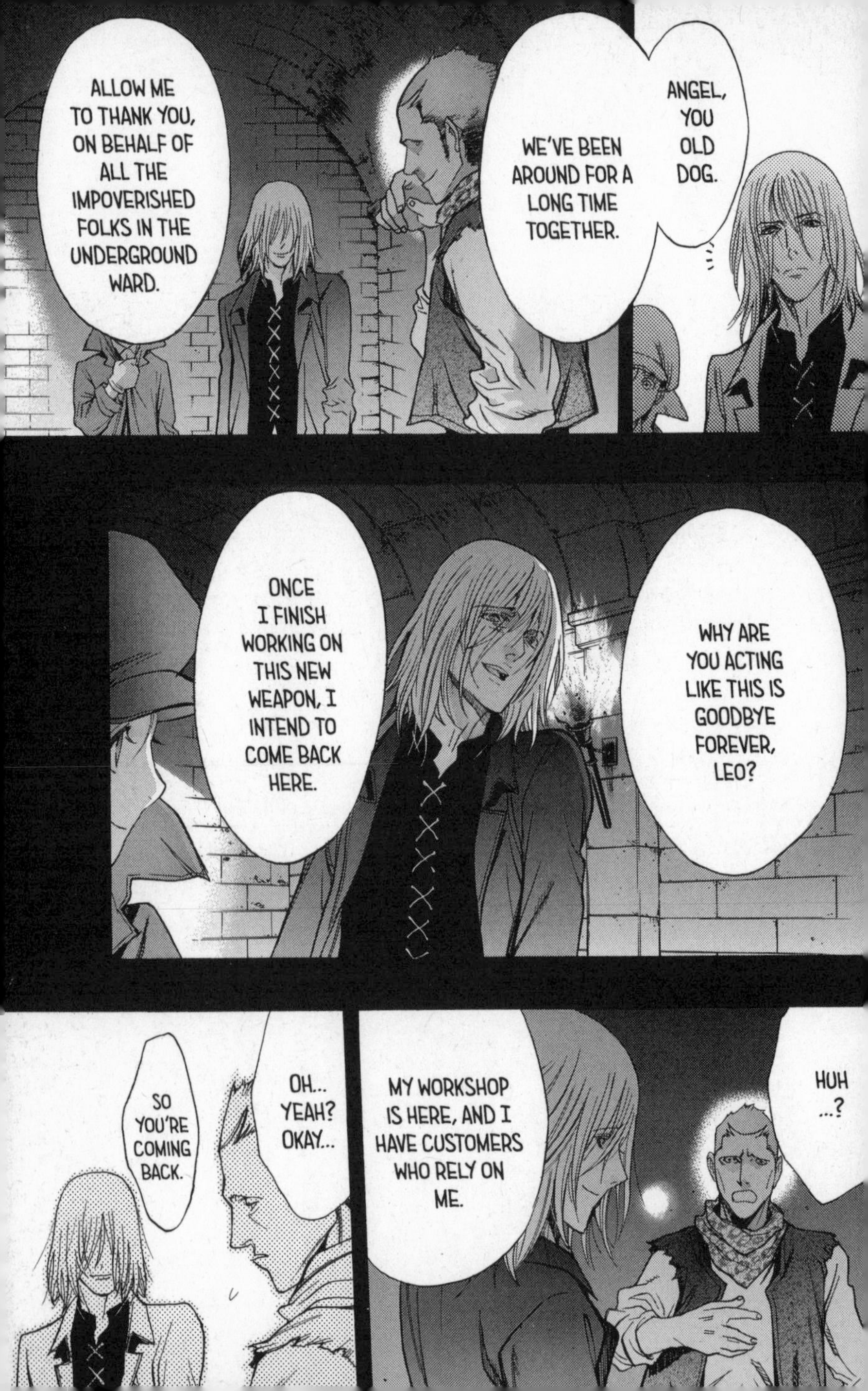
ANGEL, YOU OLD DOG.
WE'VE BEEN AROUND FOR A LONG TIME TOGETHER.
ALLOW ME TO THANK YOU, ON BEHALF OF ALL THE IMPOVERISHED FOLKS IN THE UNDERGROUND WARD.
WHY ARE YOU ACTING LIKE THIS IS GOODBYE FOREVER, LEO?
ONCE I FINISH WORKING ON THIS NEW WEAPON, I INTEND TO COME BACK HERE.
HUH ...?
MY WORKSHOP IS HERE, AND I HAVE CUSTOMERS WHO RELY ON ME.
OH... YEAH? OKAY...
SO YOU'RE COMING BACK.

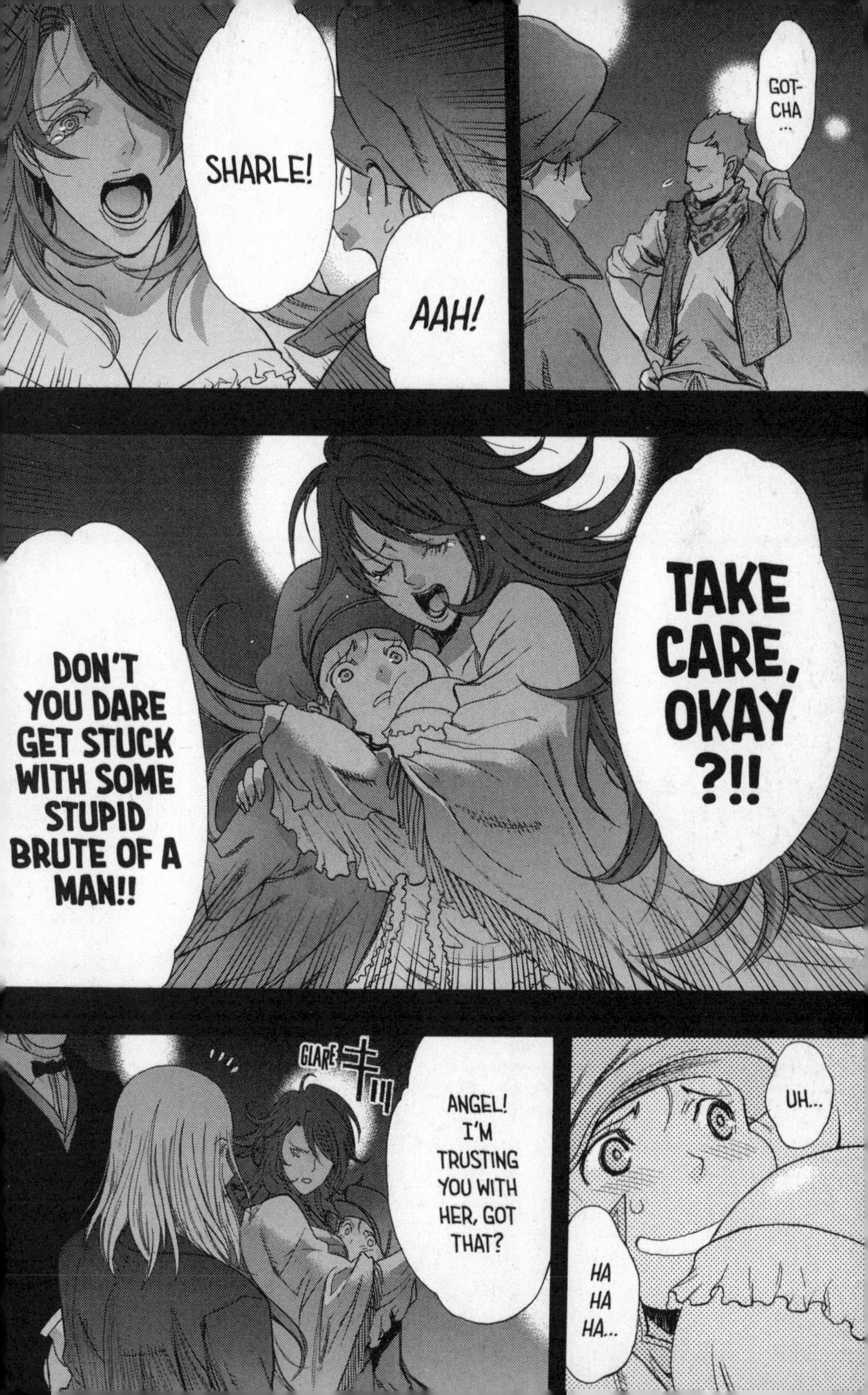
GOT-CHA...
SHARLE!
AAH!
TAKE CARE, OKAY?!!
DON'T YOU DARE GET STUCK WITH SOME STUPID BRUTE OF A MAN!!
UH...
HA HA HA...
GLARE
ANGEL! I'M TRUSTING YOU WITH HER, GOT THAT?

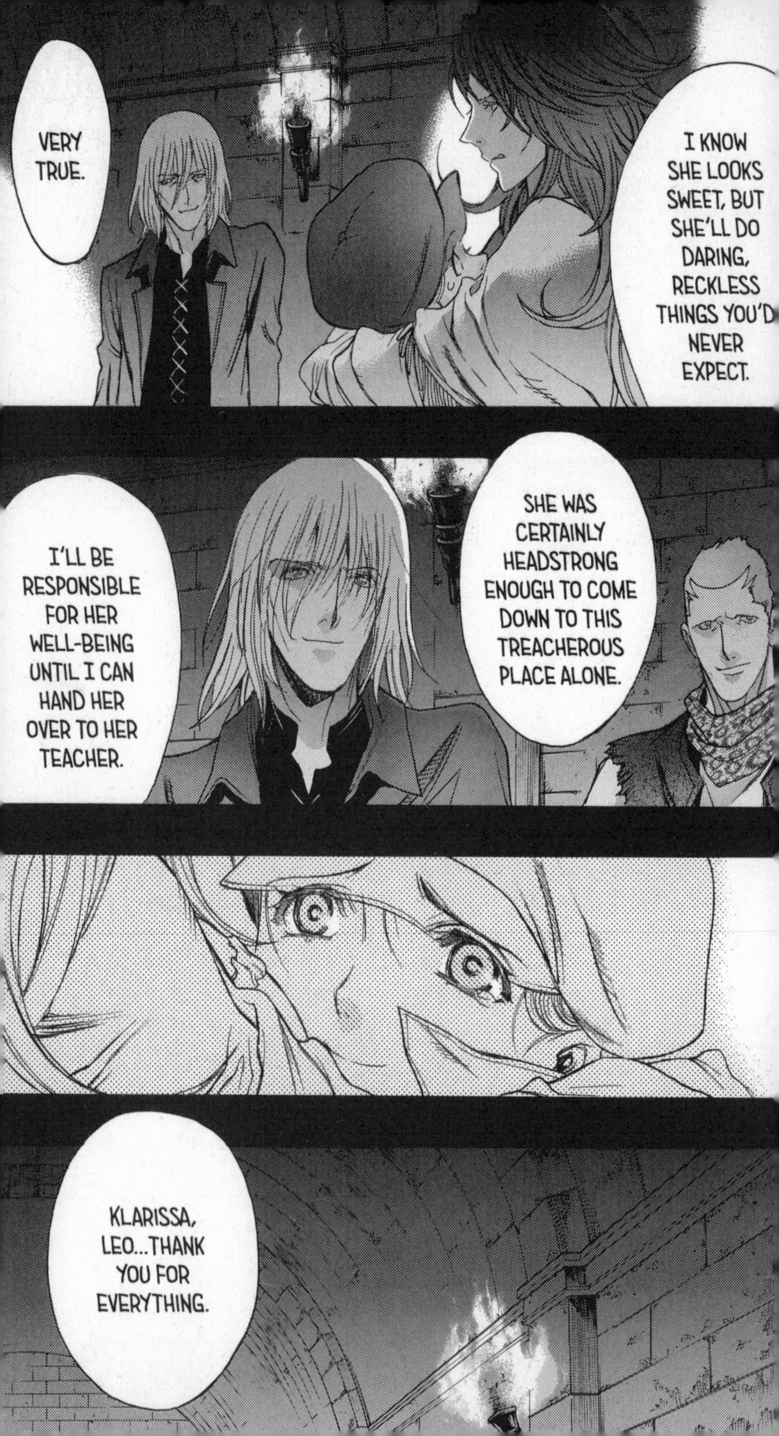
I KNOW SHE LOOKS SWEET, BUT SHE'LL DO DARING, RECKLESS THINGS YOU'D NEVER EXPECT.
VERY TRUE.
SHE WAS CERTAINLY HEADSTRONG ENOUGH TO COME DOWN TO THIS TREACHEROUS PLACE ALONE.
I'LL BE RESPONSIBLE FOR HER WELL-BEING UNTIL I CAN HAND HER OVER TO HER TEACHER.
KLARISSA, LEO...THANK YOU FOR EVERYTHING.

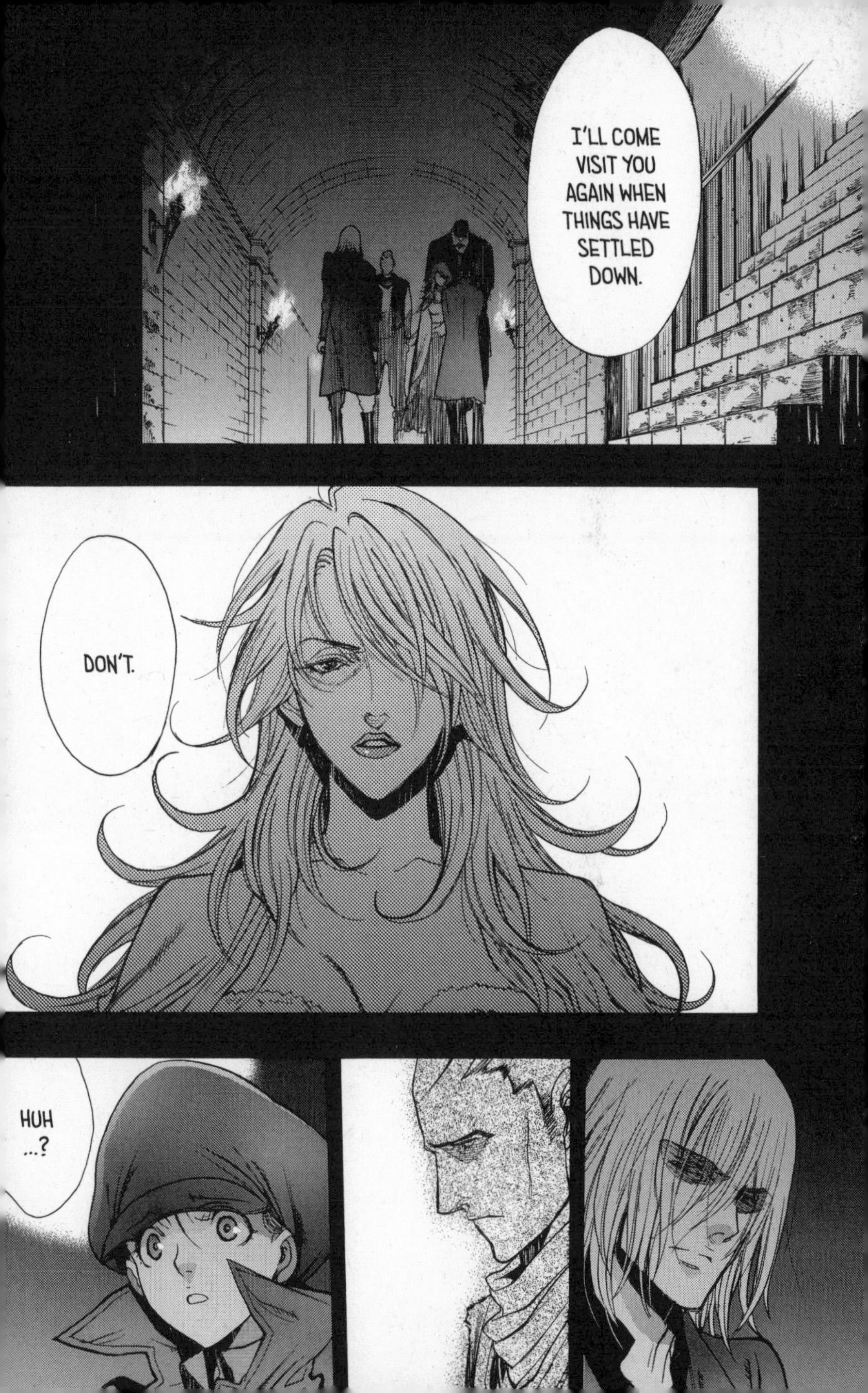
I'LL COME VISIT YOU AGAIN WHEN THINGS HAVE SETTLED DOWN.
DON'T.
HUH ...?

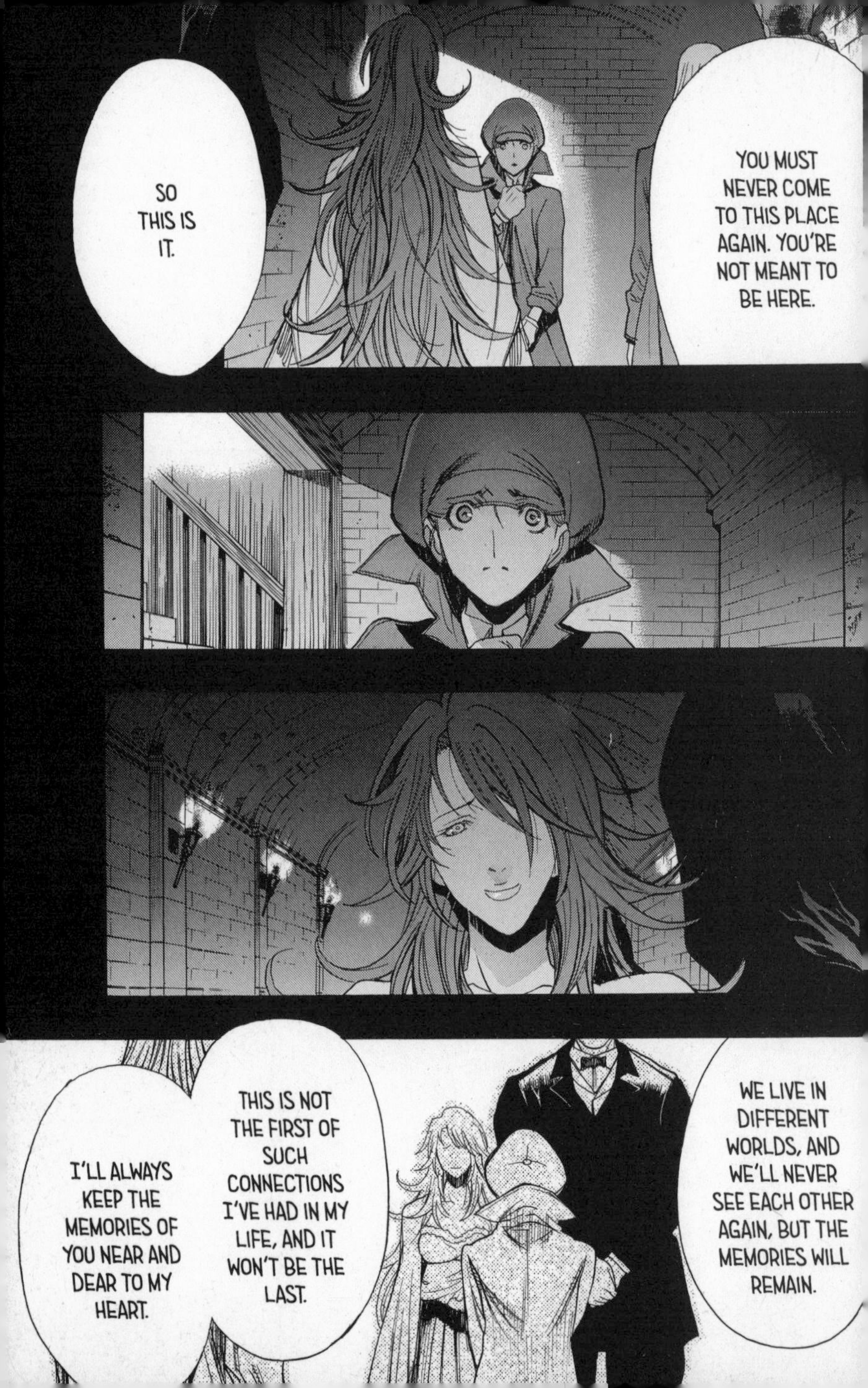
YOU MUST NEVER COME TO THIS PLACE AGAIN. YOU'RE NOT MEANT TO BE HERE.
SO THIS IS IT.
WE LIVE IN DIFFERENT WORLDS, AND WE'LL NEVER SEE EACH OTHER AGAIN, BUT THE MEMORIES WILL REMAIN.
THIS IS NOT THE FIRST OF SUCH CONNECTIONS I'VE HAD IN MY LIFE, AND IT WON'T BE THE LAST.
I'LL ALWAYS KEEP THE MEMORIES OF YOU NEAR AND DEAR TO MY HEART.

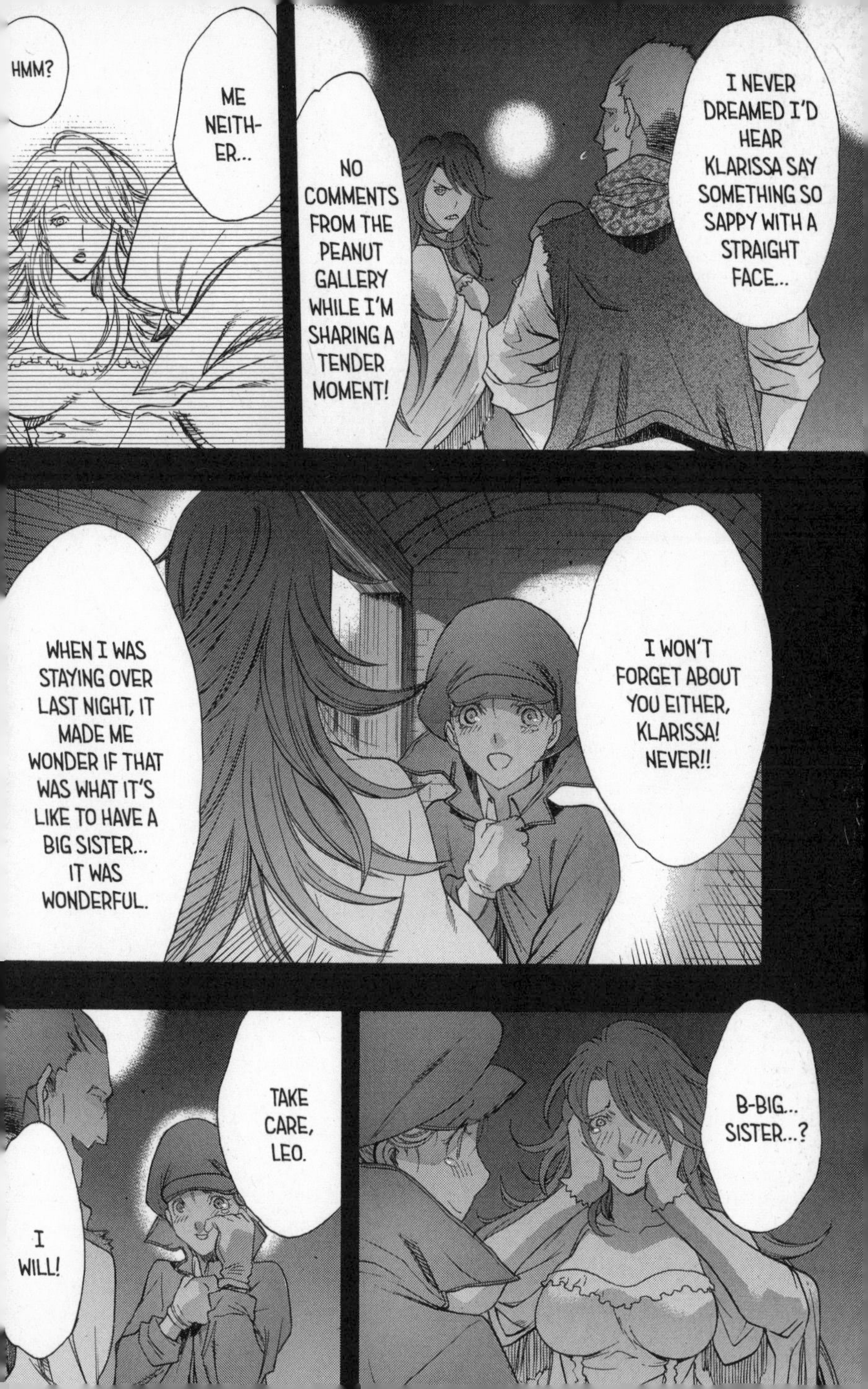
I NEVER DREAMED I'D HEAR KLARISSA SAY SOMETHING SO SAPPY WITH A STRAIGHT FACE...
NO COMMENTS FROM THE PEANUT GALLERY WHILE I'M SHARING A TENDER MOMENT!
ME NEITH-ER...
HMM?
I WON'T FORGET ABOUT YOU EITHER, KLARISSA! NEVER!!
WHEN I WAS STAYING OVER LAST NIGHT, IT MADE ME WONDER IF THAT WAS WHAT IT'S LIKE TO HAVE A BIG SISTER... IT WAS WONDERFUL.
B-BIG... SISTER...?
TAKE CARE, LEO.
I WILL!

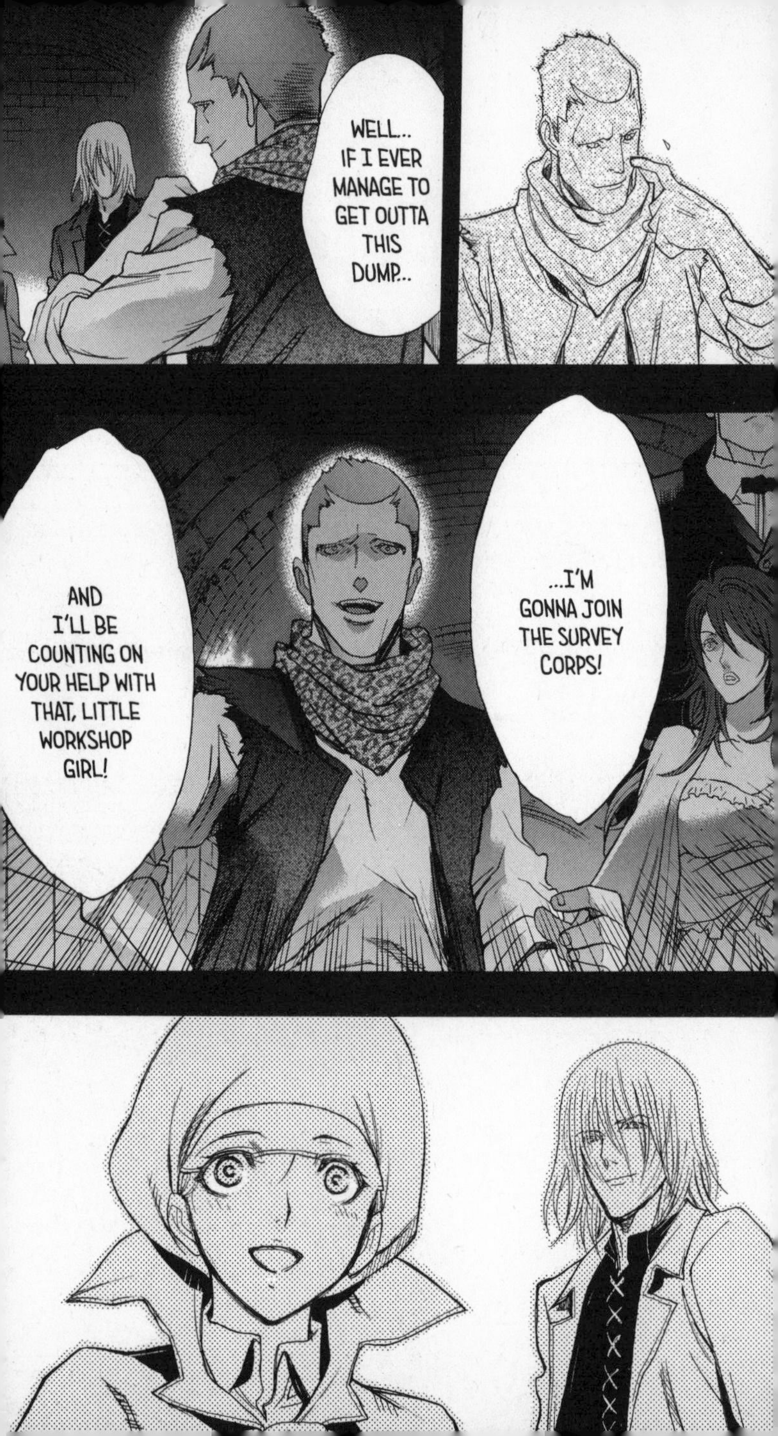
WELL... IF I EVER MANAGE TO GET OUTTA THIS DUMP...
...I'M GONNA JOIN THE SURVEY CORPS!
AND I'LL BE COUNTING ON YOUR HELP WITH THAT, LITTLE WORKSHOP GIRL!

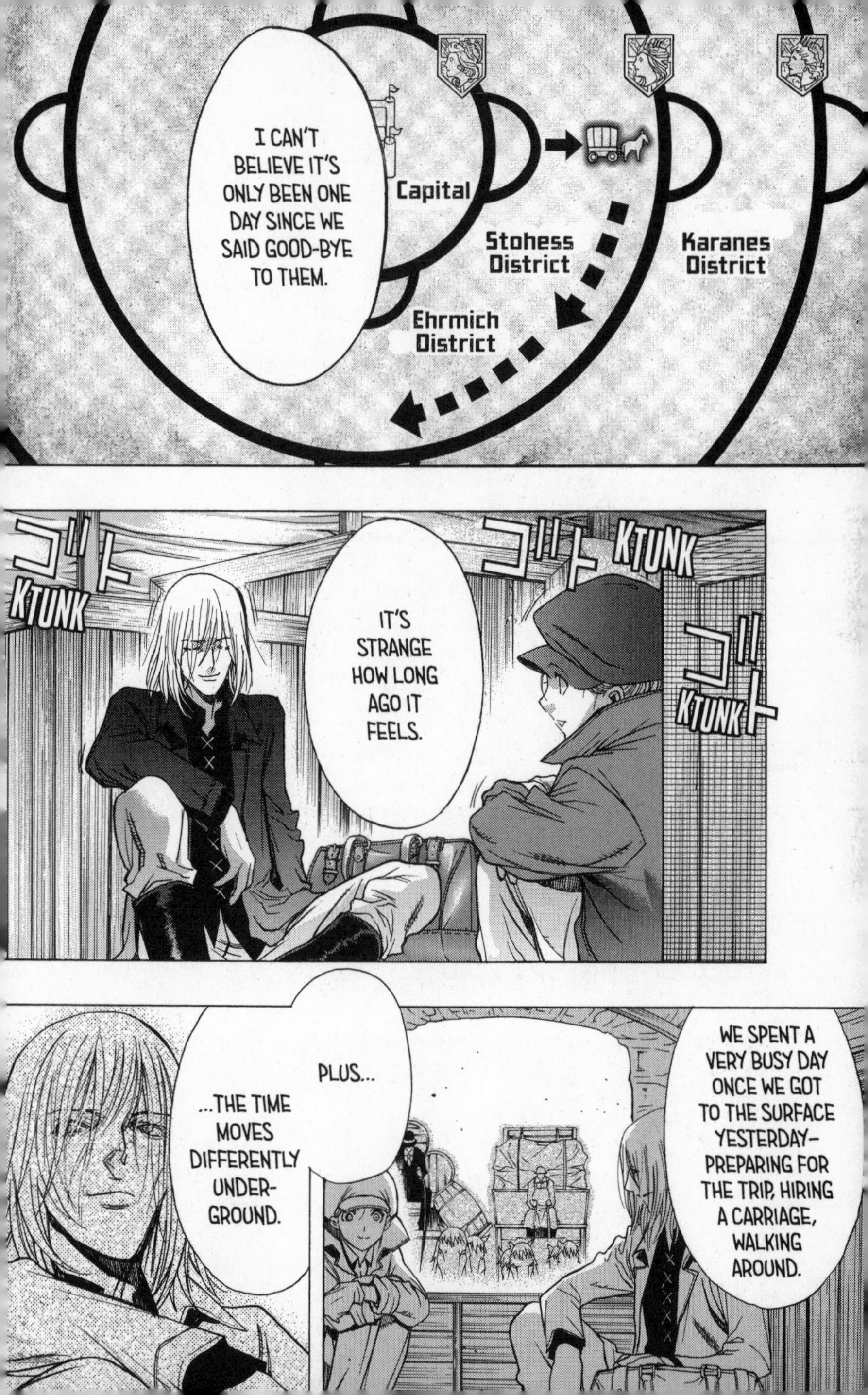

Karanes District
Capital
Stohess District
I CAN'T BELIEVE IT'S ONLY BEEN ONE DAY SINCE WE SAID GOOD-BYE TO THEM.
Ehrmich District
ゴット KTUNK
ゴット KTUNK
IT'S STRANGE HOW LONG AGO IT FEELS.
ゴット KTUNK
WE SPENT A VERY BUSY DAY ONCE WE GOT TO THE SURFACE YESTERDAY—PREPARING FOR THE TRIP, HIRING A CARRIAGE, WALKING AROUND.
PLUS...
...THE TIME MOVES DIFFERENTLY UNDER-GROUND.

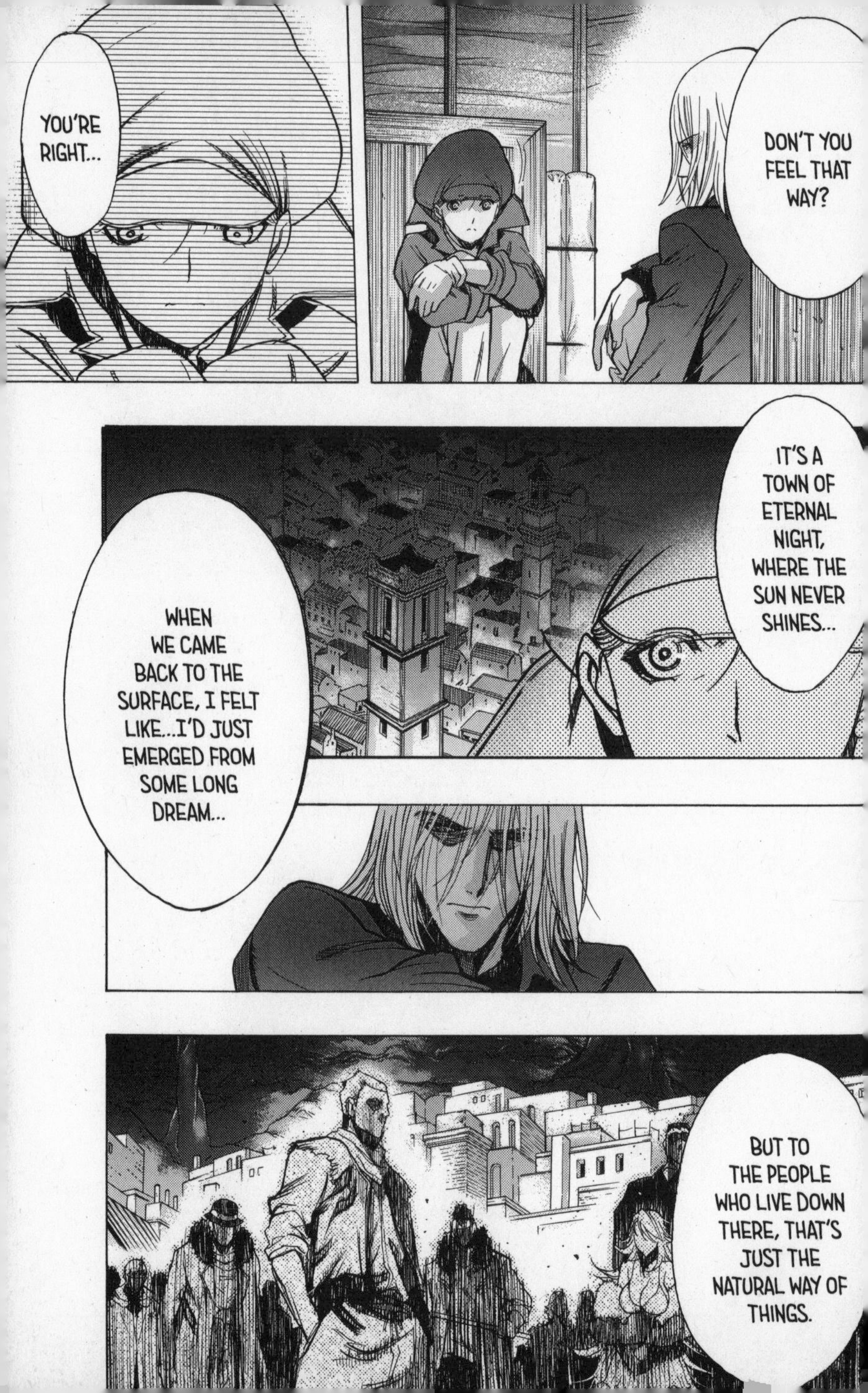
DON'T YOU FEEL THAT WAY?
YOU'RE RIGHT...
IT'S A TOWN OF ETERNAL NIGHT, WHERE THE SUN NEVER SHINES...
WHEN WE CAME BACK TO THE SURFACE, I FELT LIKE...I'D JUST EMERGED FROM SOME LONG DREAM...
BUT TO THE PEOPLE WHO LIVE DOWN THERE, THAT'S JUST THE NATURAL WAY OF THINGS.

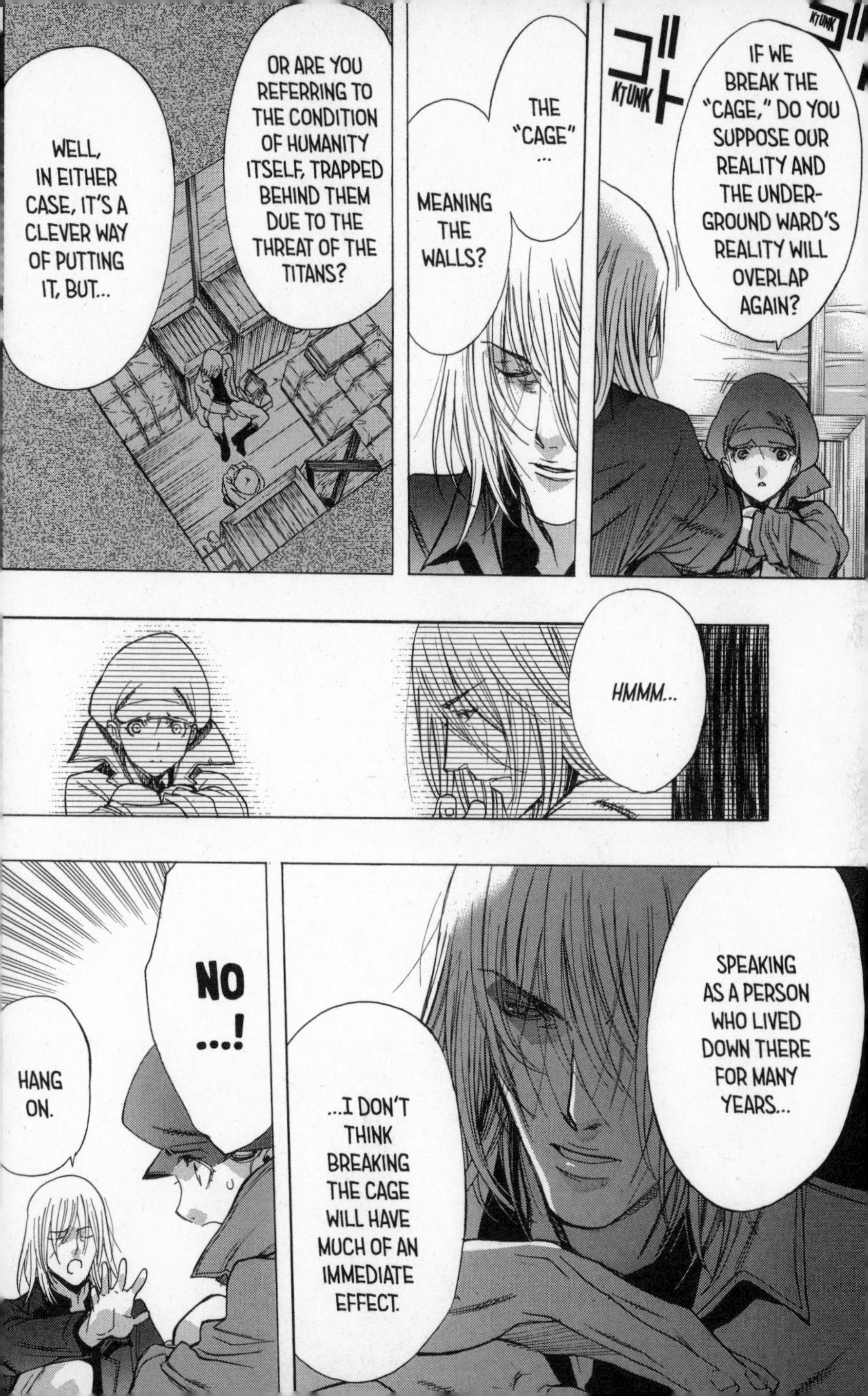
KTUNK
KTUNK
IF WE BREAK THE "CAGE," DO YOU SUPPOSE OUR REALITY AND THE UNDER-GROUND WARD'S REALITY WILL OVERLAP AGAIN?
THE "CAGE"...
MEANING THE WALLS?
OR ARE YOU REFERRING TO THE CONDITION OF HUMANITY ITSELF, TRAPPED BEHIND THEM DUE TO THE THREAT OF THE TITANS?
WELL, IN EITHER CASE, IT'S A CLEVER WAY OF PUTTING IT, BUT...
HMMM...
SPEAKING AS A PERSON WHO LIVED DOWN THERE FOR MANY YEARS...
...I DON'T THINK BREAKING THE CAGE WILL HAVE MUCH OF AN IMMEDIATE EFFECT.
NO...!
HANG ON.

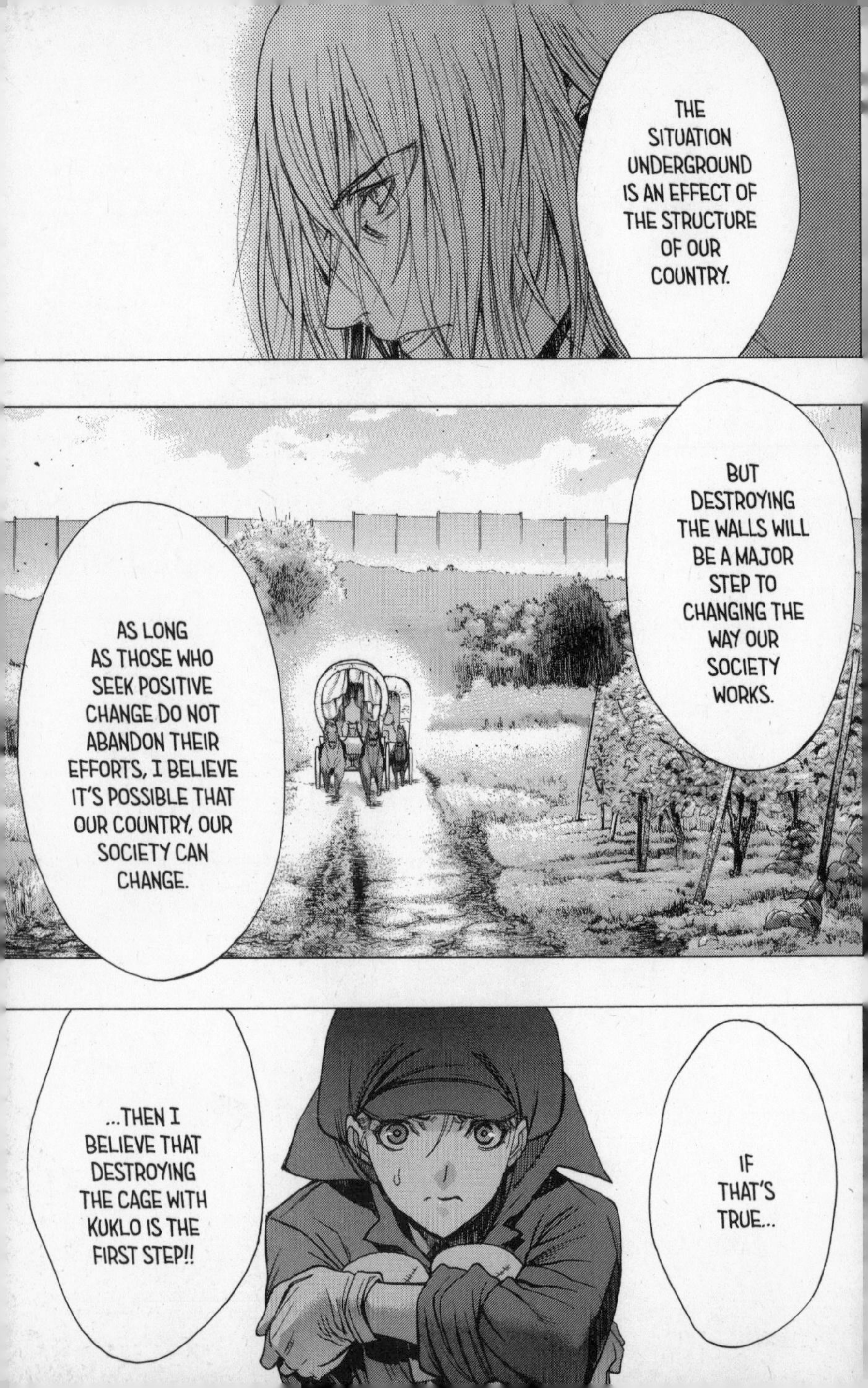
THE SITUATION UNDERGROUND IS AN EFFECT OF THE STRUCTURE OF OUR COUNTRY.
BUT DESTROYING THE WALLS WILL BE A MAJOR STEP TO CHANGING THE WAY OUR SOCIETY WORKS.
AS LONG AS THOSE WHO SEEK POSITIVE CHANGE DO NOT ABANDON THEIR EFFORTS, I BELIEVE IT'S POSSIBLE THAT OUR COUNTRY, OUR SOCIETY CAN CHANGE.
IF THAT'S TRUE...
...THEN I BELIEVE THAT DESTROYING THE CAGE WITH KUKLO IS THE FIRST STEP!!

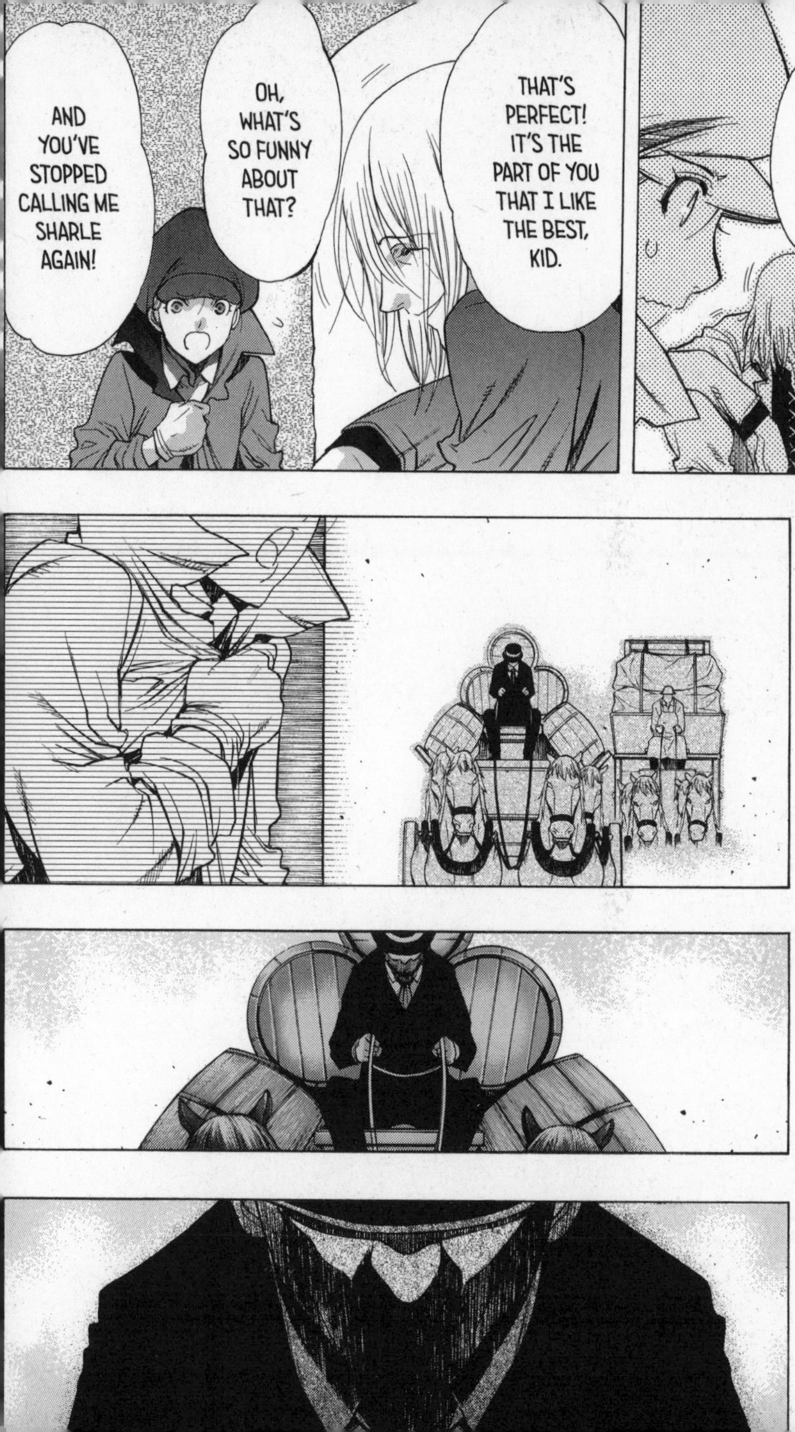
HEH HEH...
THAT'S PERFECT! IT'S THE PART OF YOU THAT I LIKE THE BEST, KID.
OH, WHAT'S SO FUNNY ABOUT THAT?
AND YOU'VE STOPPED CALLING ME SHARLE AGAIN!

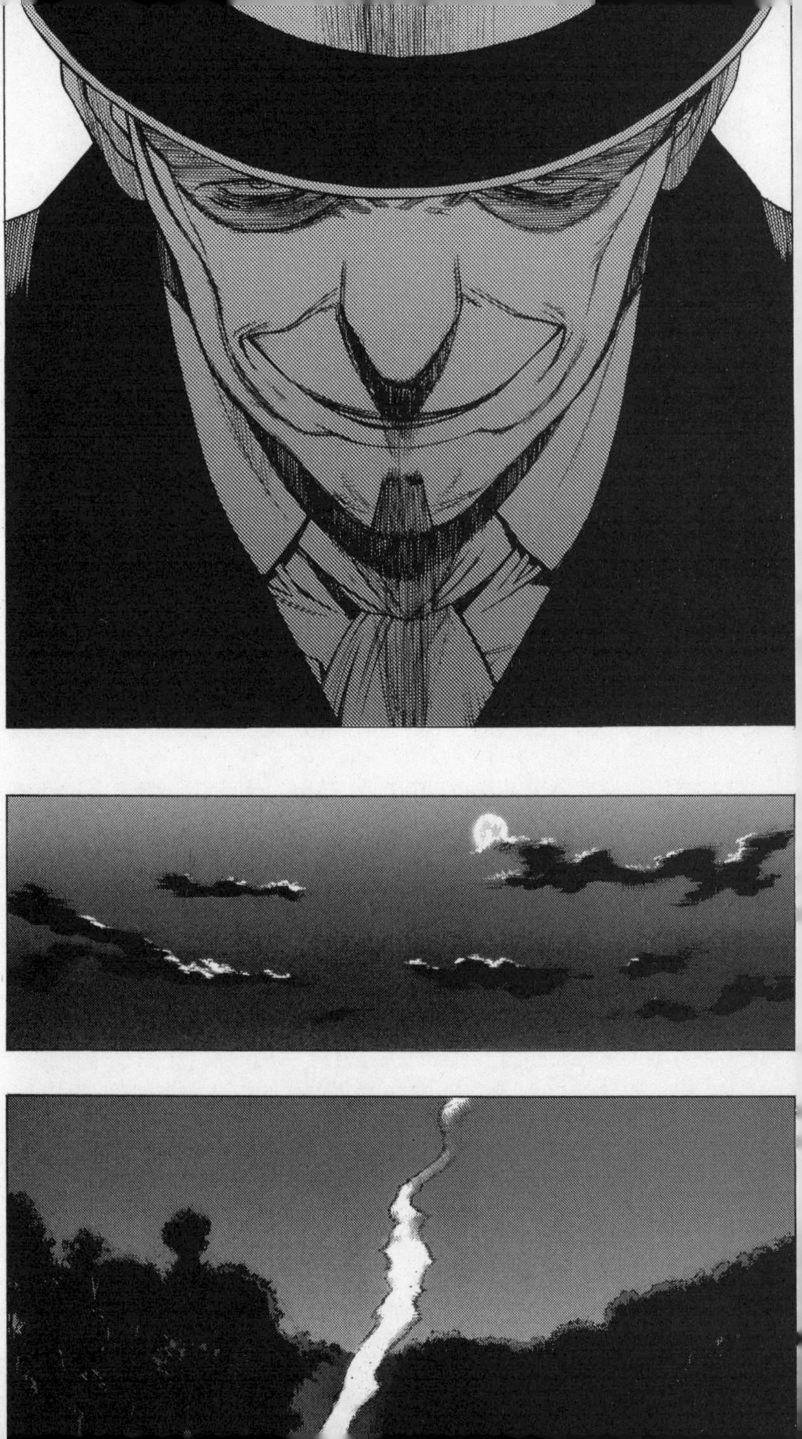

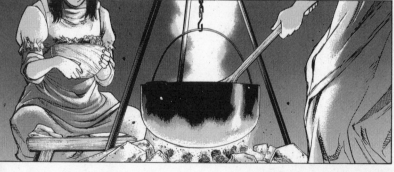

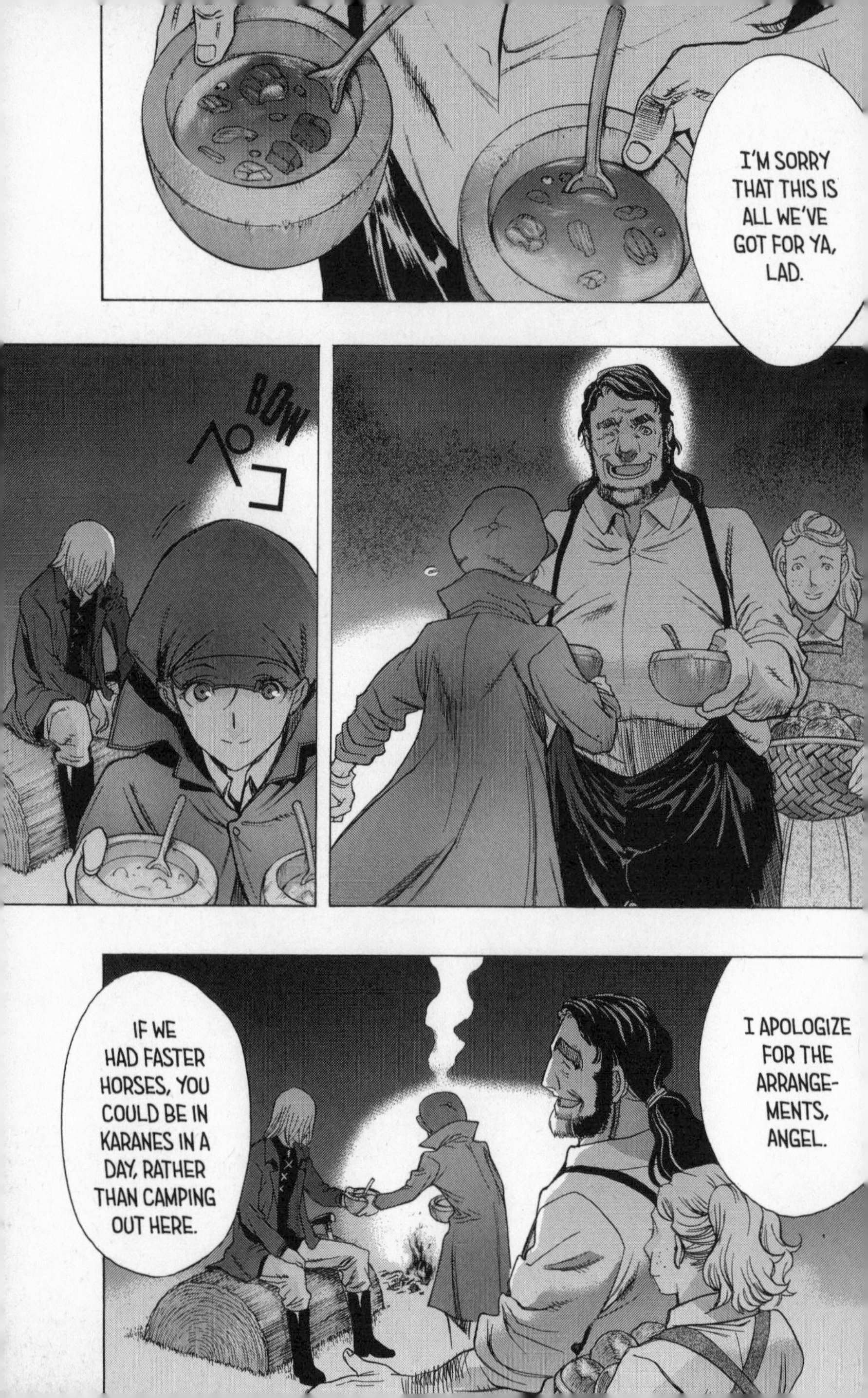

I'M SORRY THAT THIS IS ALL WE'VE GOT FOR YA, LAD.
BOW
ペコ
I APOLOGIZE FOR THE ARRANGE- MENTS, ANGEL.
IF WE HAD FASTER HORSES, YOU COULD BE IN KARANES IN A DAY, RATHER THAN CAMPING OUT HERE.

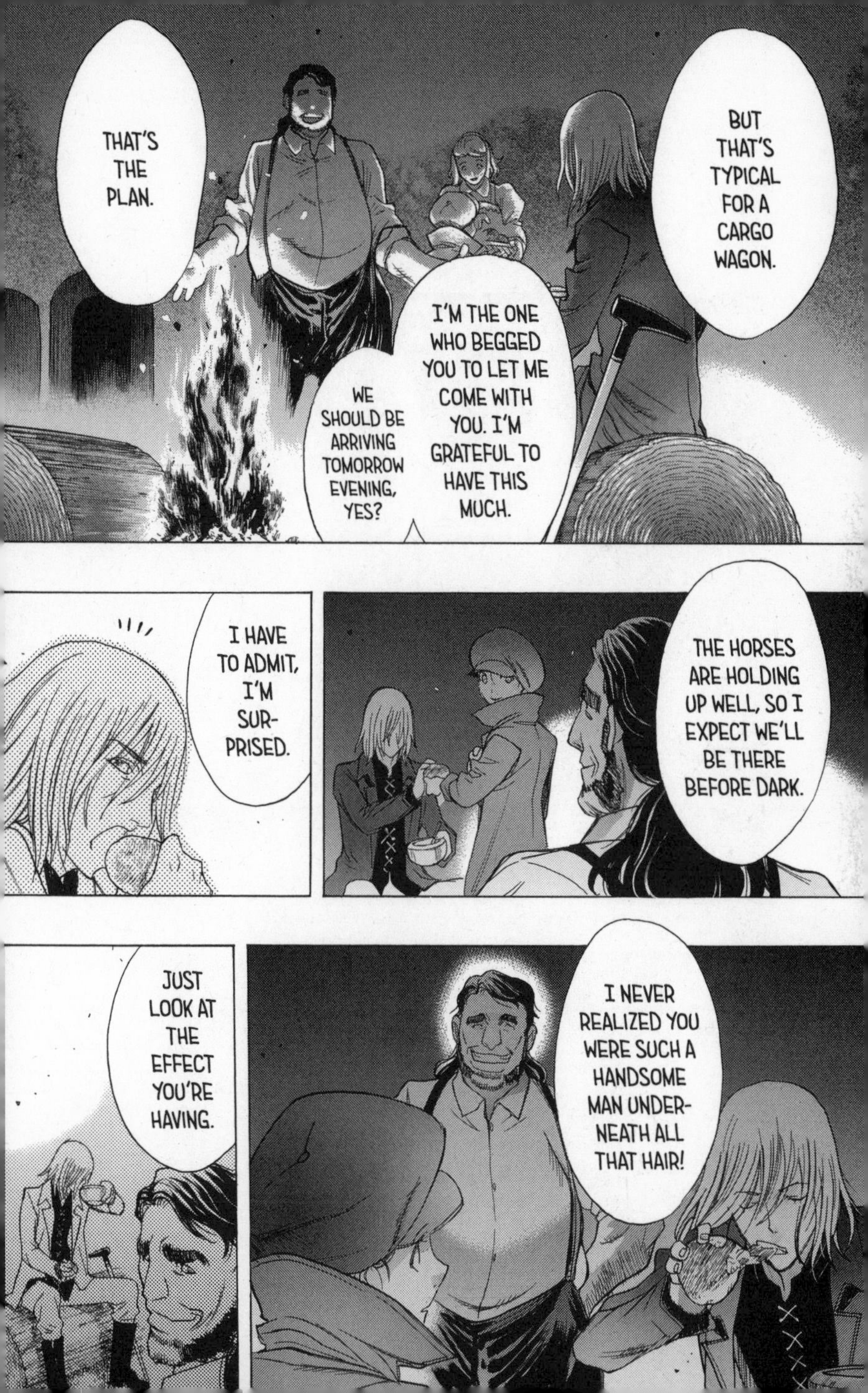
BUT THAT'S TYPICAL FOR A CARGO WAGON.
THAT'S THE PLAN.
I'M THE ONE WHO BEGGED YOU TO LET ME COME WITH YOU. I'M GRATEFUL TO HAVE THIS MUCH.
WE SHOULD BE ARRIVING TOMORROW EVENING, YES?
THE HORSES ARE HOLDING UP WELL, SO I EXPECT WE'LL BE THERE BEFORE DARK.
I HAVE TO ADMIT, I'M SUR-PRISED.
I NEVER REALIZED YOU WERE SUCH A HANDSOME MAN UNDER-NEATH ALL THAT HAIR!
JUST LOOK AT THE EFFECT YOU'RE HAVING.

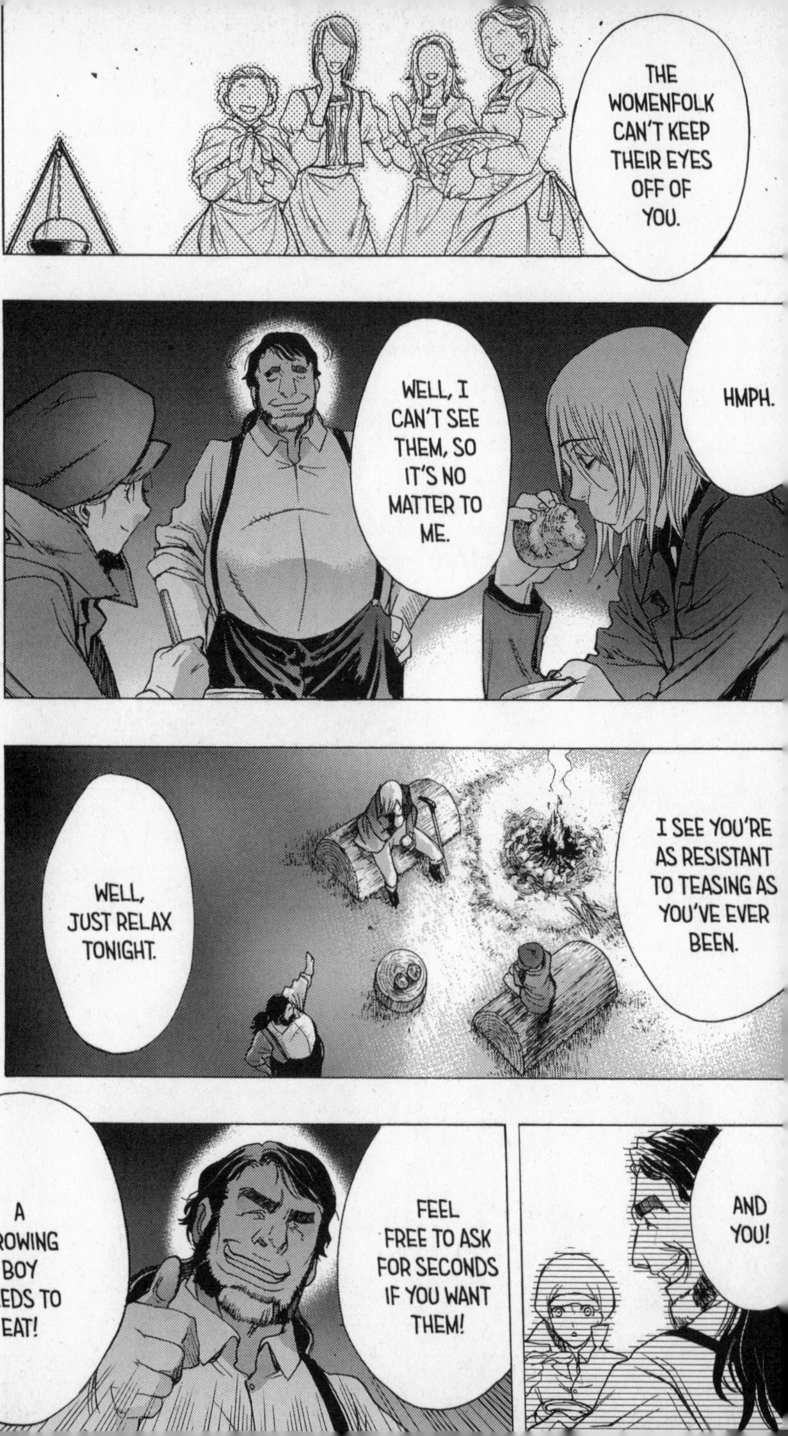
THE WOMENFOLK CAN'T KEEP THEIR EYES OFF OF YOU.
HMPH.
WELL, I CAN'T SEE THEM, SO IT'S NO MATTER TO ME.
I SEE YOU'RE AS RESISTANT TO TEASING AS YOU'VE EVER BEEN.
WELL, JUST RELAX TONIGHT.
AND YOU!
FEEL FREE TO ASK FOR SECONDS IF YOU WANT THEM!
A GROWING BOY NEEDS TO EAT!

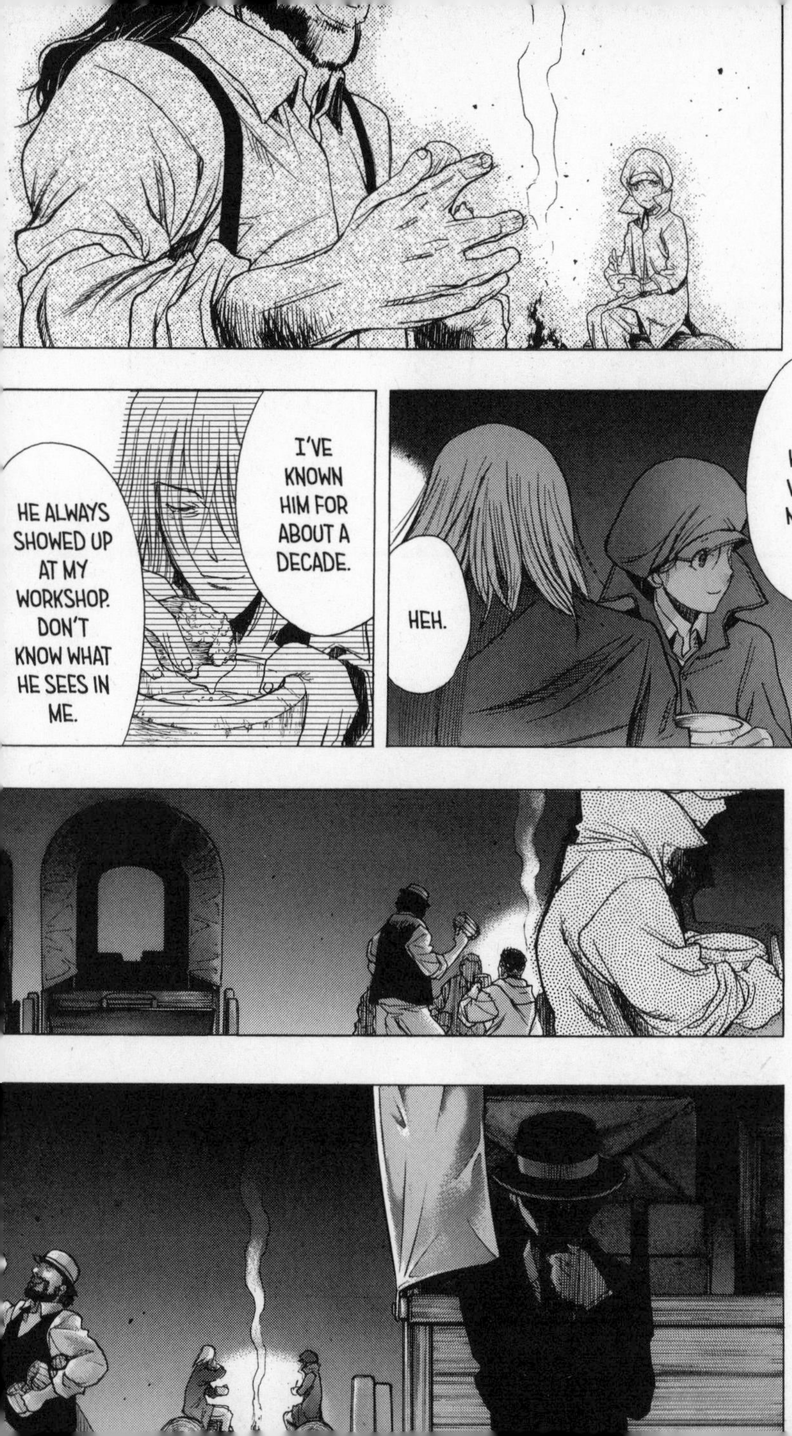
HE'S VERY NICE.
HEH.
I'VE KNOWN HIM FOR ABOUT A DECADE.
HE ALWAYS SHOWED UP AT MY WORKSHOP. DON'T KNOW WHAT HE SEES IN ME.

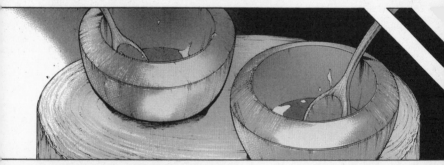

PCHAK

SO...MISS SHARLE.
ABOUT
XENOPHON'S
NEW DEVICE...THE
ONE YOU WERE
TELLING ME
ABOUT YESTER-
DAY.

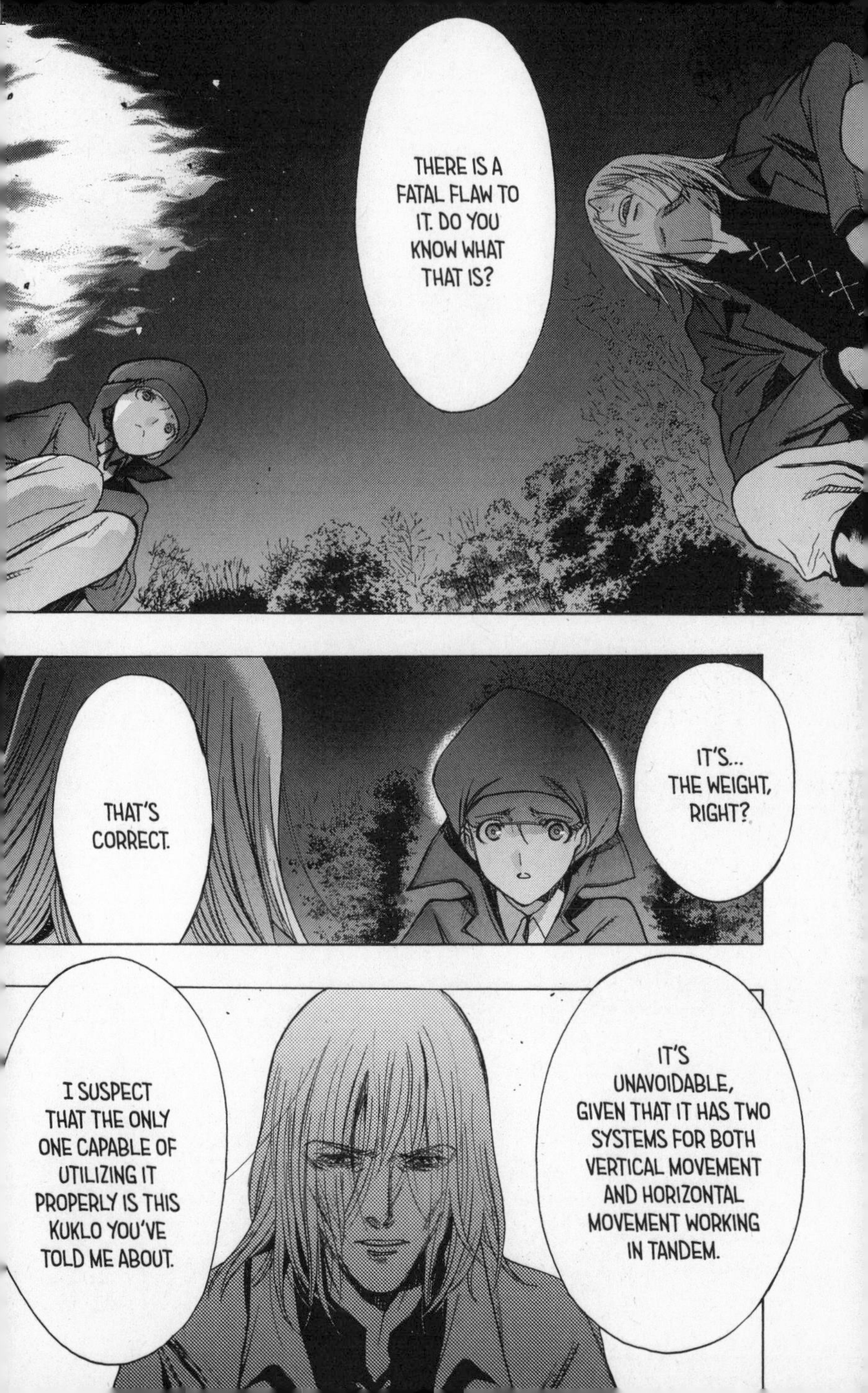
THERE IS A FATAL FLAW TO IT. DO YOU KNOW WHAT THAT IS?
IT'S... THE WEIGHT, RIGHT?
THAT'S CORRECT.
IT'S UNAVOIDABLE, GIVEN THAT IT HAS TWO SYSTEMS FOR BOTH VERTICAL MOVEMENT AND HORIZONTAL MOVEMENT WORKING IN TANDEM.
I SUSPECT THAT THE ONLY ONE CAPABLE OF UTILIZING IT PROPERLY IS THIS KUKLO YOU'VE TOLD ME ABOUT.

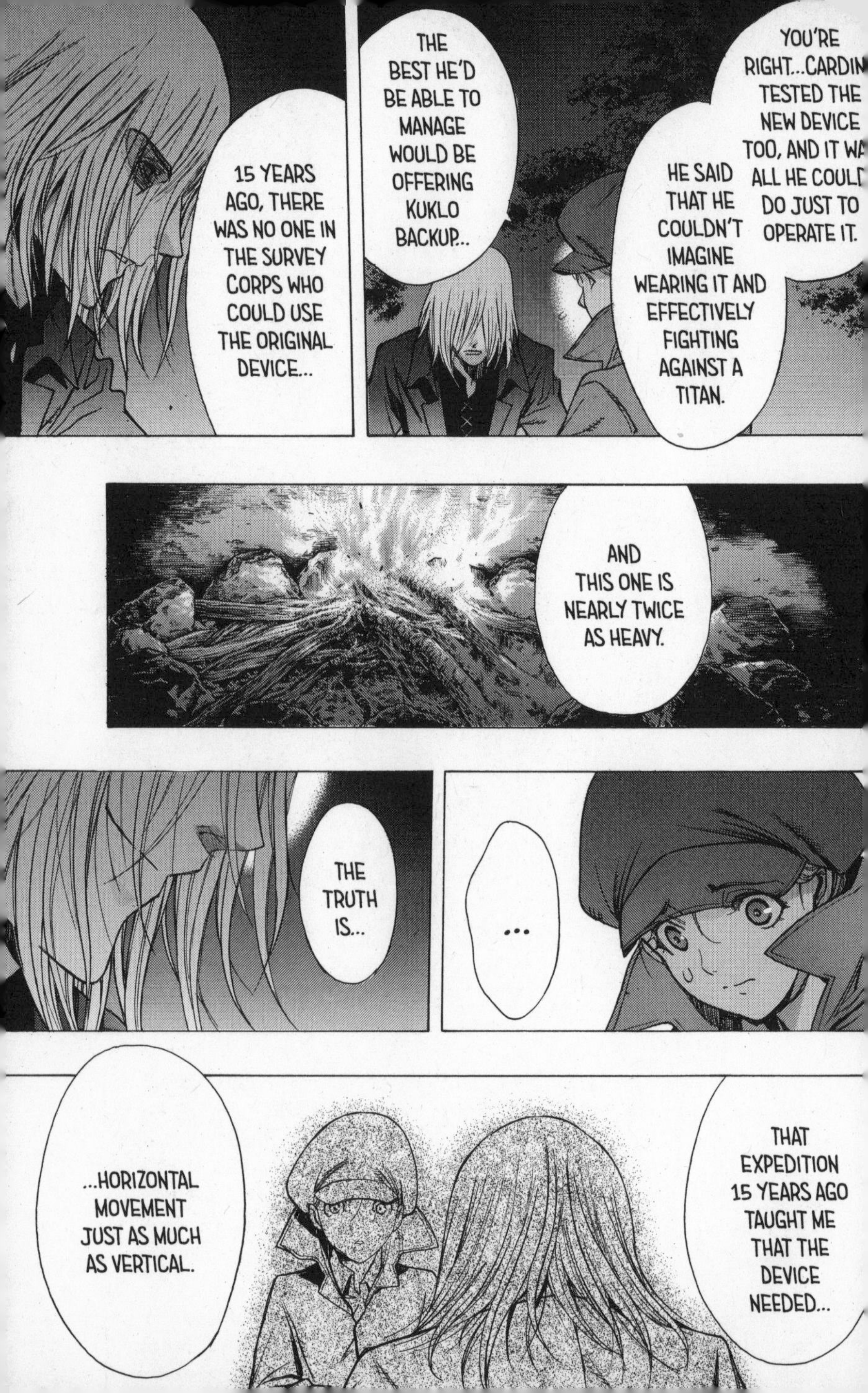
YOU'RE RIGHT...CARDIN TESTED THE NEW DEVICE TOO, AND IT WA ALL HE COULD DO JUST TO OPERATE IT.
HE SAID THAT HE COULDN'T IMAGINE WEARING IT AND EFFECTIVELY FIGHTING AGAINST A TITAN.
THE BEST HE'D BE ABLE TO MANAGE WOULD BE OFFERING KUKLO BACKUP...
15 YEARS AGO, THERE WAS NO ONE IN THE SURVEY CORPS WHO COULD USE THE ORIGINAL DEVICE...
AND THIS ONE IS NEARLY TWICE AS HEAVY.
...
THE TRUTH IS...
THAT EXPEDITION 15 YEARS AGO TAUGHT ME THAT THE DEVICE NEEDED...
...HORIZONTAL MOVEMENT JUST AS MUCH AS VERTICAL.

AND BEFORE I LOST MY EYESIGHT, I SPOKE WITH XENOPHON AND SUGGESTED A DESIGN THAT WOULD COMBINE BOTH CAPABILITIES.

THEN, YOU MEAN ...!

THAT'S RIGHT... I UNDERSTOOD THE FLAW.

IN FACT, I WANT TO APPLAUD XENOPHON'S WORK IN REDUCING THE WEIGHT OF THE NEW MODEL TO LESS THAN TWICE THAT OF THE ONE BEFORE.

BUT WE OUGHT TO CHANGE OUR WAY OF THINKING!!

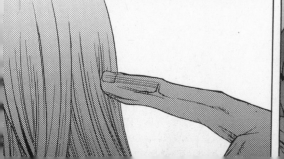

...WHAT DO YOU ...?

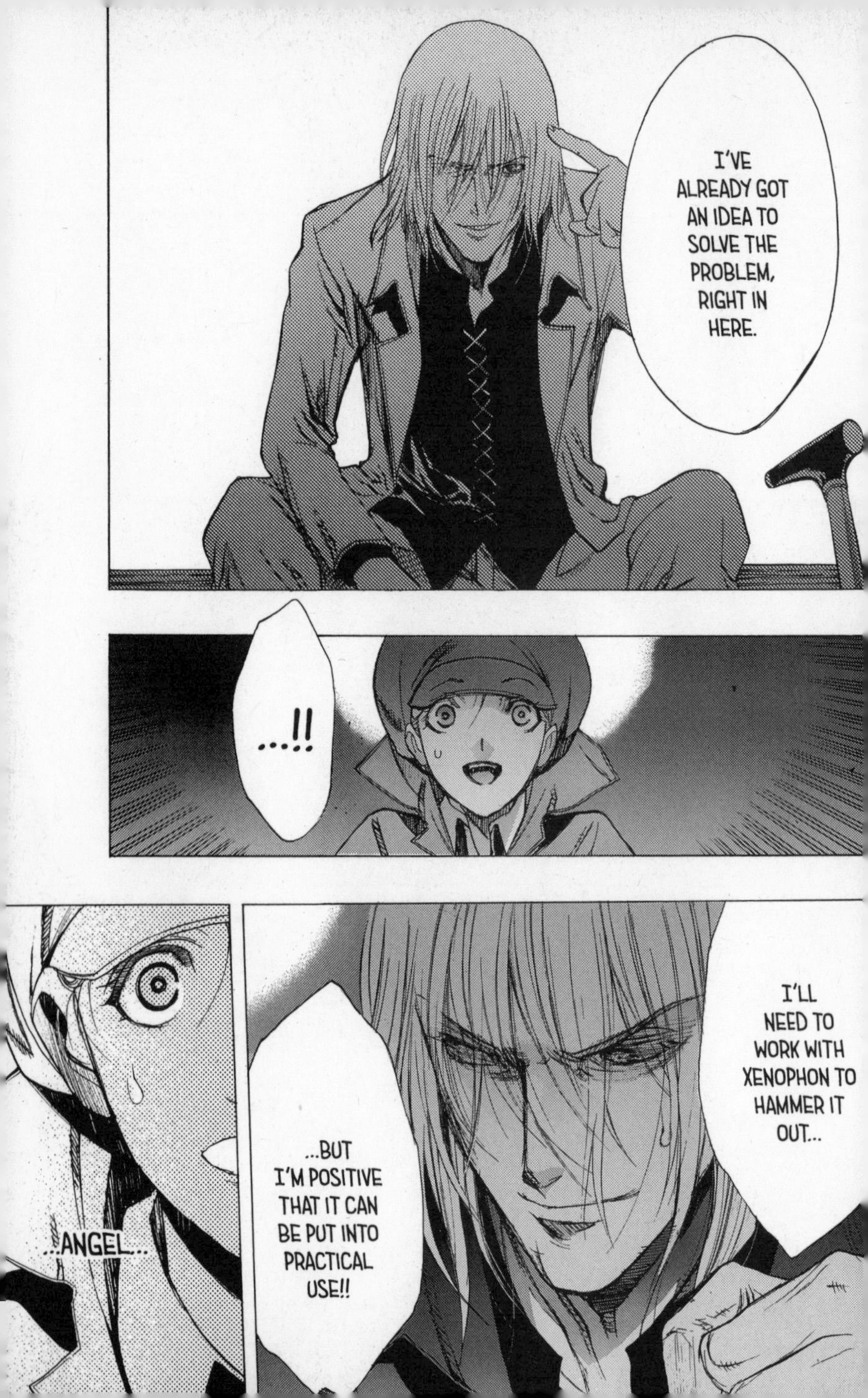
I'VE ALREADY GOT AN IDEA TO SOLVE THE PROBLEM, RIGHT IN HERE.
...!!
I'LL NEED TO WORK WITH XENOPHON TO HAMMER IT OUT...
...BUT I'M POSITIVE THAT IT CAN BE PUT INTO PRACTICAL USE!!
...ANGEL...

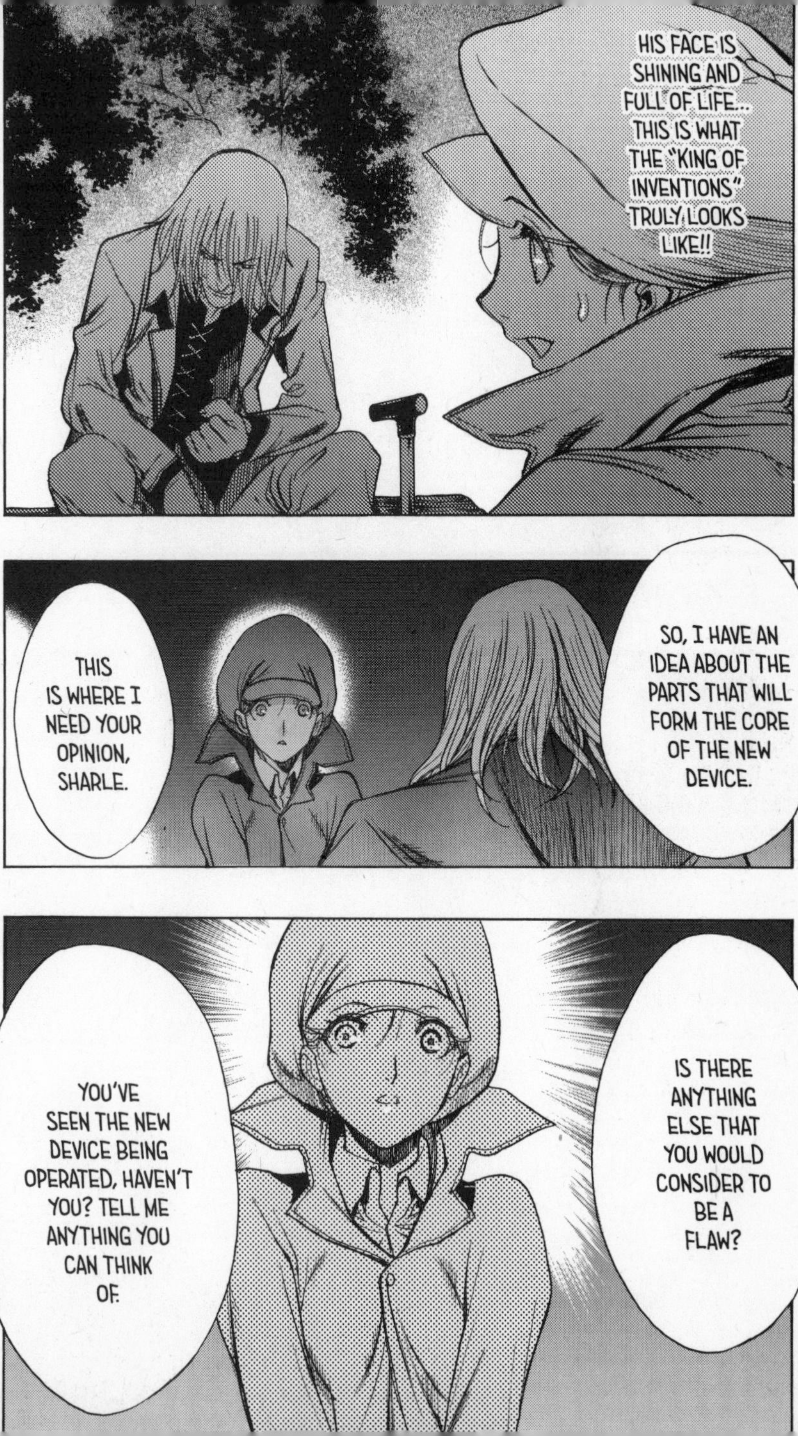
HIS FACE IS SHINING AND FULL OF LIFE... THIS IS WHAT THE "KING OF INVENTIONS" TRULY LOOKS LIKE!!
SO, I HAVE AN IDEA ABOUT THE PARTS THAT WILL FORM THE CORE OF THE NEW DEVICE.
THIS IS WHERE I NEED YOUR OPINION, SHARLE.
IS THERE ANYTHING ELSE THAT YOU WOULD CONSIDER TO BE A FLAW?
YOU'VE SEEN THE NEW DEVICE BEING OPERATED, HAVEN'T YOU? TELL ME ANYTHING YOU CAN THINK OF.

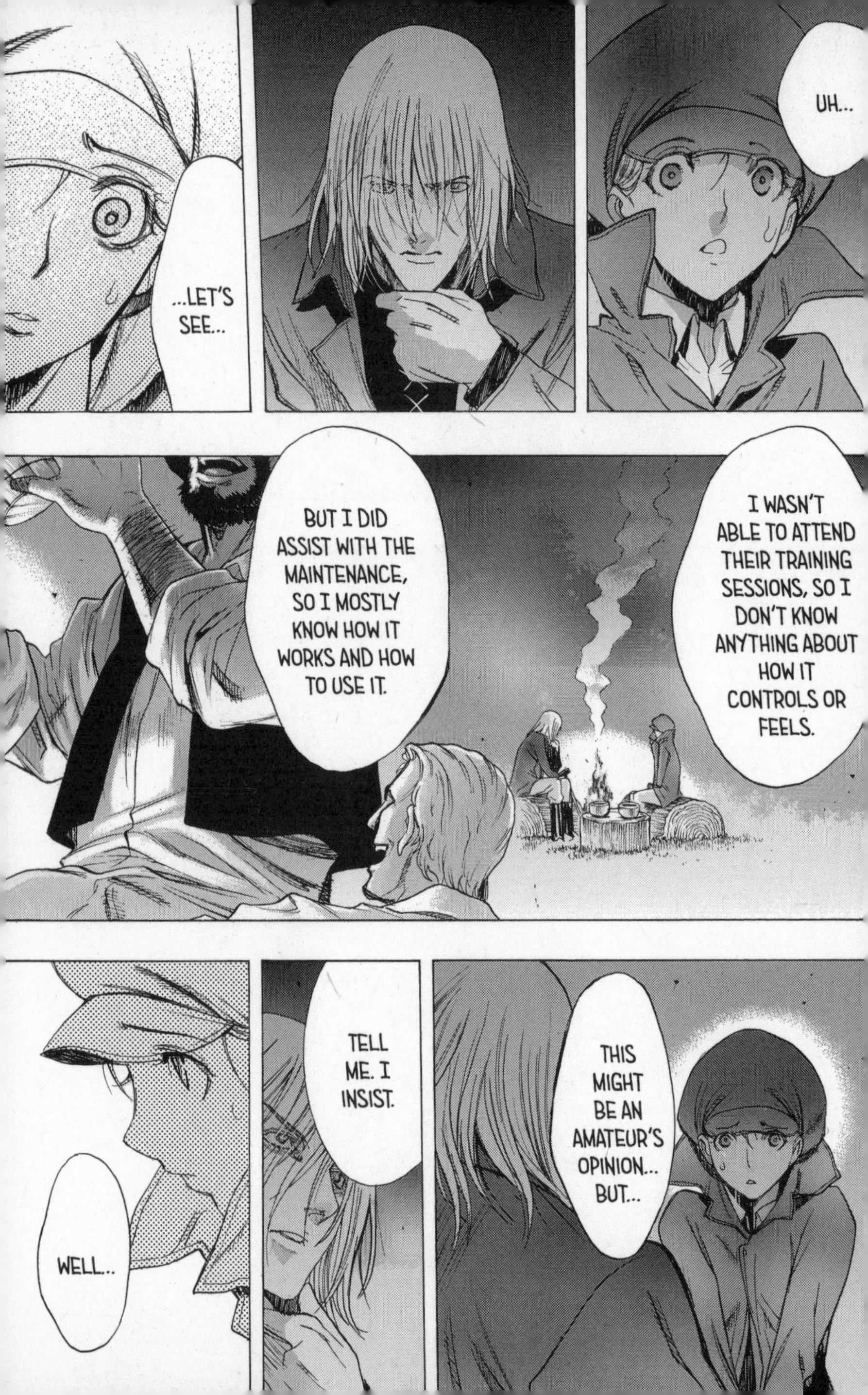
UH...
...LET'S SEE...
I WASN'T ABLE TO ATTEND THEIR TRAINING SESSIONS, SO I DON'T KNOW ANYTHING ABOUT HOW IT CONTROLS OR FEELS.
BUT I DID ASSIST WITH THE MAINTENANCE, SO I MOSTLY KNOW HOW IT WORKS AND HOW TO USE IT.
THIS MIGHT BE AN AMATEUR'S OPINION... BUT...
TELL ME. I INSIST.
WELL...

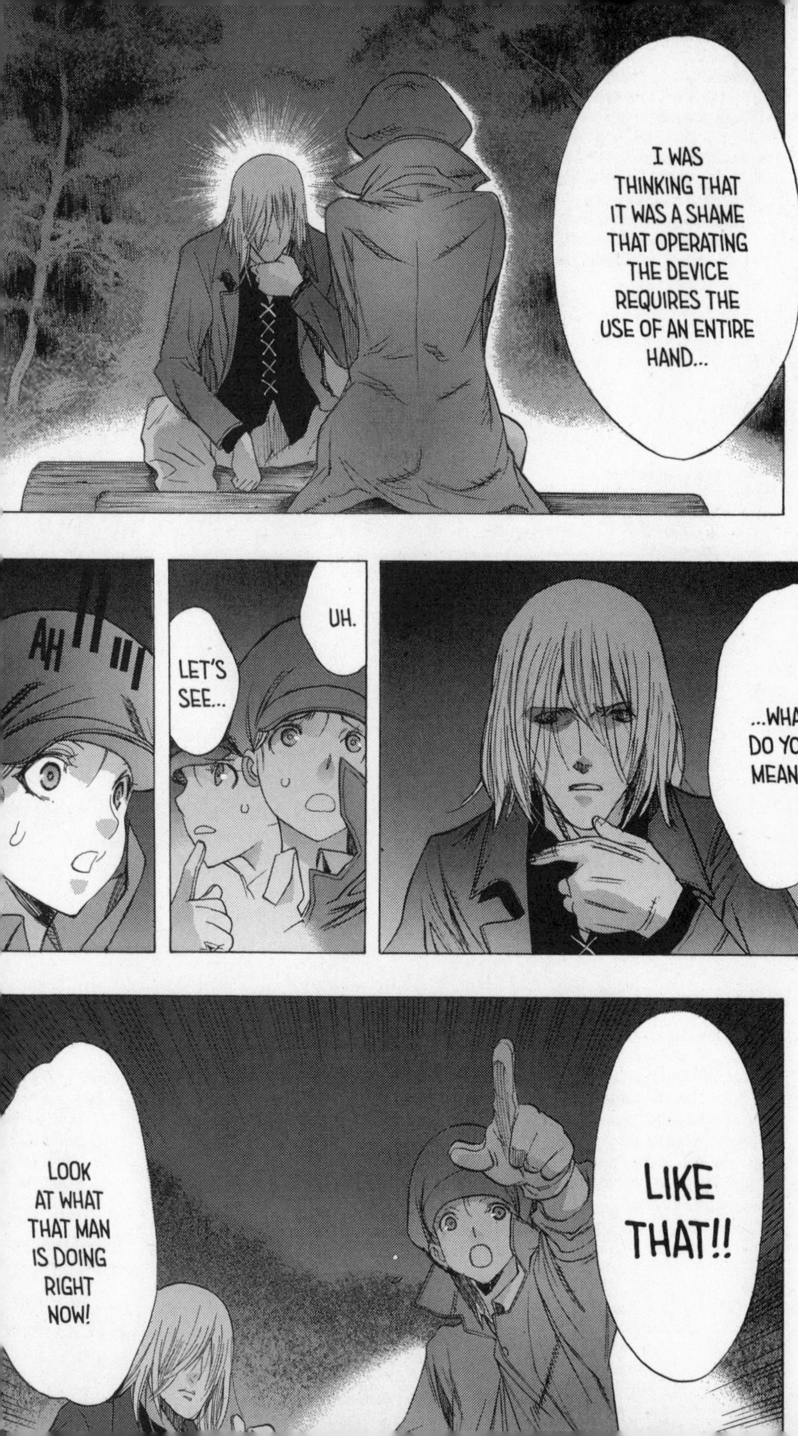
I WAS THINKING THAT IT WAS A SHAME THAT OPERATING THE DEVICE REQUIRES THE USE OF AN ENTIRE HAND...
...WHAT DO YOU MEAN?
UH.
LET'S SEE...
AH!!
LIKE THAT!!
LOOK AT WHAT THAT MAN IS DOING RIGHT NOW!

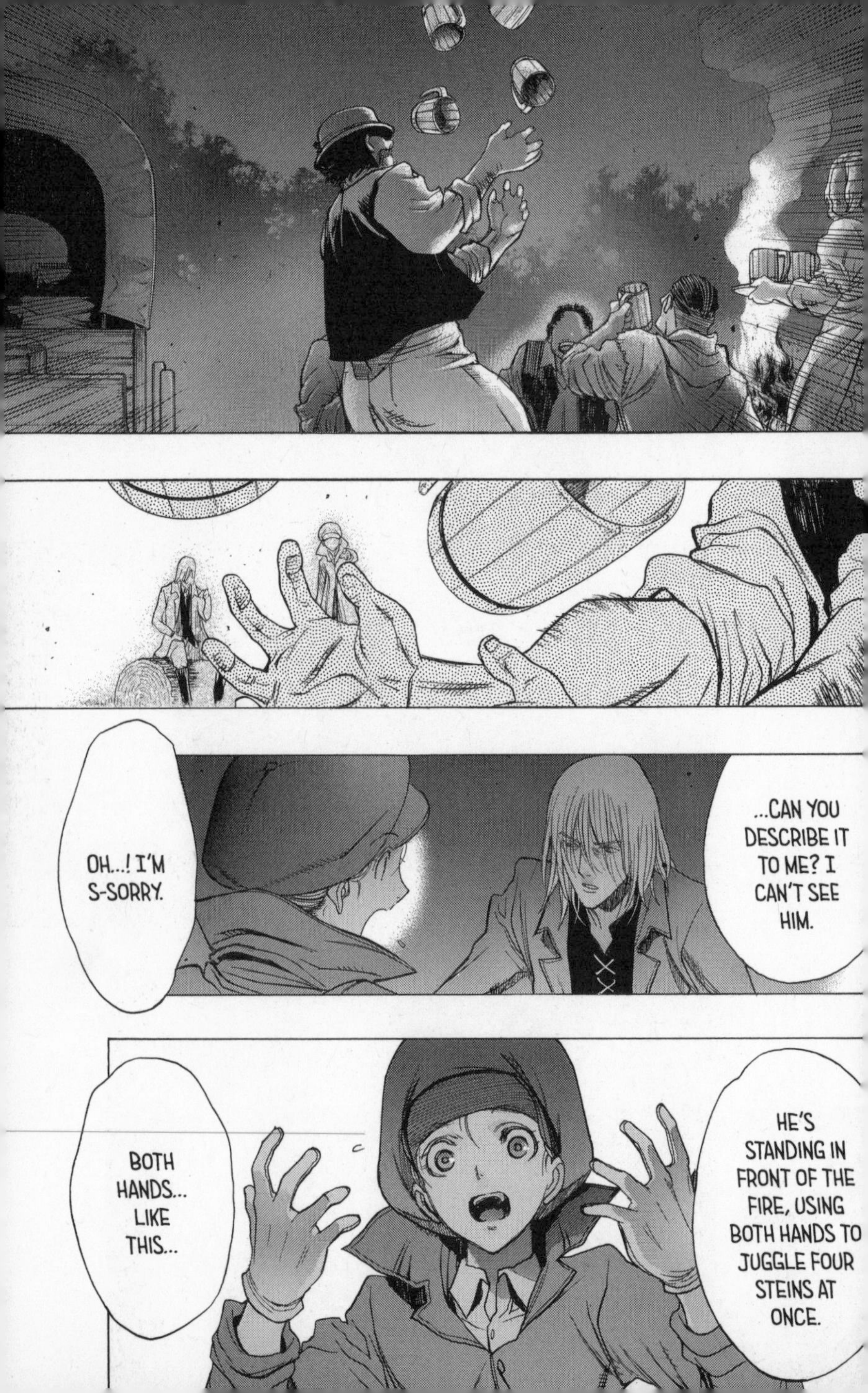
...CAN YOU DESCRIBE IT TO ME? I CAN'T SEE HIM.
OH...! I'M S-SORRY.
HE'S STANDING IN FRONT OF THE FIRE, USING BOTH HANDS TO JUGGLE FOUR STEINS AT ONCE.
BOTH HANDS... LIKE THIS...

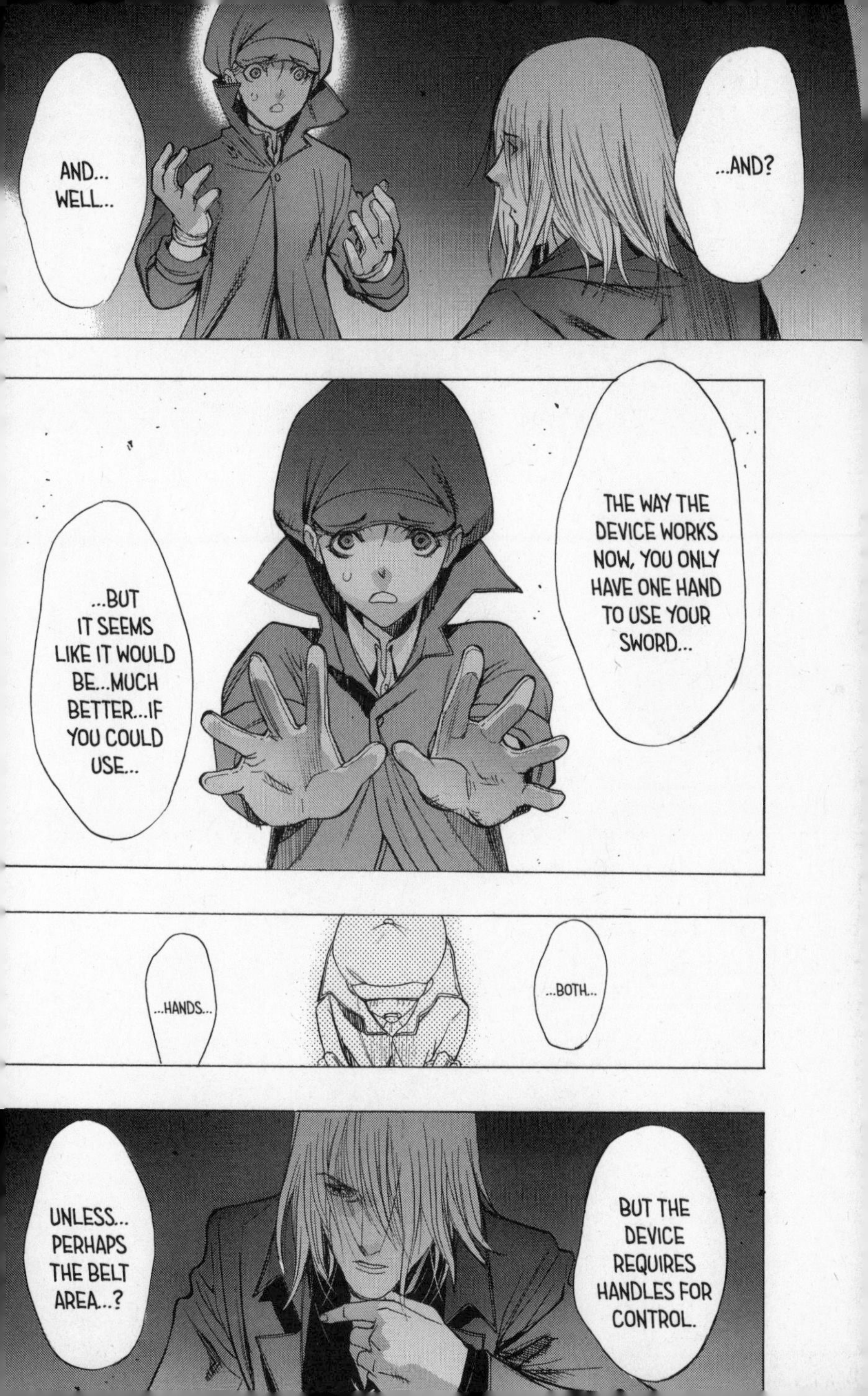
...AND?
AND... WELL...
THE WAY THE DEVICE WORKS NOW, YOU ONLY HAVE ONE HAND TO USE YOUR SWORD...
...BUT IT SEEMS LIKE IT WOULD BE...MUCH BETTER...IF YOU COULD USE...
...BOTH...
...HANDS...
BUT THE DEVICE REQUIRES HANDLES FOR CONTROL.
UNLESS... PERHAPS THE BELT AREA...?

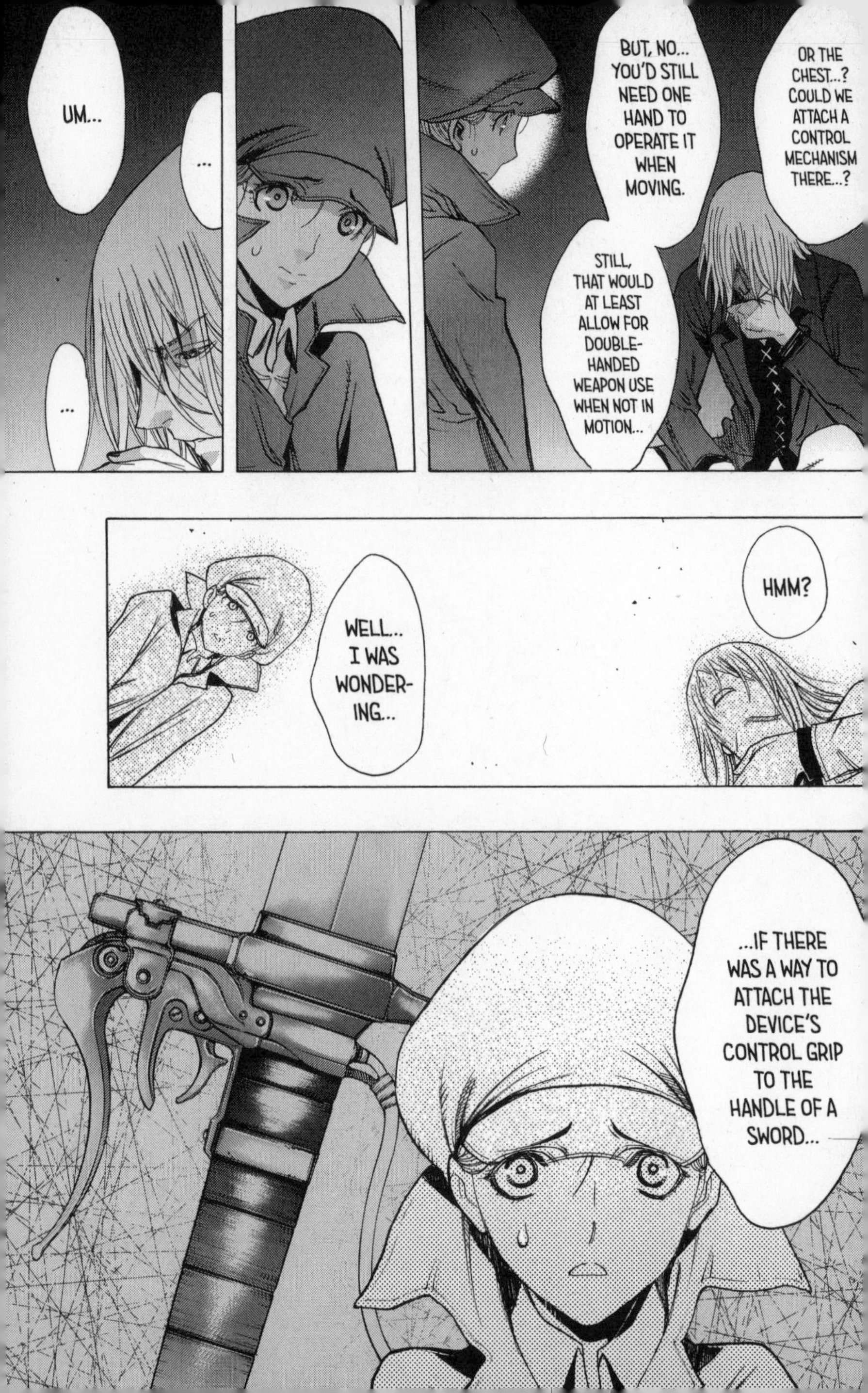
OR THE CHEST...? COULD WE ATTACH A CONTROL MECHANISM THERE...?
BUT, NO... YOU'D STILL NEED ONE HAND TO OPERATE IT WHEN MOVING.
STILL, THAT WOULD AT LEAST ALLOW FOR DOUBLE-HANDED WEAPON USE WHEN NOT IN MOTION...
UM...
...
...
HMM?
WELL... I WAS WONDER-ING...
...IF THERE WAS A WAY TO ATTACH THE DEVICE'S CONTROL GRIP TO THE HANDLE OF A SWORD...

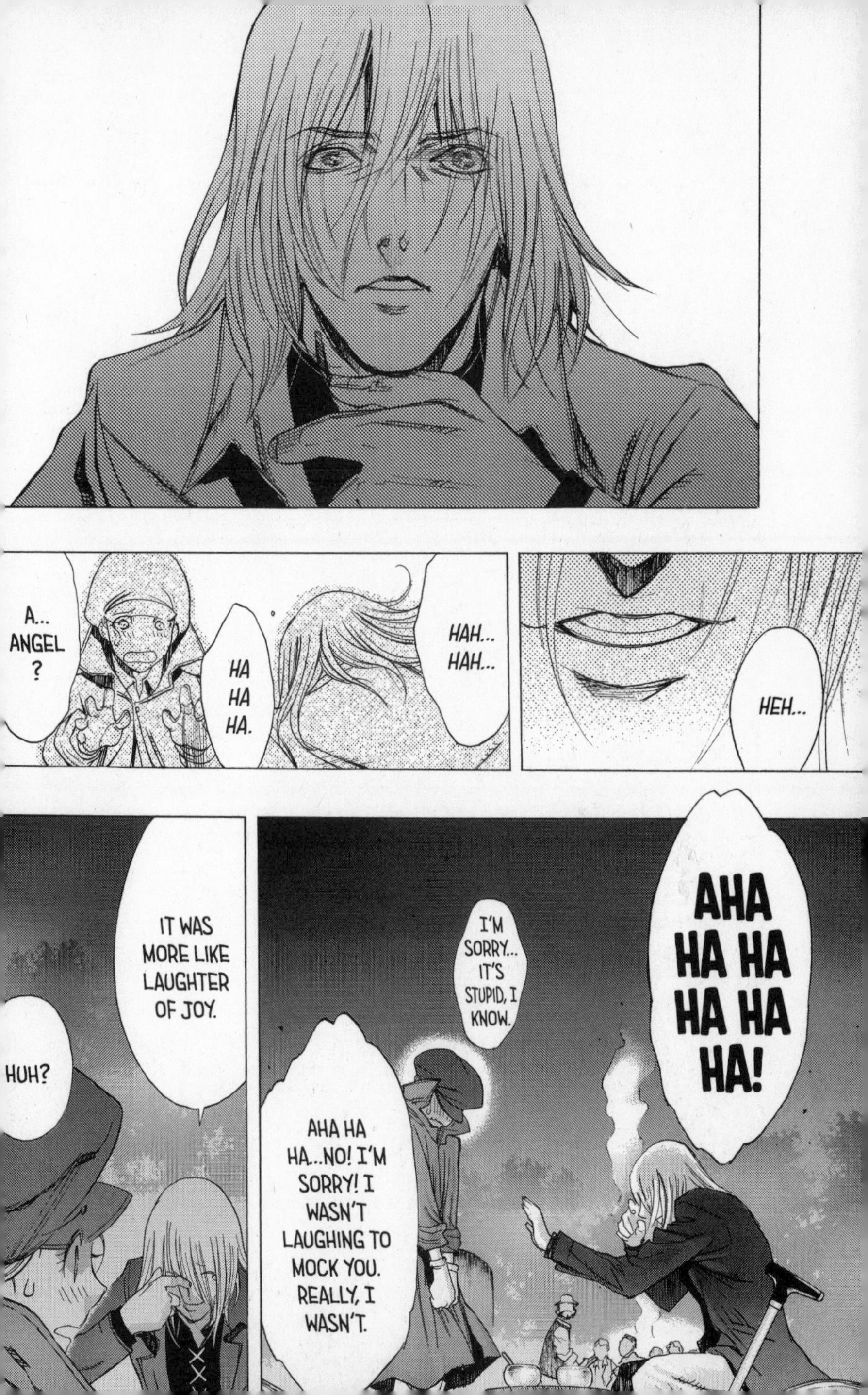
HEH...
HAH... HAH...
HA HA HA.
A... ANGEL?
AHA HA HA HA HA HA HA!
I'M SORRY... IT'S STUPID, I KNOW.
AHA HA HA...NO! I'M SORRY! I WASN'T LAUGHING TO MOCK YOU. REALLY, I WASN'T.
IT WAS MORE LIKE LAUGHTER OF JOY.
HUH?

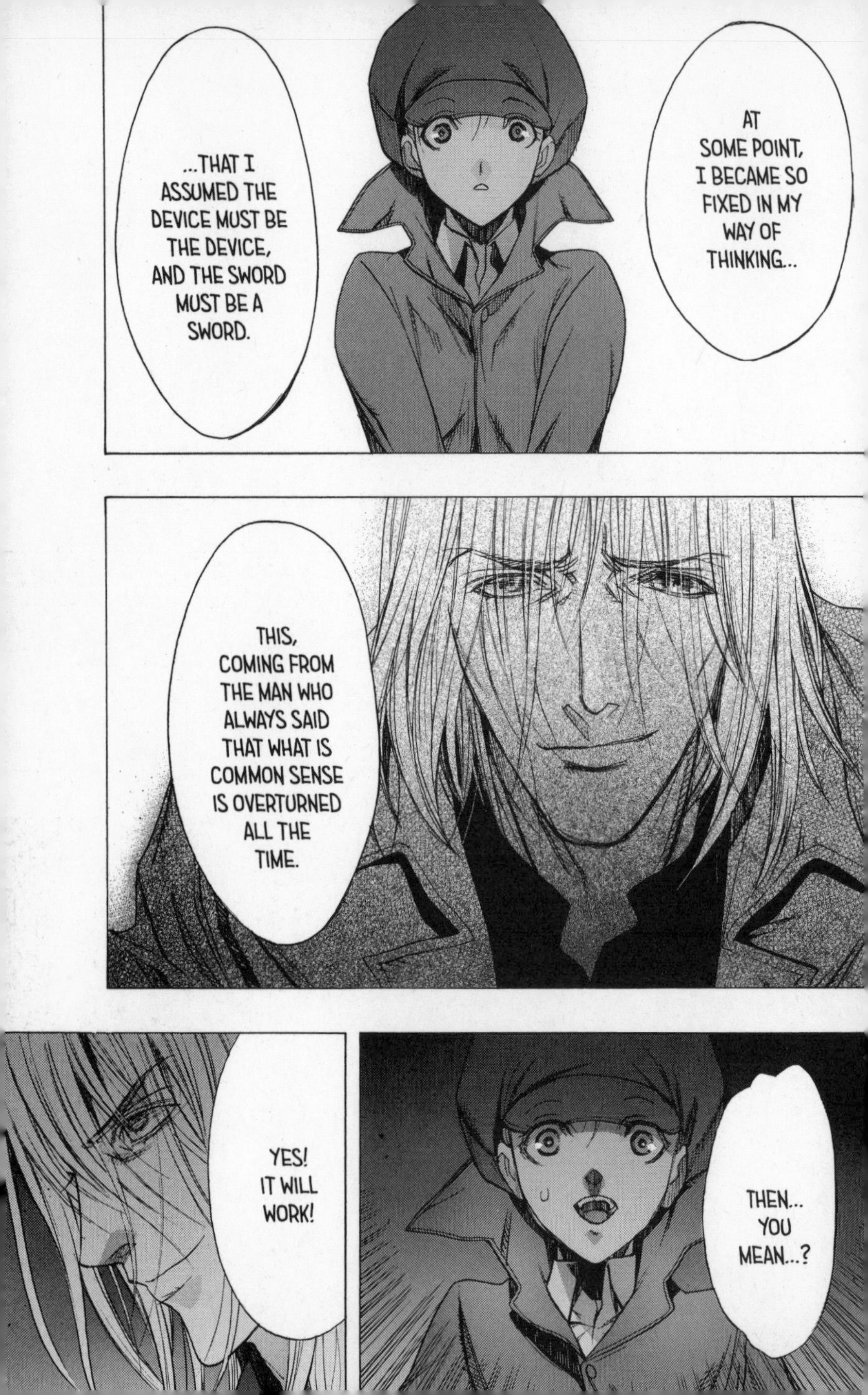
AT SOME POINT, I BECAME SO FIXED IN MY WAY OF THINKING...
...THAT I ASSUMED THE DEVICE MUST BE THE DEVICE, AND THE SWORD MUST BE A SWORD.
THIS, COMING FROM THE MAN WHO ALWAYS SAID THAT WHAT IS COMMON SENSE IS OVERTURNED ALL THE TIME.
THEN... YOU MEAN...?
YES! IT WILL WORK!

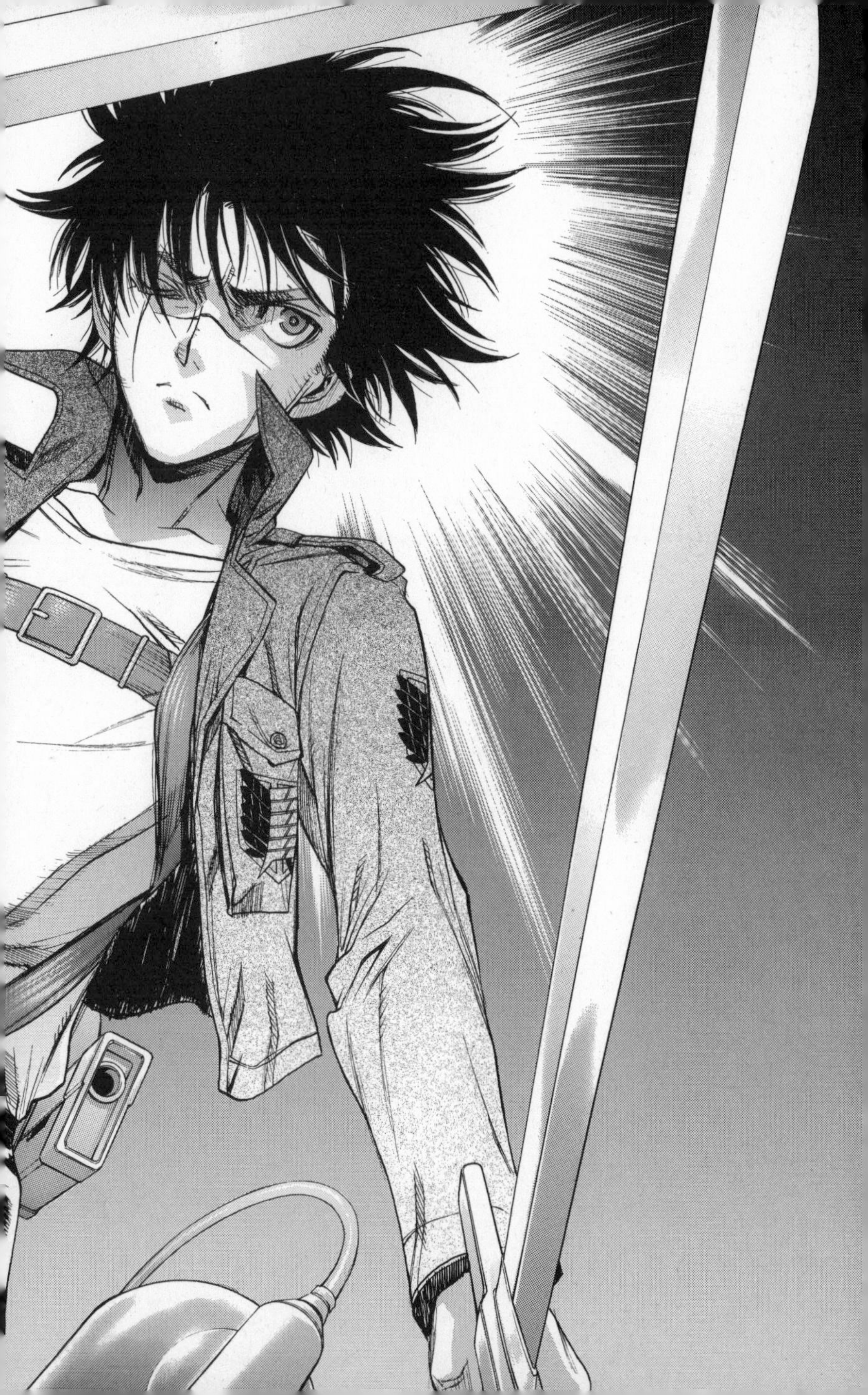

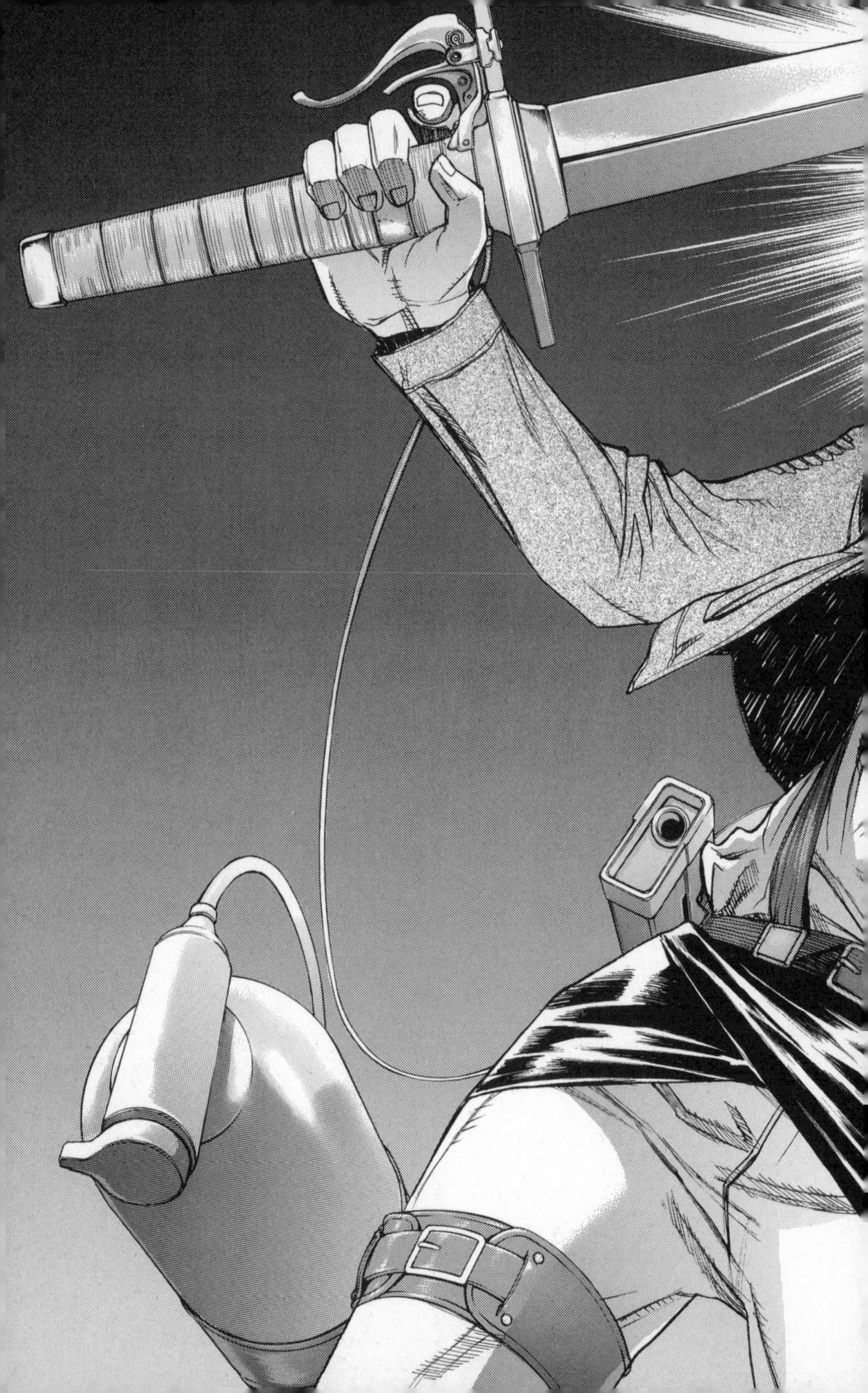

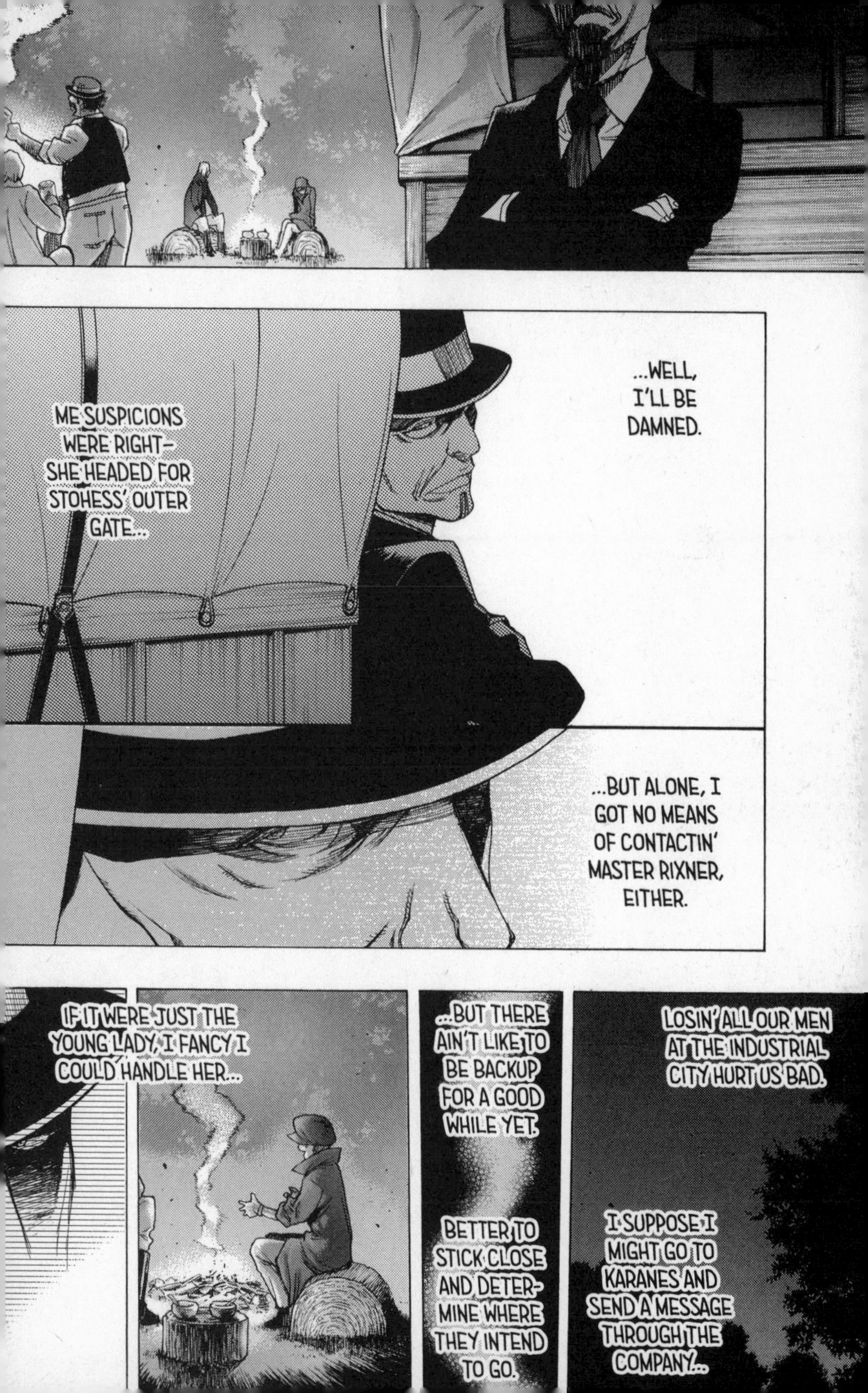

ME SUSPICIONS WERE RIGHT—SHE HEADED FOR STOHESS' OUTER GATE...
...WELL, I'LL BE DAMNED.
...BUT ALONE, I GOT NO MEANS OF CONTACTIN' MASTER RIXNER, EITHER.
IF IT WERE JUST THE YOUNG LADY, I FANCY I COULD HANDLE HER...
...BUT THERE AIN'T LIKE TO BE BACKUP FOR A GOOD WHILE YET.
BETTER TO STICK CLOSE AND DETERMINE WHERE THEY INTEND TO GO.
LOSIN' ALL OUR MEN AT THE INDUSTRIAL CITY HURT US BAD.
I SUPPOSE I MIGHT GO TO KARANES AND SEND A MESSAGE THROUGH THE COMPANY...

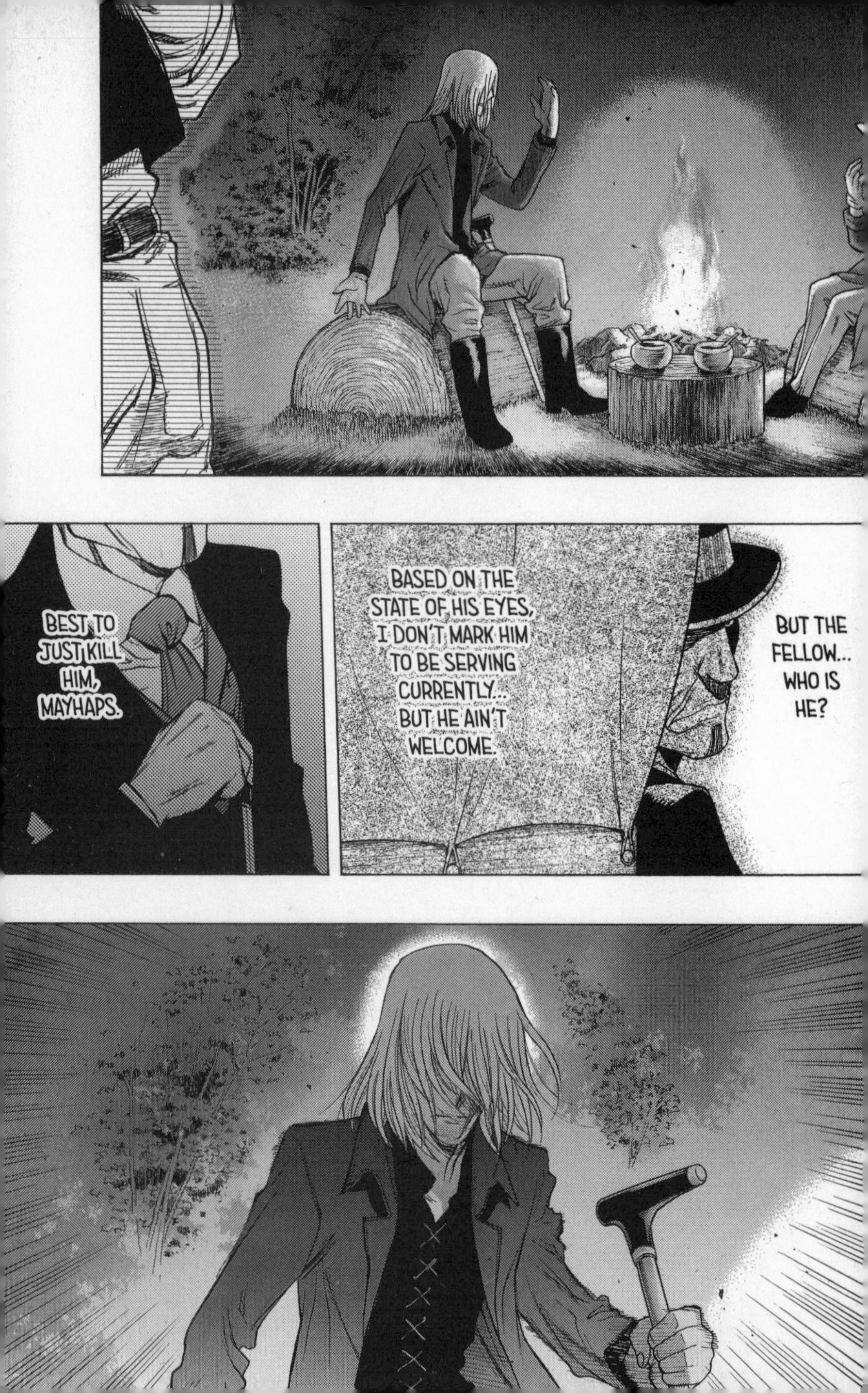
BUT THE FELLOW... WHO IS HE?
BASED ON THE STATE OF HIS EYES, I DON'T MARK HIM TO BE SERVING CURRENTLY... BUT HE AIN'T WELCOME.
BEST TO JUST KILL HIM, MAYHAPS.

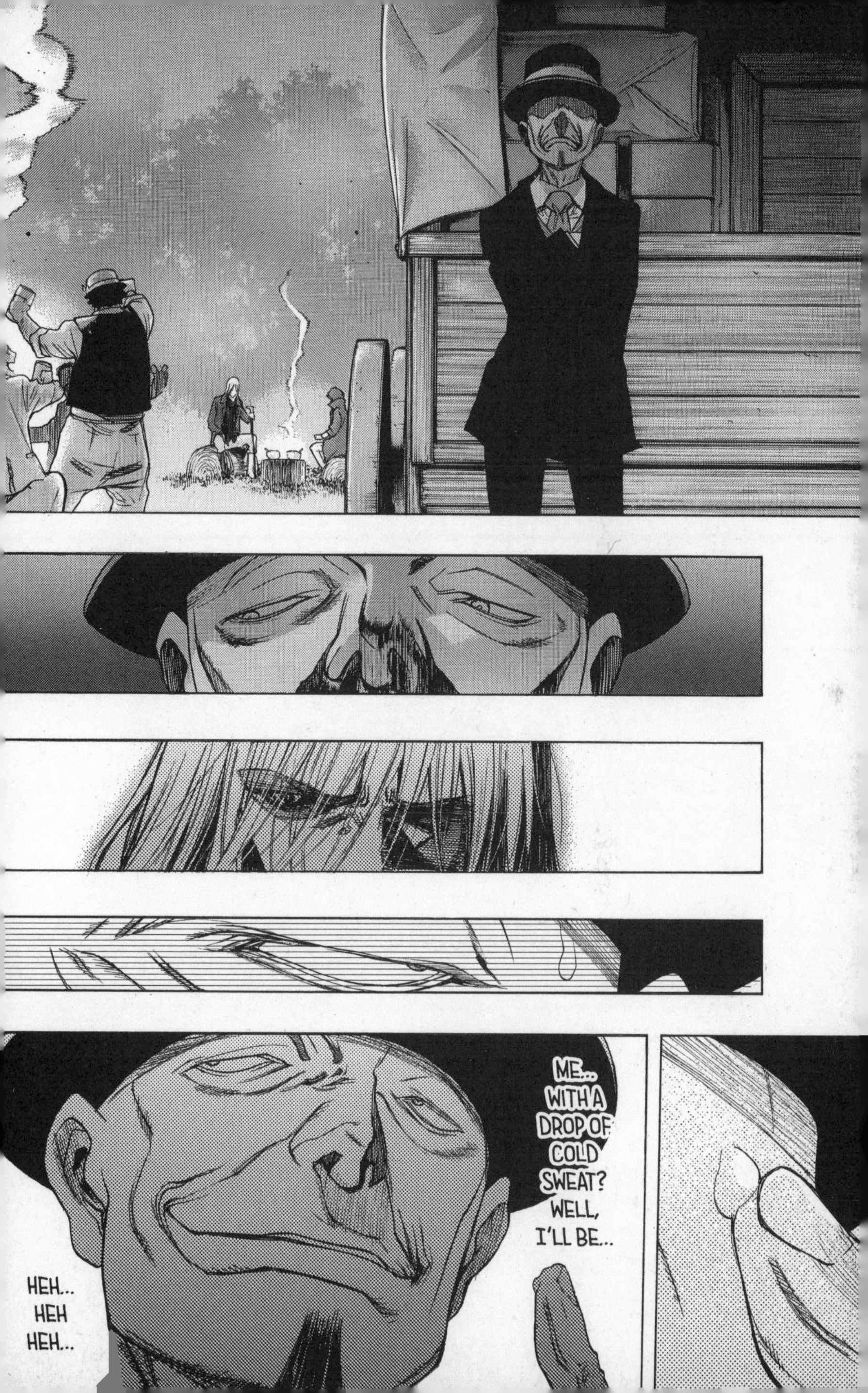
ME... WITH A DROP OF COLD SWEAT? WELL, I'LL BE...
HEH... HEH HEH...

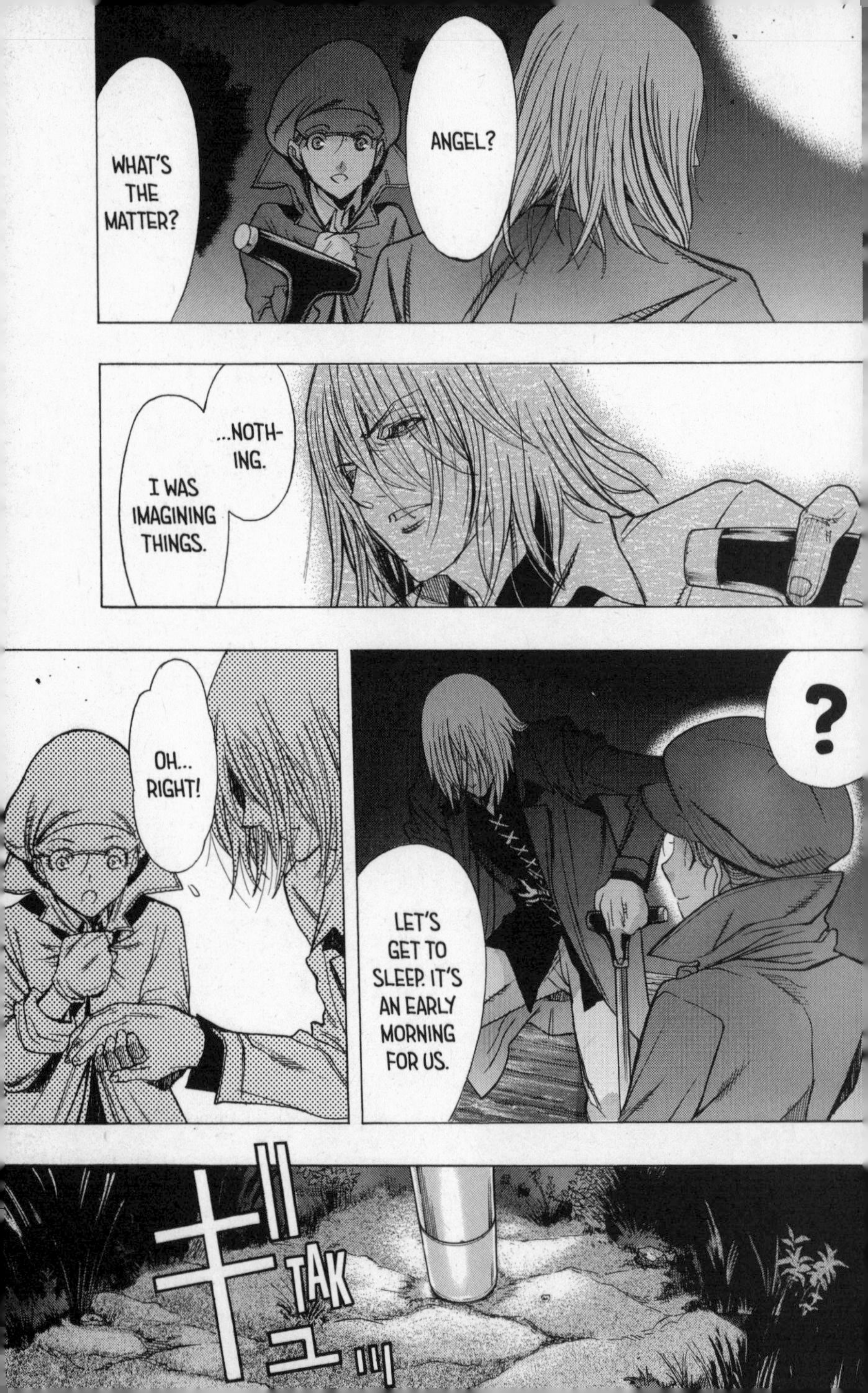
ANGEL?
WHAT'S THE MATTER?
...NOTH-ING.
I WAS IMAGINING THINGS.
?
LET'S GET TO SLEEP. IT'S AN EARLY MORNING FOR US.
OH... RIGHT!
TAK

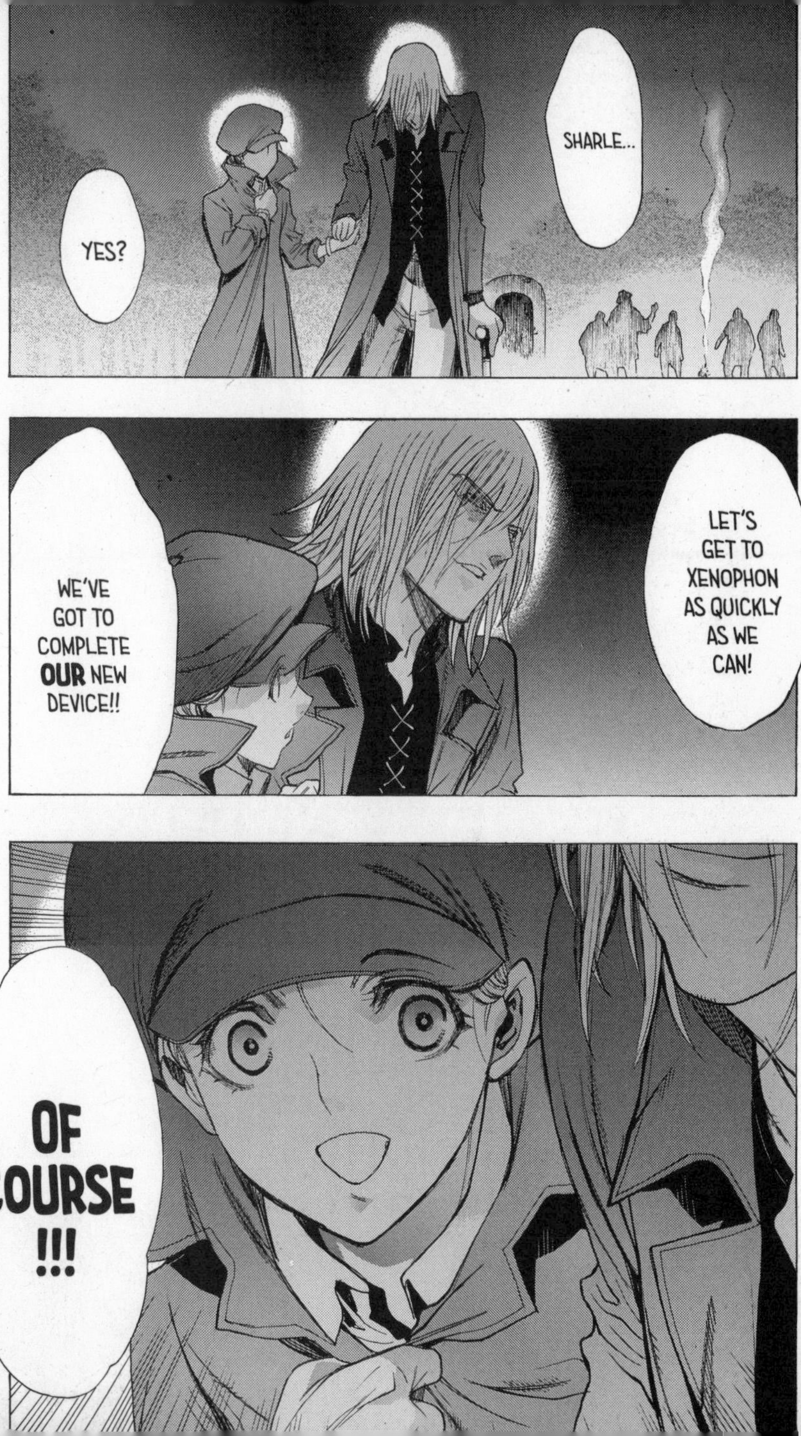
SHARLE...
YES?
LET'S GET TO XENOPHON AS QUICKLY AS WE CAN!
WE'VE GOT TO COMPLETE **OUR** NEW DEVICE!!
OF COURSE!!!

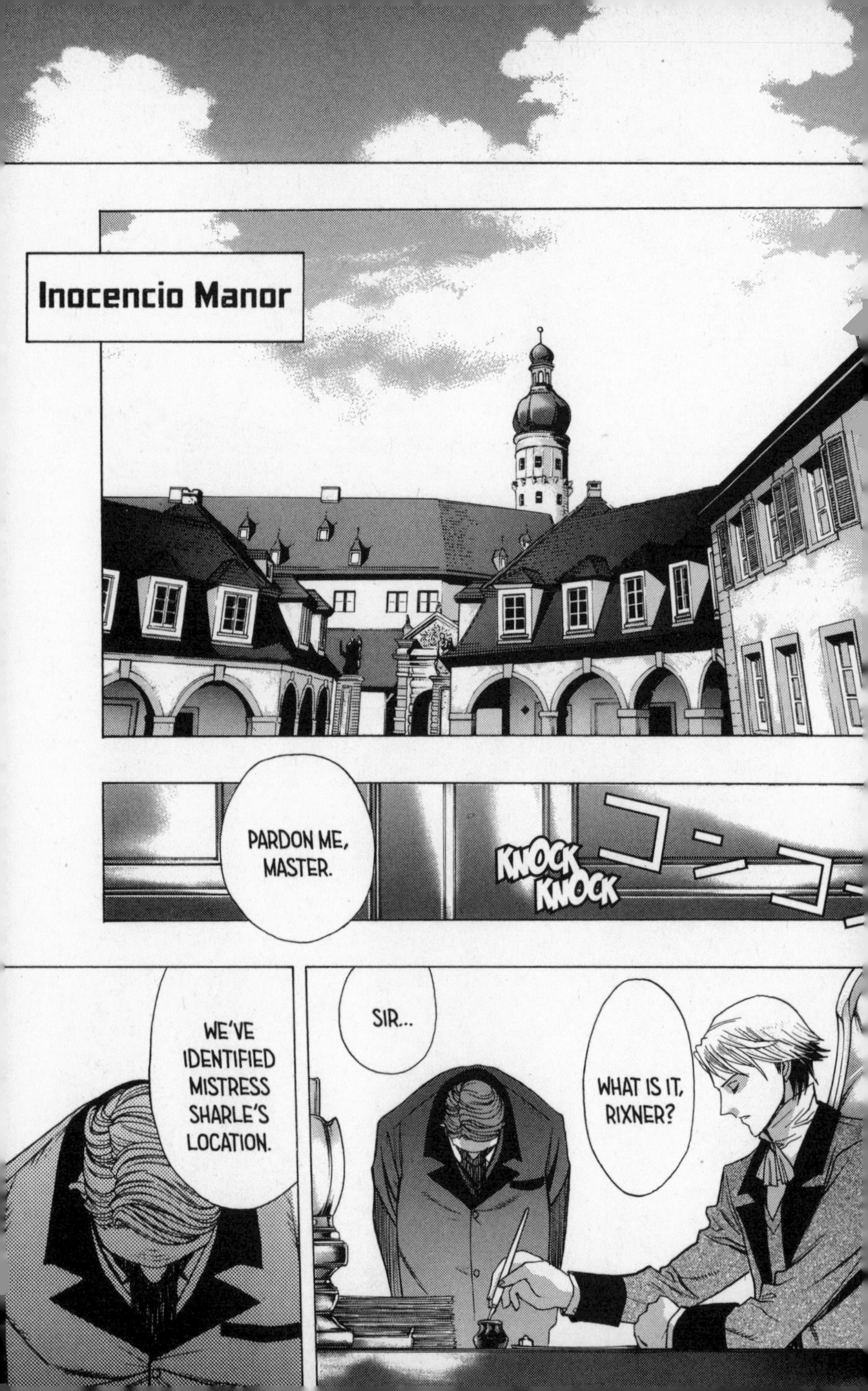
Inocencio Manor
KNOCK KNOCK
PARDON ME, MASTER.
WHAT IS IT, RIXNER?
SIR...
WE'VE IDENTIFIED MISTRESS SHARLE'S LOCATION.

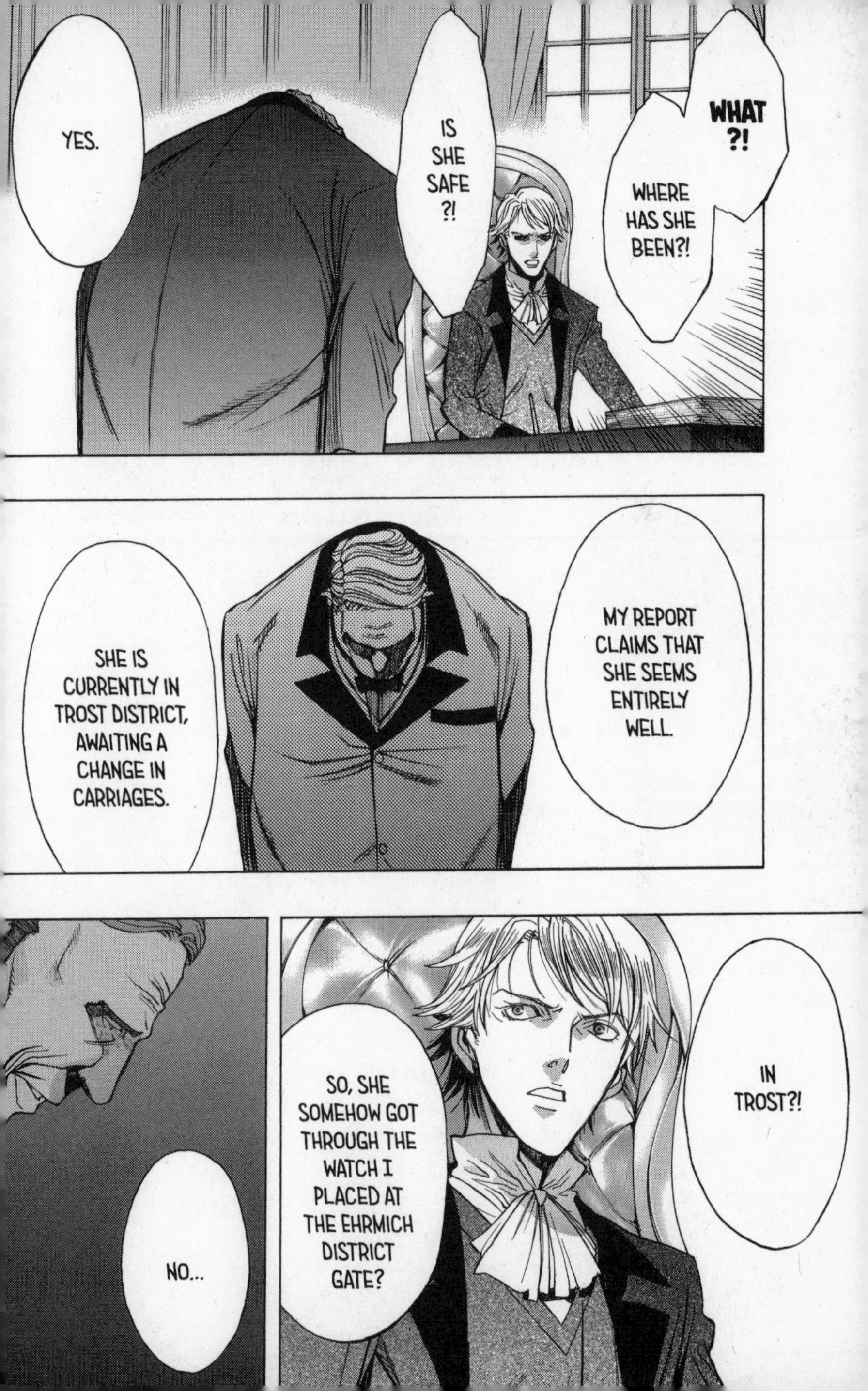
WHAT ?!
WHERE HAS SHE BEEN?!
IS SHE SAFE ?!
YES.
MY REPORT CLAIMS THAT SHE SEEMS ENTIRELY WELL.
SHE IS CURRENTLY IN TROST DISTRICT, AWAITING A CHANGE IN CARRIAGES.
IN TROST?!
SO, SHE SOMEHOW GOT THROUGH THE WATCH I PLACED AT THE EHRMICH DISTRICT GATE?
NO...

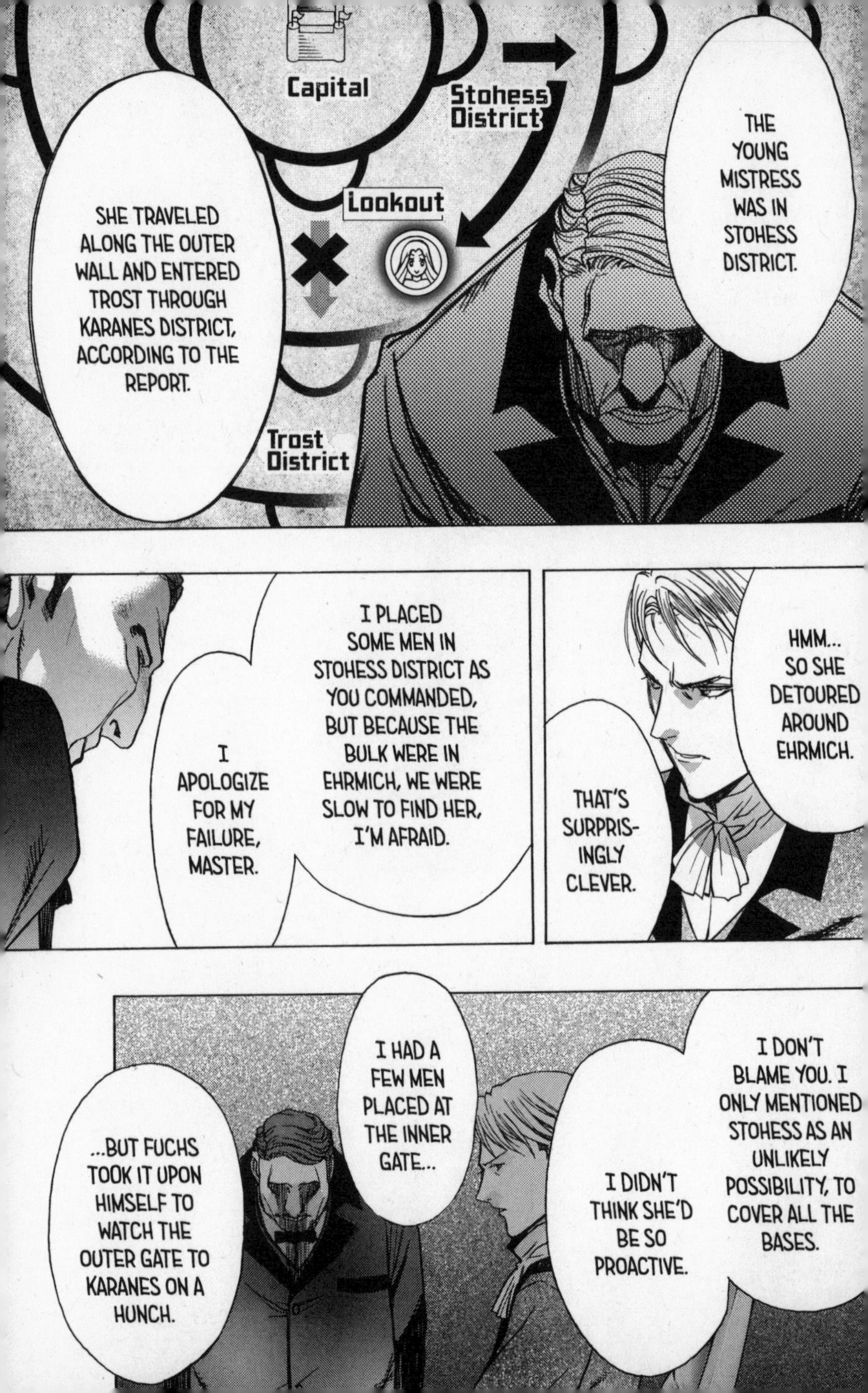
Capital
Stohess District
Lookout
Trost District
THE YOUNG MISTRESS WAS IN STOHESS DISTRICT.
SHE TRAVELED ALONG THE OUTER WALL AND ENTERED TROST THROUGH KARANES DISTRICT, ACCORDING TO THE REPORT.
HMM... SO SHE DETOURED AROUND EHRMICH.
THAT'S SURPRIS-INGLY CLEVER.
I PLACED SOME MEN IN STOHESS DISTRICT AS YOU COMMANDED, BUT BECAUSE THE BULK WERE IN EHRMICH, WE WERE SLOW TO FIND HER, I'M AFRAID.
I APOLOGIZE FOR MY FAILURE, MASTER.
I DON'T BLAME YOU. I ONLY MENTIONED STOHESS AS AN UNLIKELY POSSIBILITY, TO COVER ALL THE BASES.
I DIDN'T THINK SHE'D BE SO PROACTIVE.
I HAD A FEW MEN PLACED AT THE INNER GATE...
...BUT FUCHS TOOK IT UPON HIMSELF TO WATCH THE OUTER GATE TO KARANES ON A HUNCH.

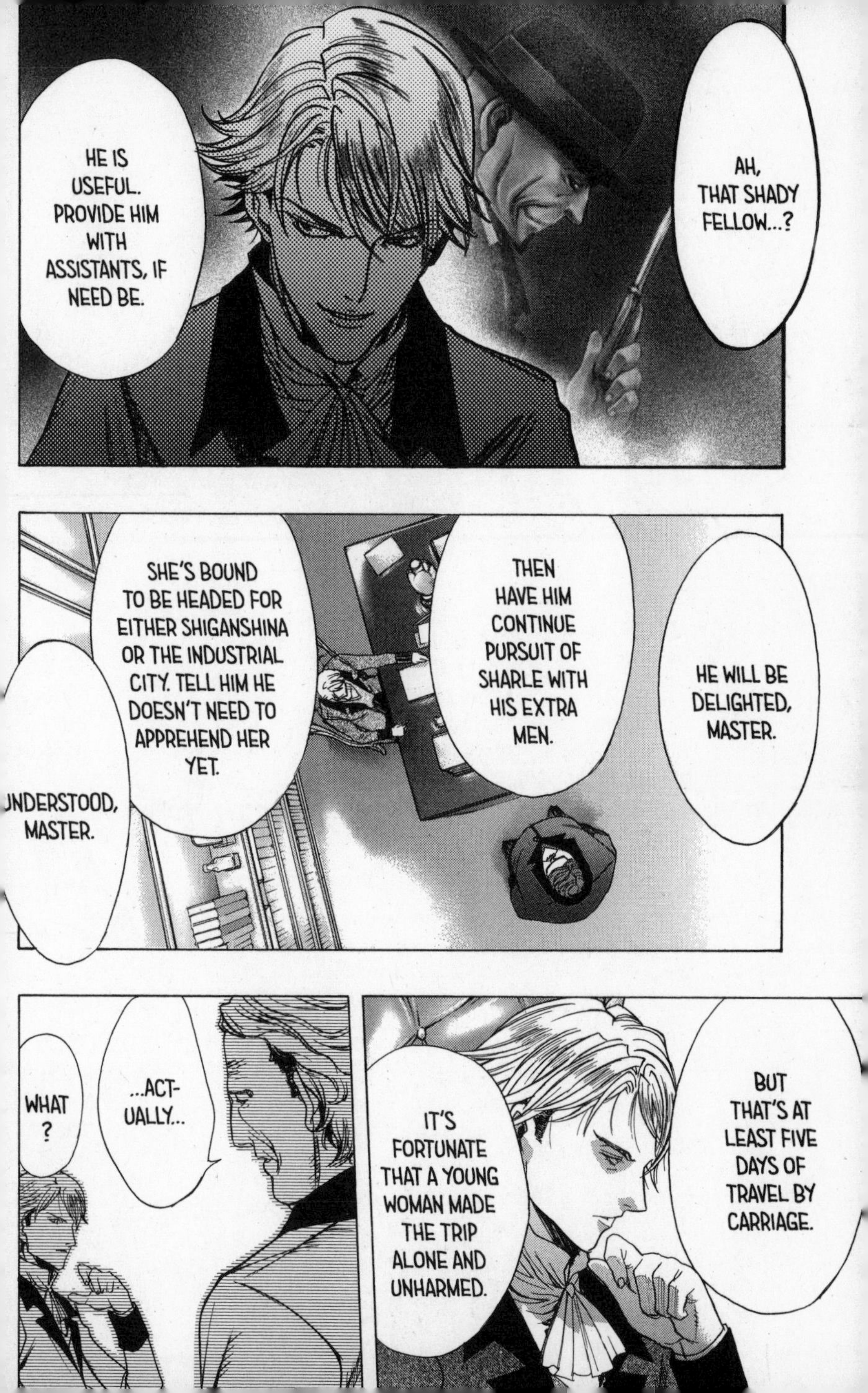
AH, THAT SHADY FELLOW...?
HE IS USEFUL. PROVIDE HIM WITH ASSISTANTS, IF NEED BE.
THEN HAVE HIM CONTINUE PURSUIT OF SHARLE WITH HIS EXTRA MEN.
HE WILL BE DELIGHTED, MASTER.
SHE'S BOUND TO BE HEADED FOR EITHER SHIGANSHINA OR THE INDUSTRIAL CITY. TELL HIM HE DOESN'T NEED TO APPREHEND HER YET.
UNDERSTOOD, MASTER.
BUT THAT'S AT LEAST FIVE DAYS OF TRAVEL BY CARRIAGE.
IT'S FORTUNATE THAT A YOUNG WOMAN MADE THE TRIP ALONE AND UNHARMED.
...ACT-UALLY...
WHAT?

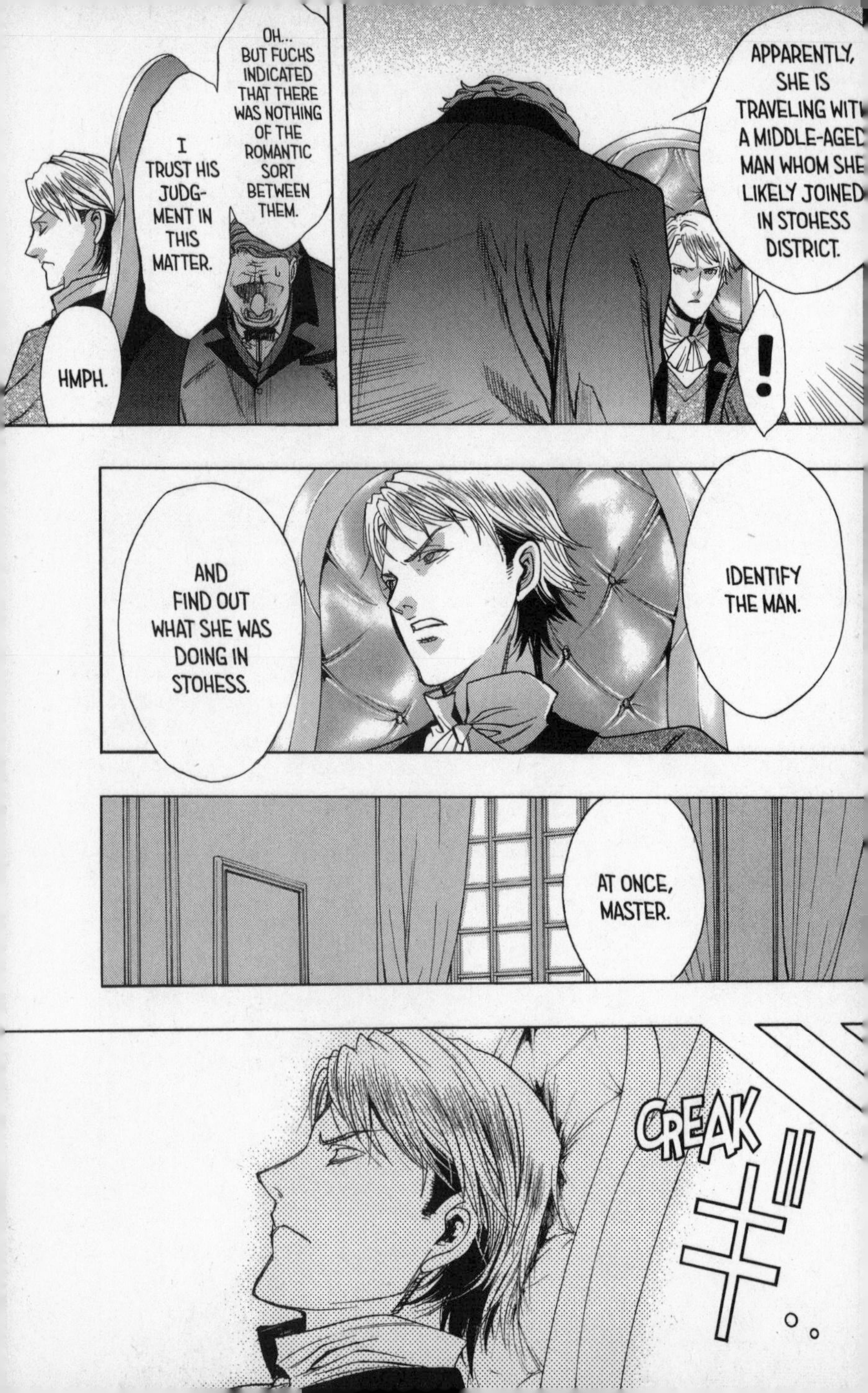
APPARENTLY, SHE IS TRAVELING WITH A MIDDLE-AGED MAN WHOM SHE LIKELY JOINED IN STOHESS DISTRICT.
!
OH... BUT FUCHS INDICATED THAT THERE WAS NOTHING OF THE ROMANTIC SORT BETWEEN THEM.
I TRUST HIS JUDGMENT IN THIS MATTER.
HMPH.
IDENTIFY THE MAN.
AND FIND OUT WHAT SHE WAS DOING IN STOHESS.
AT ONCE, MASTER.
CREAK

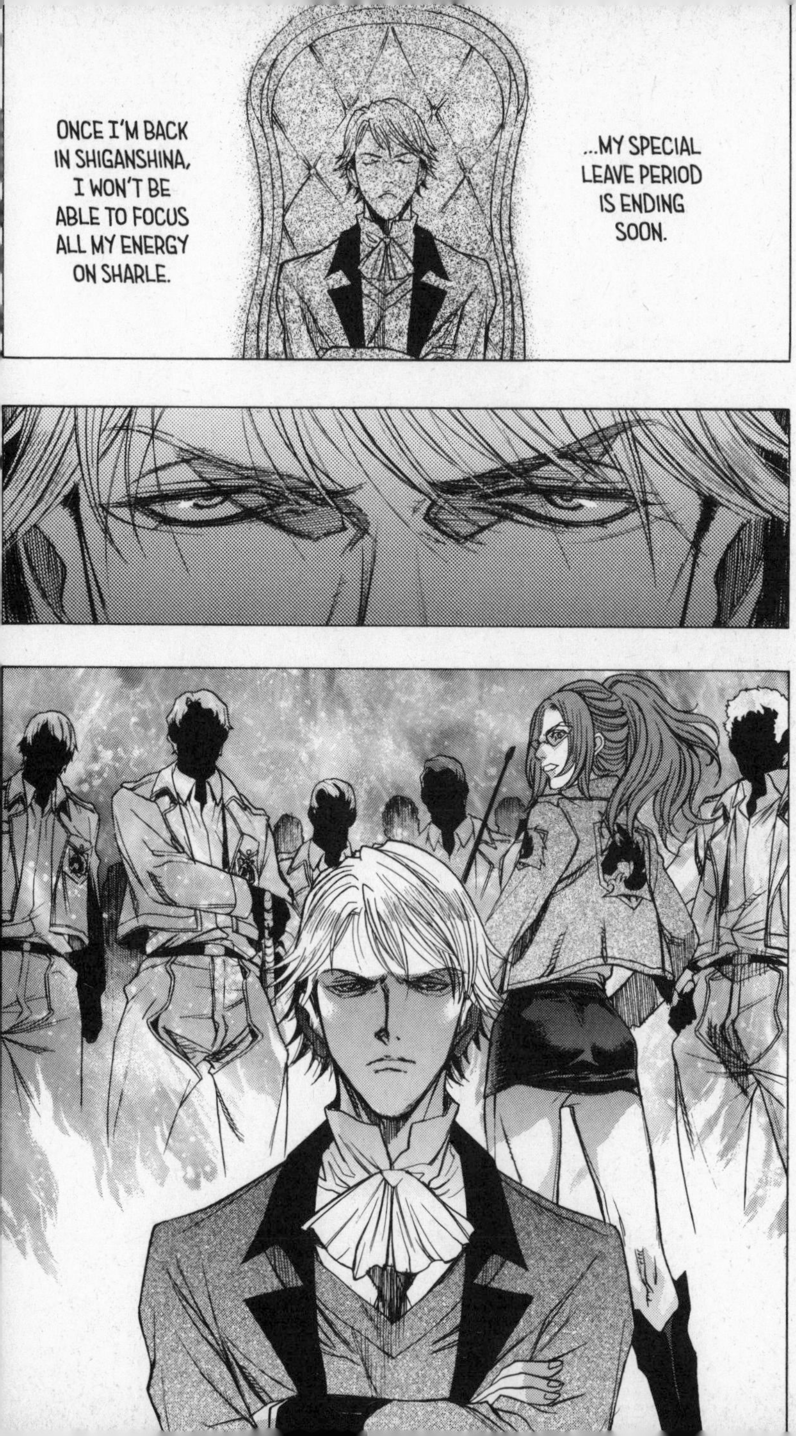
...MY SPECIAL LEAVE PERIOD IS ENDING SOON.
ONCE I'M BACK IN SHIGANSHINA, I WON'T BE ABLE TO FOCUS ALL MY ENERGY ON SHARLE.

Chapter 42: Traveling Skies · End

ATTACK
on TITAN
BEFORE THE FALL

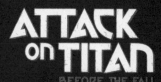

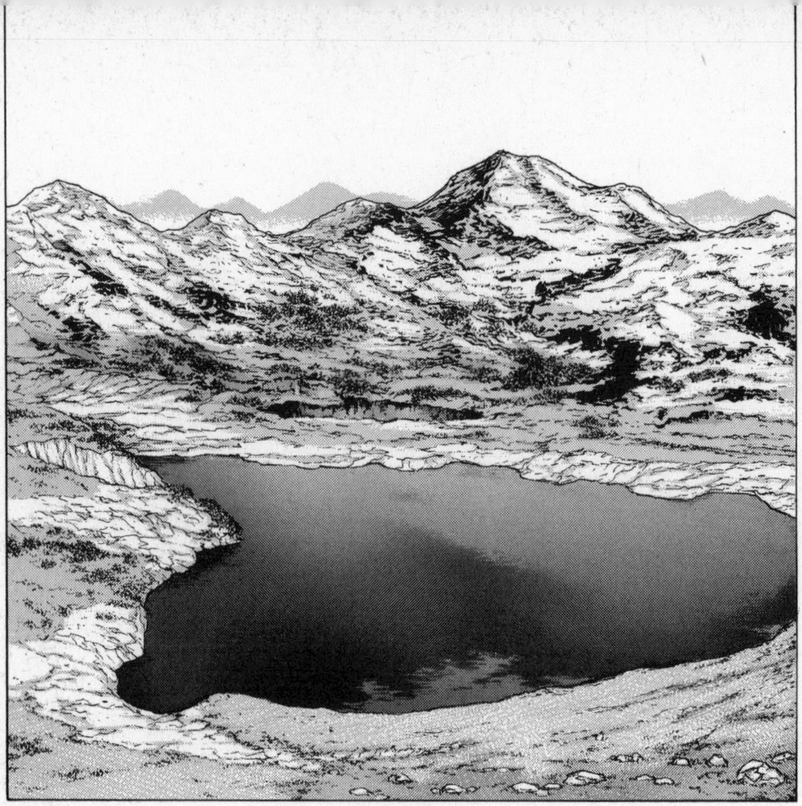
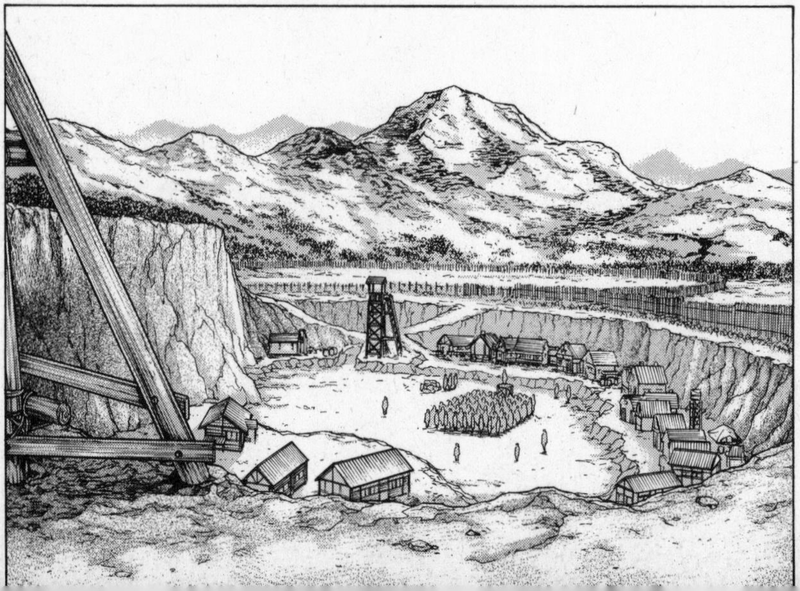

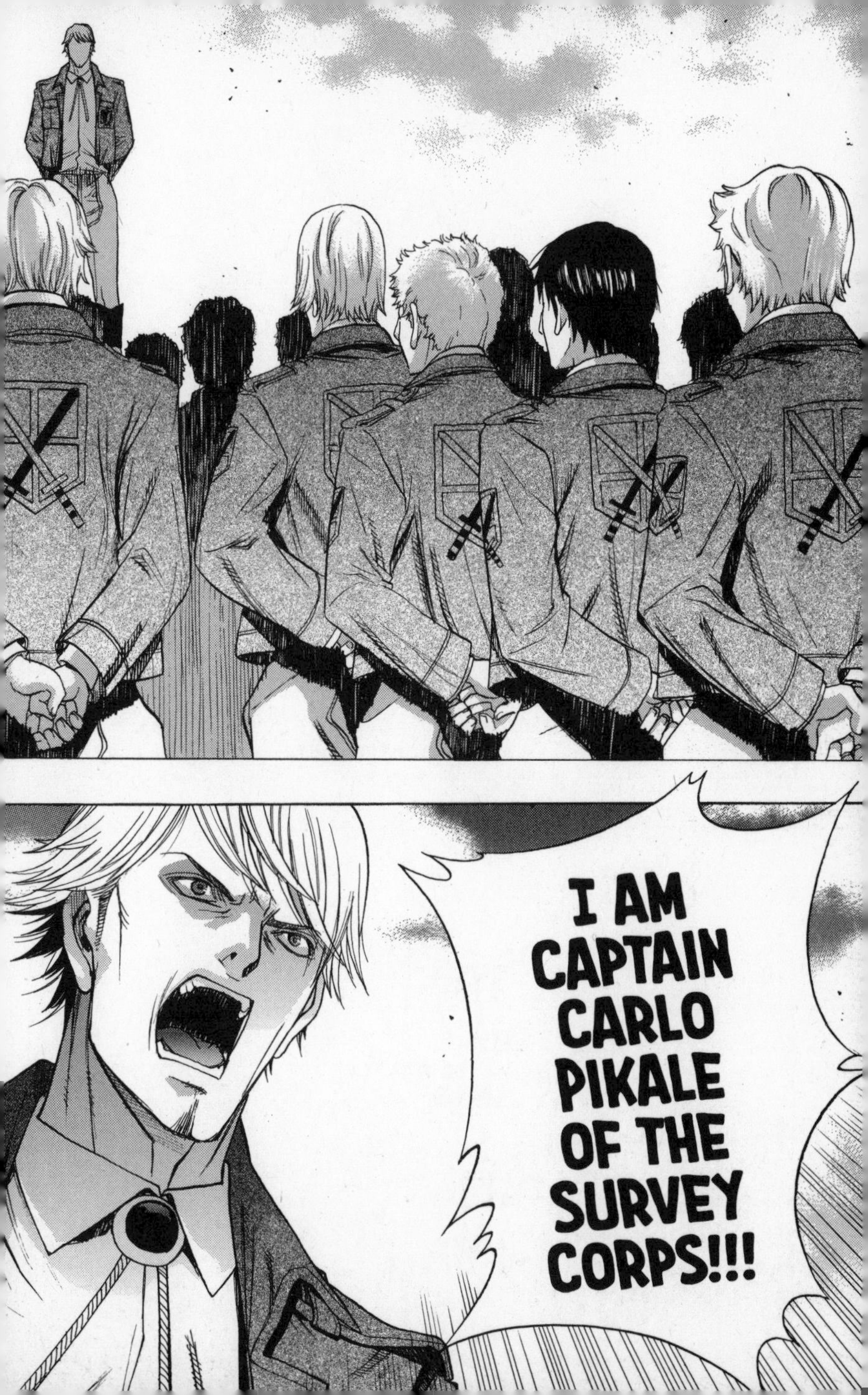
I AM CAPTAIN CARLO PIKALE OF THE SURVEY CORPS!!!

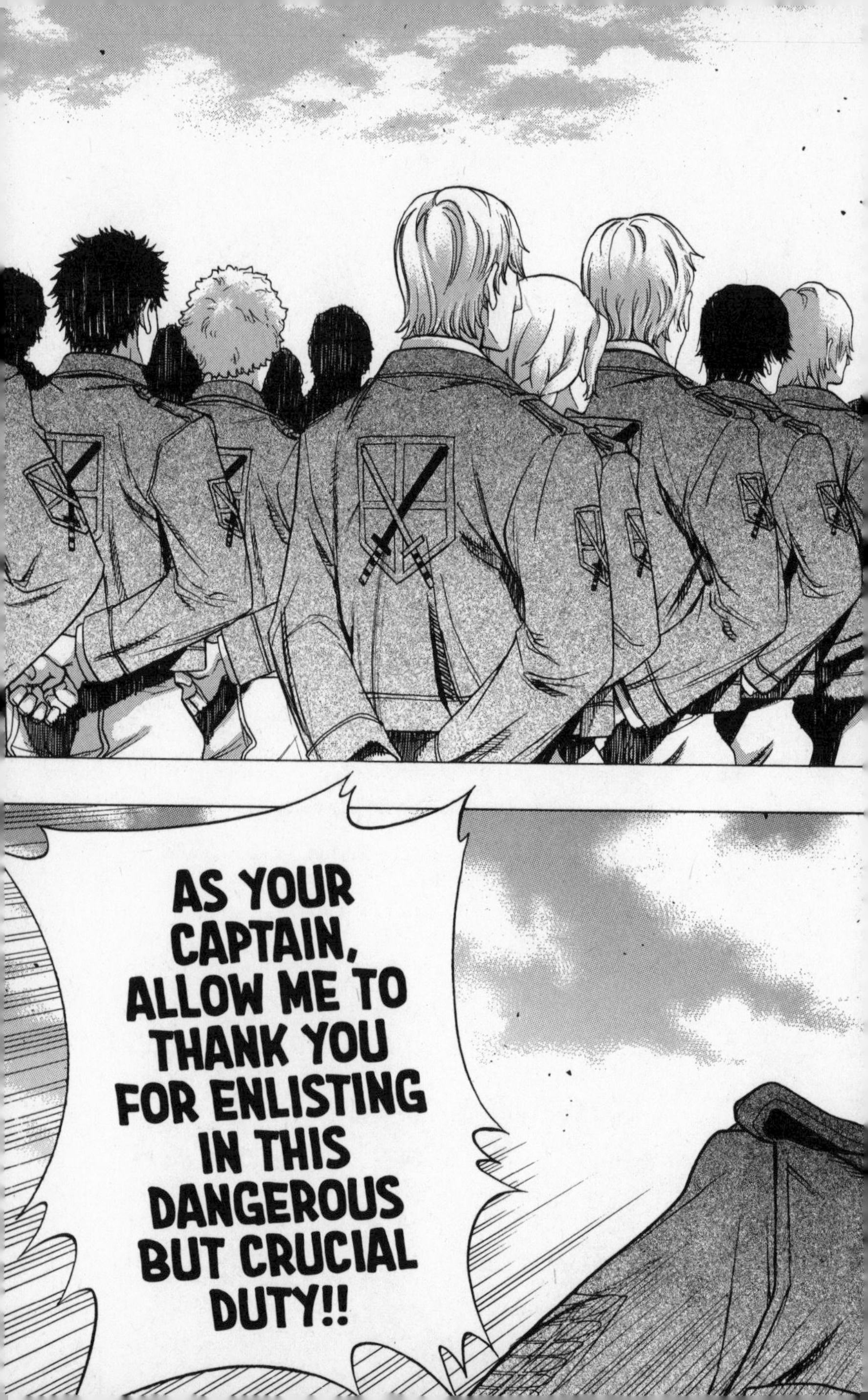
AS YOUR CAPTAIN, ALLOW ME TO THANK YOU FOR ENLISTING IN THIS DANGEROUS BUT CRUCIAL DUTY!!

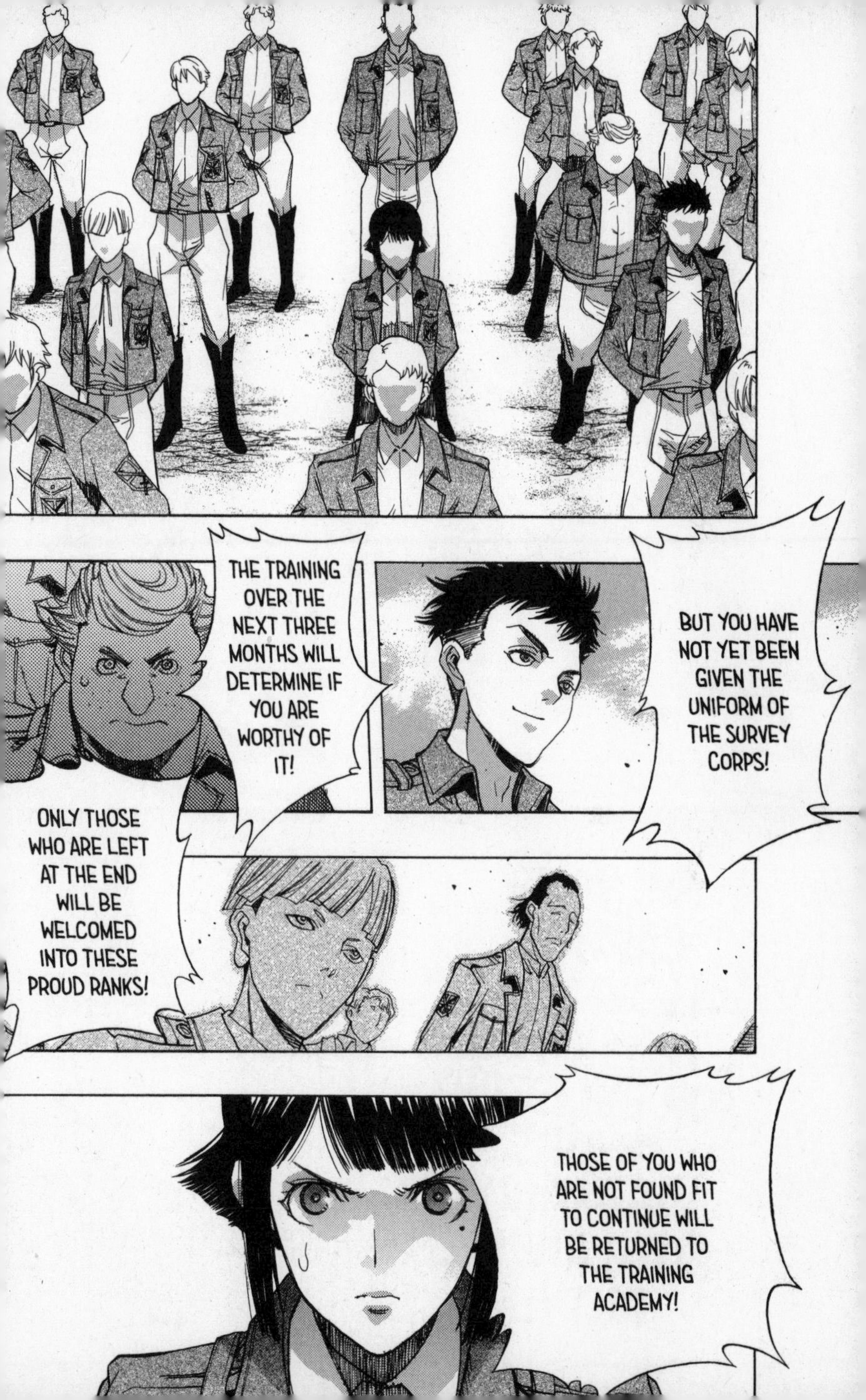

BUT YOU HAVE NOT YET BEEN GIVEN THE UNIFORM OF THE SURVEY CORPS!
THE TRAINING OVER THE NEXT THREE MONTHS WILL DETERMINE IF YOU ARE WORTHY OF IT!
ONLY THOSE WHO ARE LEFT AT THE END WILL BE WELCOMED INTO THESE PROUD RANKS!
THOSE OF YOU WHO ARE NOT FOUND FIT TO CONTINUE WILL BE RETURNED TO THE TRAINING ACADEMY!

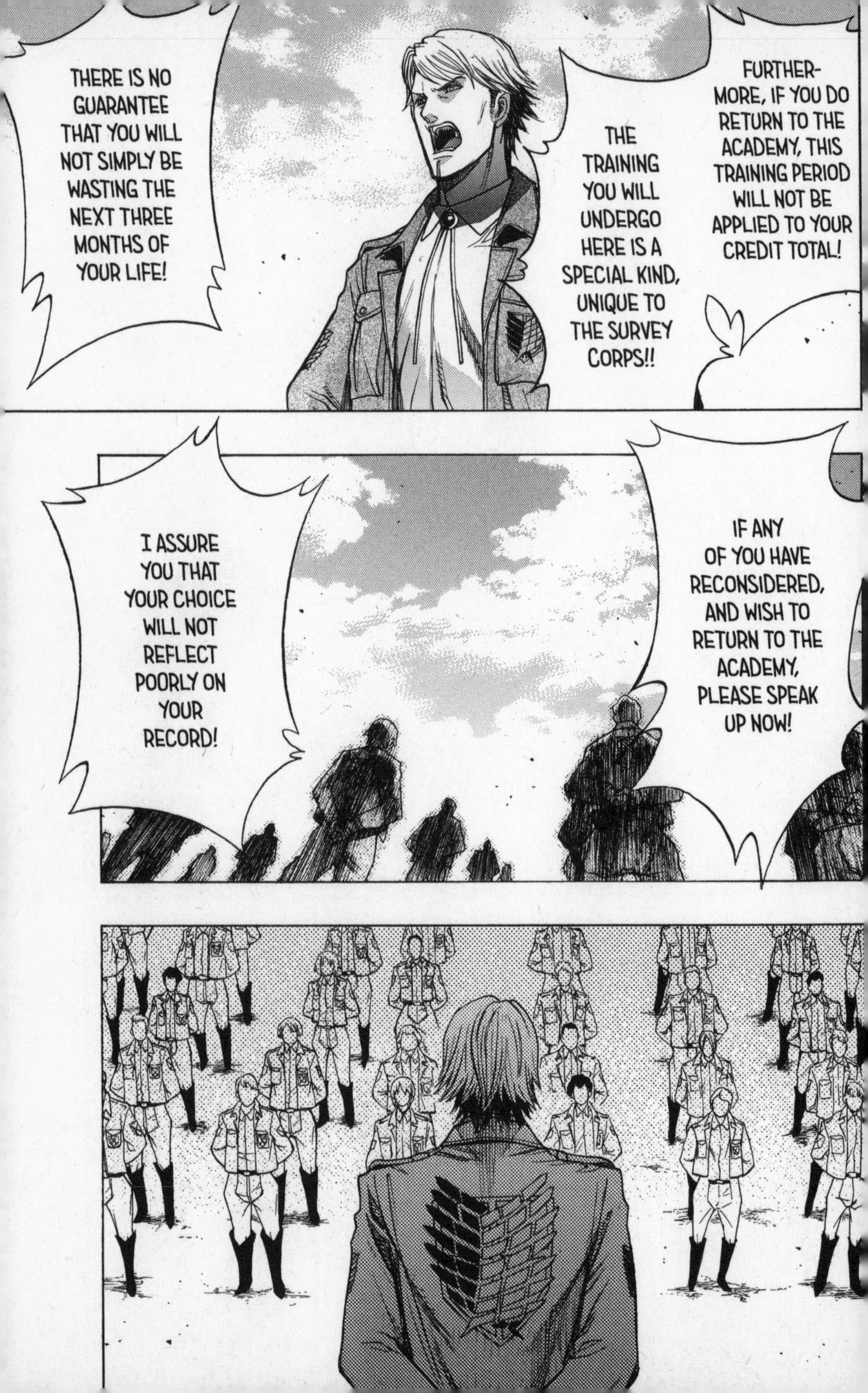
FURTHER-MORE, IF YOU DO RETURN TO THE ACADEMY, THIS TRAINING PERIOD WILL NOT BE APPLIED TO YOUR CREDIT TOTAL!
THE TRAINING YOU WILL UNDERGO HERE IS A SPECIAL KIND, UNIQUE TO THE SURVEY CORPS!!
THERE IS NO GUARANTEE THAT YOU WILL NOT SIMPLY BE WASTING THE NEXT THREE MONTHS OF YOUR LIFE!
IF ANY OF YOU HAVE RECONSIDERED, AND WISH TO RETURN TO THE ACADEMY, PLEASE SPEAK UP NOW!
I ASSURE YOU THAT YOUR CHOICE WILL NOT REFLECT POORLY ON YOUR RECORD!

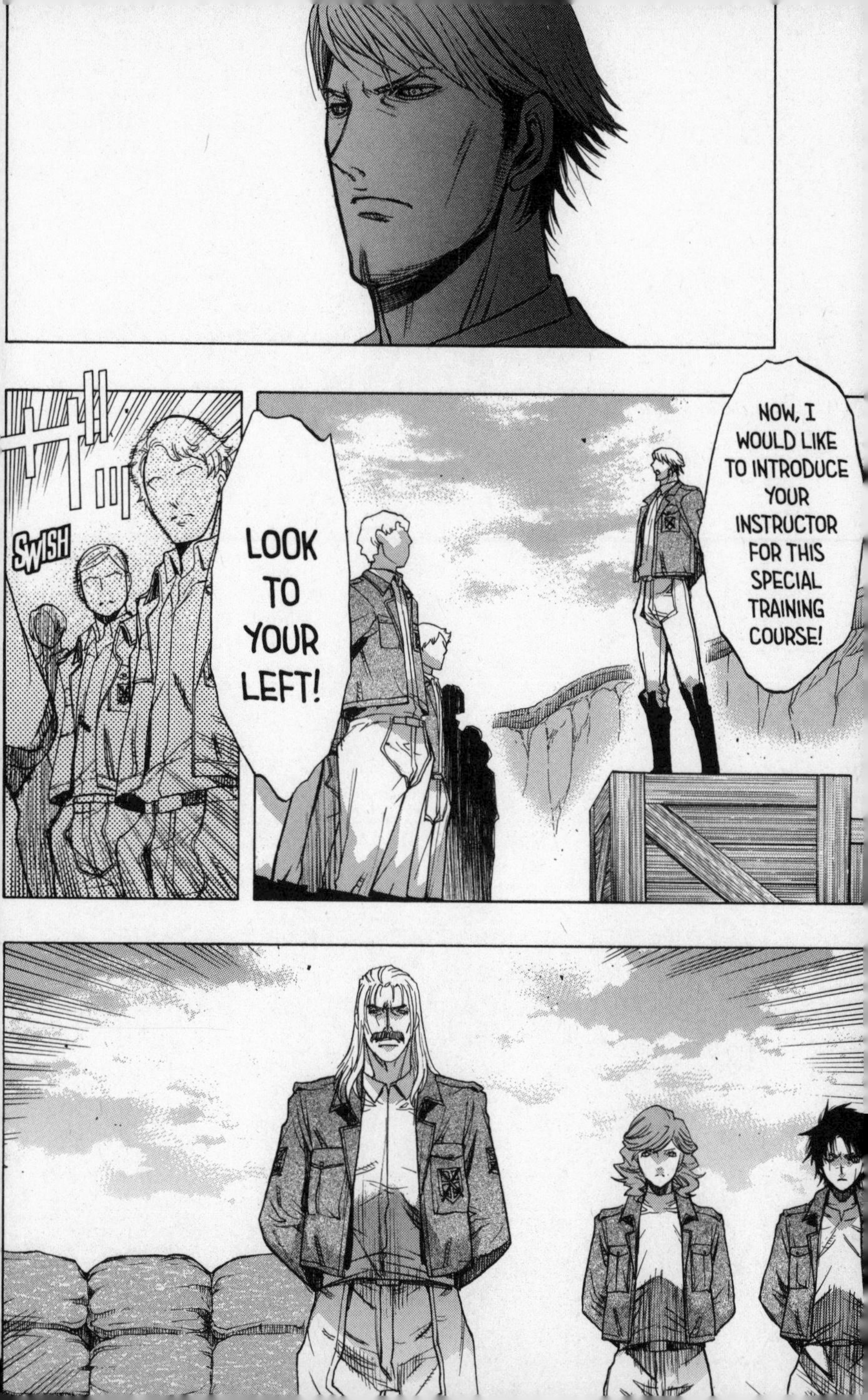
NOW, I WOULD LIKE TO INTRODUCE YOUR INSTRUCTOR FOR THIS SPECIAL TRAINING COURSE!
LOOK TO YOUR LEFT!
SWISH

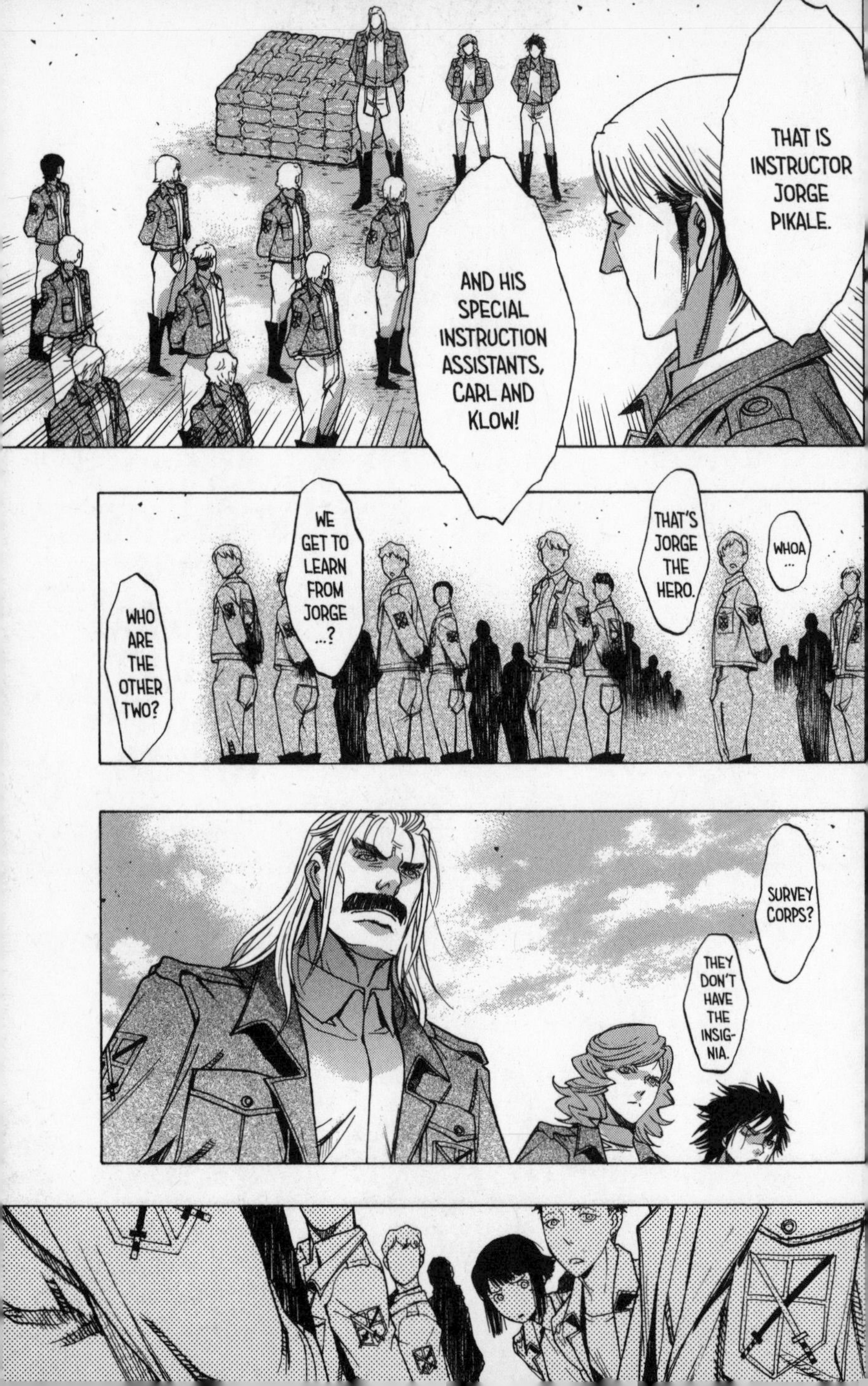
THAT IS INSTRUCTOR JORGE PIKALE.
AND HIS SPECIAL INSTRUCTION ASSISTANTS, CARL AND KLOW!
WHOA...
THAT'S JORGE THE HERO.
WE GET TO LEARN FROM JORGE...?
WHO ARE THE OTHER TWO?
SURVEY CORPS?
THEY DON'T HAVE THE INSIG-NIA.

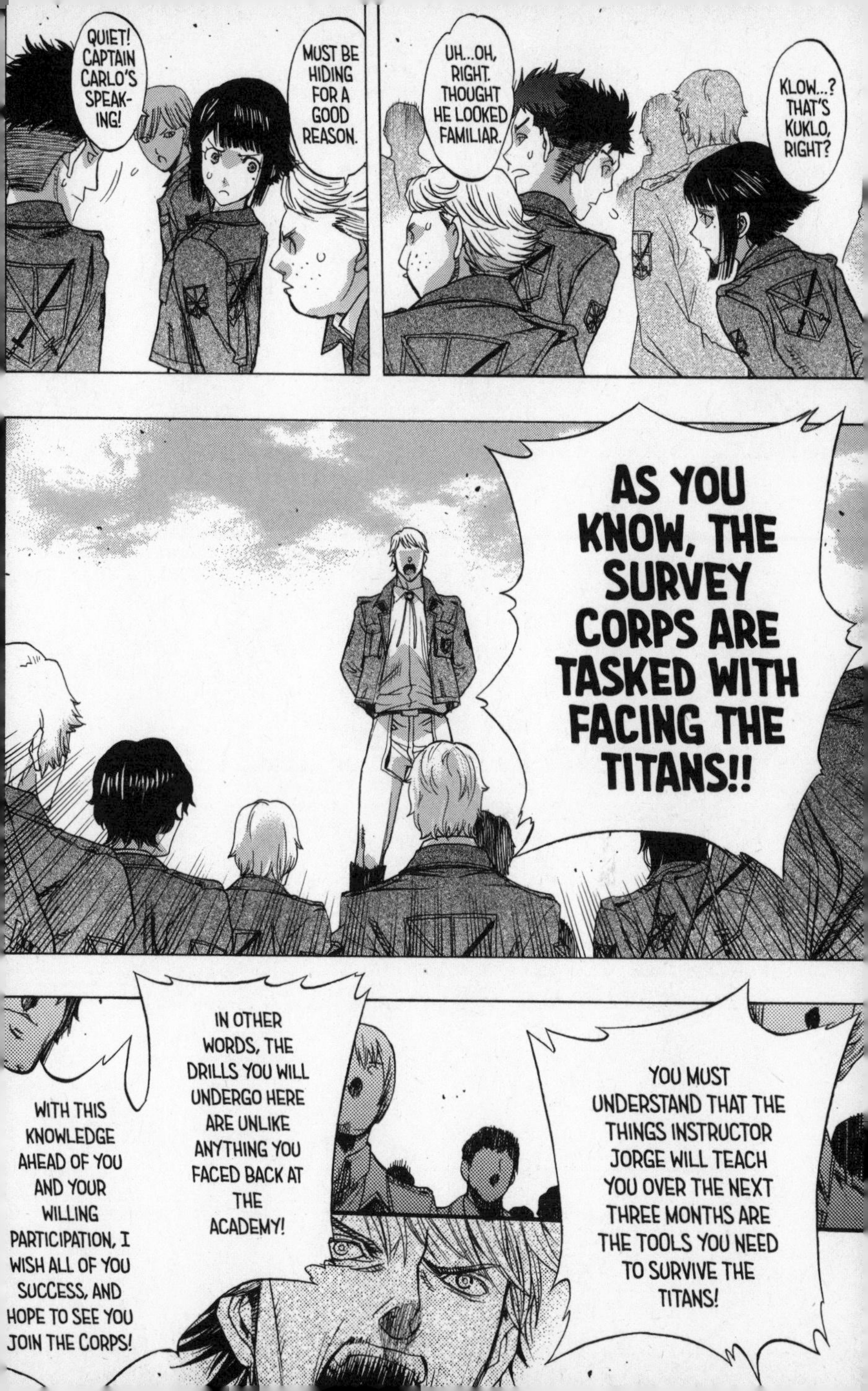
KLOW...? THAT'S KUKLO, RIGHT?
UH...OH, RIGHT. THOUGHT HE LOOKED FAMILIAR.
MUST BE HIDING FOR A GOOD REASON.
QUIET! CAPTAIN CARLO'S SPEAK-ING!
AS YOU KNOW, THE SURVEY CORPS ARE TASKED WITH FACING THE TITANS!!
YOU MUST UNDERSTAND THAT THE THINGS INSTRUCTOR JORGE WILL TEACH YOU OVER THE NEXT THREE MONTHS ARE THE TOOLS YOU NEED TO SURVIVE THE TITANS!
IN OTHER WORDS, THE DRILLS YOU WILL UNDERGO HERE ARE UNLIKE ANYTHING YOU FACED BACK AT THE ACADEMY!
WITH THIS KNOWLEDGE AHEAD OF YOU AND YOUR WILLING PARTICIPATION, I WISH ALL OF YOU SUCCESS, AND HOPE TO SEE YOU JOIN THE CORPS!

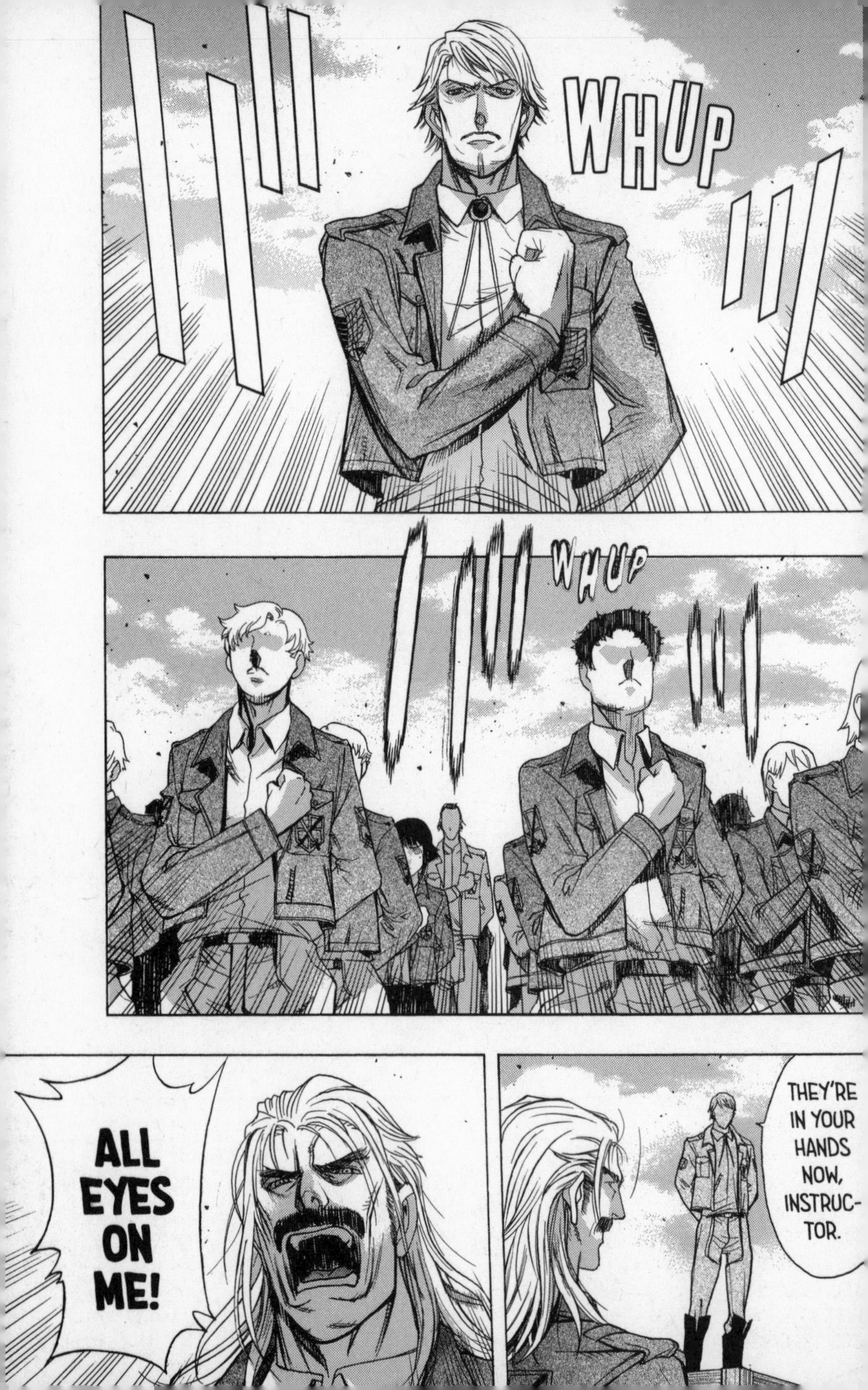
WHUP
WHUP
THEY'RE IN YOUR HANDS NOW, INSTRUCTOR.
ALL EYES ON ME!

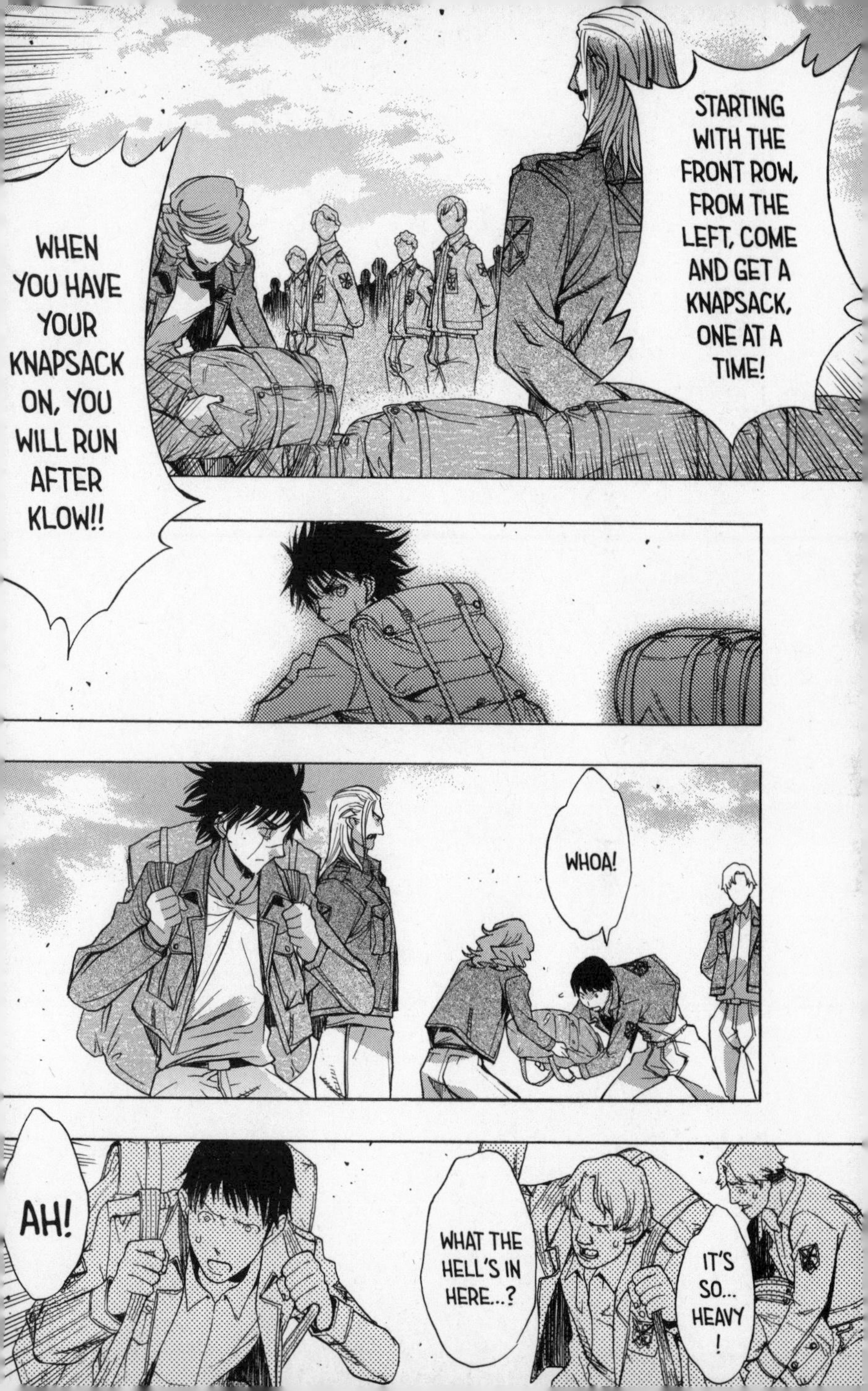
STARTING WITH THE FRONT ROW, FROM THE LEFT, COME AND GET A KNAPSACK, ONE AT A TIME!
WHEN YOU HAVE YOUR KNAPSACK ON, YOU WILL RUN AFTER KLOW!!
WHOA!
IT'S SO... HEAVY!
WHAT THE HELL'S IN HERE...?
AH!

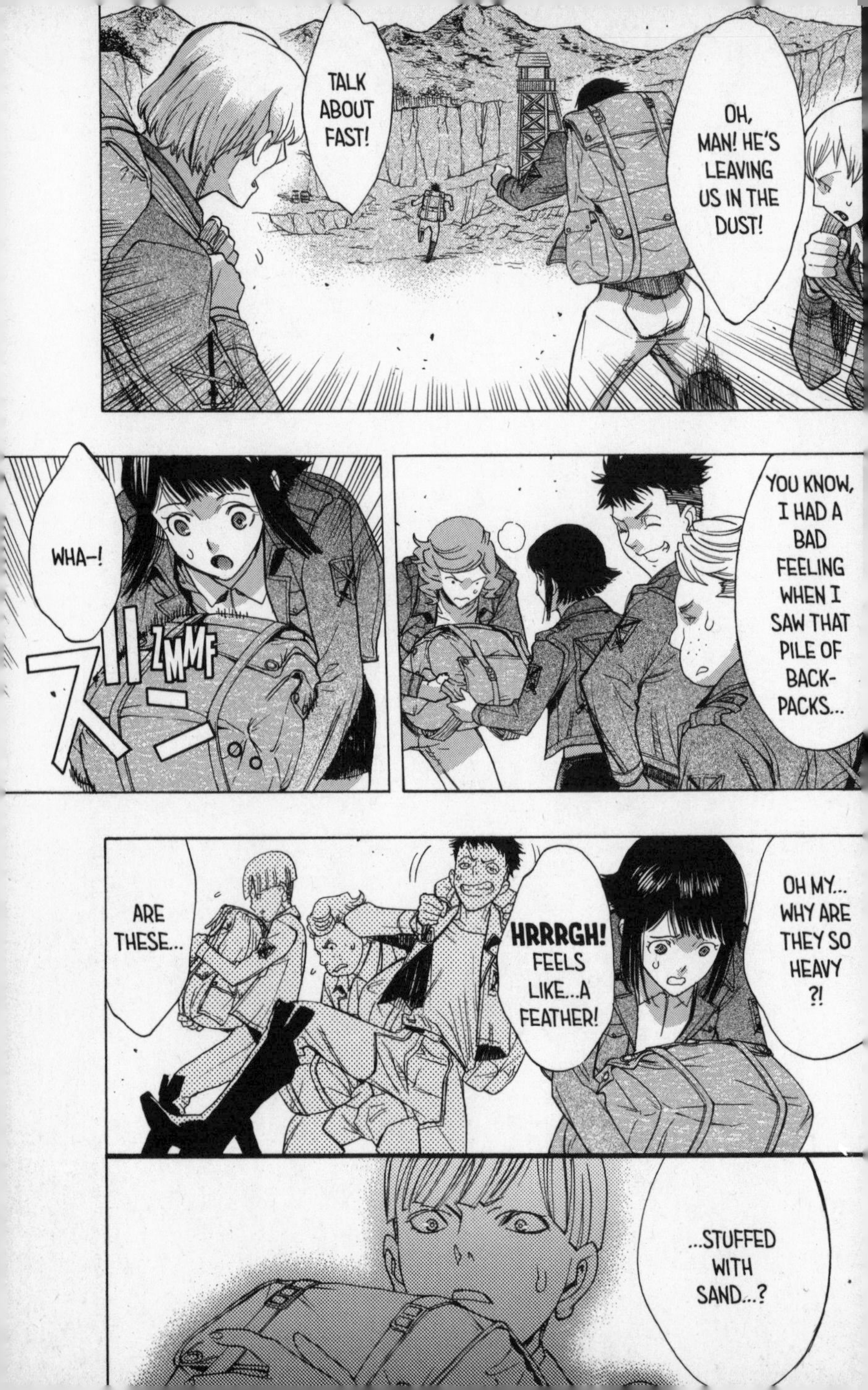
OH, MAN! HE'S LEAVING US IN THE DUST!
TALK ABOUT FAST!
YOU KNOW, I HAD A BAD FEELING WHEN I SAW THAT PILE OF BACK-PACKS...
WHA-!
ZMMF
OH MY... WHY ARE THEY SO HEAVY ?!
HRRRGH! FEELS LIKE...A FEATHER!
ARE THESE...
...STUFFED WITH SAND...?

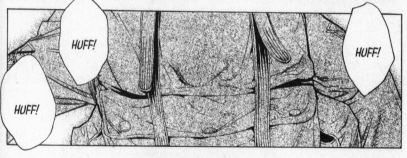

HUFF!

HUFF!

HUFF!

THIS IS JUST...

...LOGISTICS TRAINING, ISN'T IT...?

HUFF!

HUFF!

HUFF!

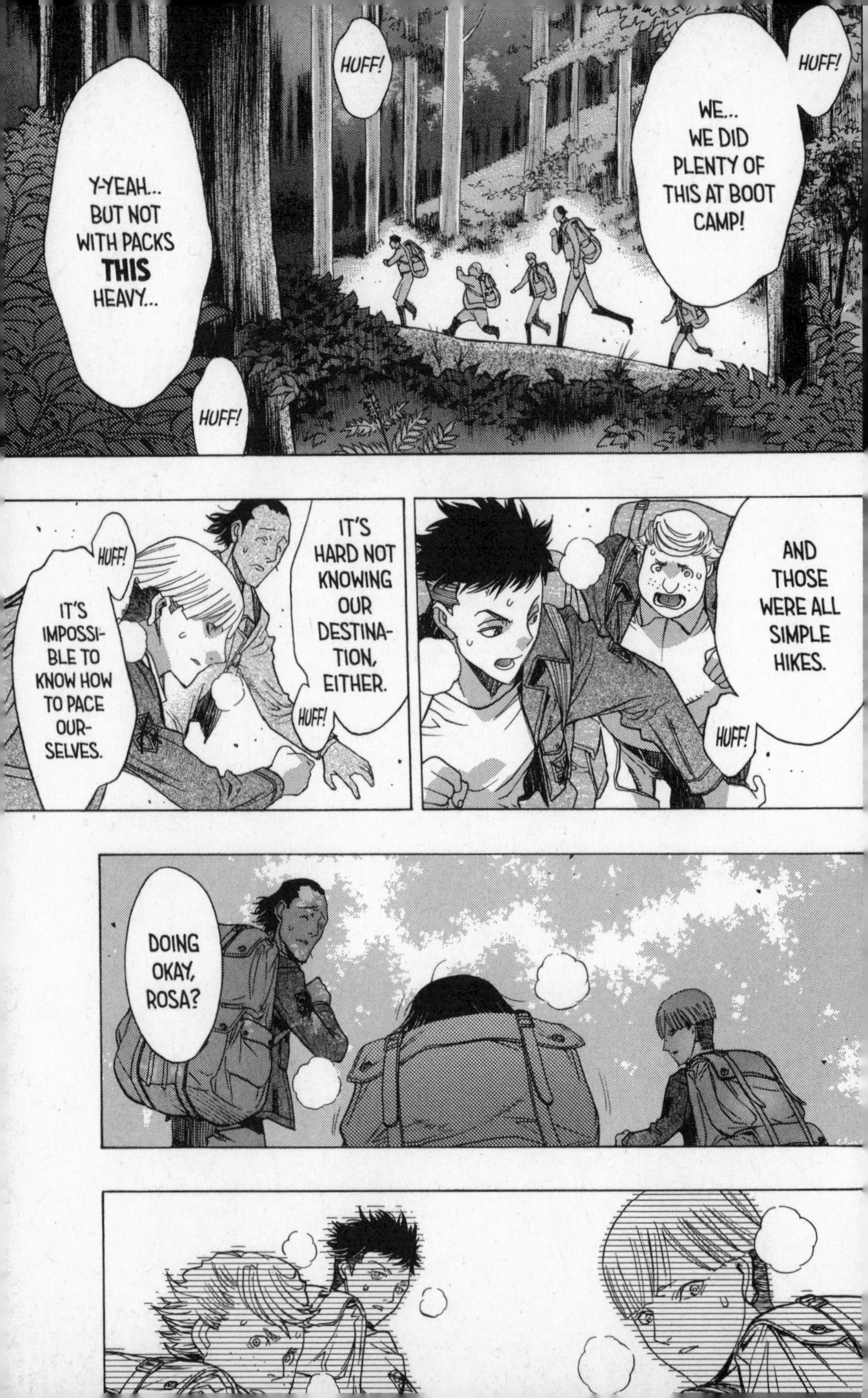
HUFF!
WE... WE DID PLENTY OF THIS AT BOOT CAMP!
HUFF!
Y-YEAH... BUT NOT WITH PACKS **THIS** HEAVY...
HUFF!
AND THOSE WERE ALL SIMPLE HIKES.
HUFF!
IT'S HARD NOT KNOWING OUR DESTINATION, EITHER.
HUFF!
HUFF!
IT'S IMPOSSIBLE TO KNOW HOW TO PACE OURSELVES.
DOING OKAY, ROSA?

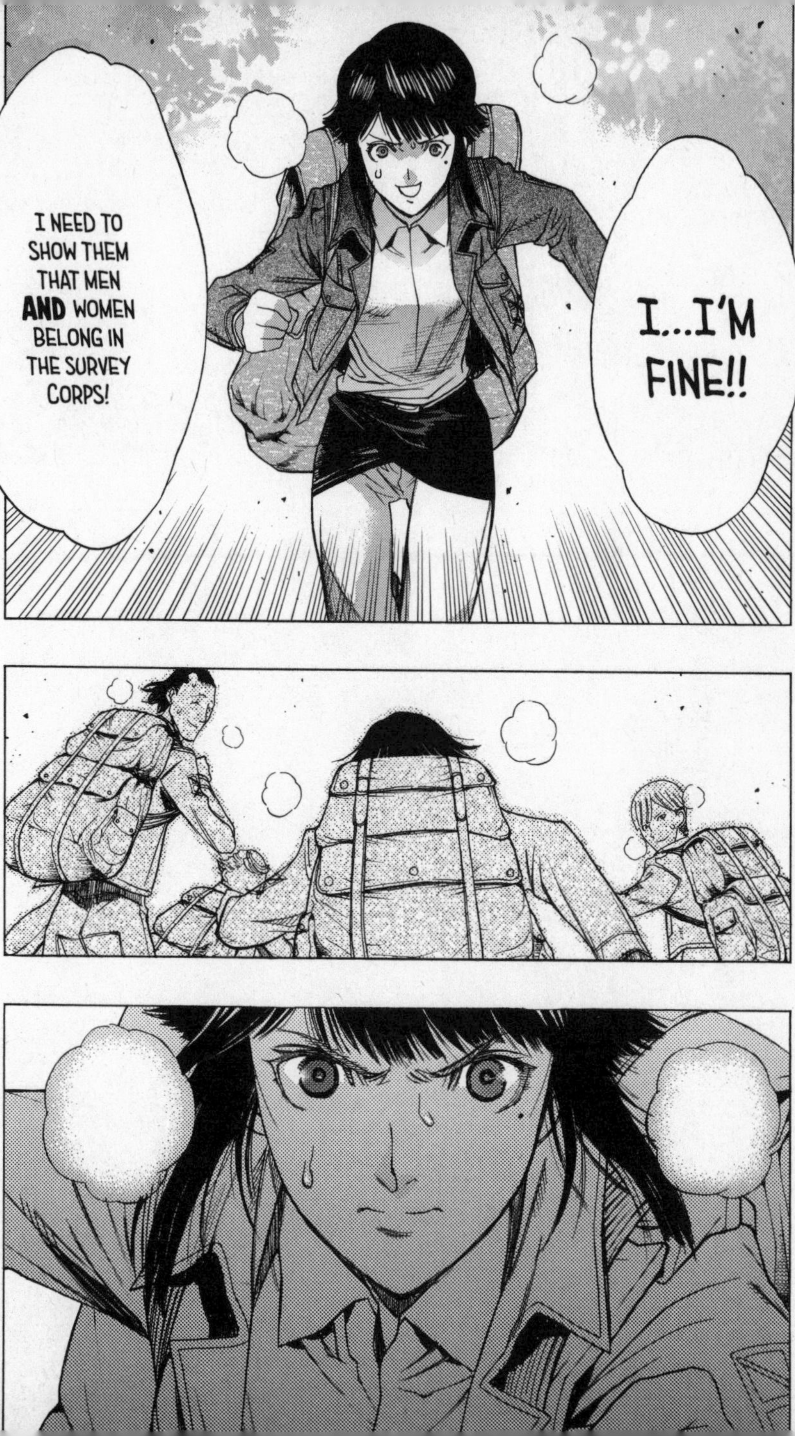
I...I'M FINE!!
I NEED TO SHOW THEM THAT MEN AND WOMEN BELONG IN THE SURVEY CORPS!

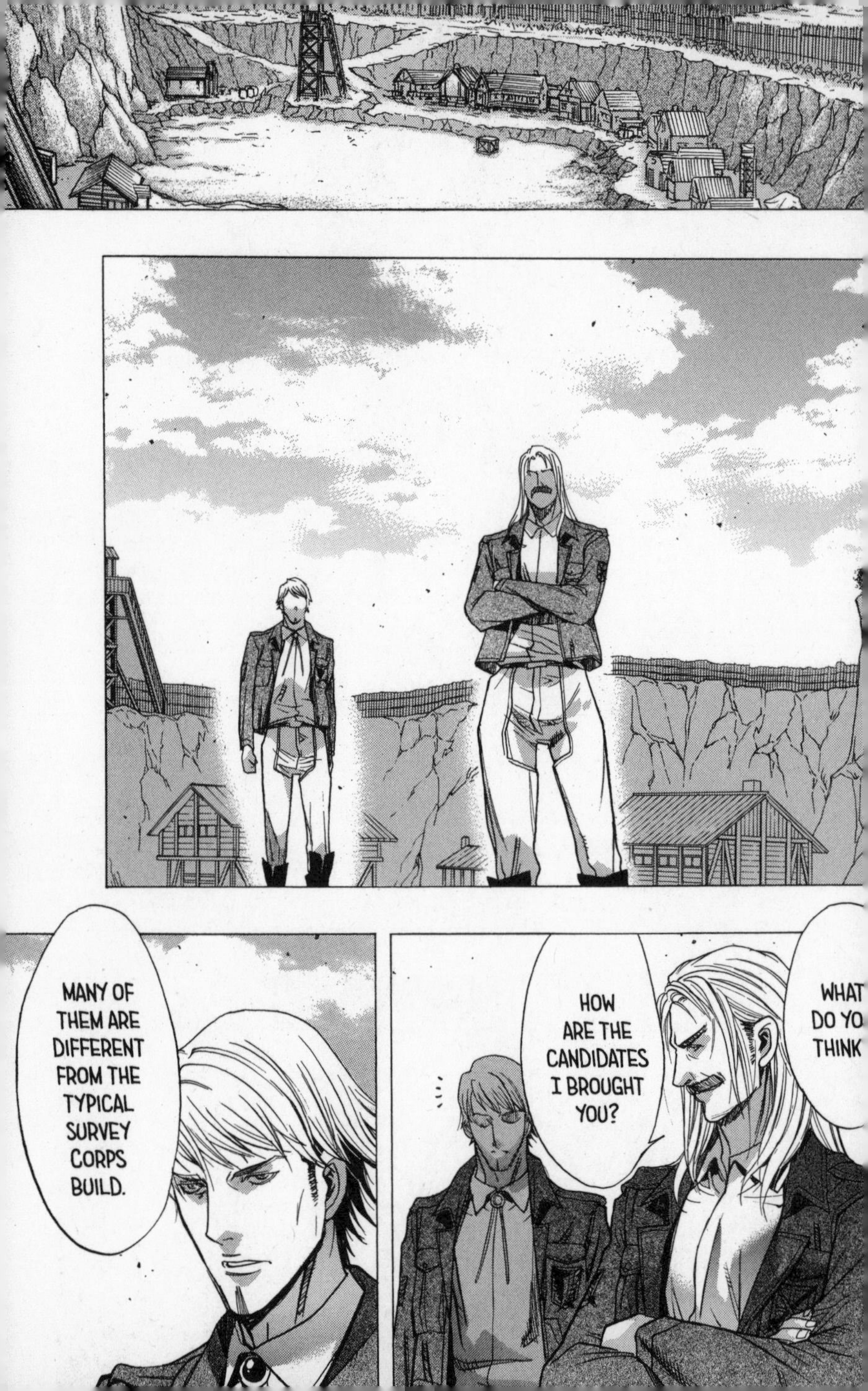
WHAT DO YO THINK
HOW ARE THE CANDIDATES I BROUGHT YOU?
MANY OF THEM ARE DIFFERENT FROM THE TYPICAL SURVEY CORPS BUILD.

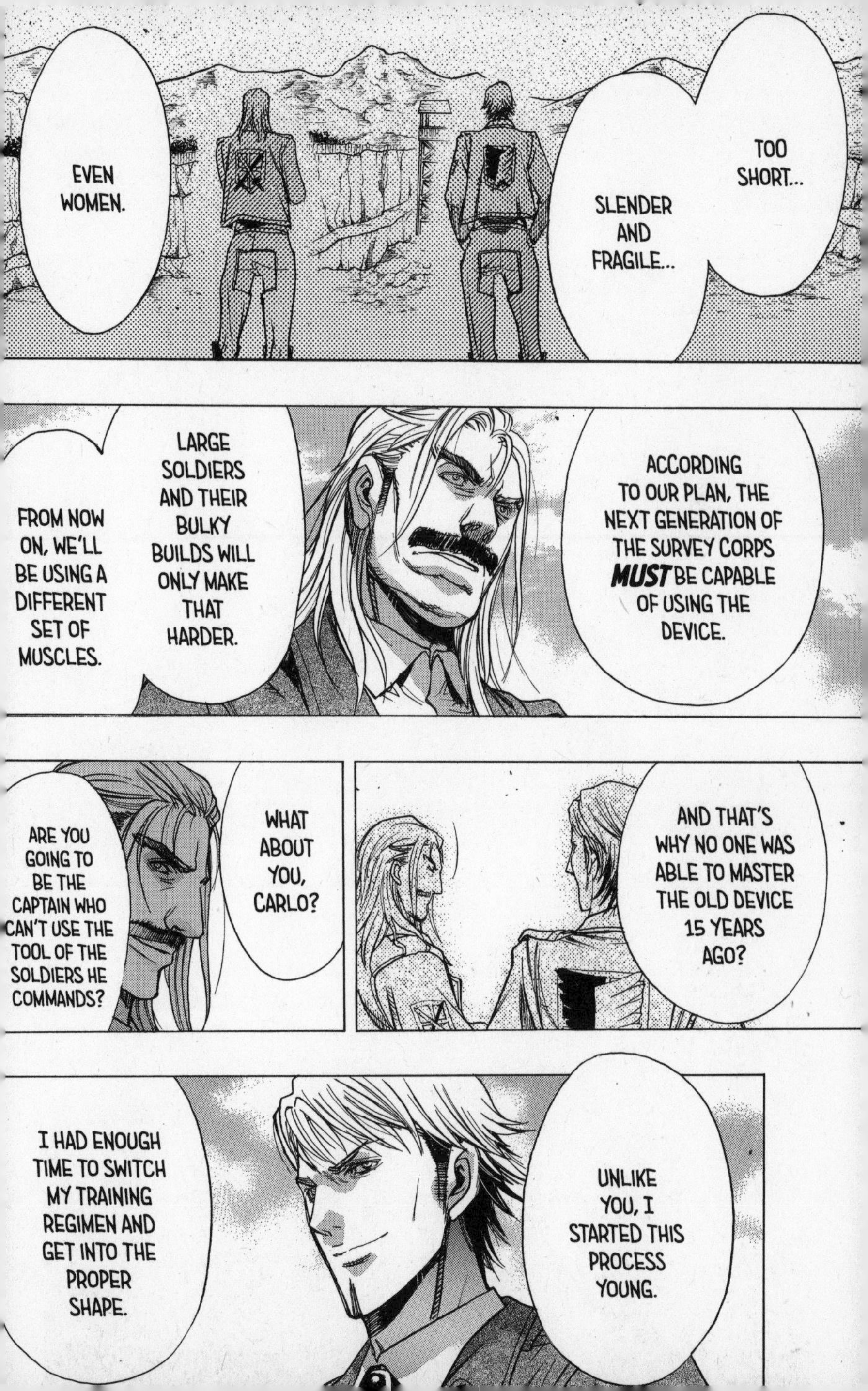
TOO SHORT...
SLENDER AND FRAGILE...
EVEN WOMEN.
ACCORDING TO OUR PLAN, THE NEXT GENERATION OF THE SURVEY CORPS **MUST** BE CAPABLE OF USING THE DEVICE.
LARGE SOLDIERS AND THEIR BULKY BUILDS WILL ONLY MAKE THAT HARDER.
FROM NOW ON, WE'LL BE USING A DIFFERENT SET OF MUSCLES.
AND THAT'S WHY NO ONE WAS ABLE TO MASTER THE OLD DEVICE 15 YEARS AGO?
WHAT ABOUT YOU, CARLO?
ARE YOU GOING TO BE THE CAPTAIN WHO CAN'T USE THE TOOL OF THE SOLDIERS HE COMMANDS?
UNLIKE YOU, I STARTED THIS PROCESS YOUNG.
I HAD ENOUGH TIME TO SWITCH MY TRAINING REGIMEN AND GET INTO THE PROPER SHAPE.

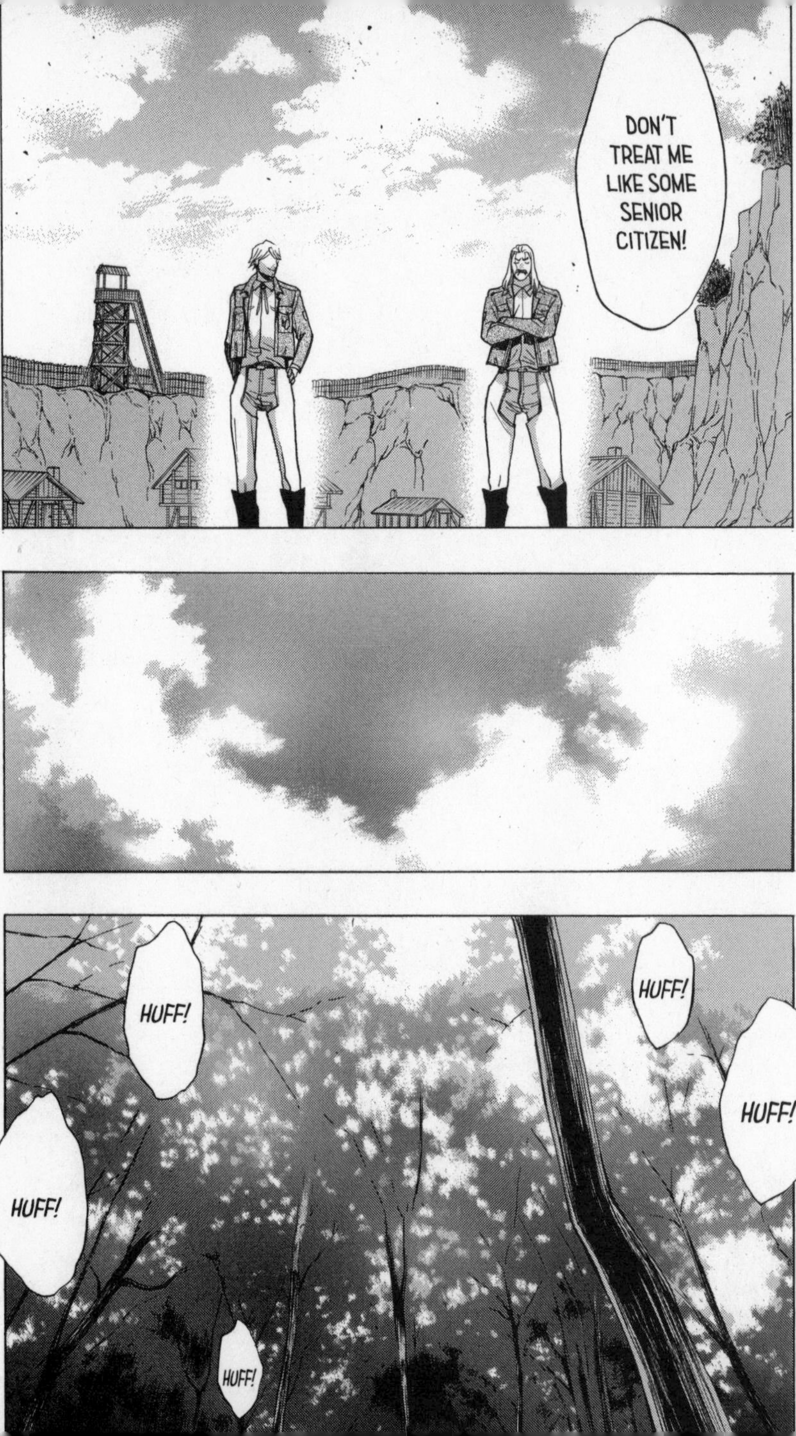
DON'T TREAT ME LIKE SOME SENIOR CITIZEN!
HUFF!
HUFF!
HUFF!
HUFF!
HUFF!

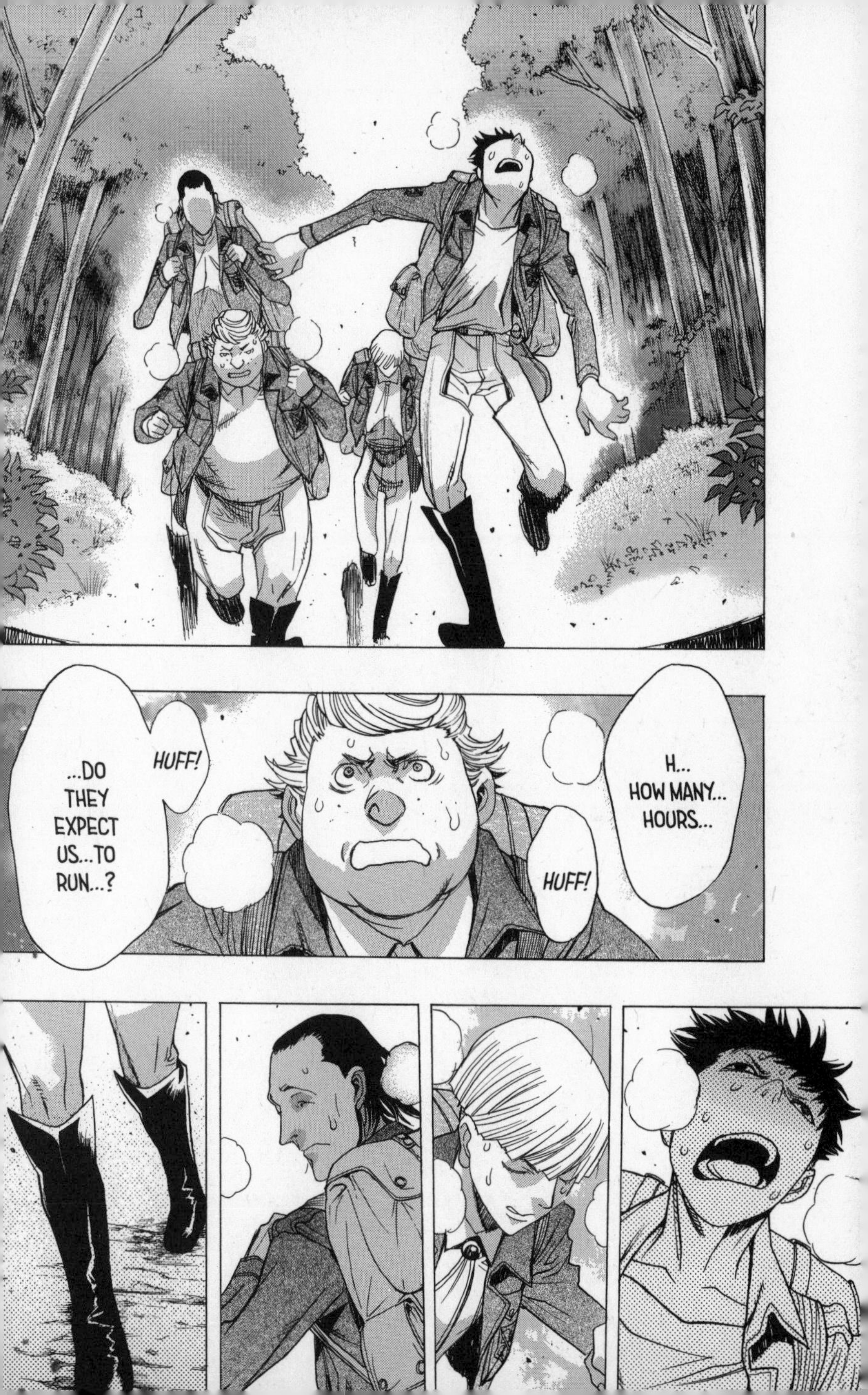
H... HOW MANY... HOURS...
HUFF!
HUFF!
...DO THEY EXPECT US...TO RUN...?

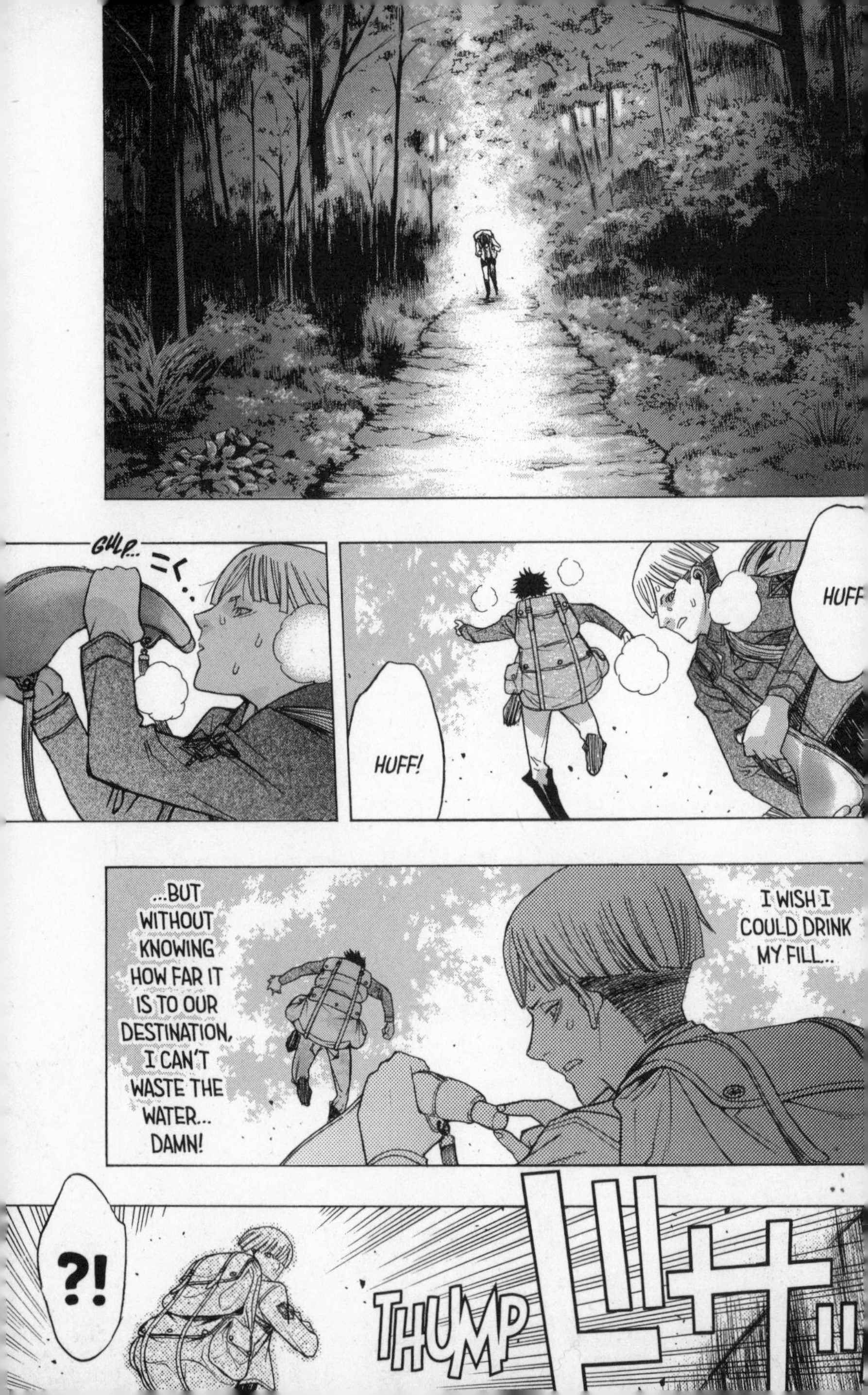
HUFF
HUFF!
GULP...
I WISH I COULD DRINK MY FILL...
...BUT WITHOUT KNOWING HOW FAR IT IS TO OUR DESTINATION, I CAN'T WASTE THE WATER... DAMN!
THUMP
?!

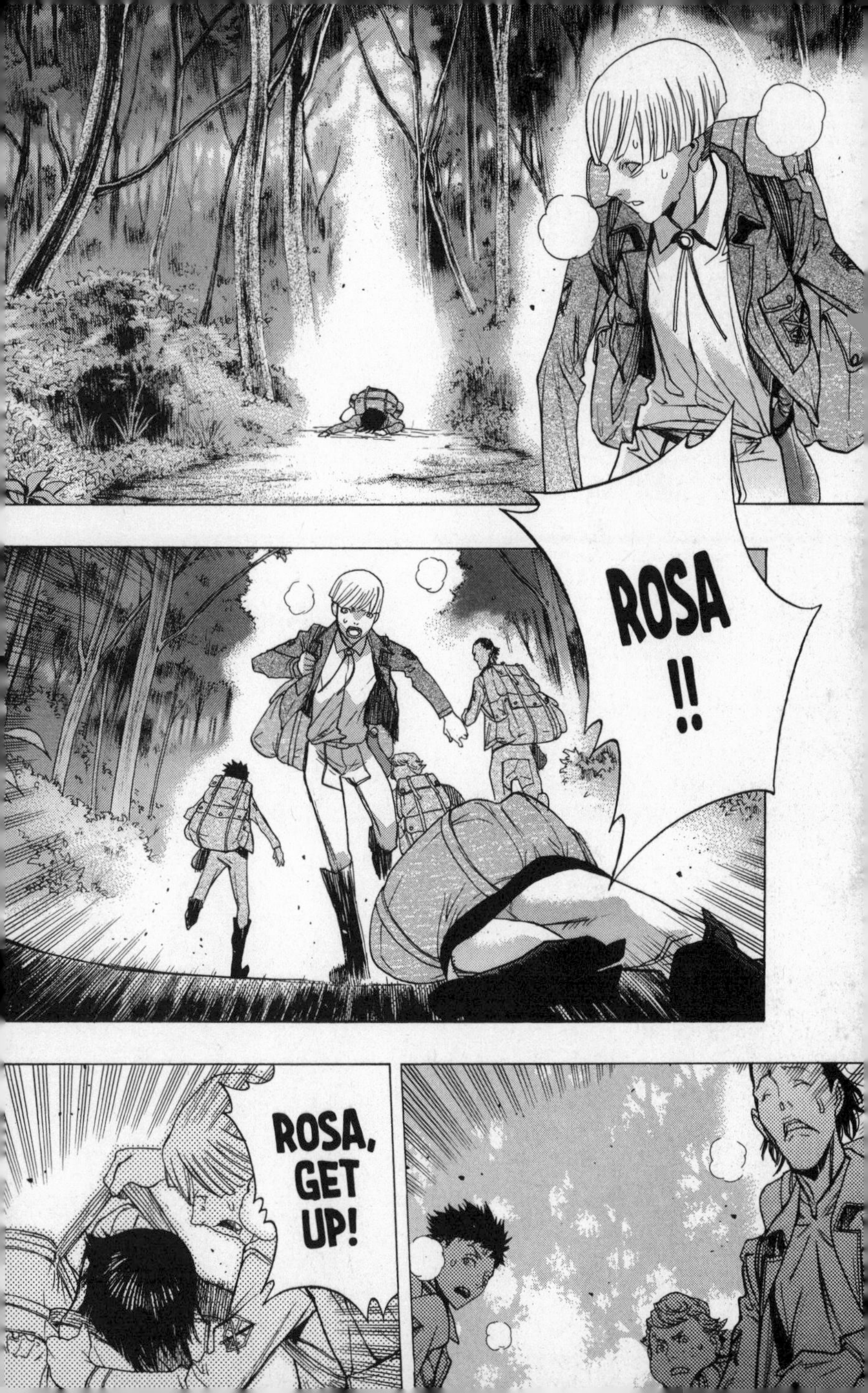
ROSA !!
ROSA, GET UP!

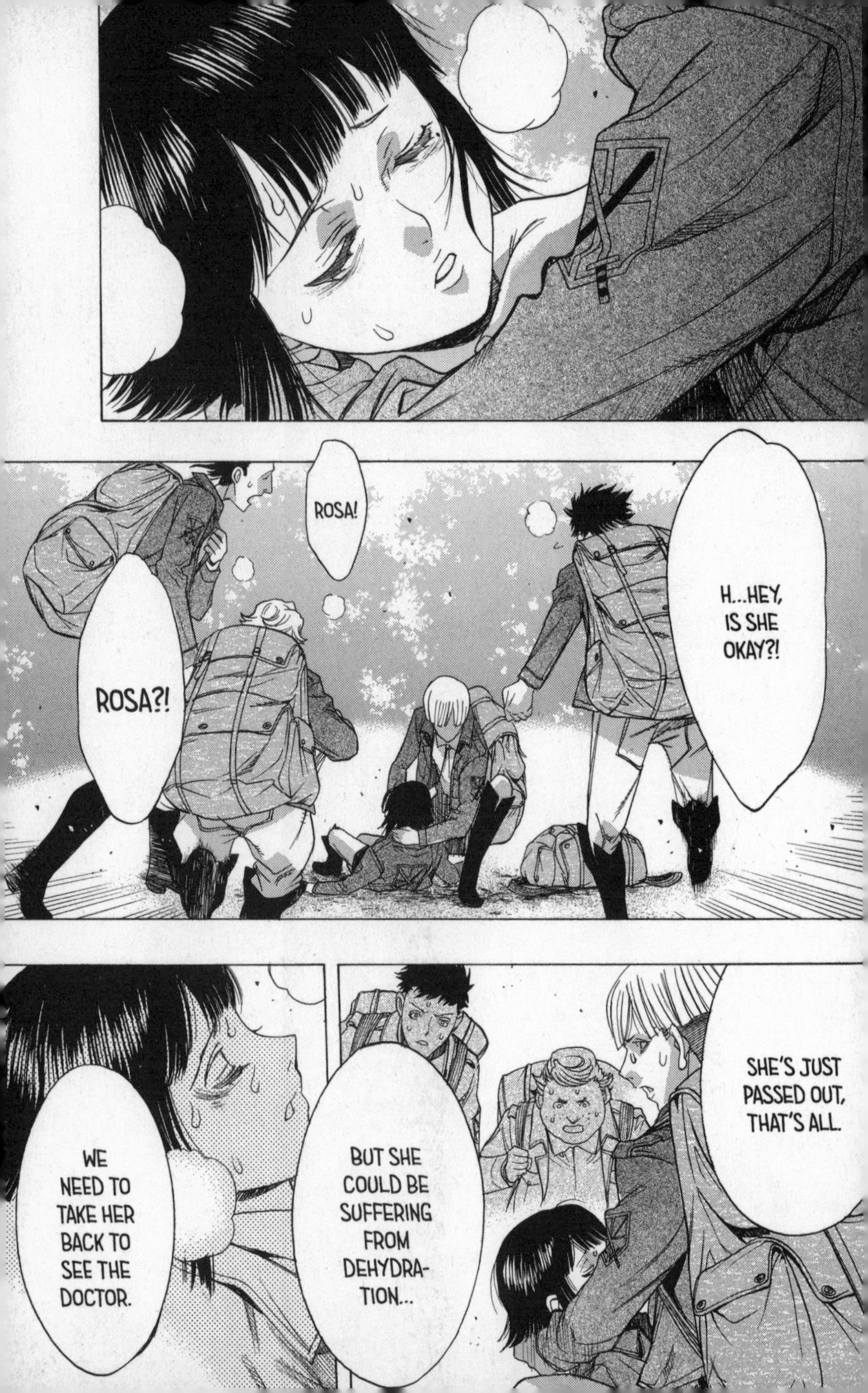
H...HEY, IS SHE OKAY?!
ROSA!
ROSA?!
SHE'S JUST PASSED OUT, THAT'S ALL.
BUT SHE COULD BE SUFFERING FROM DEHYDRATION...
WE NEED TO TAKE HER BACK TO SEE THE DOCTOR.

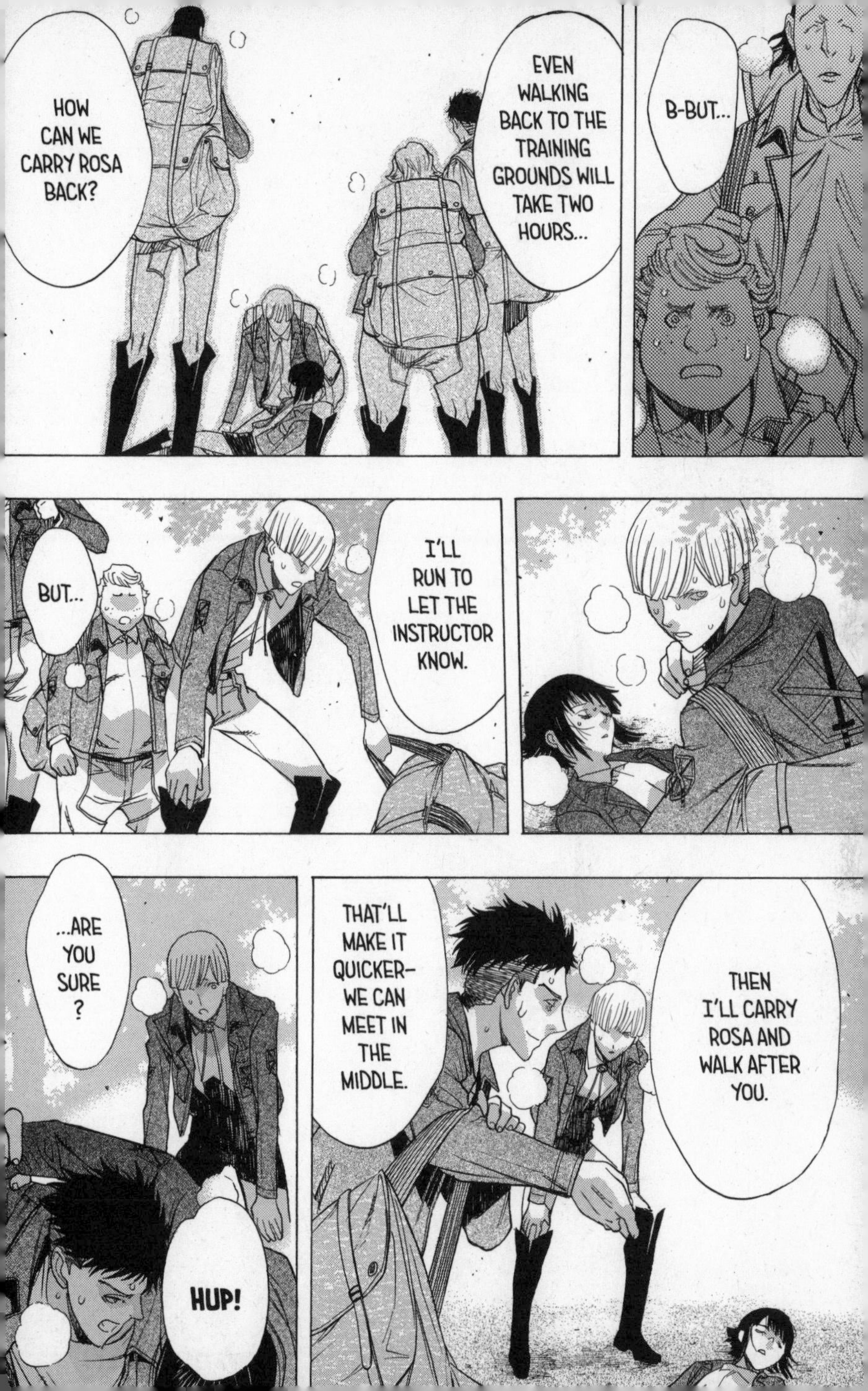
B-BUT...
EVEN WALKING BACK TO THE TRAINING GROUNDS WILL TAKE TWO HOURS...
HOW CAN WE CARRY ROSA BACK?
I'LL RUN TO LET THE INSTRUCTOR KNOW.
BUT...
THEN I'LL CARRY ROSA AND WALK AFTER YOU.
THAT'LL MAKE IT QUICKER—WE CAN MEET IN THE MIDDLE.
...ARE YOU SURE?
HUP!

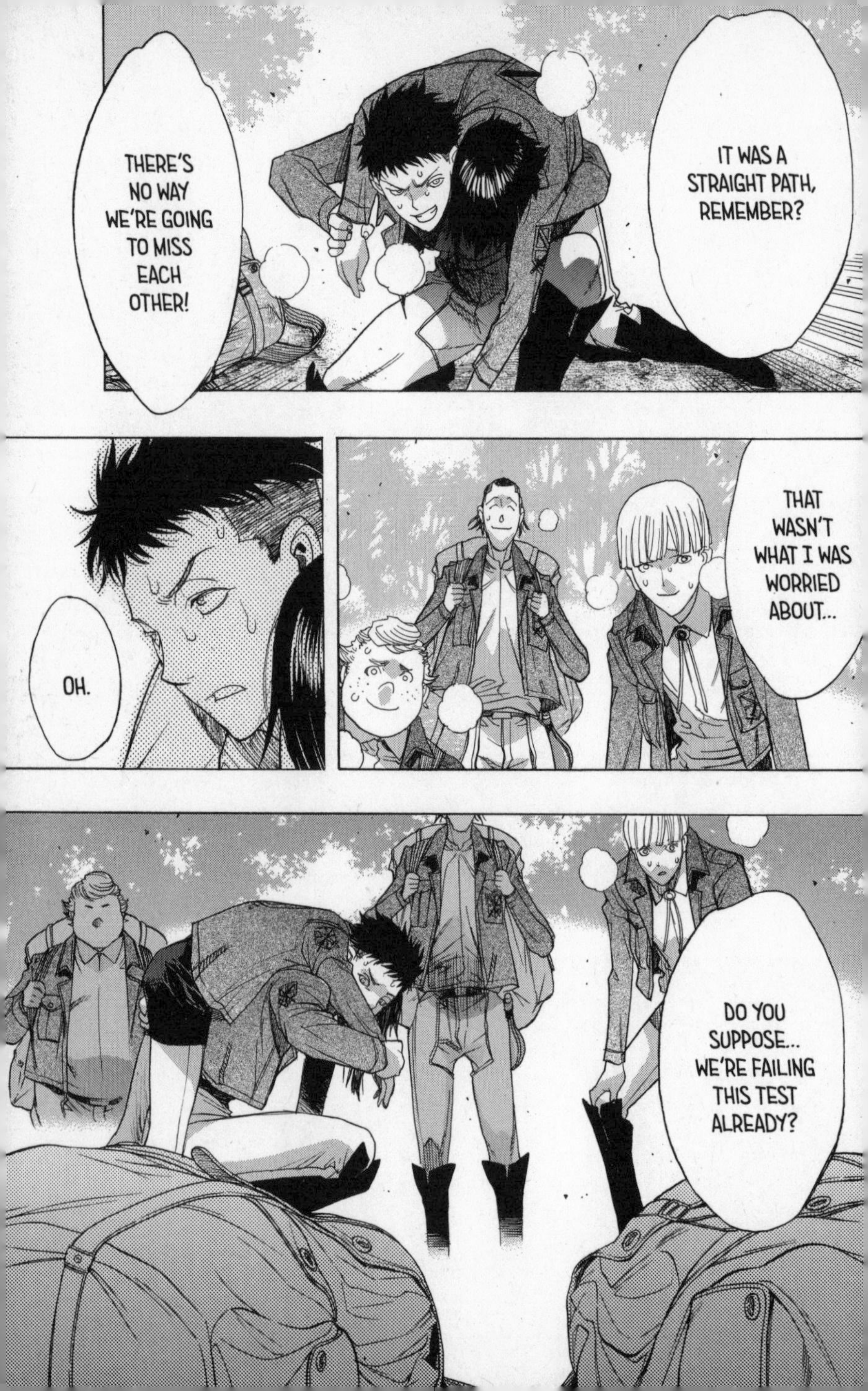
IT WAS A STRAIGHT PATH, REMEMBER?
THERE'S NO WAY WE'RE GOING TO MISS EACH OTHER!
THAT WASN'T WHAT I WAS WORRIED ABOUT...
OH.
DO YOU SUPPOSE... WE'RE FAILING THIS TEST ALREADY?

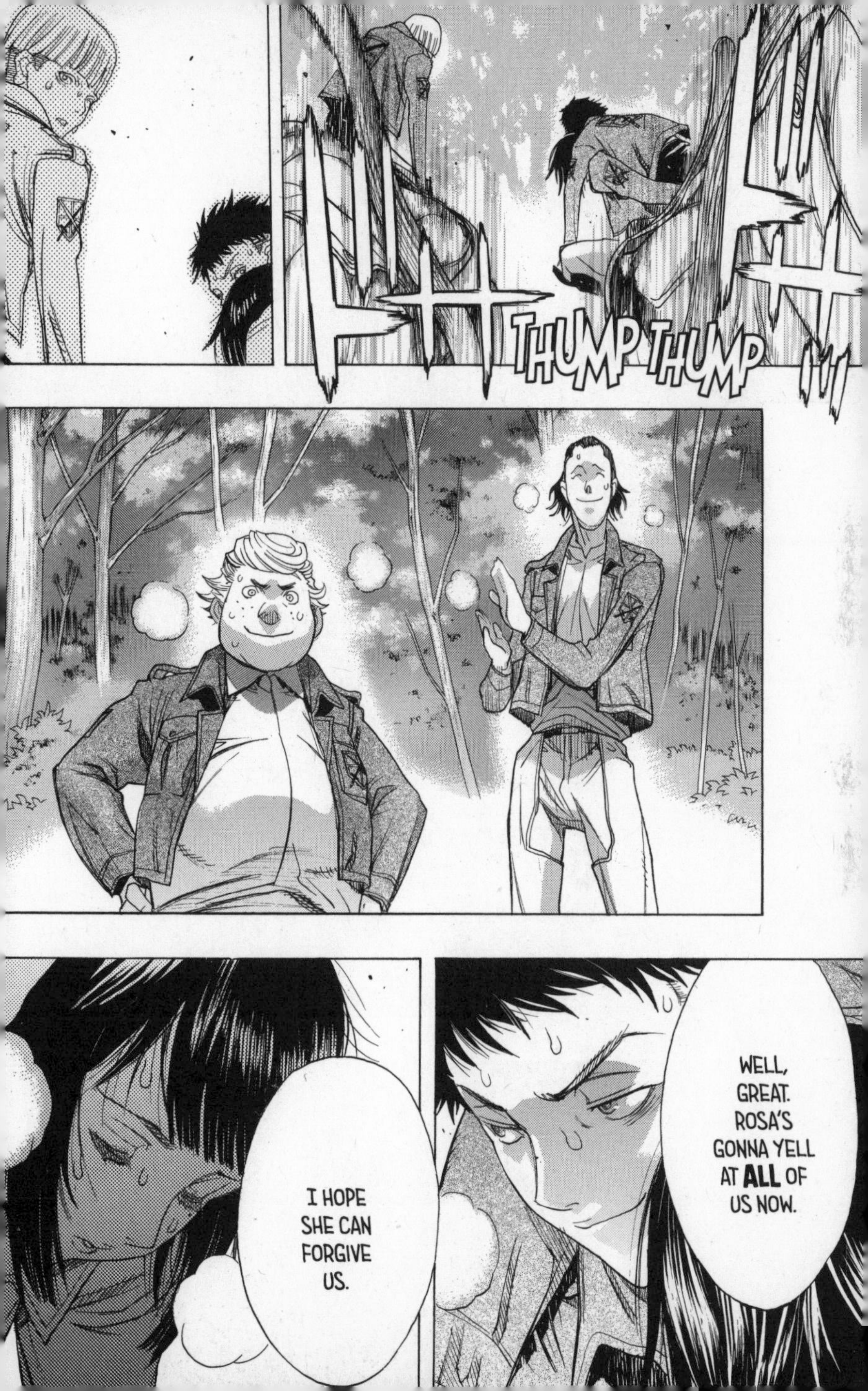
THUMP THUMP
WELL, GREAT. ROSA'S GONNA YELL AT **ALL** OF US NOW.
I HOPE SHE CAN FORGIVE US.

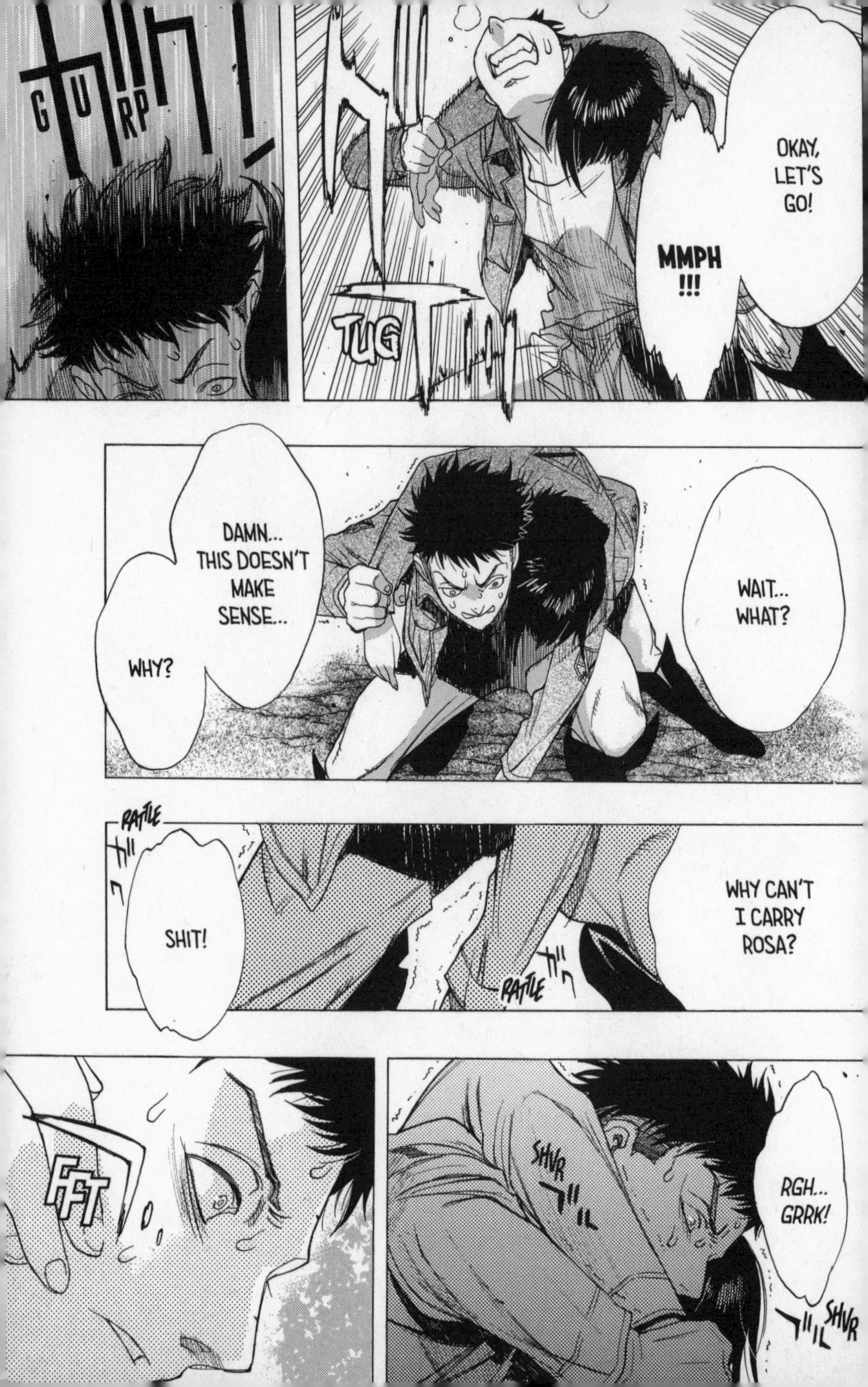
OKAY, LET'S GO!
MMPH !!!
TUG
GURP
WAIT... WHAT?
DAMN... THIS DOESN'T MAKE SENSE...
WHY?
WHY CAN'T I CARRY ROSA?
RATTLE
RATTLE
SHIT!
RGH... GRRK!
SHVR
SHVR
FFT

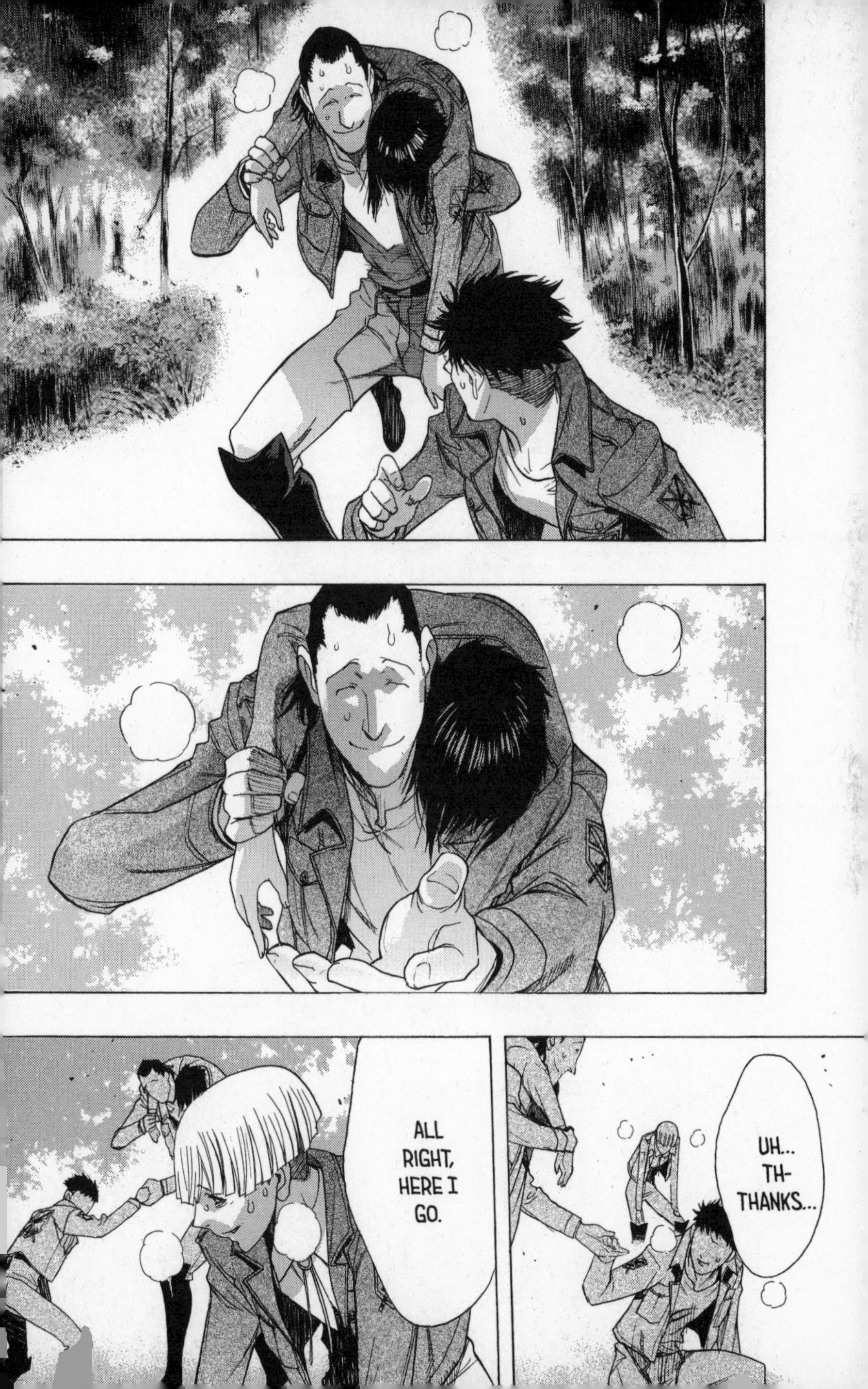
UH... TH-THANKS...
ALL RIGHT, HERE I GO.

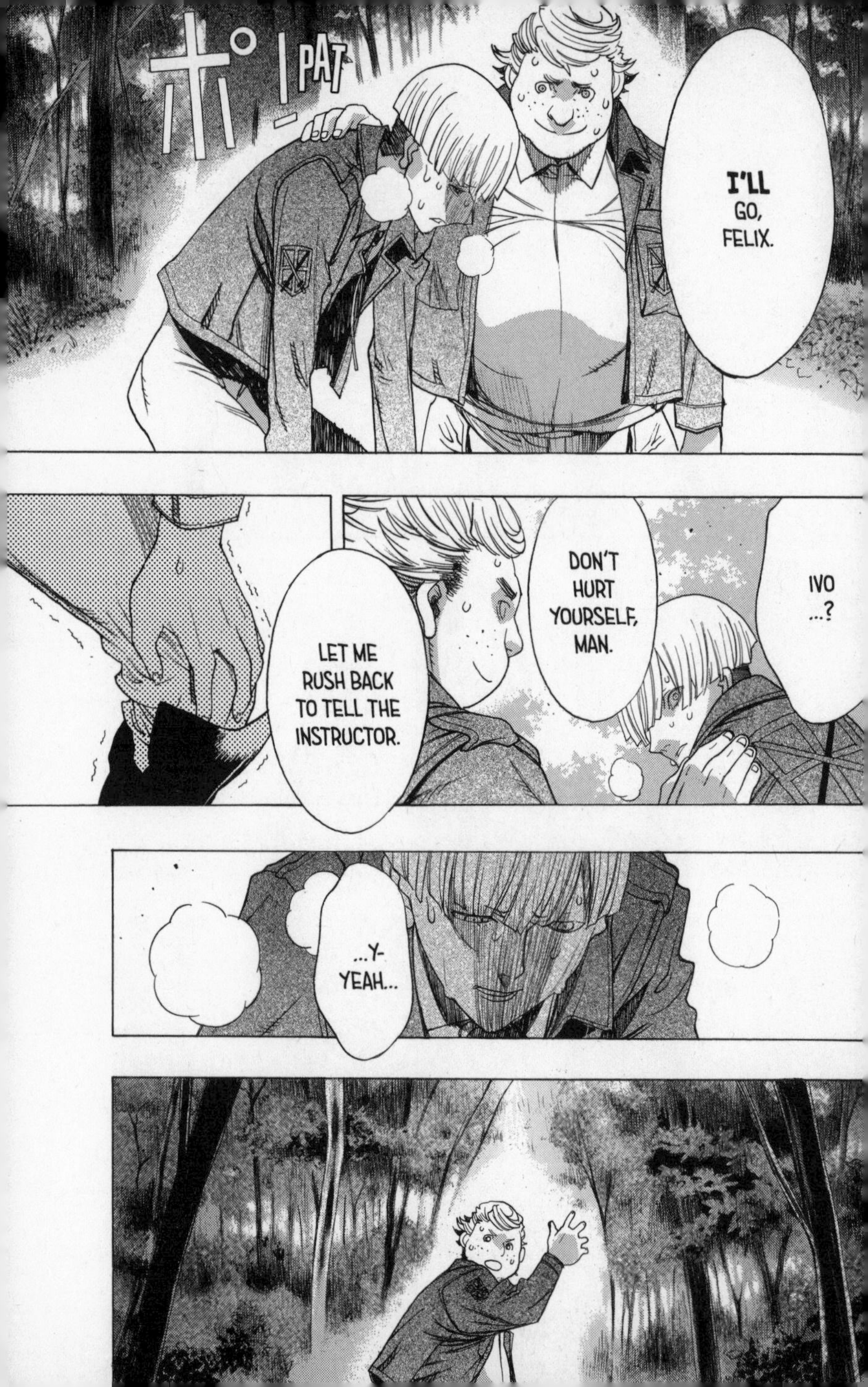

ポー
PAT
I'LL GO, FELIX.
IVO ...?
DON'T HURT YOURSELF, MAN.
LET ME RUSH BACK TO TELL THE INSTRUCTOR.
...Y-YEAH...

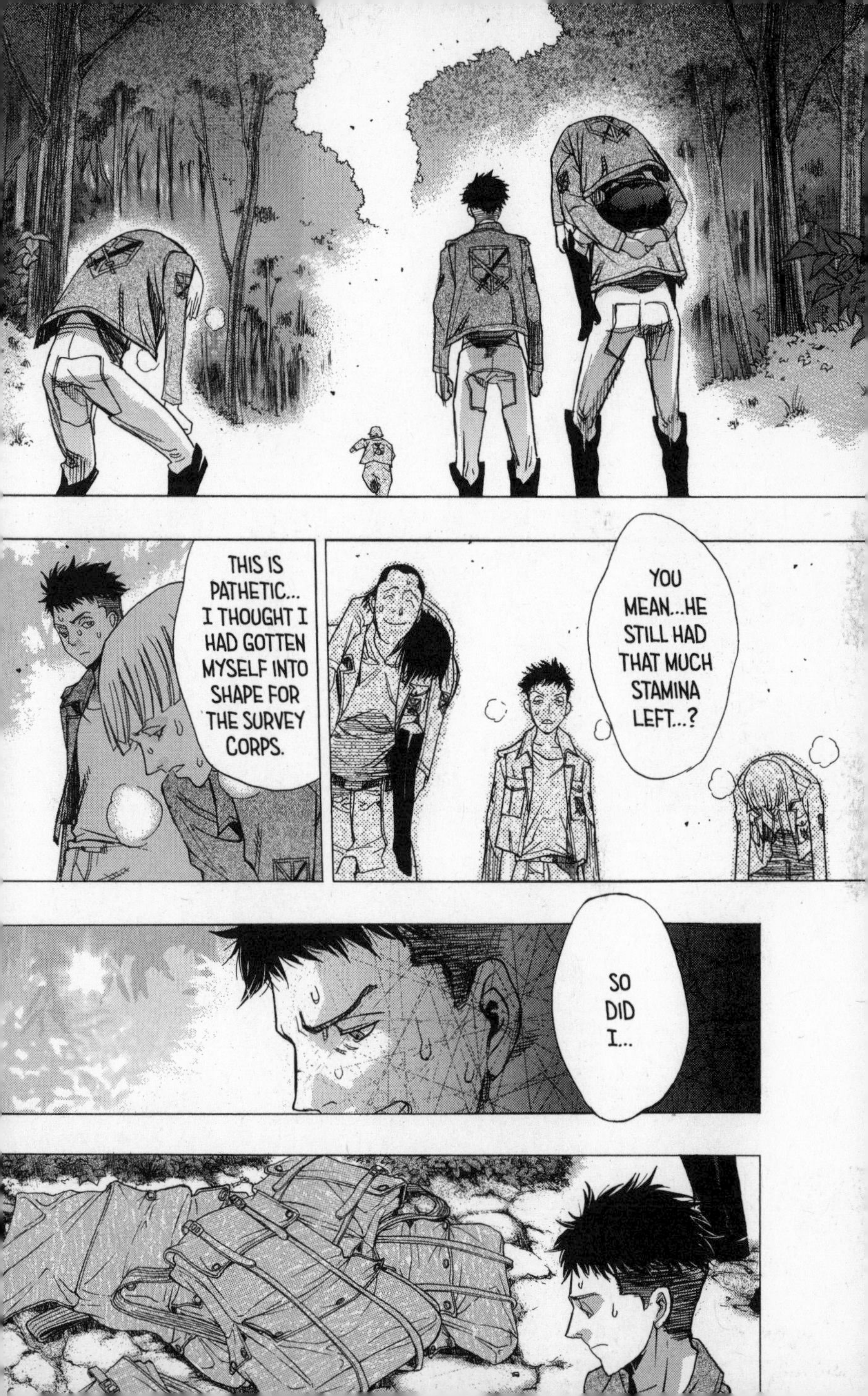
YOU MEAN...HE STILL HAD THAT MUCH STAMINA LEFT...?
THIS IS PATHETIC... I THOUGHT I HAD GOTTEN MYSELF INTO SHAPE FOR THE SURVEY CORPS.
SO DID I...

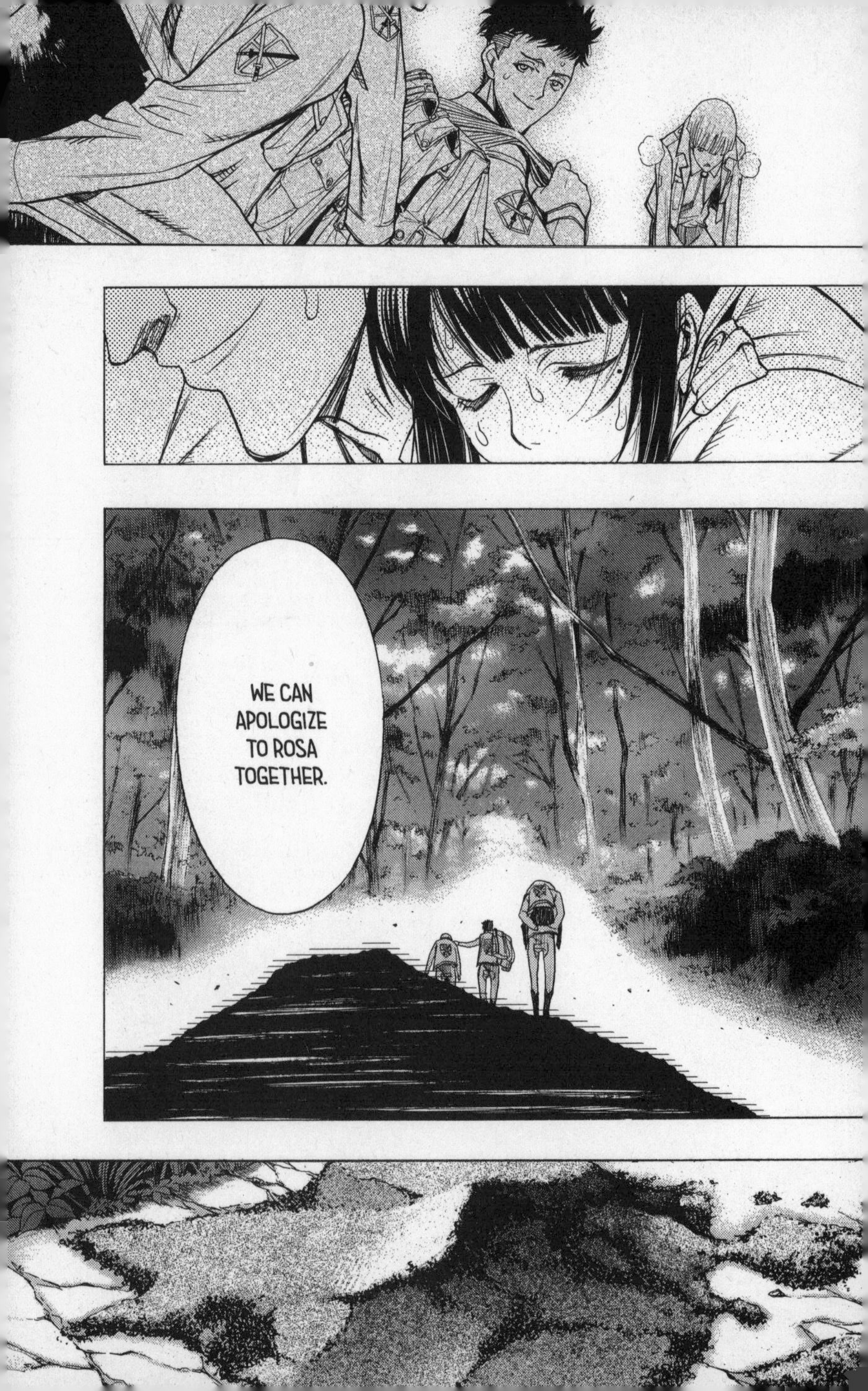
WE CAN APOLOGIZE TO ROSA TOGETHER.

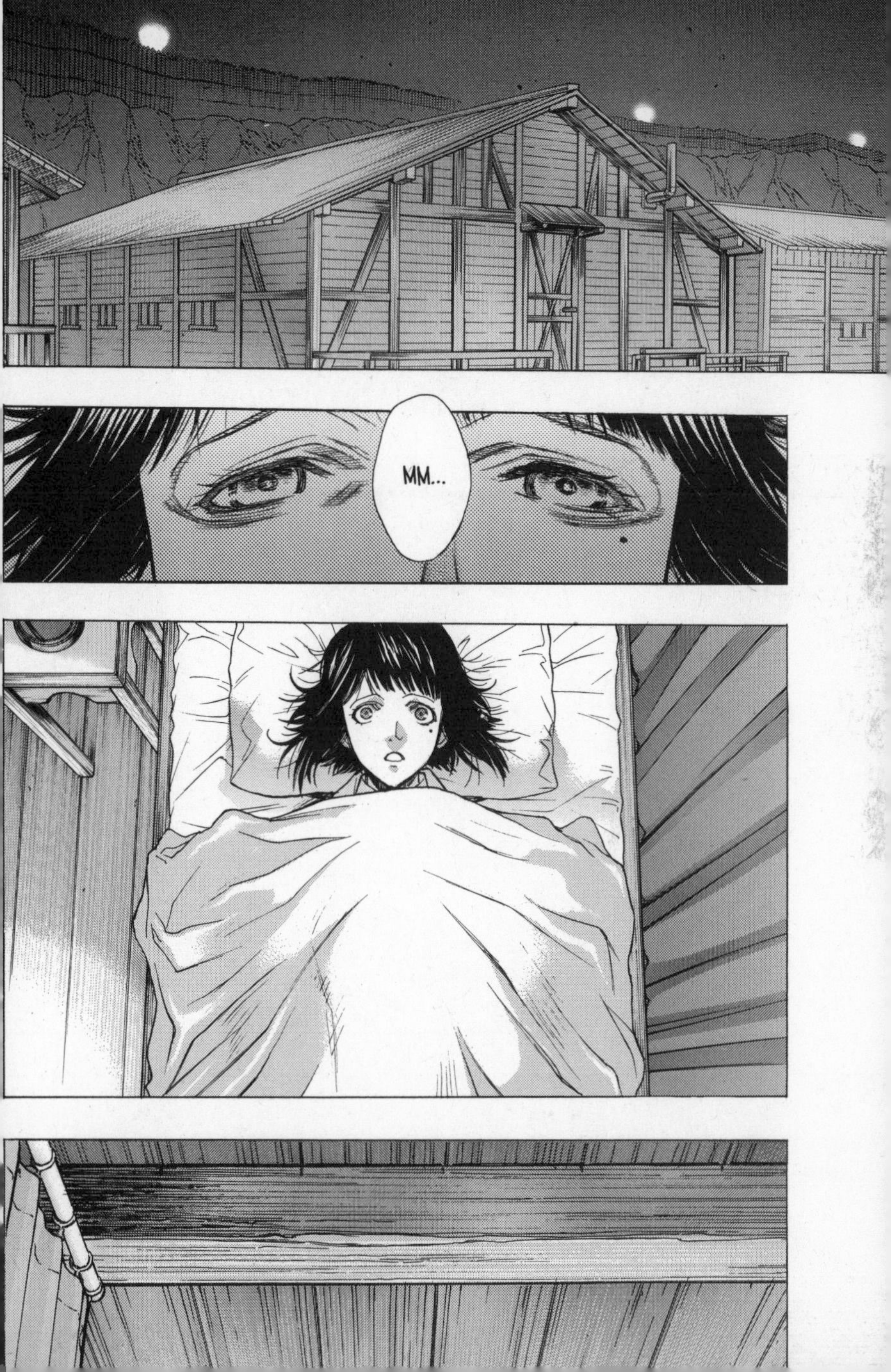
MM...

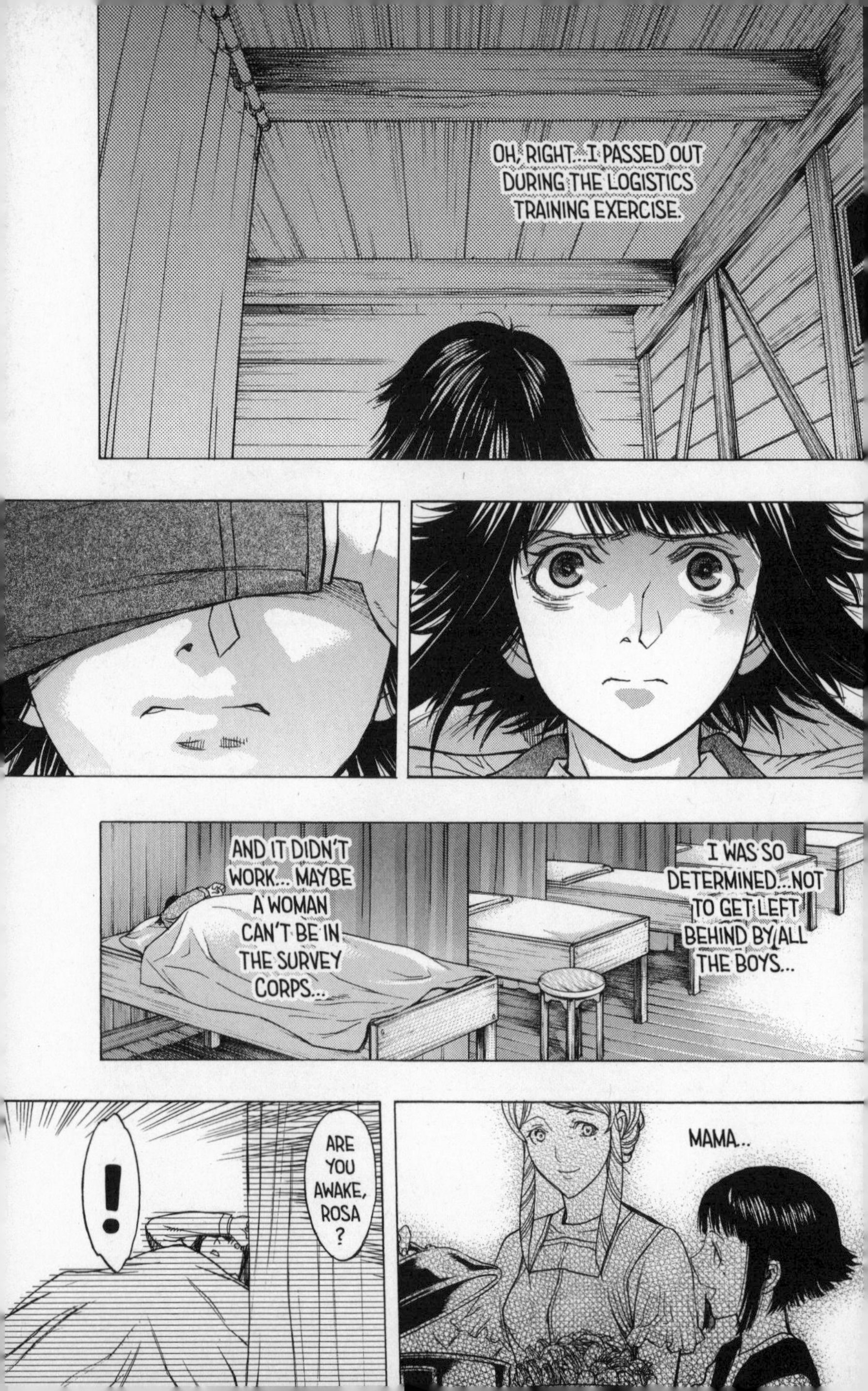
OH, RIGHT...I PASSED OUT DURING THE LOGISTICS TRAINING EXERCISE.
I WAS SO DETERMINED...NOT TO GET LEFT BEHIND BY ALL THE BOYS...
AND IT DIDN'T WORK... MAYBE A WOMAN CAN'T BE IN THE SURVEY CORPS...
MAMA...
ARE YOU AWAKE, ROSA?
!

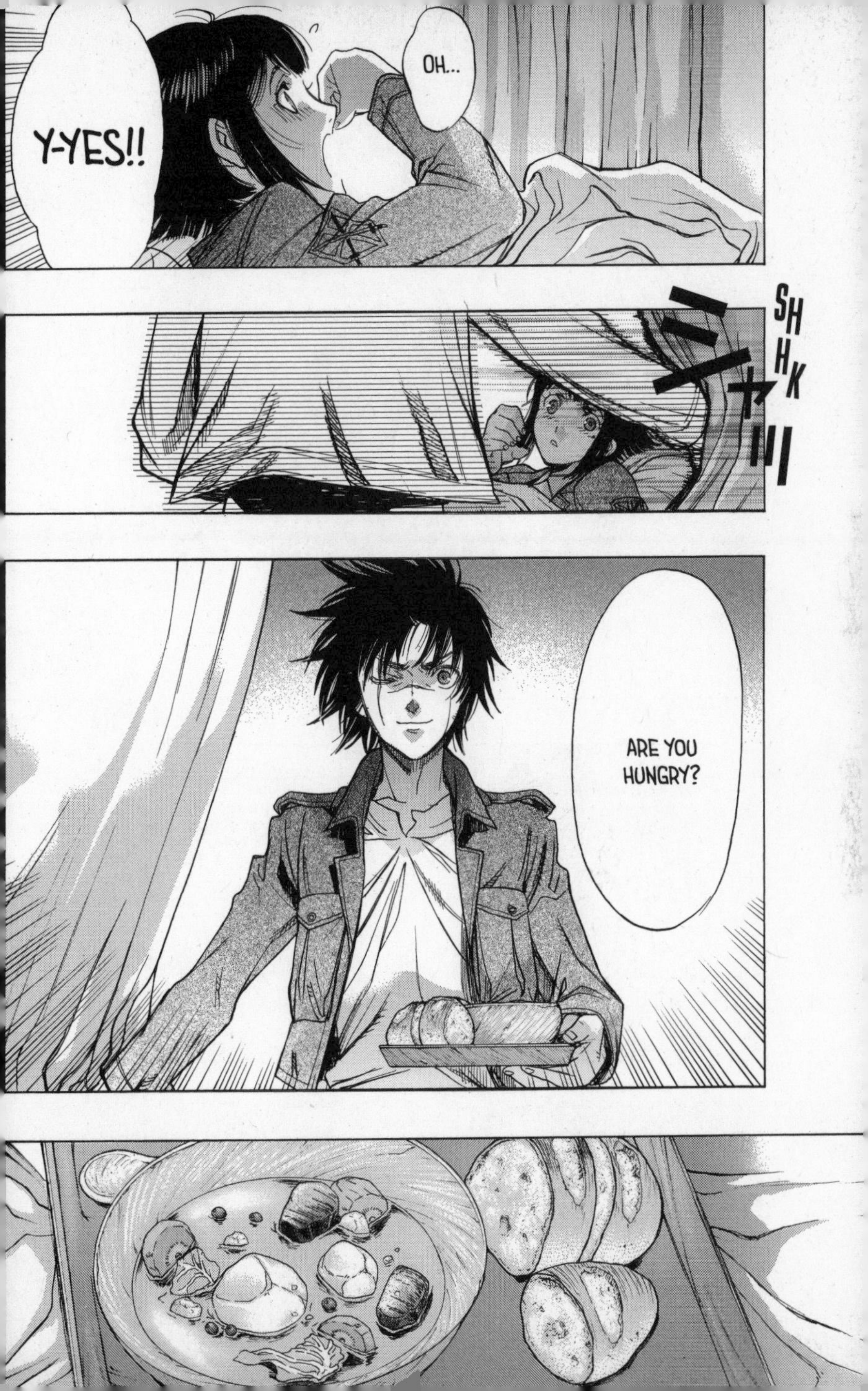
OH...
Y-YES!!
SHHK
ARE YOU HUNGRY?

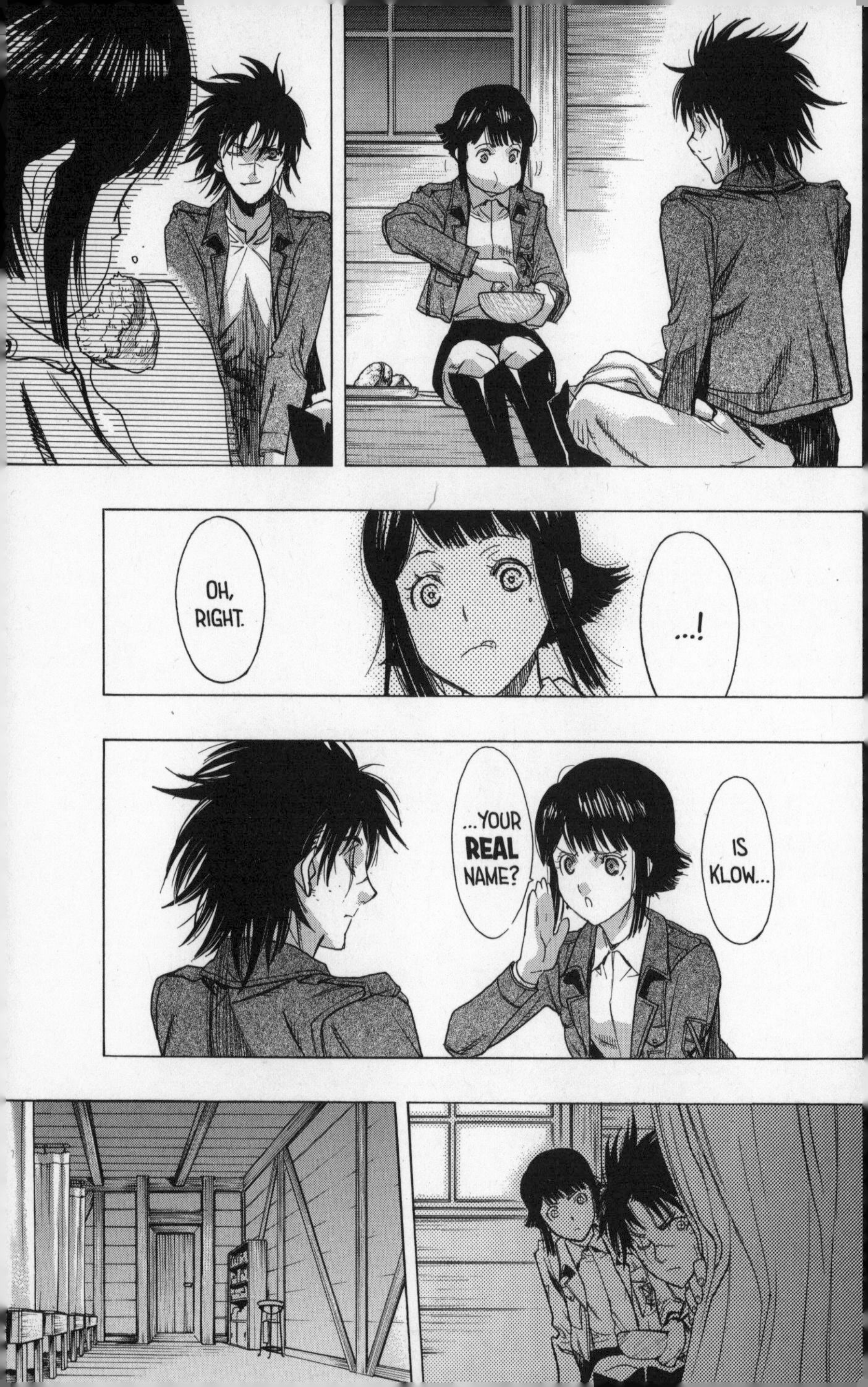
...!
OH, RIGHT.
IS KLOW...
...YOUR REAL NAME?

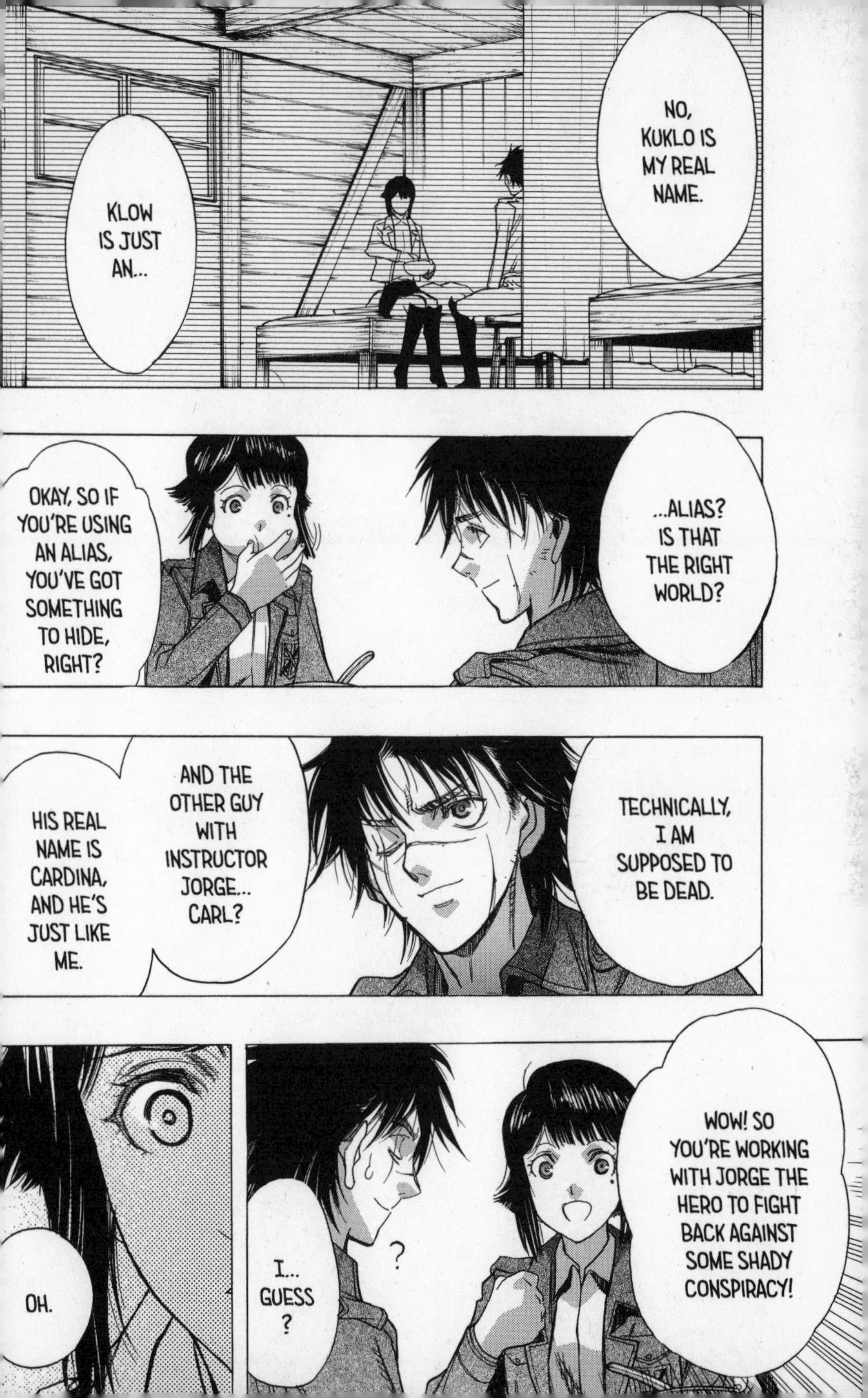
NO, KUKLO IS MY REAL NAME.
KLOW IS JUST AN...
...ALIAS? IS THAT THE RIGHT WORLD?
OKAY, SO IF YOU'RE USING AN ALIAS, YOU'VE GOT SOMETHING TO HIDE, RIGHT?
TECHNICALLY, I AM SUPPOSED TO BE DEAD.
AND THE OTHER GUY WITH INSTRUCTOR JORGE... CARL?
HIS REAL NAME IS CARDINA, AND HE'S JUST LIKE ME.
WOW! SO YOU'RE WORKING WITH JORGE THE HERO TO FIGHT BACK AGAINST SOME SHADY CONSPIRACY!
?
I... GUESS ?
OH.

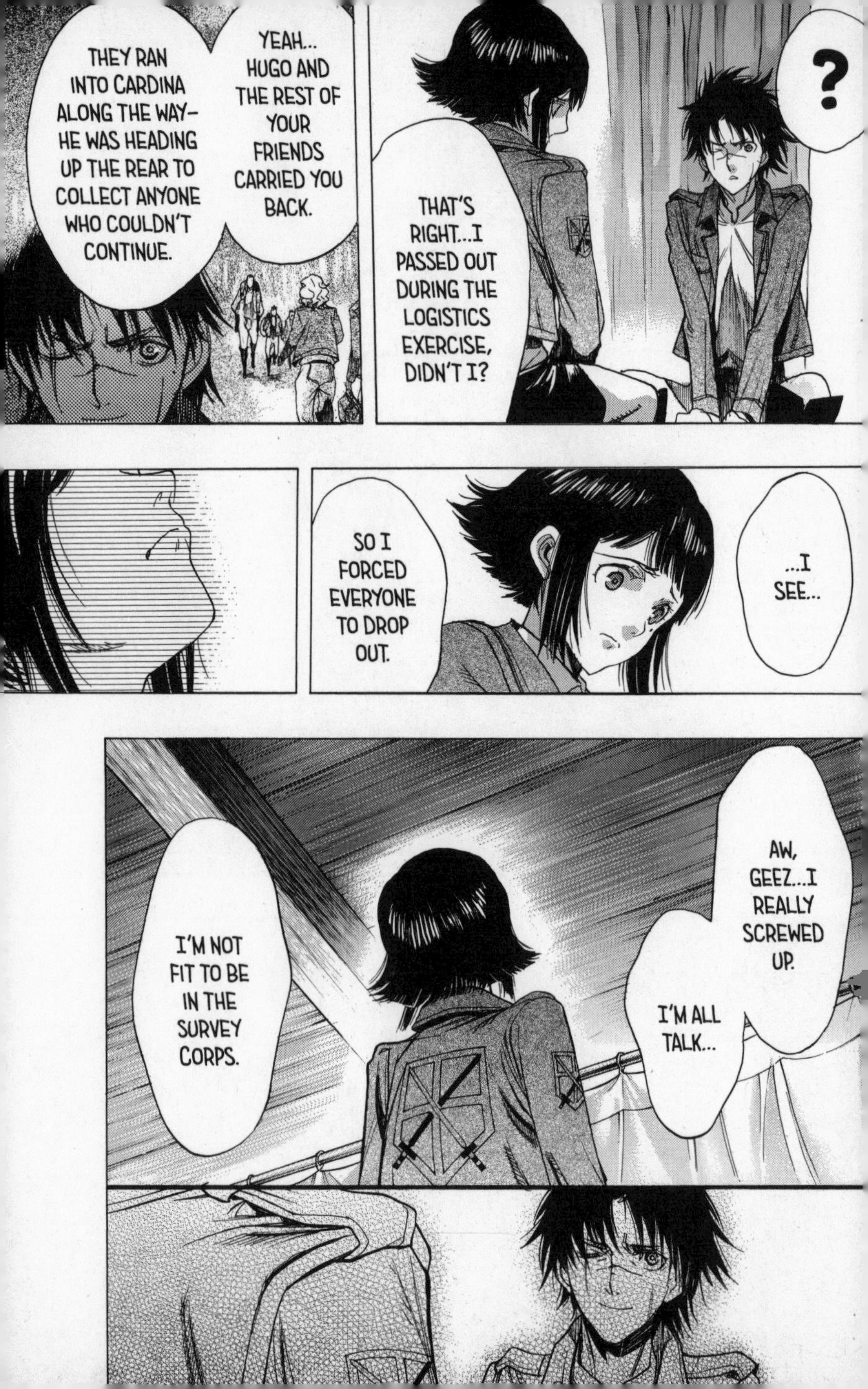
?
THAT'S RIGHT...I PASSED OUT DURING THE LOGISTICS EXERCISE, DIDN'T I?
YEAH... HUGO AND THE REST OF YOUR FRIENDS CARRIED YOU BACK.
THEY RAN INTO CARDINA ALONG THE WAY–HE WAS HEADING UP THE REAR TO COLLECT ANYONE WHO COULDN'T CONTINUE.
...I SEE...
SO I FORCED EVERYONE TO DROP OUT.
AW, GEEZ...I REALLY SCREWED UP.
I'M ALL TALK...
I'M NOT FIT TO BE IN THE SURVEY CORPS.

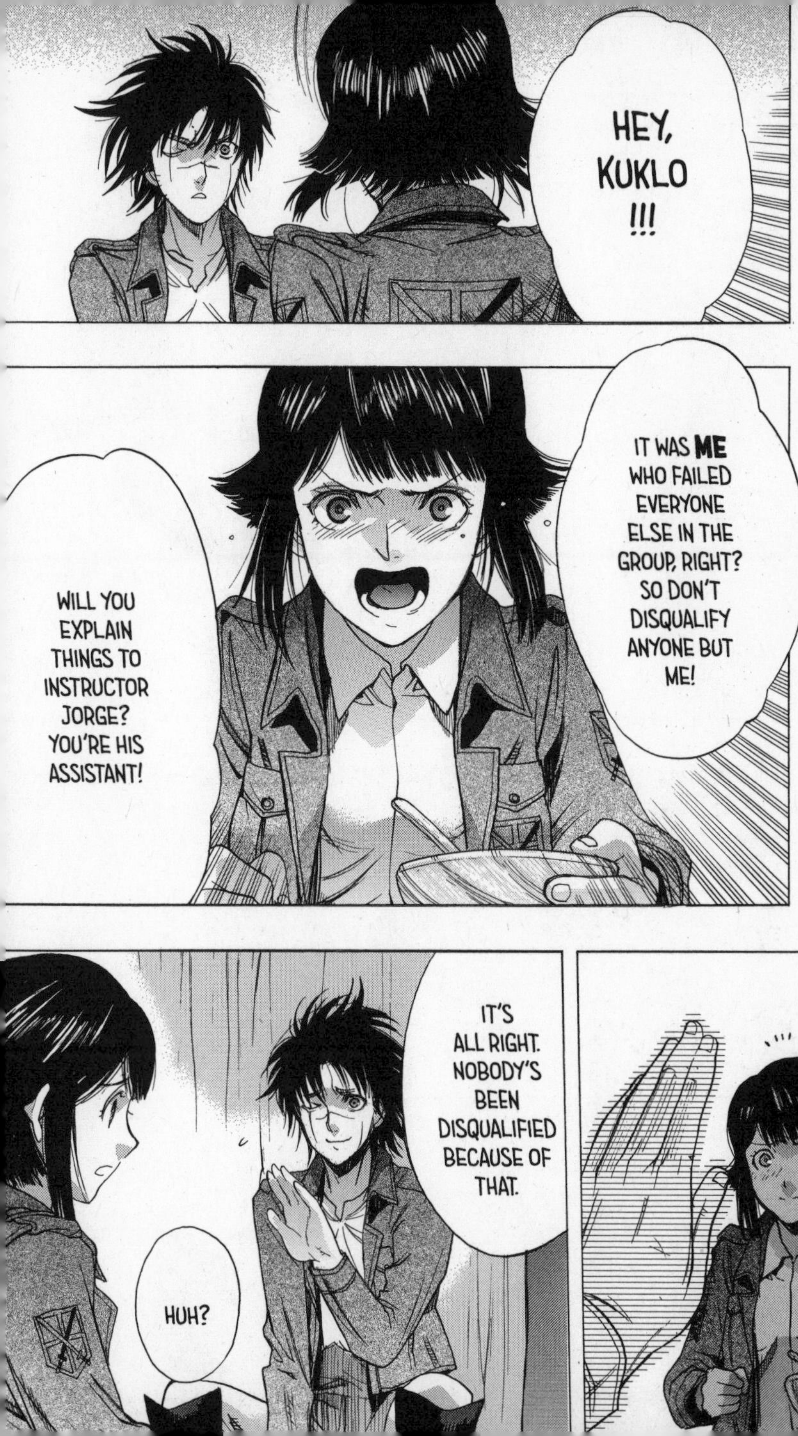
HEY, KUKLO !!!
IT WAS **ME** WHO FAILED EVERYONE ELSE IN THE GROUP, RIGHT? SO DON'T DISQUALIFY ANYONE BUT ME!
WILL YOU EXPLAIN THINGS TO INSTRUCTOR JORGE? YOU'RE HIS ASSISTANT!
IT'S ALL RIGHT. NOBODY'S BEEN DISQUALIFIED BECAUSE OF THAT.
HUH?

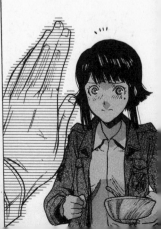

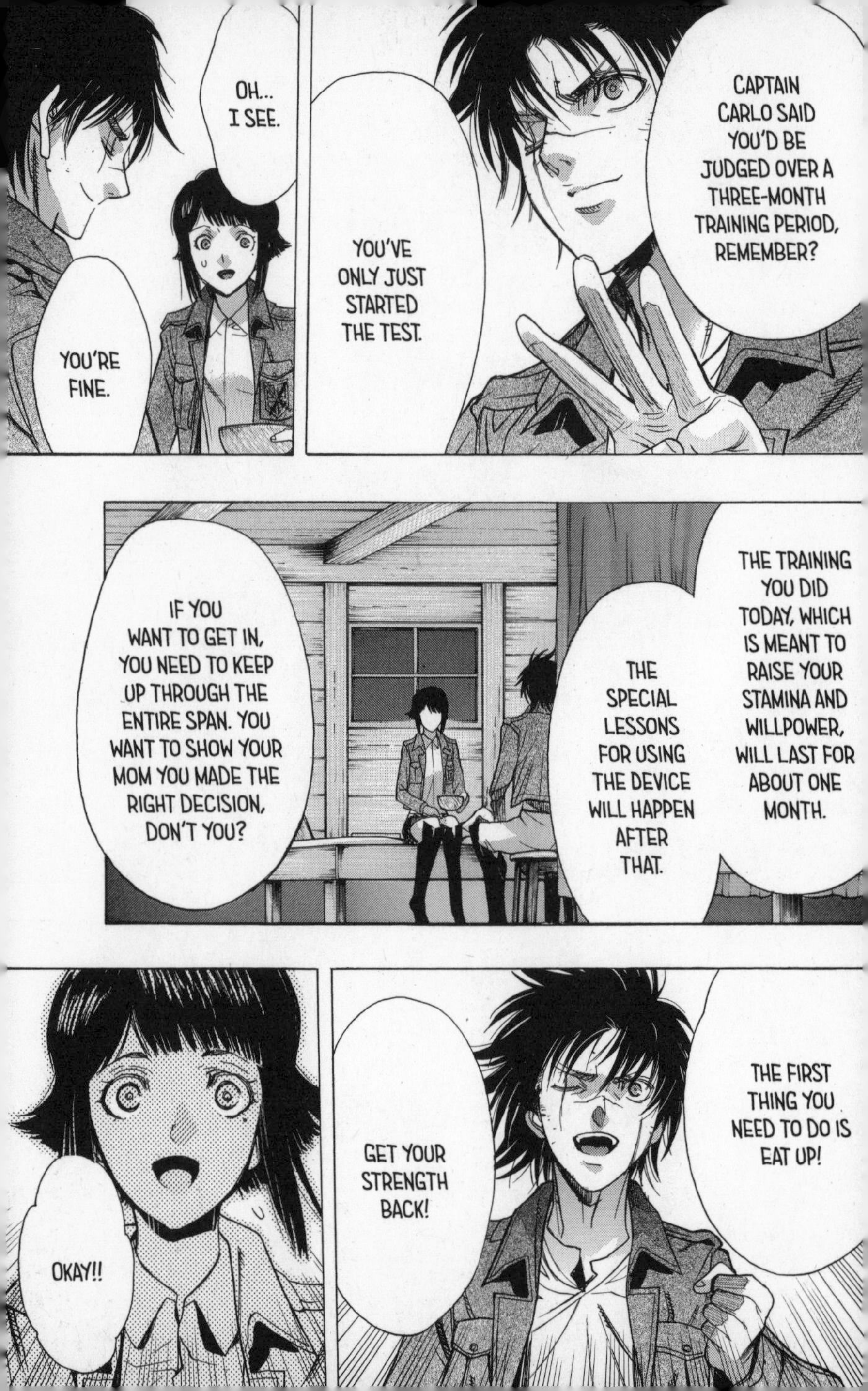
CAPTAIN CARLO SAID YOU'D BE JUDGED OVER A THREE-MONTH TRAINING PERIOD, REMEMBER?
YOU'VE ONLY JUST STARTED THE TEST.
OH... I SEE.
YOU'RE FINE.
THE TRAINING YOU DID TODAY, WHICH IS MEANT TO RAISE YOUR STAMINA AND WILLPOWER, WILL LAST FOR ABOUT ONE MONTH.
THE SPECIAL LESSONS FOR USING THE DEVICE WILL HAPPEN AFTER THAT.
IF YOU WANT TO GET IN, YOU NEED TO KEEP UP THROUGH THE ENTIRE SPAN. YOU WANT TO SHOW YOUR MOM YOU MADE THE RIGHT DECISION, DON'T YOU?
THE FIRST THING YOU NEED TO DO IS EAT UP!
GET YOUR STRENGTH BACK!
OKAY!!

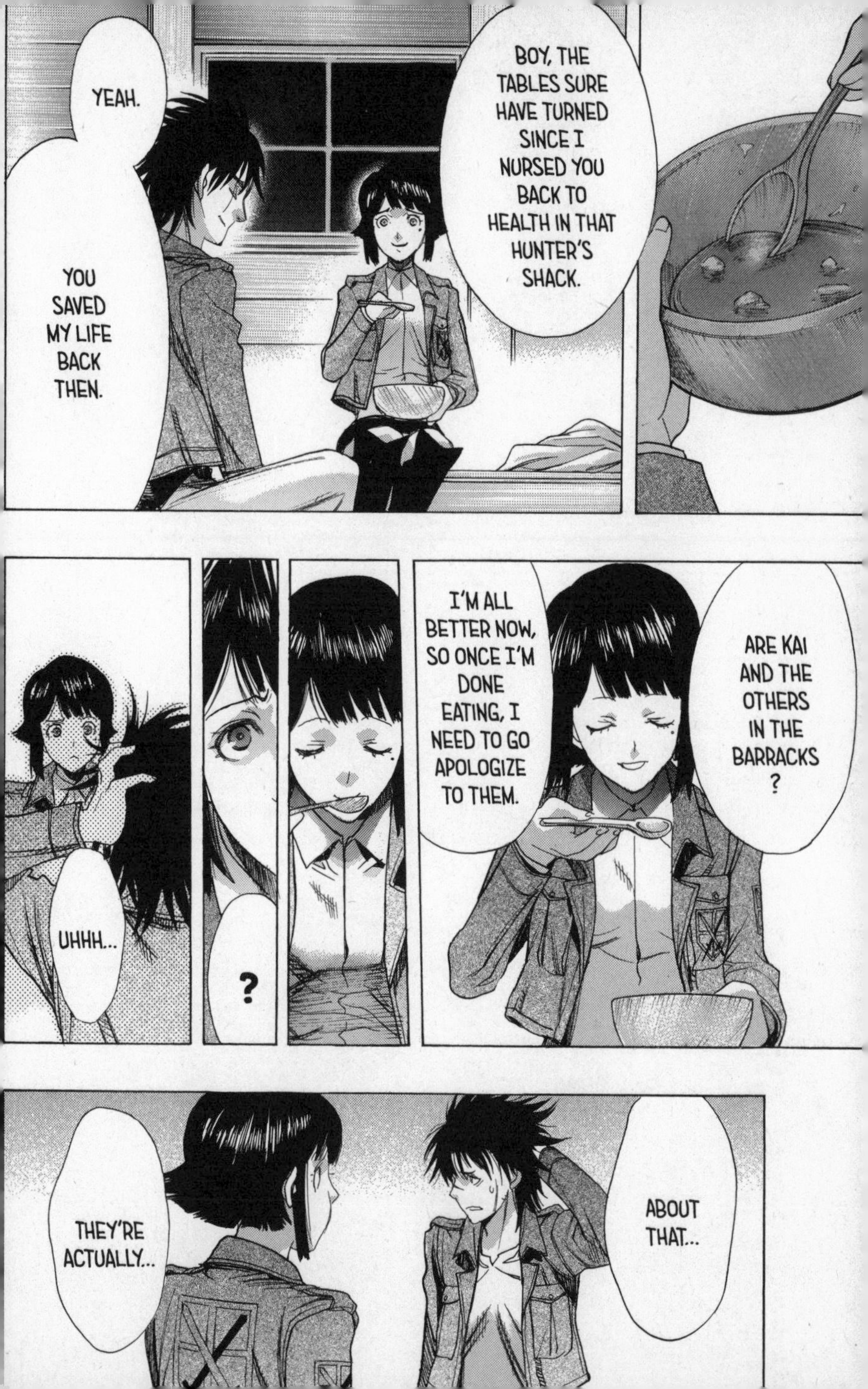
BOY, THE TABLES SURE HAVE TURNED SINCE I NURSED YOU BACK TO HEALTH IN THAT HUNTER'S SHACK.
YEAH.
YOU SAVED MY LIFE BACK THEN.
ARE KAI AND THE OTHERS IN THE BARRACKS ?
I'M ALL BETTER NOW, SO ONCE I'M DONE EATING, I NEED TO GO APOLOGIZE TO THEM.
?
UHHH...
ABOUT THAT...
THEY'RE ACTUALLY...

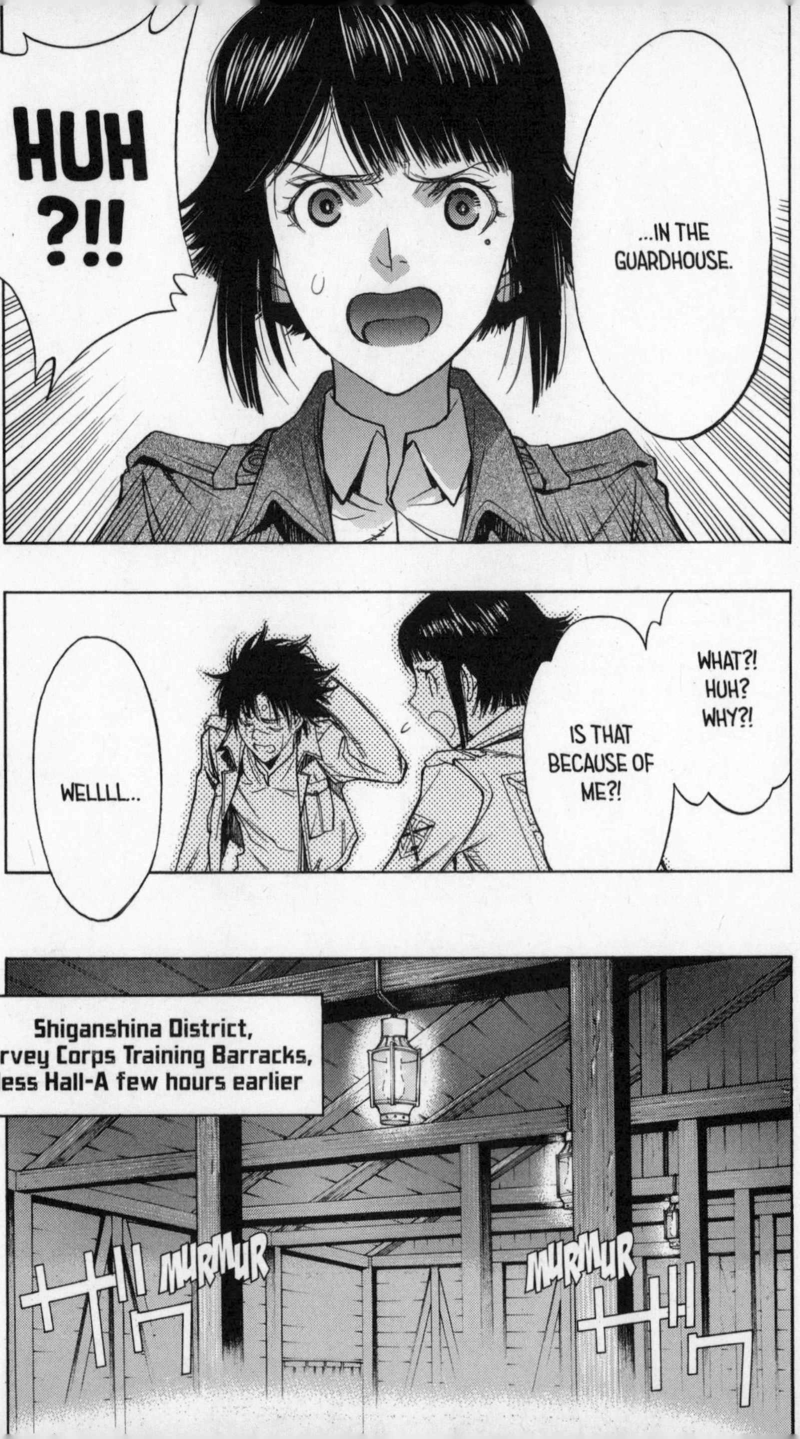
...IN THE GUARDHOUSE.
HUH?!!
WHAT?! HUH? WHY?!
IS THAT BECAUSE OF ME?!
WELLLL..
Shiganshina District, Survey Corps Training Barracks, Mess Hall-A few hours earlier
MURMUR
MURMUR

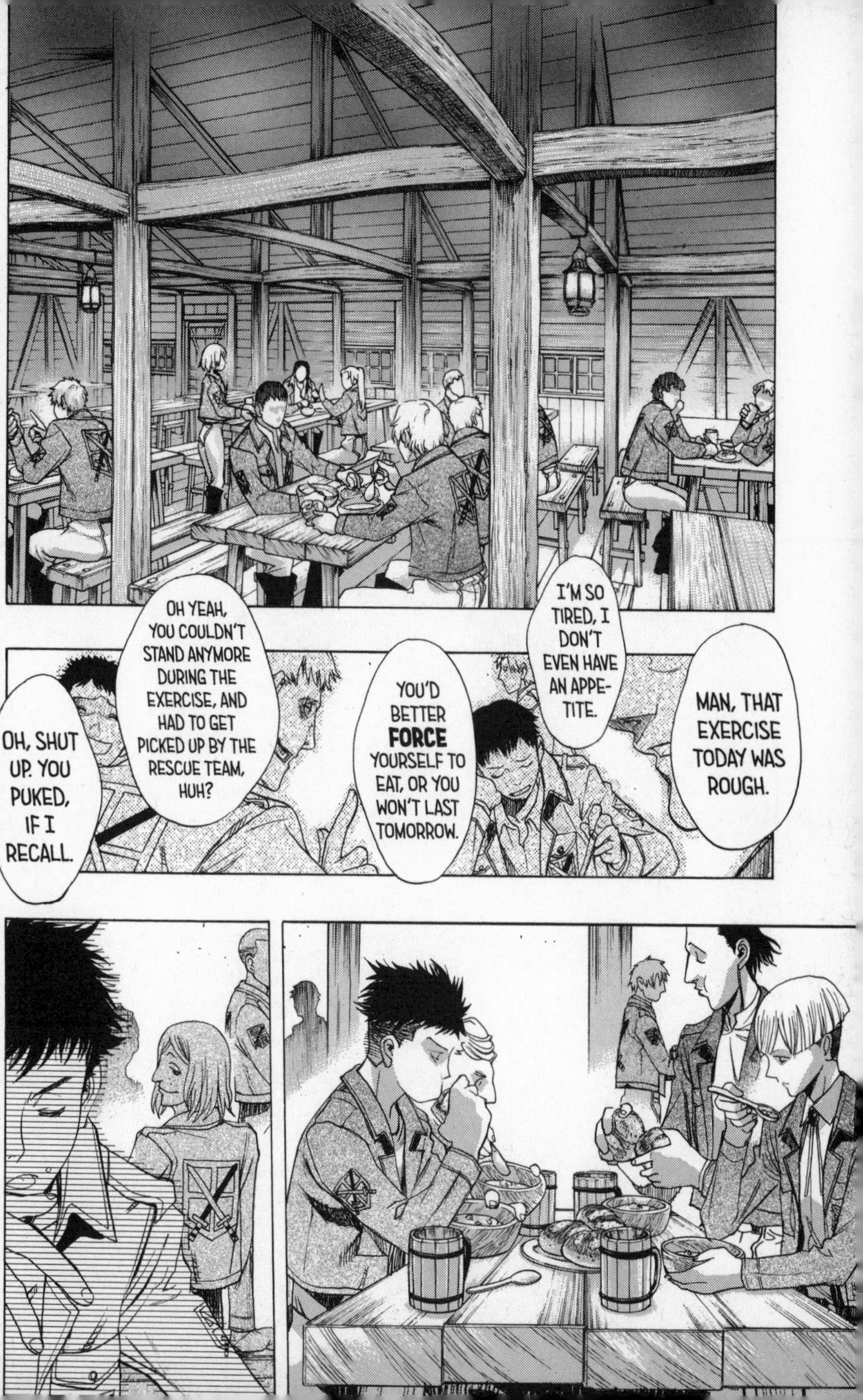
MAN, THAT EXERCISE TODAY WAS ROUGH.
I'M SO TIRED, I DON'T EVEN HAVE AN APPE-TITE.
YOU'D BETTER **FORCE** YOURSELF TO EAT, OR YOU WON'T LAST TOMORROW.
OH YEAH, YOU COULDN'T STAND ANYMORE DURING THE EXERCISE, AND HAD TO GET PICKED UP BY THE RESCUE TEAM, HUH?
OH, SHUT UP. YOU PUKED, IF I RECALL.

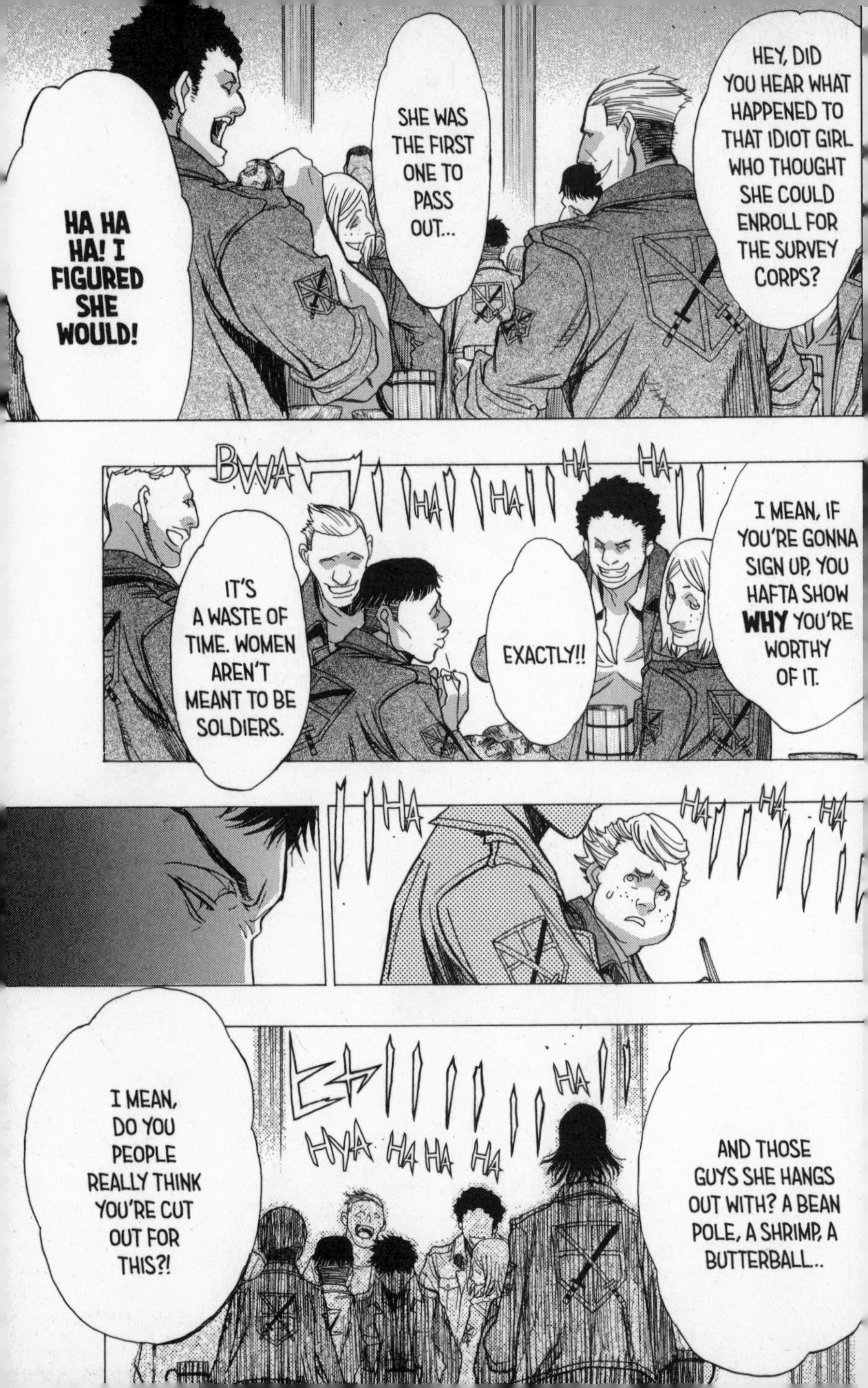
HEY, DID YOU HEAR WHAT HAPPENED TO THAT IDIOT GIRL WHO THOUGHT SHE COULD ENROLL FOR THE SURVEY CORPS?
SHE WAS THE FIRST ONE TO PASS OUT...
HA HA HA! I FIGURED SHE WOULD!
BWA HA HA HA HA
I MEAN, IF YOU'RE GONNA SIGN UP, YOU HAFTA SHOW **WHY** YOU'RE WORTHY OF IT.
EXACTLY!!
IT'S A WASTE OF TIME. WOMEN AREN'T MEANT TO BE SOLDIERS.
HA HA HA
HA
AND THOSE GUYS SHE HANGS OUT WITH? A BEAN POLE, A SHRIMP, A BUTTERBALL...
HA
HYA HA HA HA
I MEAN, DO YOU PEOPLE REALLY THINK YOU'RE CUT OUT FOR THIS?!

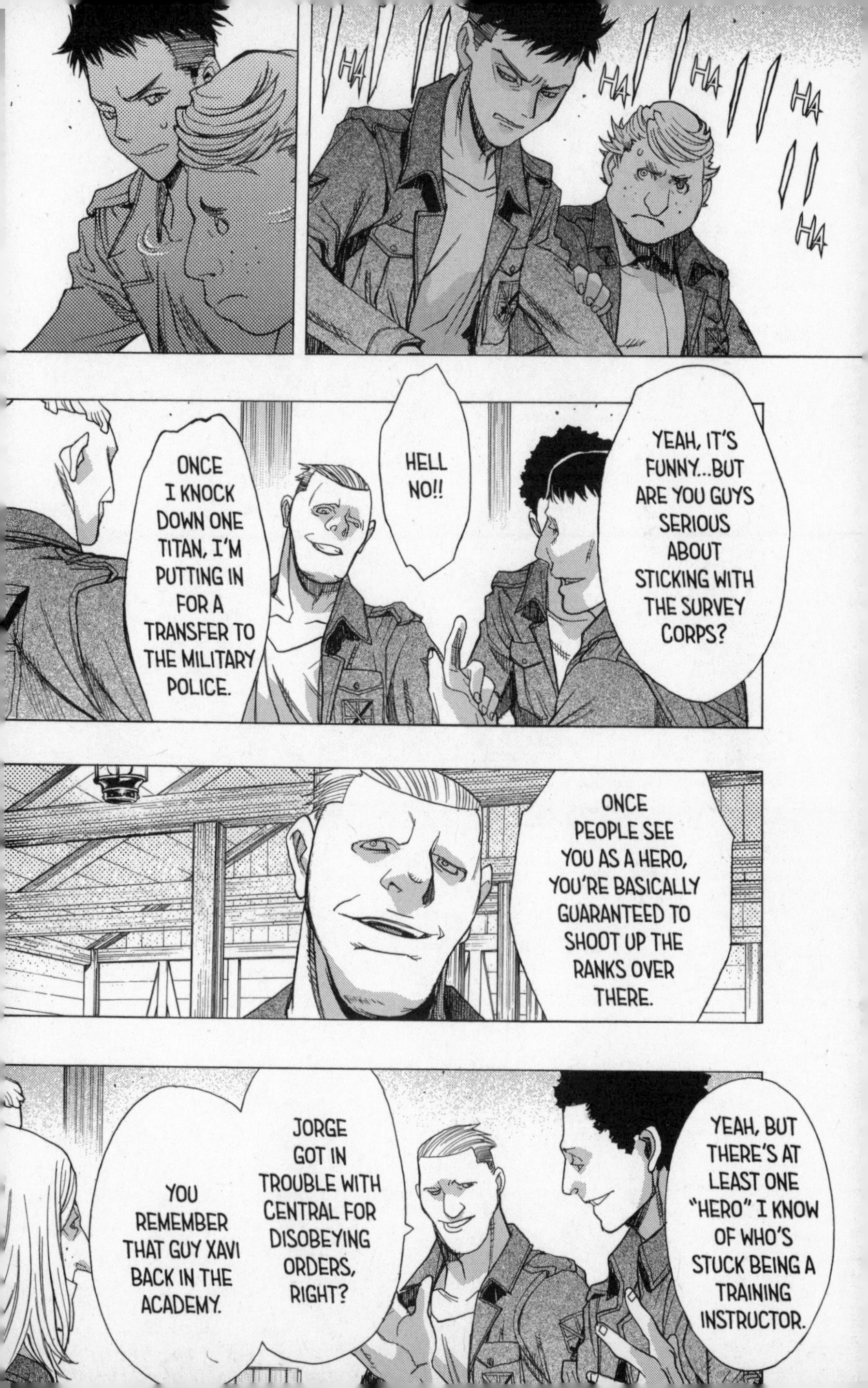
HA
HA
HA
HA
HA
YEAH, IT'S FUNNY...BUT ARE YOU GUYS SERIOUS ABOUT STICKING WITH THE SURVEY CORPS?
HELL NO!!
ONCE I KNOCK DOWN ONE TITAN, I'M PUTTING IN FOR A TRANSFER TO THE MILITARY POLICE.
ONCE PEOPLE SEE YOU AS A HERO, YOU'RE BASICALLY GUARANTEED TO SHOOT UP THE RANKS OVER THERE.
YEAH, BUT THERE'S AT LEAST ONE "HERO" I KNOW OF WHO'S STUCK BEING A TRAINING INSTRUCTOR.
JORGE GOT IN TROUBLE WITH CENTRAL FOR DISOBEYING ORDERS, RIGHT?
YOU REMEMBER THAT GUY XAVI BACK IN THE ACADEMY.

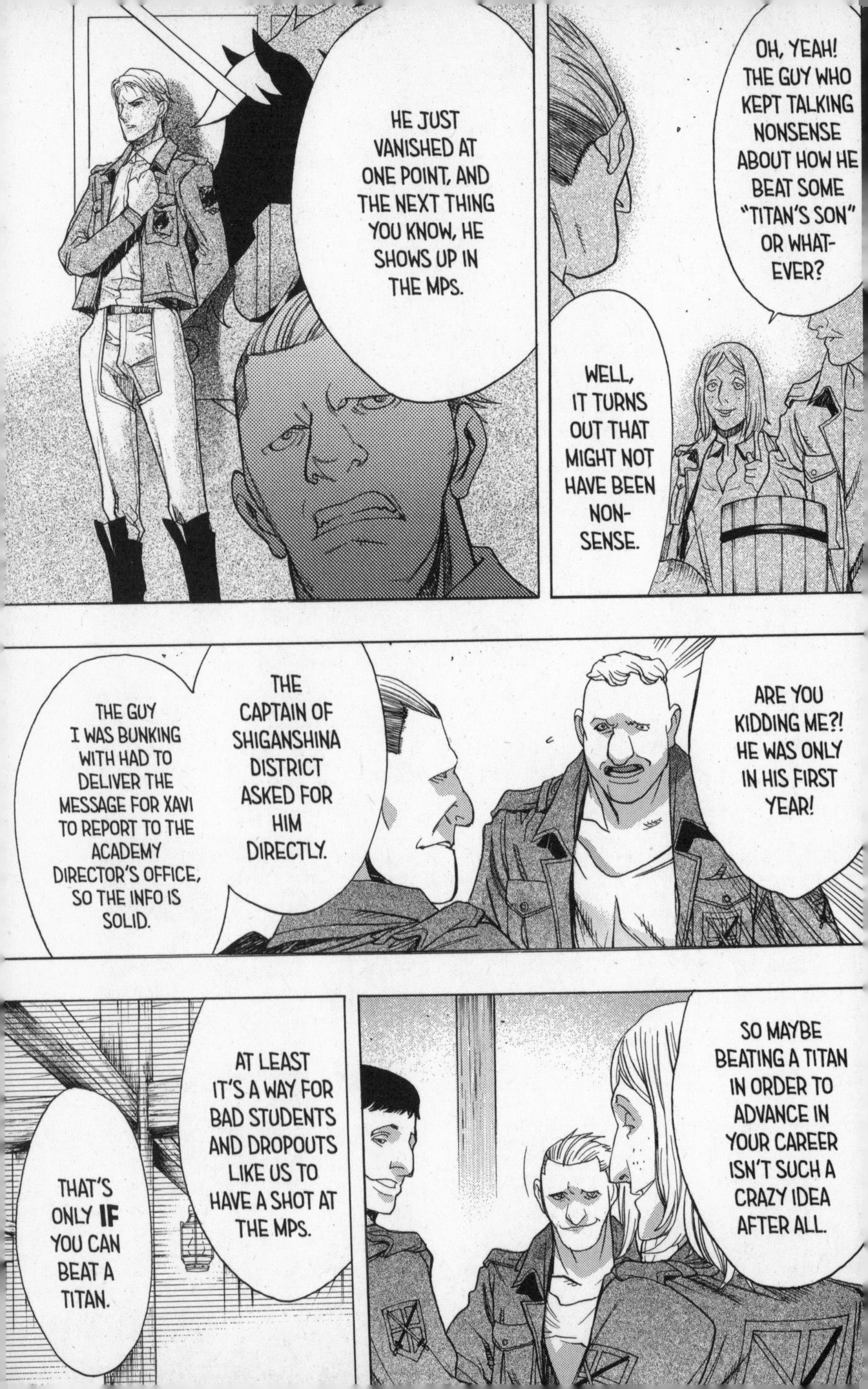
OH, YEAH! THE GUY WHO KEPT TALKING NONSENSE ABOUT HOW HE BEAT SOME "TITAN'S SON" OR WHAT-EVER?
WELL, IT TURNS OUT THAT MIGHT NOT HAVE BEEN NON-SENSE.
HE JUST VANISHED AT ONE POINT, AND THE NEXT THING YOU KNOW, HE SHOWS UP IN THE MPS.
ARE YOU KIDDING ME?! HE WAS ONLY IN HIS FIRST YEAR!
THE CAPTAIN OF SHIGANSHINA DISTRICT ASKED FOR HIM DIRECTLY.
THE GUY I WAS BUNKING WITH HAD TO DELIVER THE MESSAGE FOR XAVI TO REPORT TO THE ACADEMY DIRECTOR'S OFFICE, SO THE INFO IS SOLID.
SO MAYBE BEATING A TITAN IN ORDER TO ADVANCE IN YOUR CAREER ISN'T SUCH A CRAZY IDEA AFTER ALL.
AT LEAST IT'S A WAY FOR BAD STUDENTS AND DROPOUTS LIKE US TO HAVE A SHOT AT THE MPS.
THAT'S ONLY **IF** YOU CAN BEAT A TITAN.

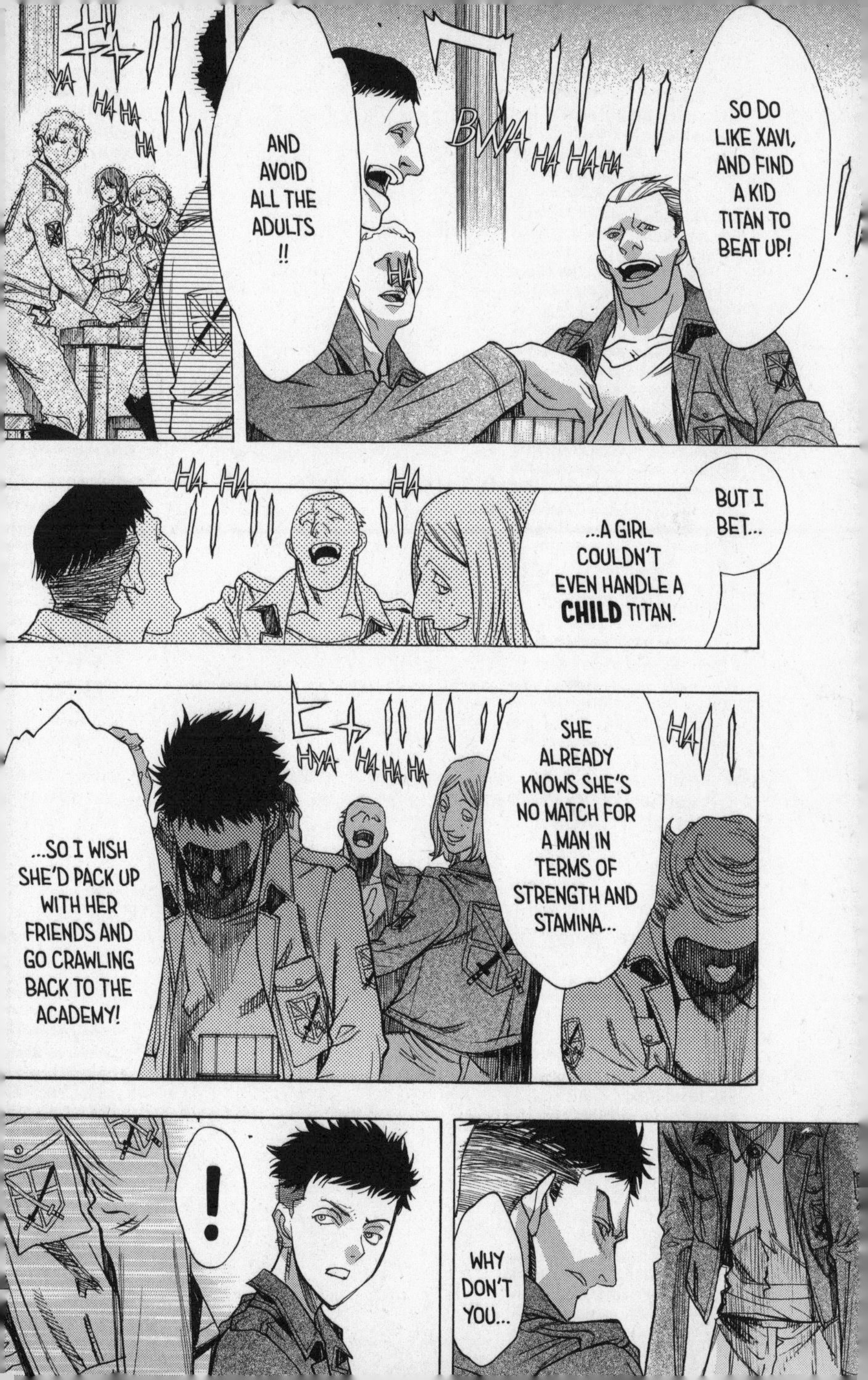
SO DO LIKE XAVI, AND FIND A KID TITAN TO BEAT UP!
BWA HA HA HA HA
HA
AND AVOID ALL THE ADULTS !!
YA HA HA HA
BUT I BET...
...A GIRL COULDN'T EVEN HANDLE A **CHILD** TITAN.
HA
HA HA
HA
SHE ALREADY KNOWS SHE'S NO MATCH FOR A MAN IN TERMS OF STRENGTH AND STAMINA...
HYA HA HA HA
...SO I WISH SHE'D PACK UP WITH HER FRIENDS AND GO CRAWLING BACK TO THE ACADEMY!
WHY DON'T YOU...
!

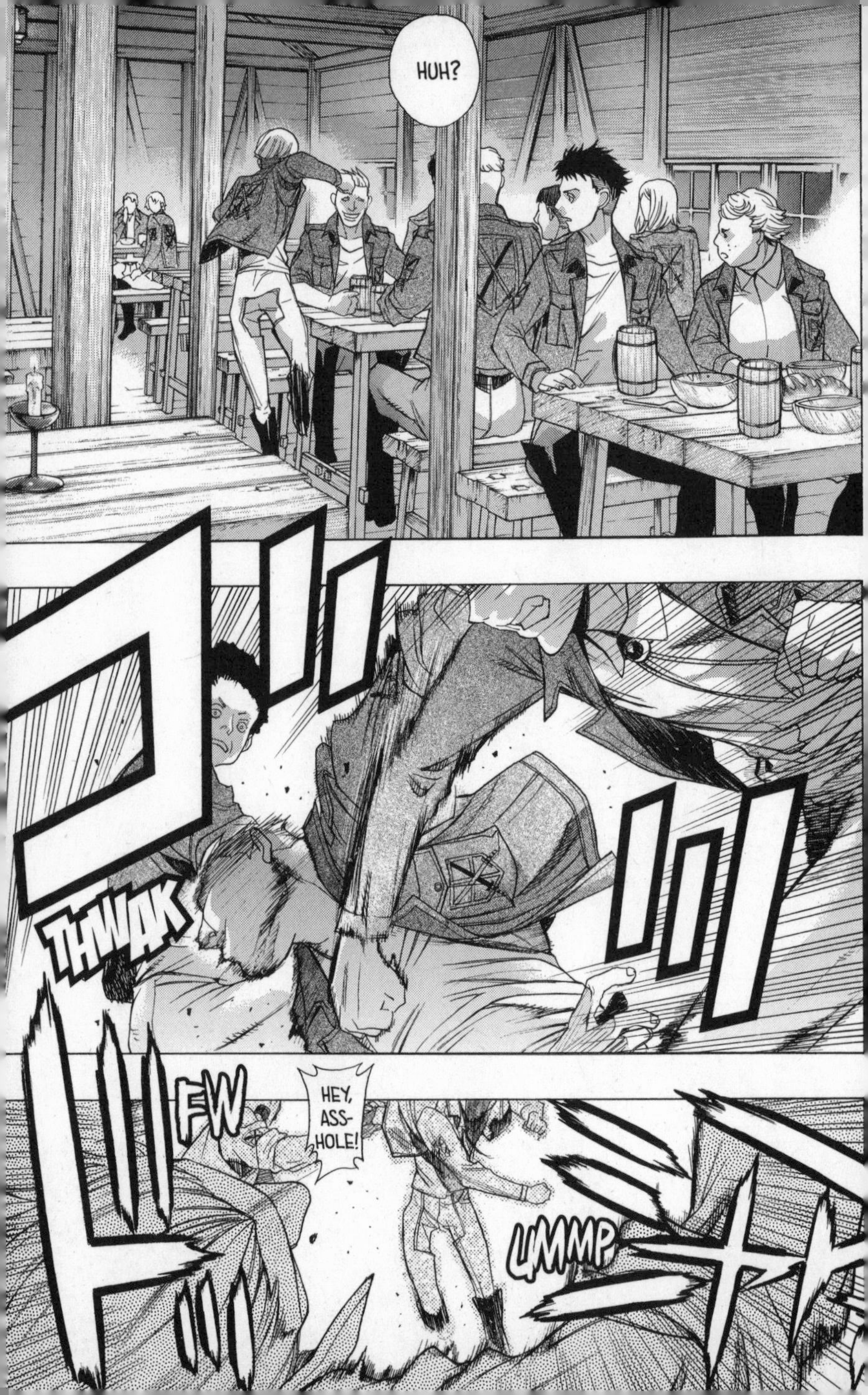
HUH?
THWAK
HEY, ASS-HOLE!
FW
UMMP

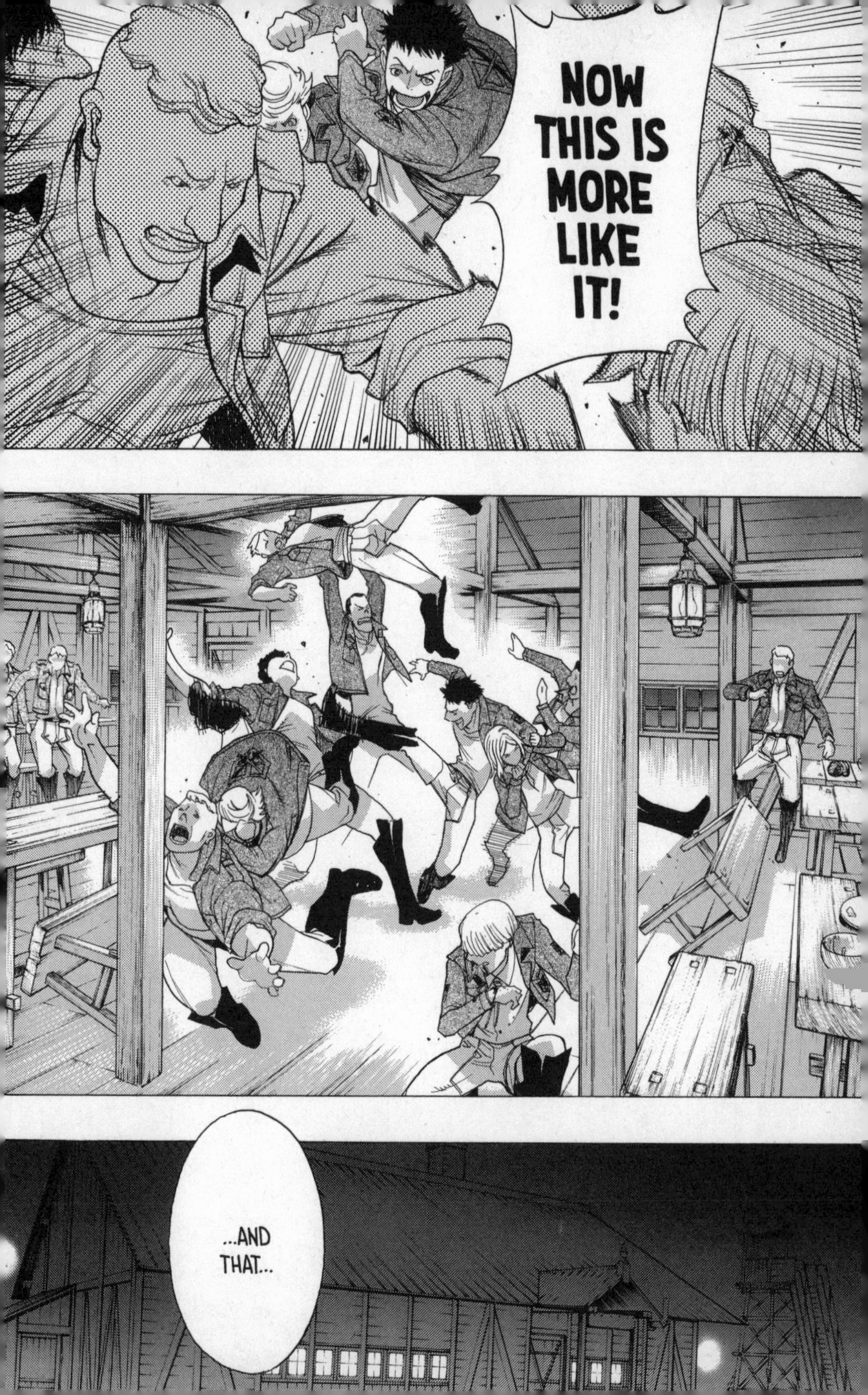
NOW THIS IS MORE LIKE IT!
...AND THAT...

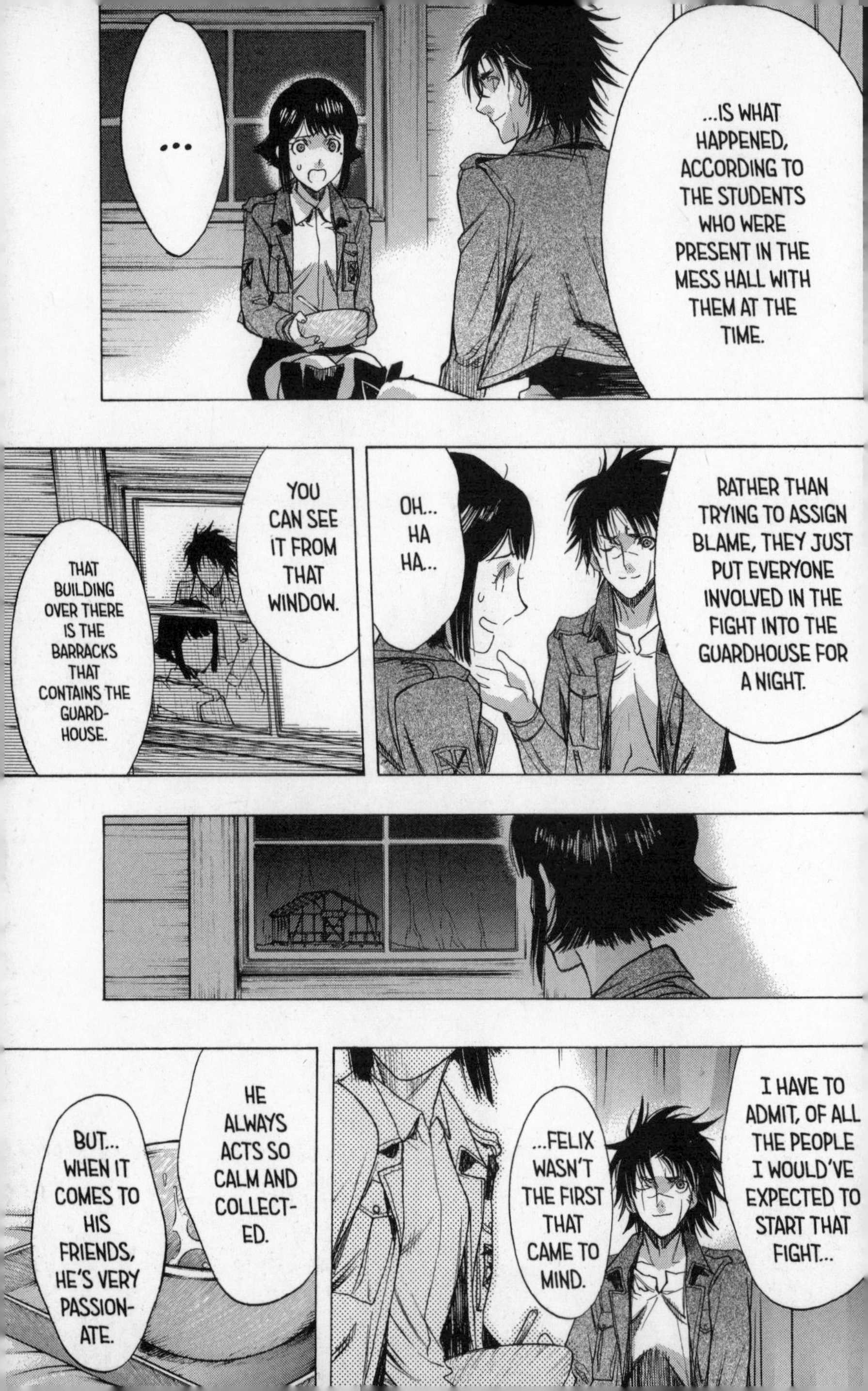
...IS WHAT HAPPENED, ACCORDING TO THE STUDENTS WHO WERE PRESENT IN THE MESS HALL WITH THEM AT THE TIME.
...
RATHER THAN TRYING TO ASSIGN BLAME, THEY JUST PUT EVERYONE INVOLVED IN THE FIGHT INTO THE GUARDHOUSE FOR A NIGHT.
OH... HA HA...
YOU CAN SEE IT FROM THAT WINDOW.
THAT BUILDING OVER THERE IS THE BARRACKS THAT CONTAINS THE GUARD-HOUSE.
I HAVE TO ADMIT, OF ALL THE PEOPLE I WOULD'VE EXPECTED TO START THAT FIGHT...
...FELIX WASN'T THE FIRST THAT CAME TO MIND.
HE ALWAYS ACTS SO CALM AND COLLECT-ED.
BUT... WHEN IT COMES TO HIS FRIENDS, HE'S VERY PASSION-ATE.

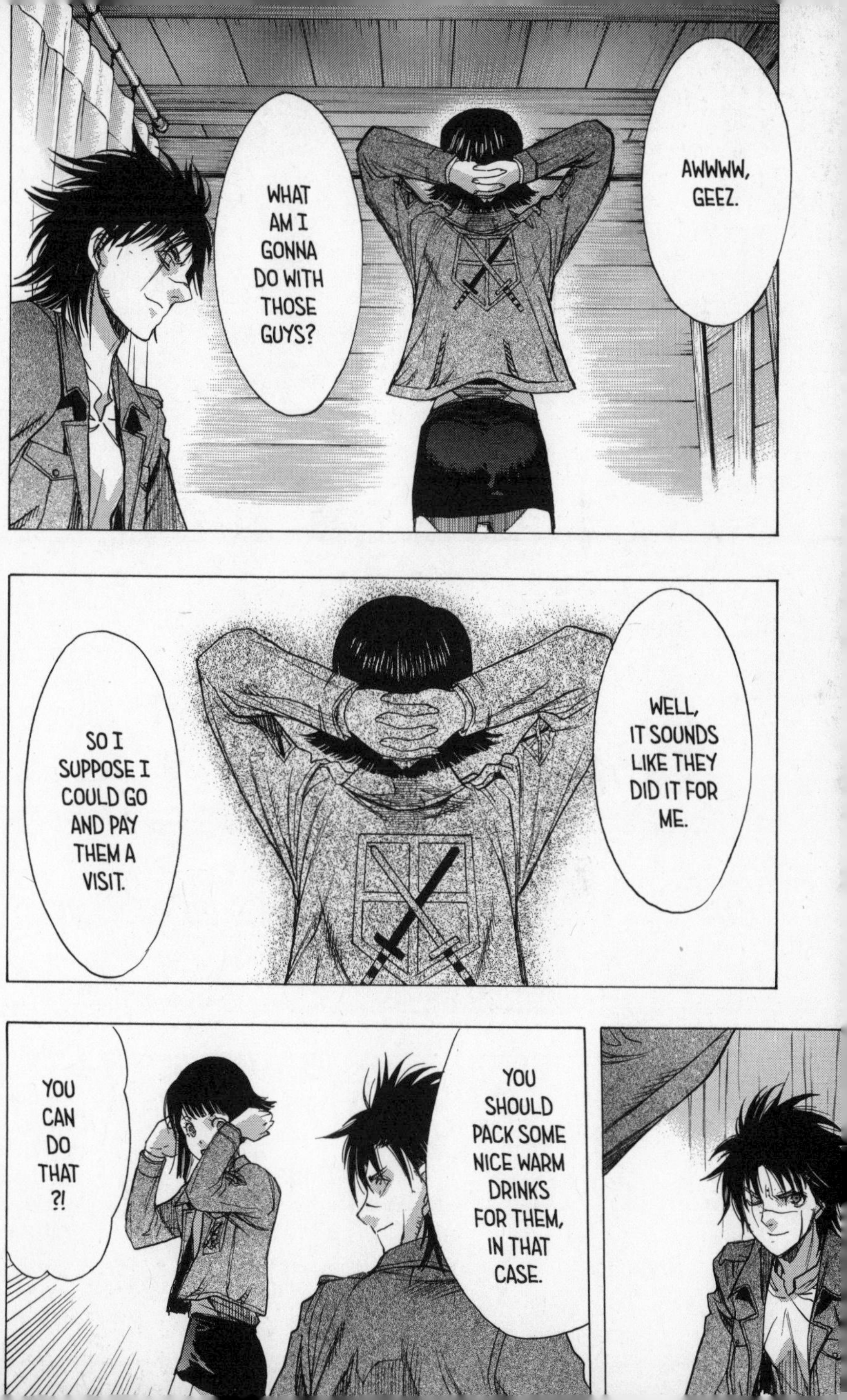
AWWWW, GEEZ.
WHAT AM I GONNA DO WITH THOSE GUYS?
WELL, IT SOUNDS LIKE THEY DID IT FOR ME.
SO I SUPPOSE I COULD GO AND PAY THEM A VISIT.
YOU SHOULD PACK SOME NICE WARM DRINKS FOR THEM, IN THAT CASE.
YOU CAN DO THAT?!

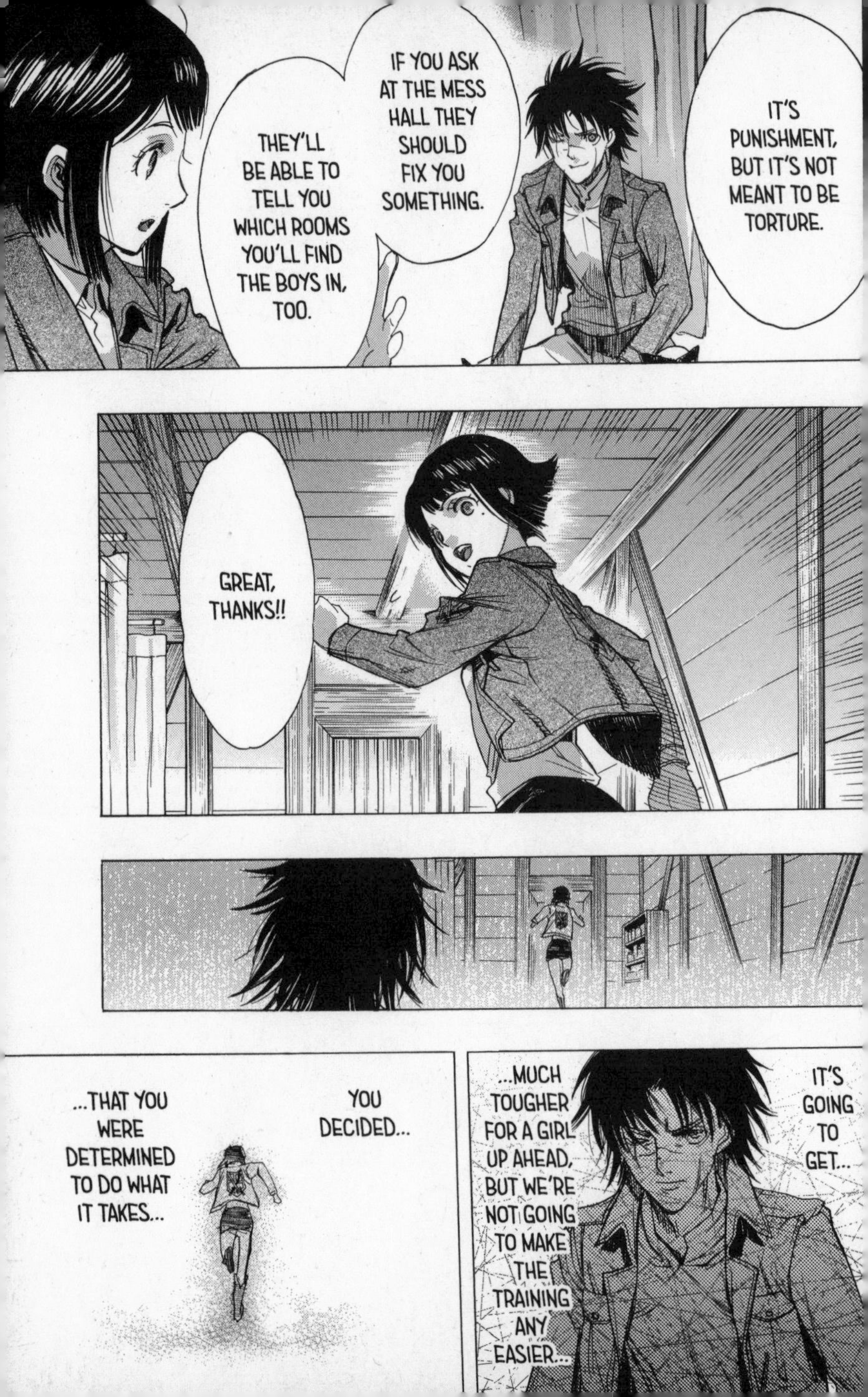
IT'S PUNISHMENT, BUT IT'S NOT MEANT TO BE TORTURE.
IF YOU ASK AT THE MESS HALL THEY SHOULD FIX YOU SOMETHING.
THEY'LL BE ABLE TO TELL YOU WHICH ROOMS YOU'LL FIND THE BOYS IN, TOO.
GREAT, THANKS!!
IT'S GOING TO GET...
...MUCH TOUGHER FOR A GIRL UP AHEAD, BUT WE'RE NOT GOING TO MAKE THE TRAINING ANY EASIER...
YOU DECIDED...
...THAT YOU WERE DETERMINED TO DO WHAT IT TAKES...

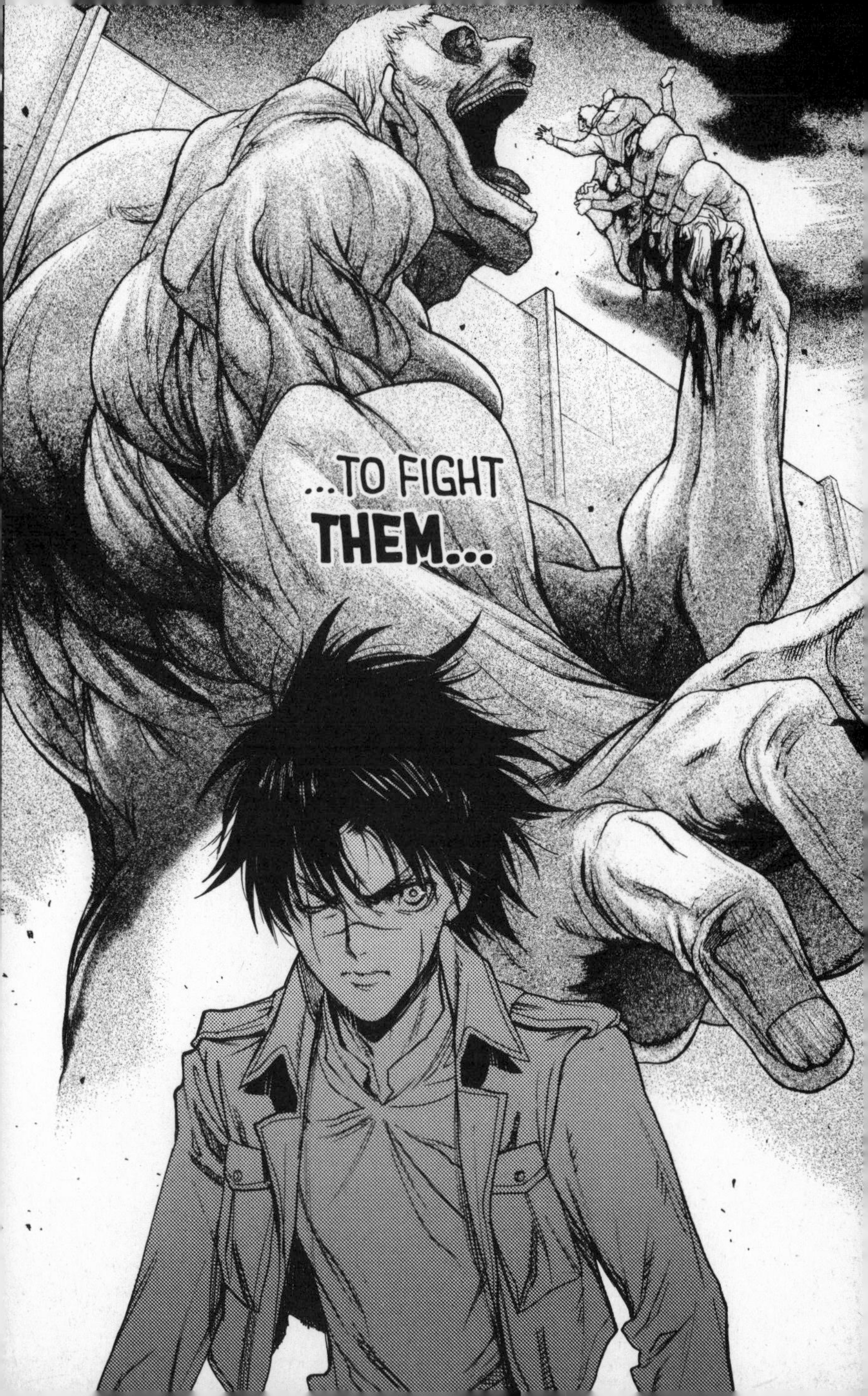
...TO FIGHT THEM...

Chapter 43: Wellspring of the Restoration · End

ATTACK on TITAN
BEFORE THE FALL

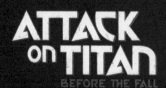

Chapter 44: Long-Awaited Weapon

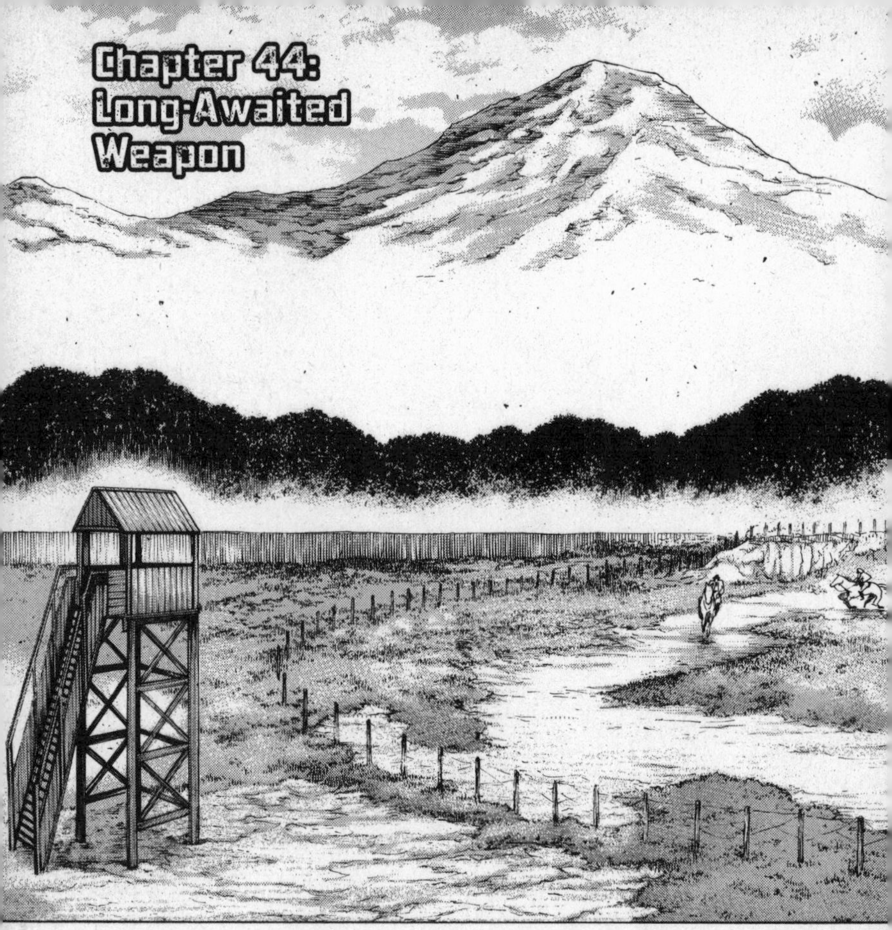

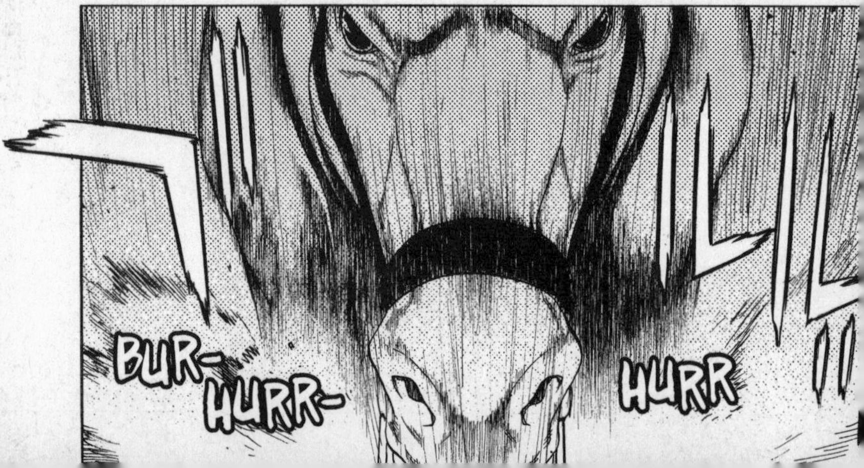
BUR-
HURR-
HURR

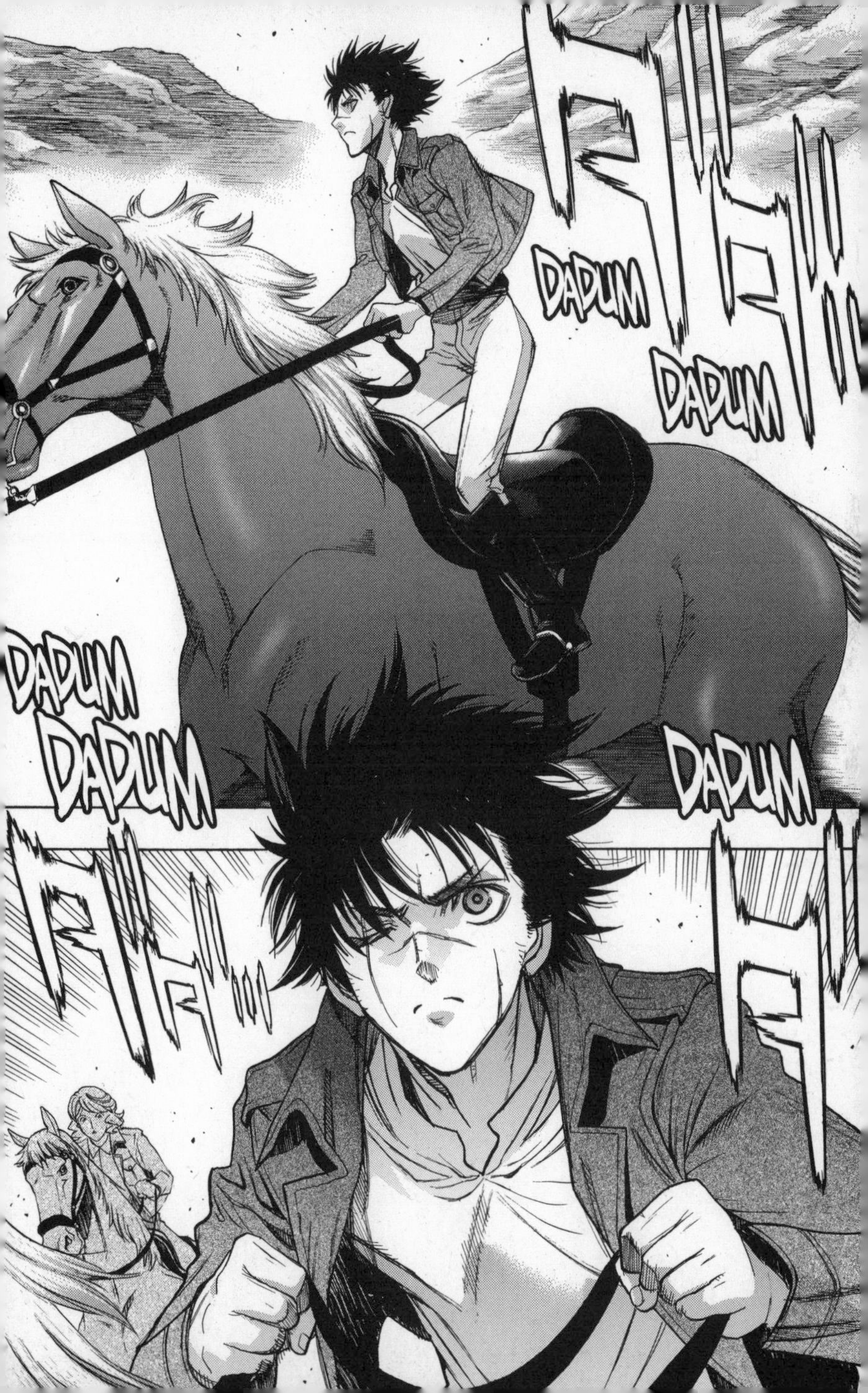
DADUM
DADUM
DADUM
DADUM
DADUM

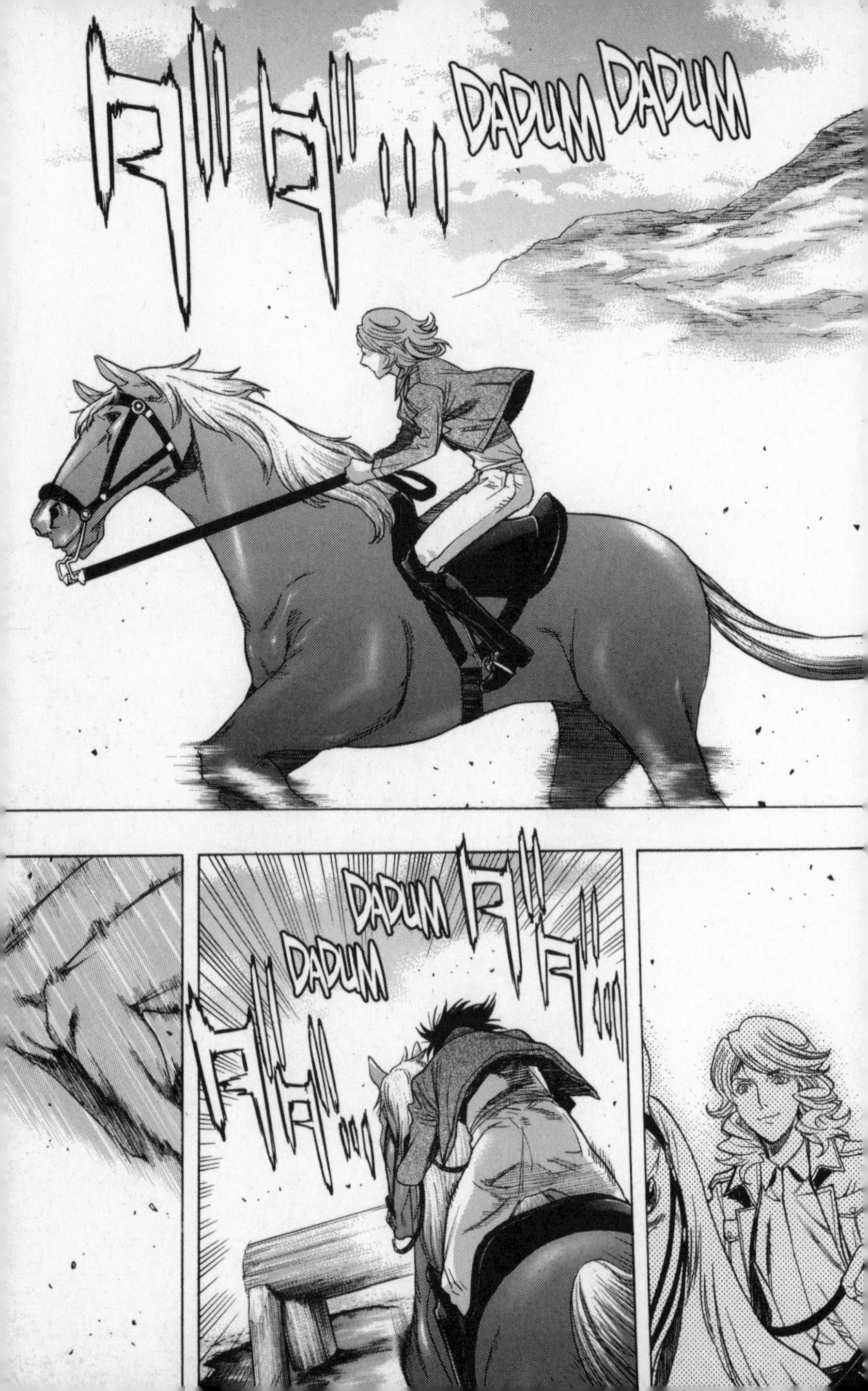
DADUM DADUM
DADUM
DADUM

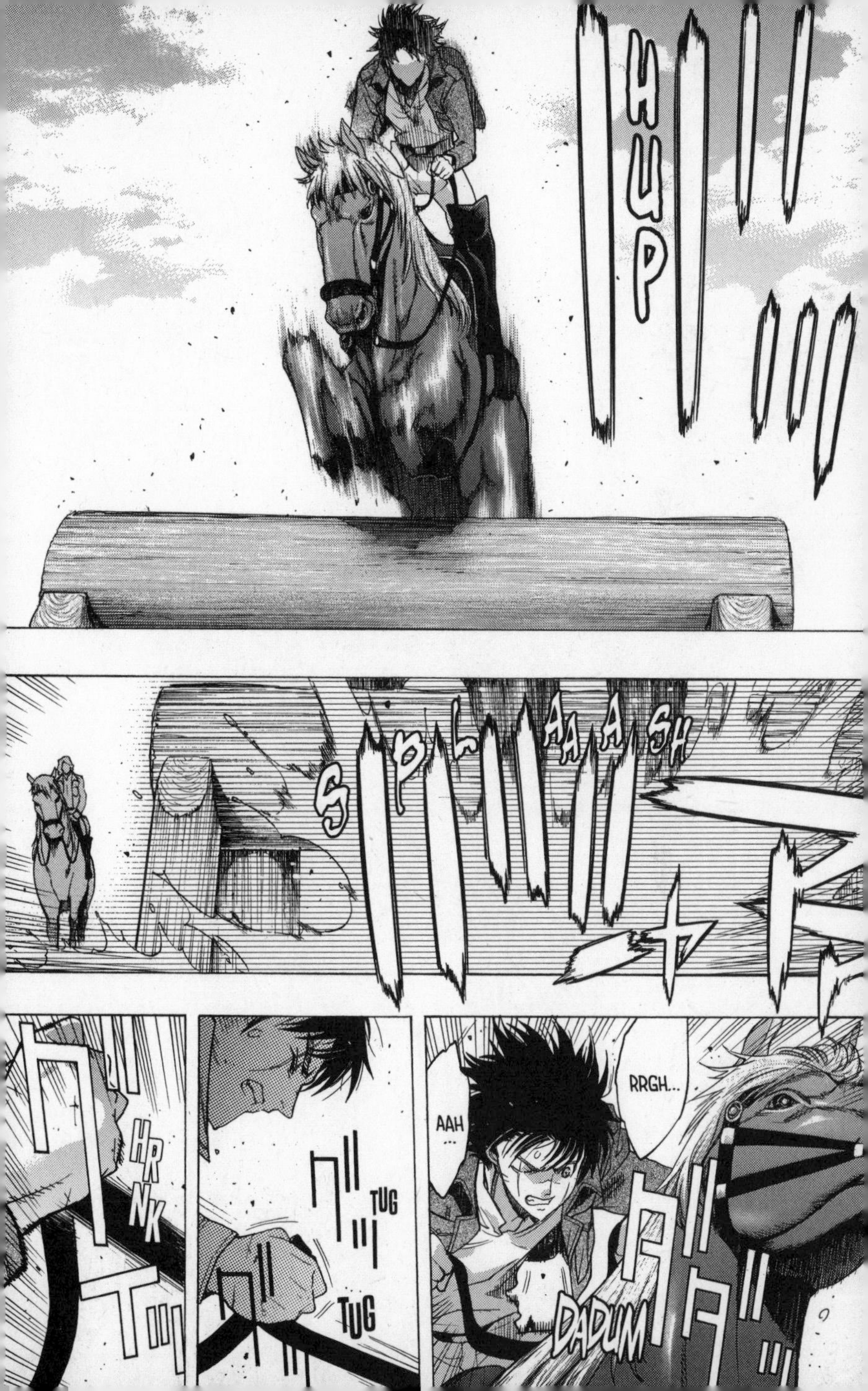
HUP
SPLAAASH
RRGH...
AAH...
DADUM
TUG
TUG
HRNK

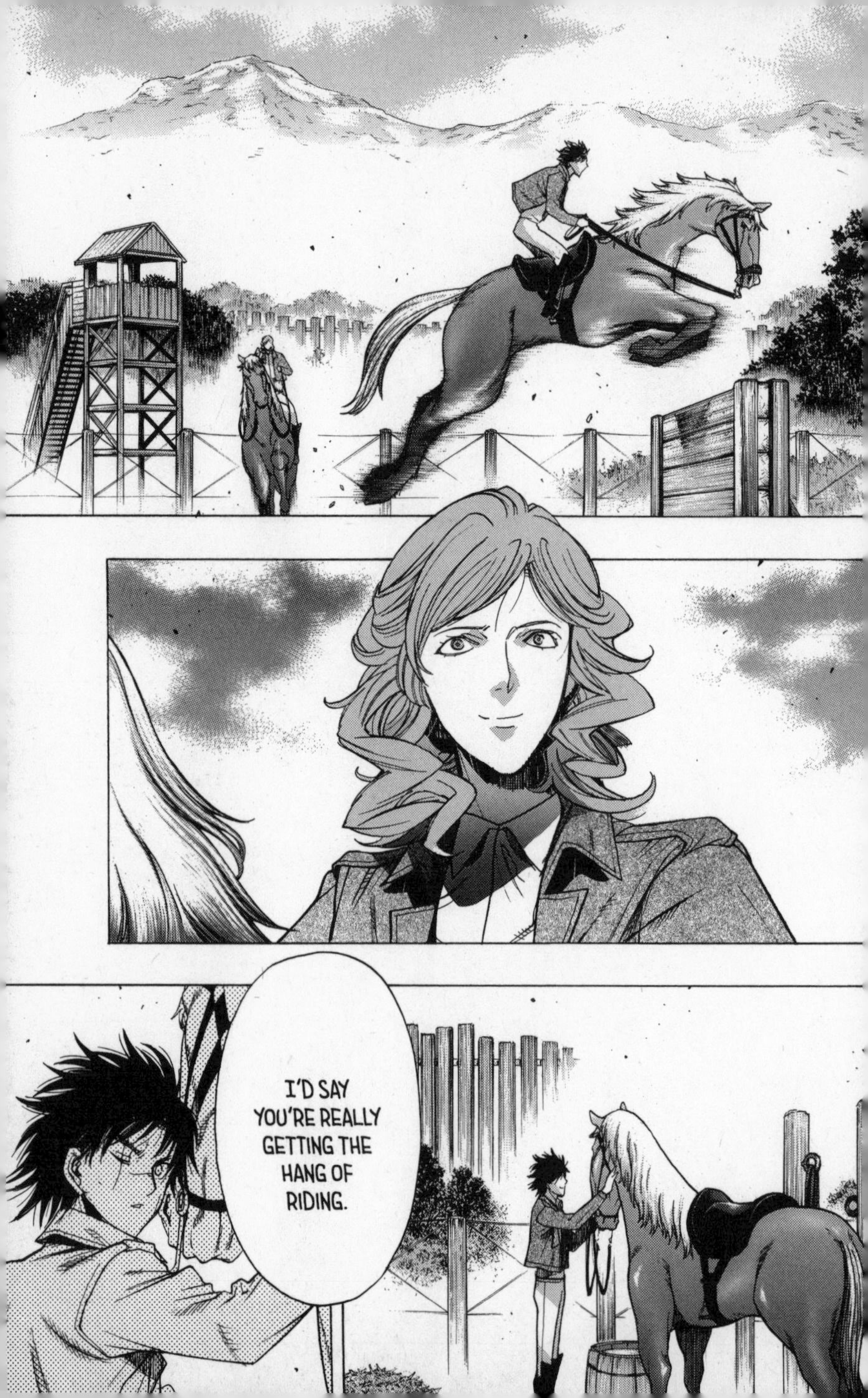
I'D SAY YOU'RE REALLY GETTING THE HANG OF RIDING.

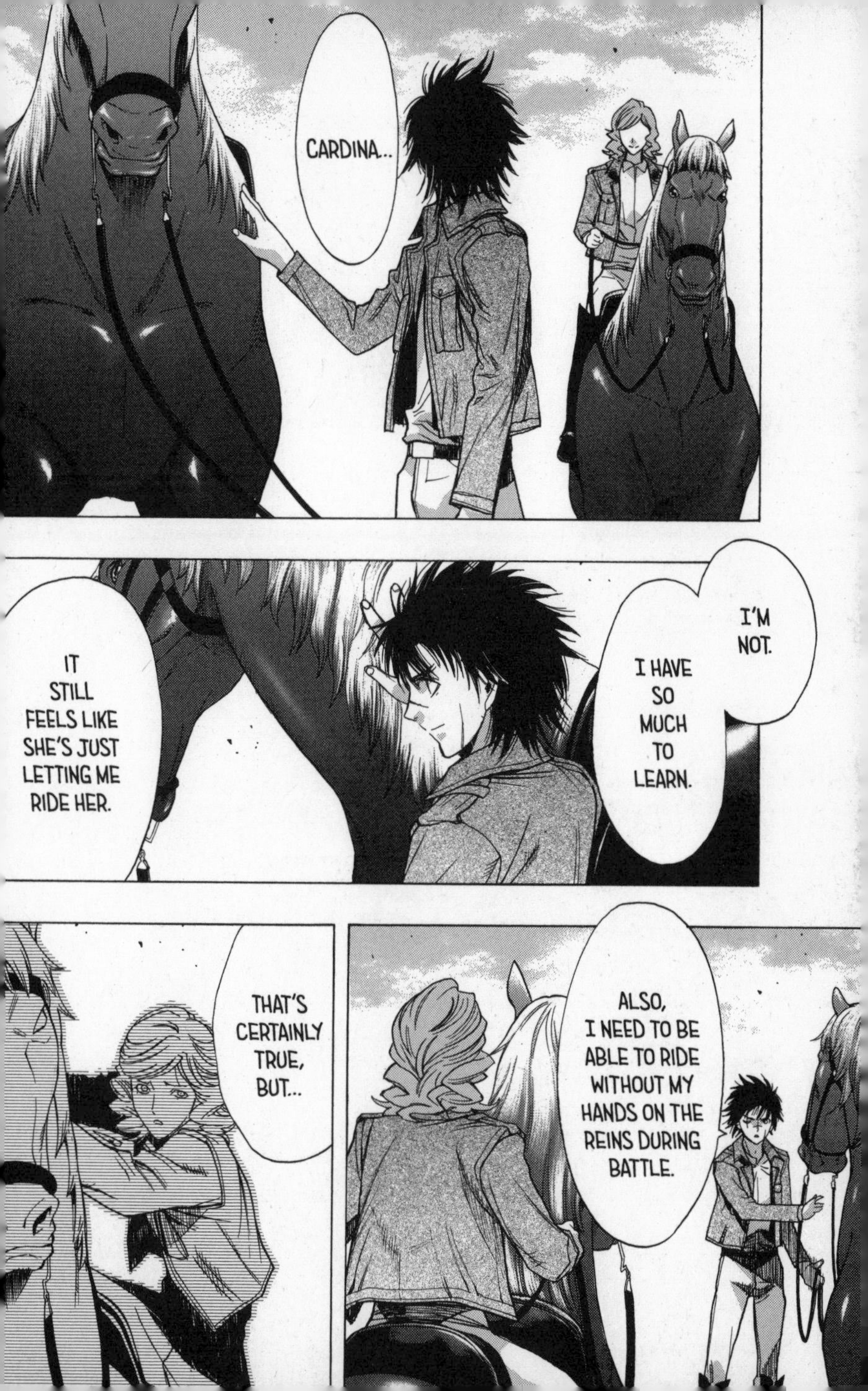
CARDINA...
I'M NOT.
I HAVE SO MUCH TO LEARN.
IT STILL FEELS LIKE SHE'S JUST LETTING ME RIDE HER.
ALSO, I NEED TO BE ABLE TO RIDE WITHOUT MY HANDS ON THE REINS DURING BATTLE.
THAT'S CERTAINLY TRUE, BUT...

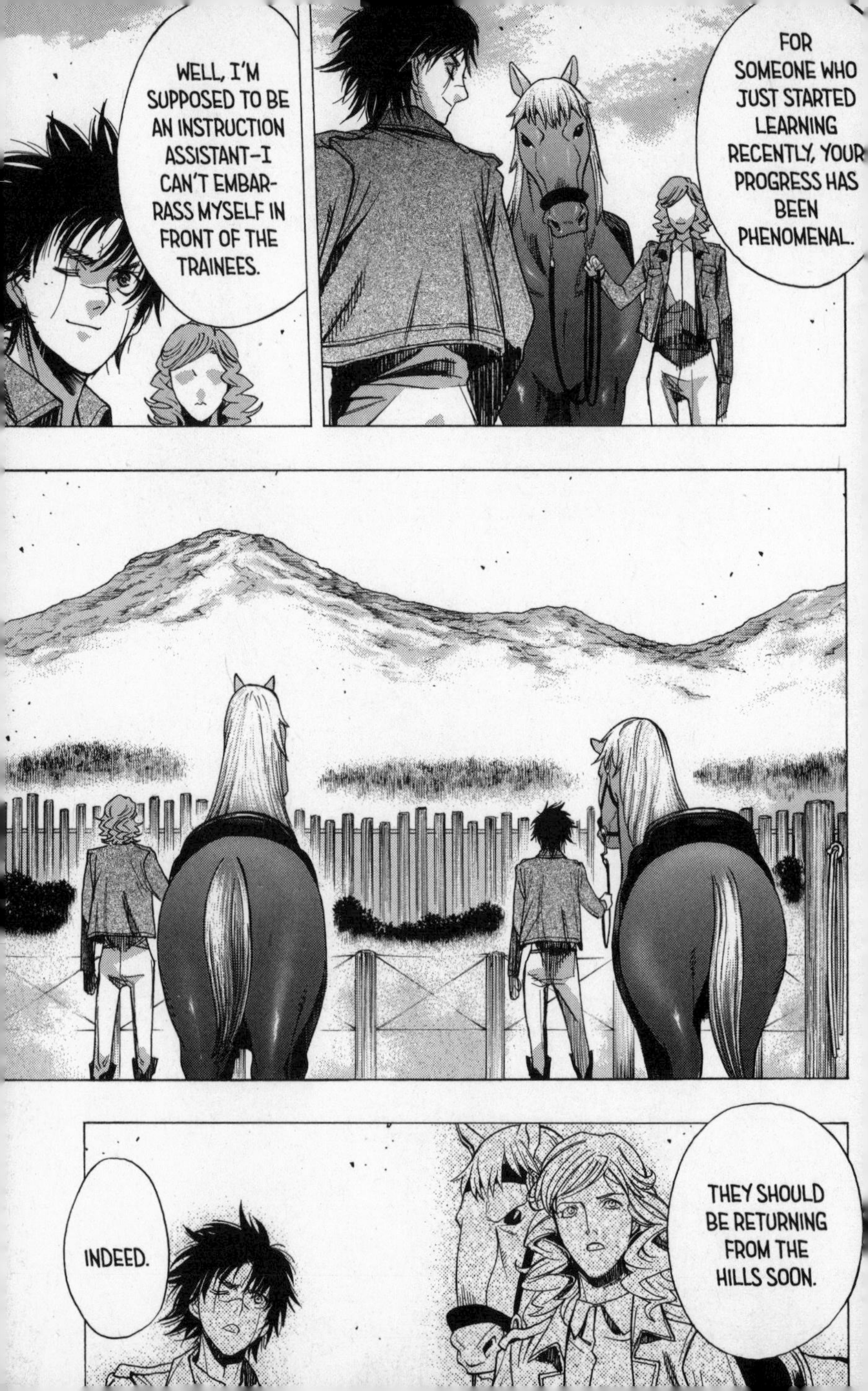
FOR SOMEONE WHO JUST STARTED LEARNING RECENTLY, YOUR PROGRESS HAS BEEN PHENOMENAL.
WELL, I'M SUPPOSED TO BE AN INSTRUCTION ASSISTANT—I CAN'T EMBARRASS MYSELF IN FRONT OF THE TRAINEES.
THEY SHOULD BE RETURNING FROM THE HILLS SOON.
INDEED.

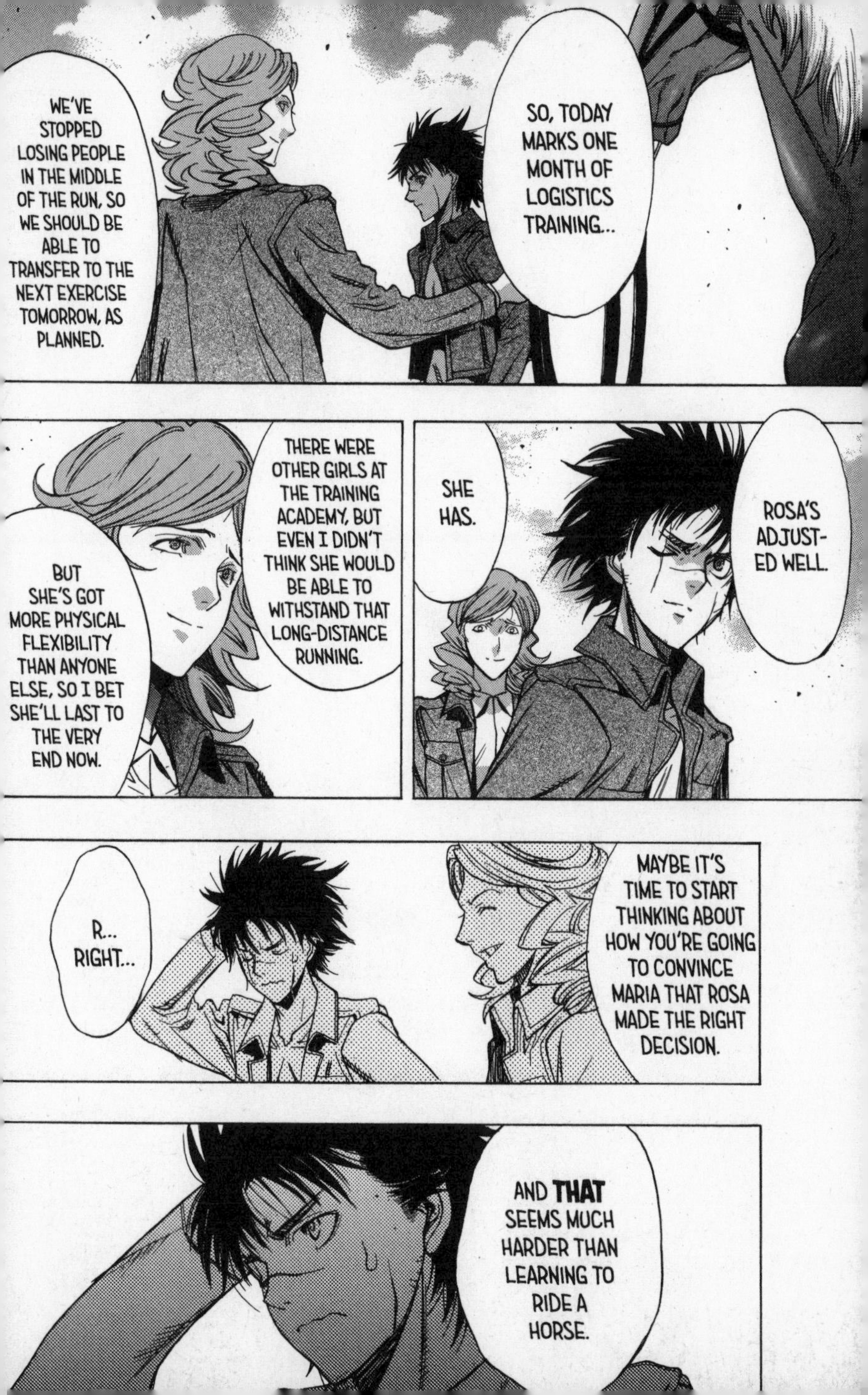
SO, TODAY MARKS ONE MONTH OF LOGISTICS TRAINING...
WE'VE STOPPED LOSING PEOPLE IN THE MIDDLE OF THE RUN, SO WE SHOULD BE ABLE TO TRANSFER TO THE NEXT EXERCISE TOMORROW, AS PLANNED.
ROSA'S ADJUST-ED WELL.
SHE HAS.
THERE WERE OTHER GIRLS AT THE TRAINING ACADEMY, BUT EVEN I DIDN'T THINK SHE WOULD BE ABLE TO WITHSTAND THAT LONG-DISTANCE RUNNING.
BUT SHE'S GOT MORE PHYSICAL FLEXIBILITY THAN ANYONE ELSE, SO I BET SHE'LL LAST TO THE VERY END NOW.
MAYBE IT'S TIME TO START THINKING ABOUT HOW YOU'RE GOING TO CONVINCE MARIA THAT ROSA MADE THE RIGHT DECISION.
R... RIGHT...
AND **THAT** SEEMS MUCH HARDER THAN LEARNING TO RIDE A HORSE.

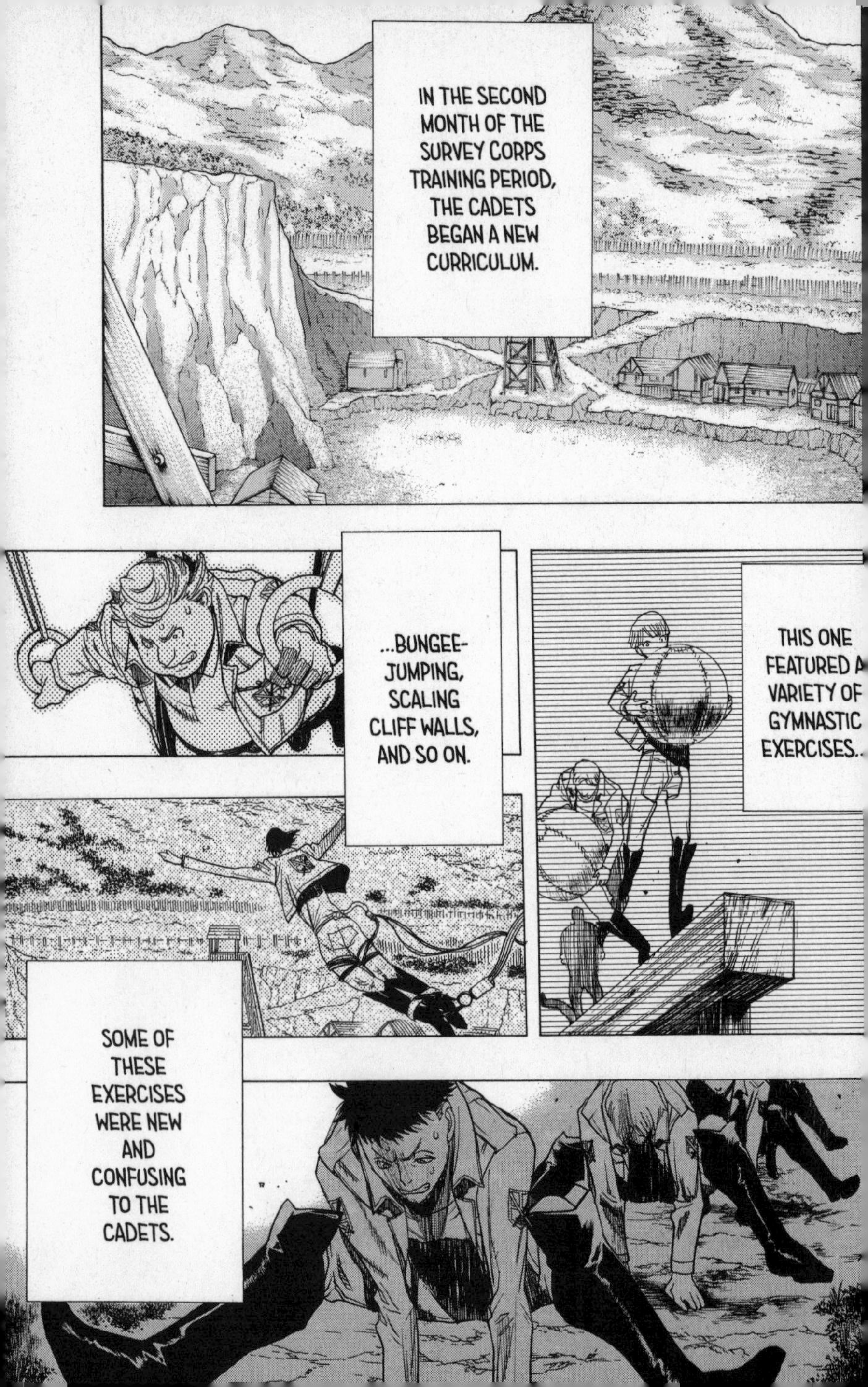
IN THE SECOND MONTH OF THE SURVEY CORPS TRAINING PERIOD, THE CADETS BEGAN A NEW CURRICULUM.
THIS ONE FEATURED A VARIETY OF GYMNASTIC EXERCISES...
...BUNGEE-JUMPING, SCALING CLIFF WALLS, AND SO ON.
SOME OF THESE EXERCISES WERE NEW AND CONFUSING TO THE CADETS.

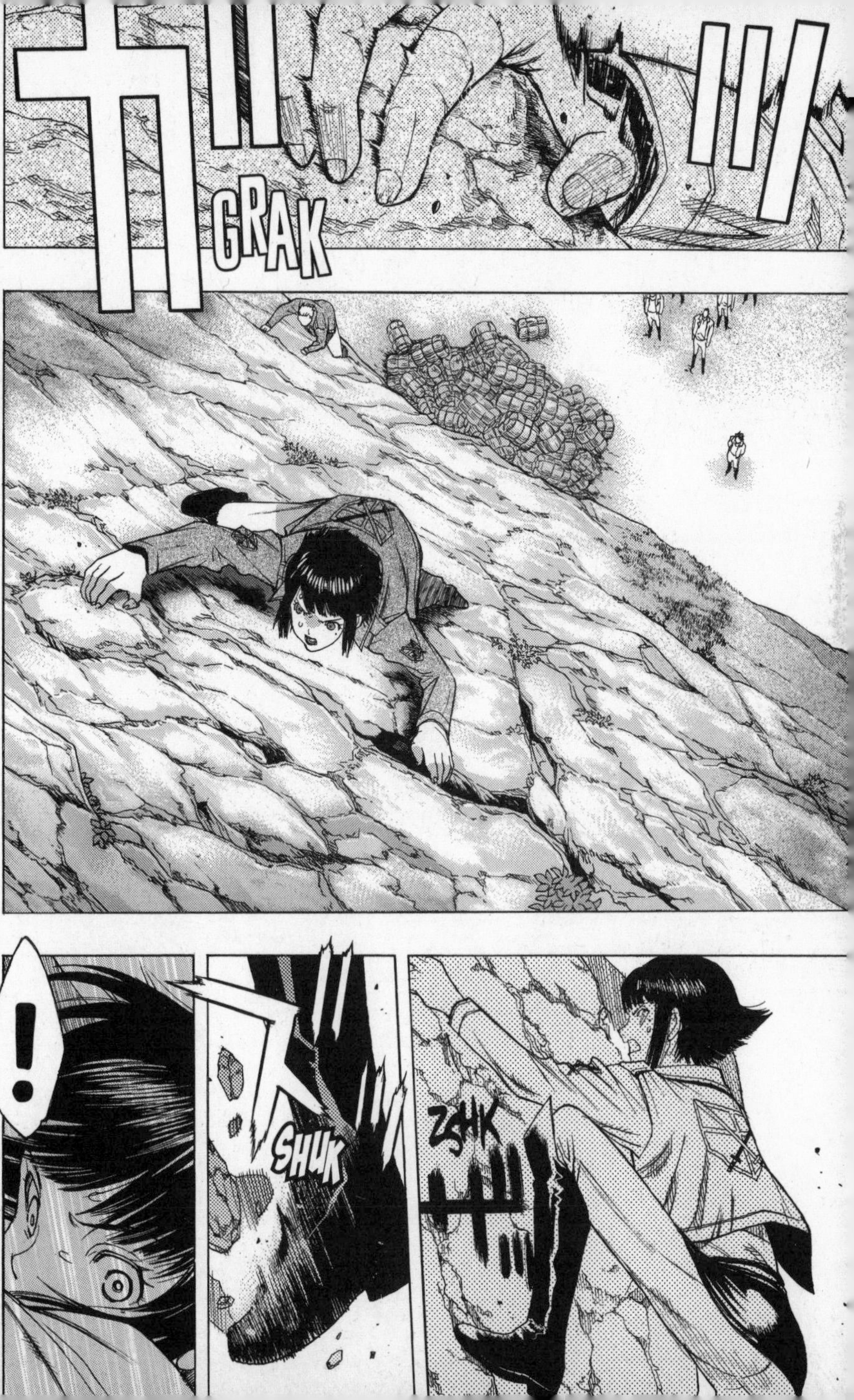
GRAK
ZSHK
SHUK
!

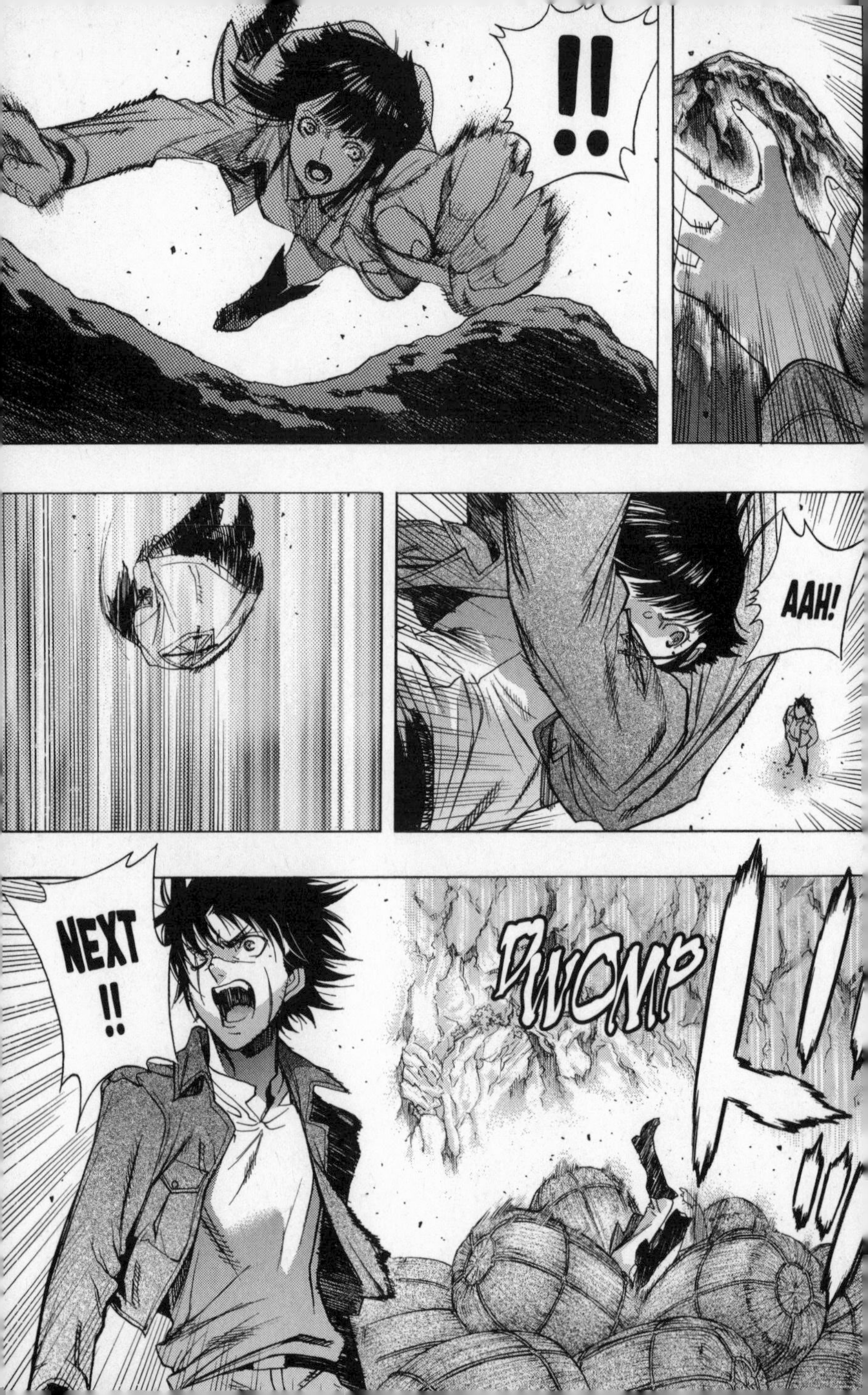
!!
AAH!
DWOMP
NEXT !!

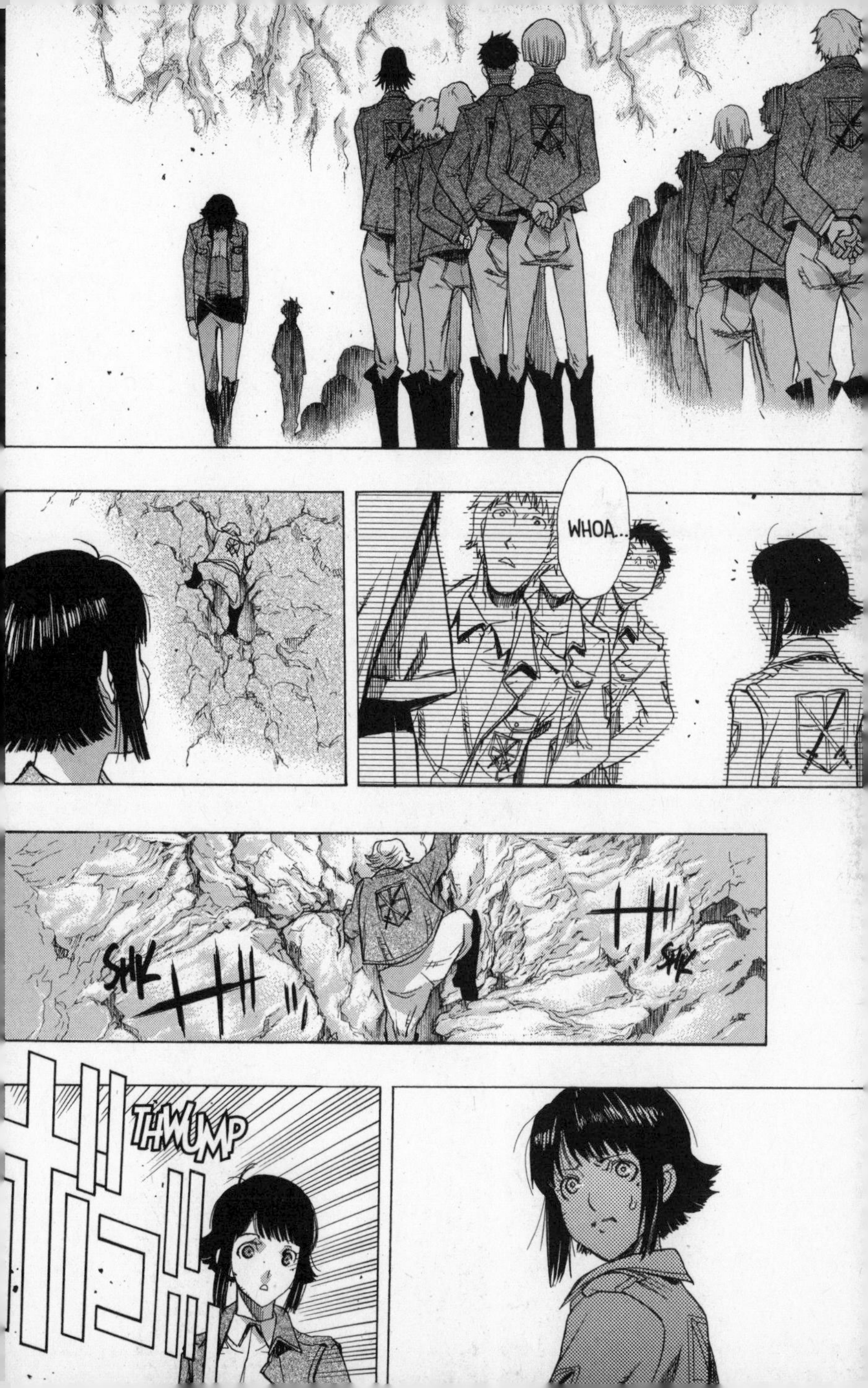
WHOA...
SHK
SHK
THWUMP

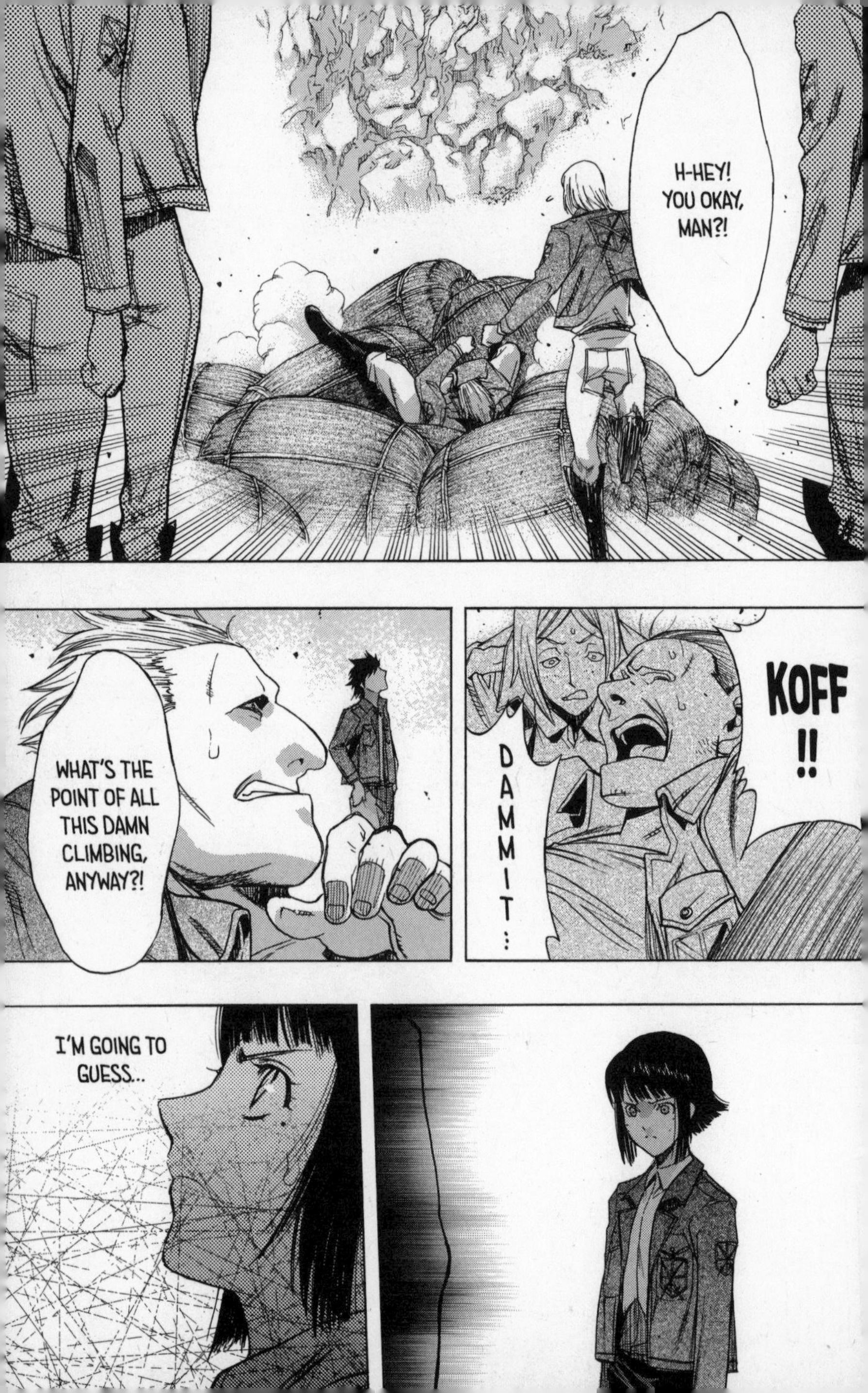
H-HEY! YOU OKAY, MAN?!
KOFF !!
DAMMIT...
WHAT'S THE POINT OF ALL THIS DAMN CLIMBING, ANYWAY?!
I'M GOING TO GUESS...

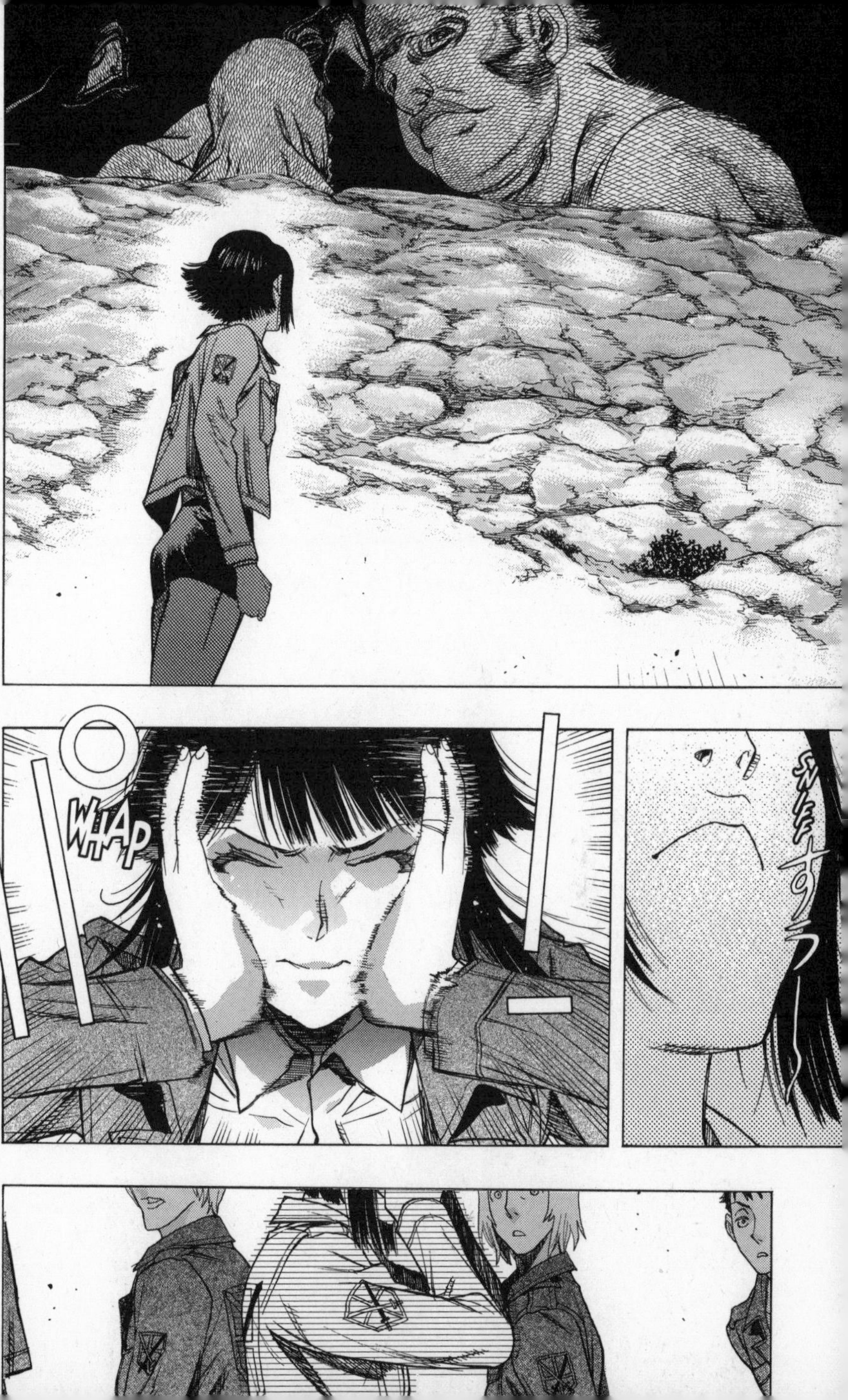
SNIFF すう
WHAP

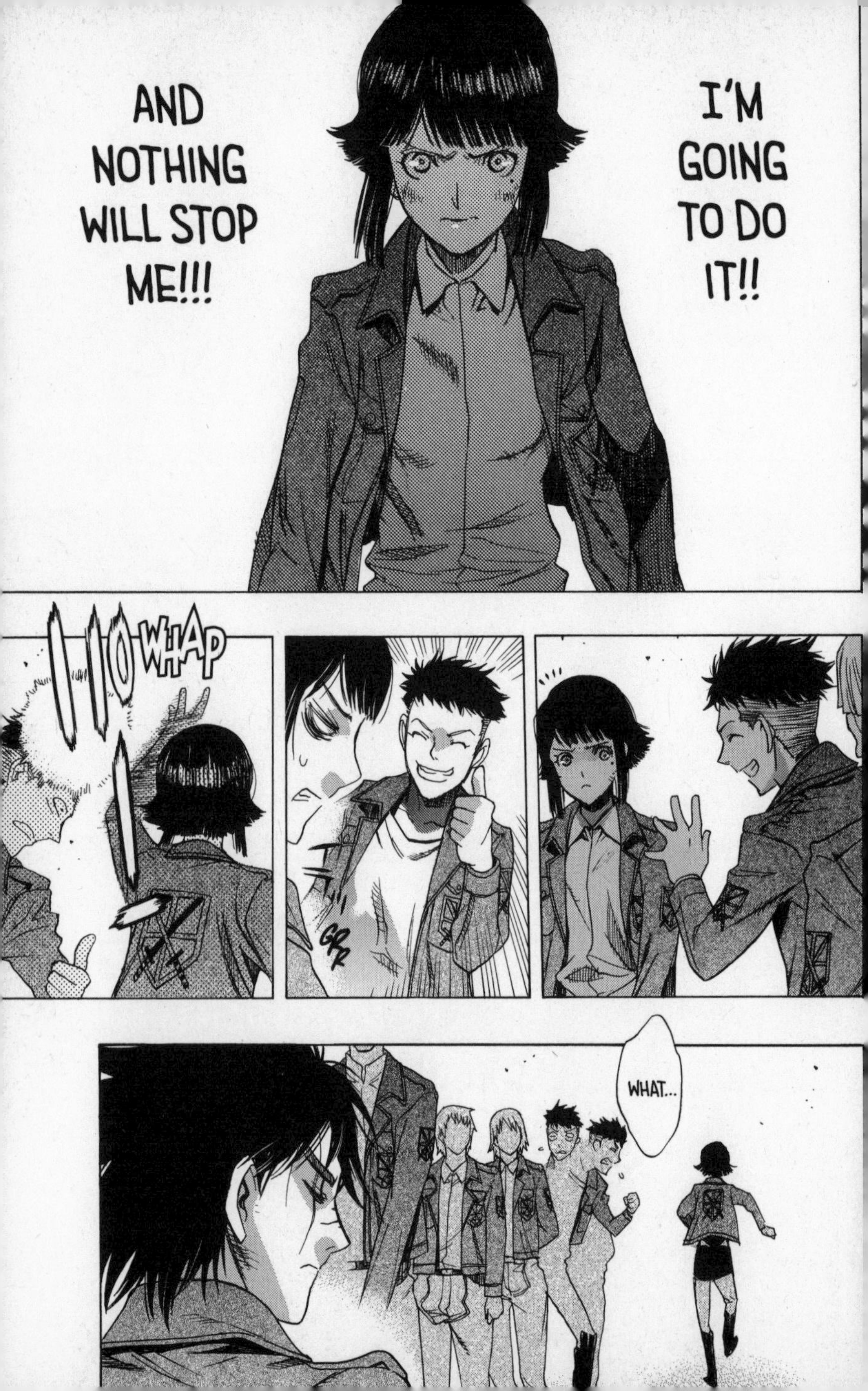
I'M GOING TO DO IT!!
AND NOTHING WILL STOP ME!!!
GRR
WHAP
WHAT...

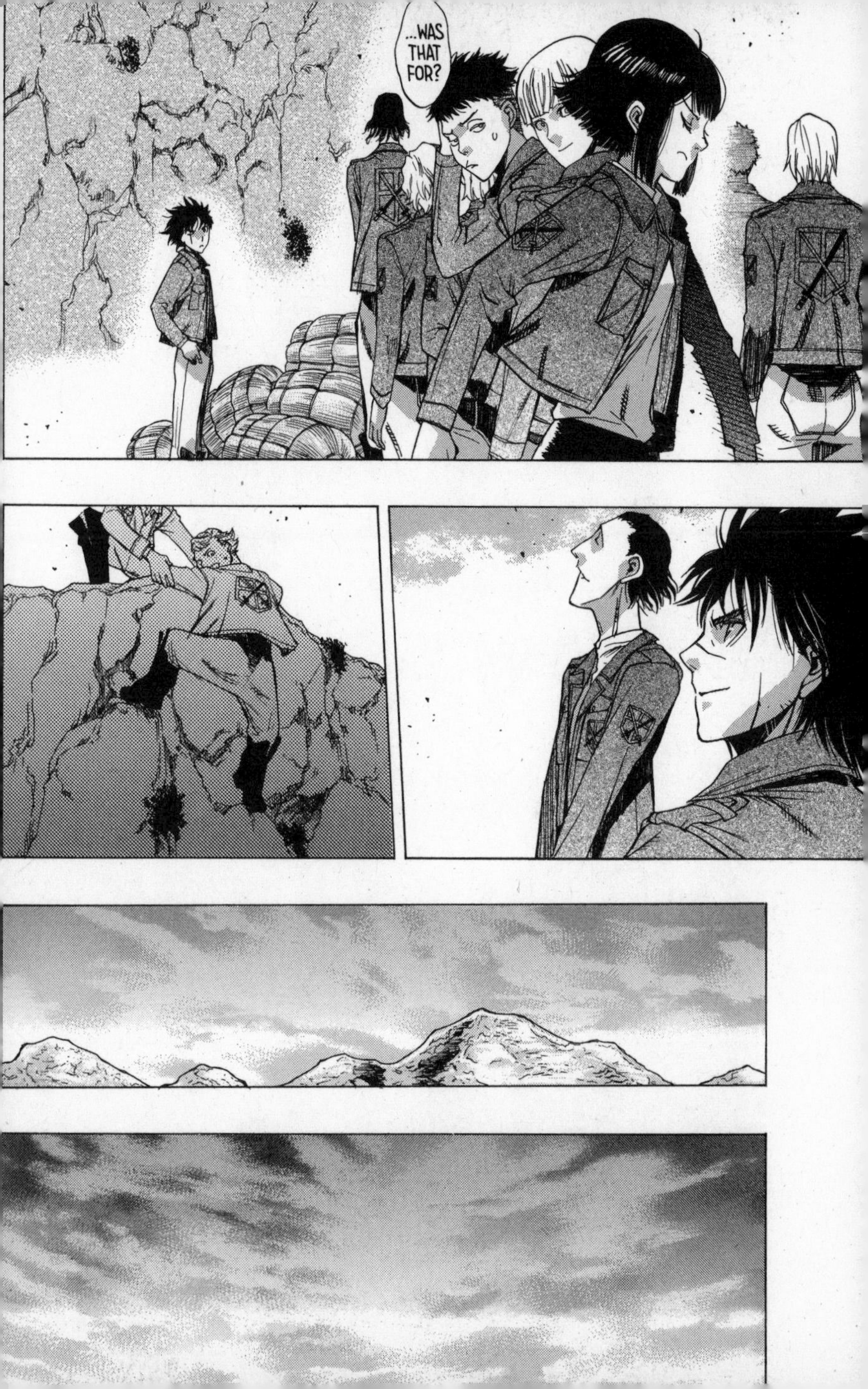
...WAS THAT FOR?

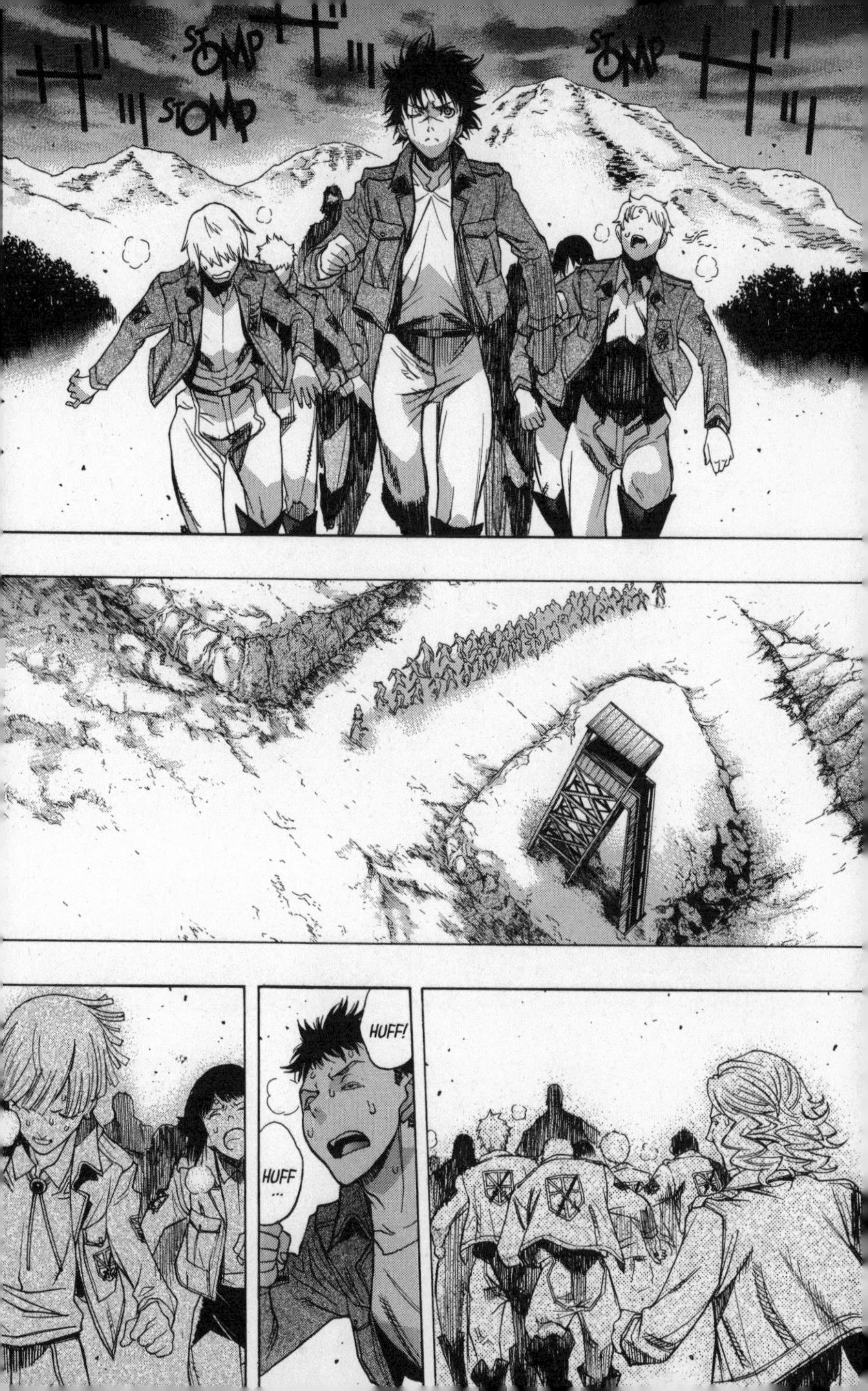
STOMP
STOMP
STOMP
HUFF!
HUFF ...

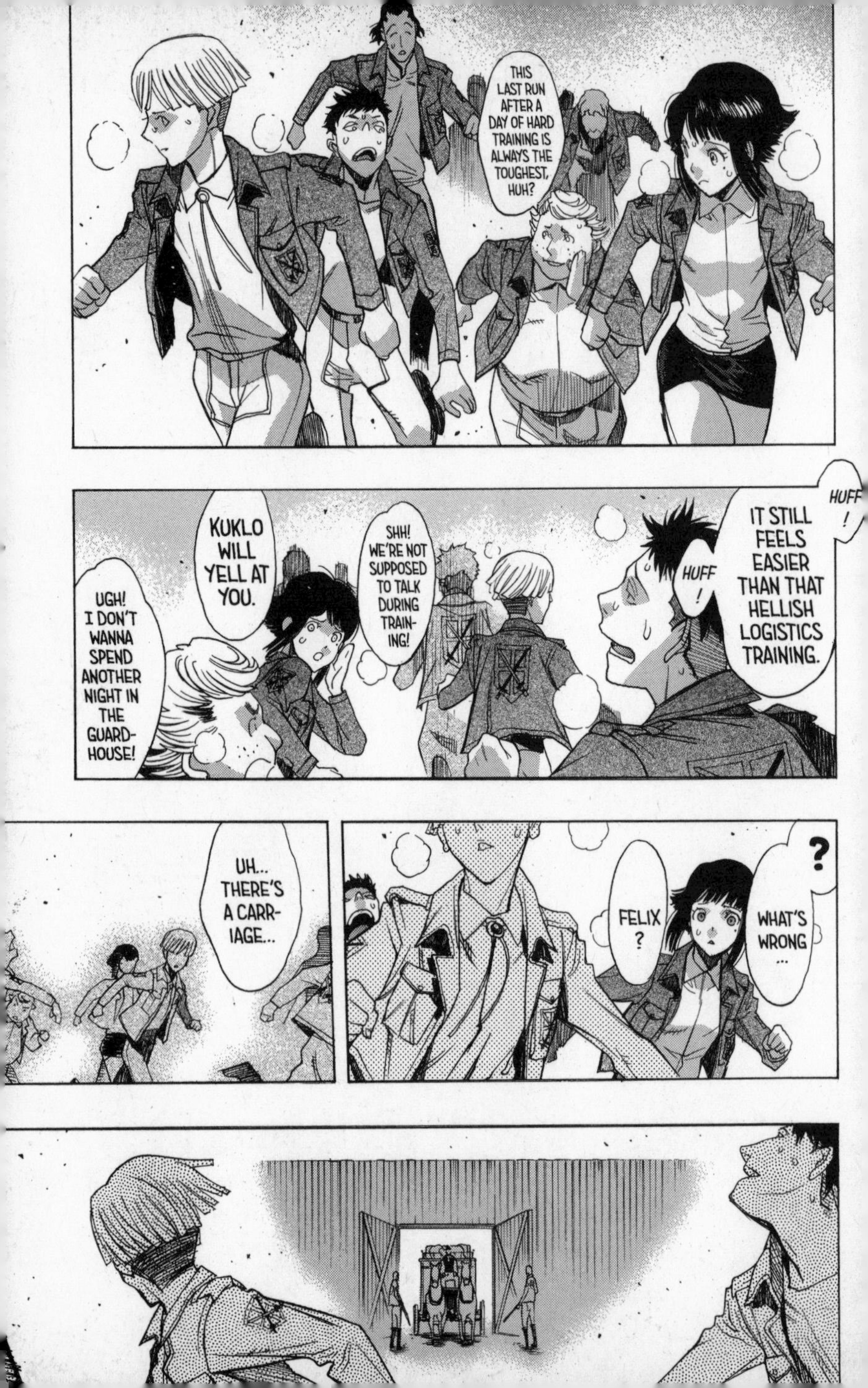
THIS LAST RUN AFTER A DAY OF HARD TRAINING IS ALWAYS THE TOUGHEST, HUH?
HUFF!
IT STILL FEELS EASIER THAN THAT HELLISH LOGISTICS TRAINING.
HUFF!
SHH! WE'RE NOT SUPPOSED TO TALK DURING TRAIN-ING!
KUKLO WILL YELL AT YOU.
UGH! I DON'T WANNA SPEND ANOTHER NIGHT IN THE GUARD-HOUSE!
?
WHAT'S WRONG ...
FELIX ?
UH... THERE'S A CARR-IAGE...

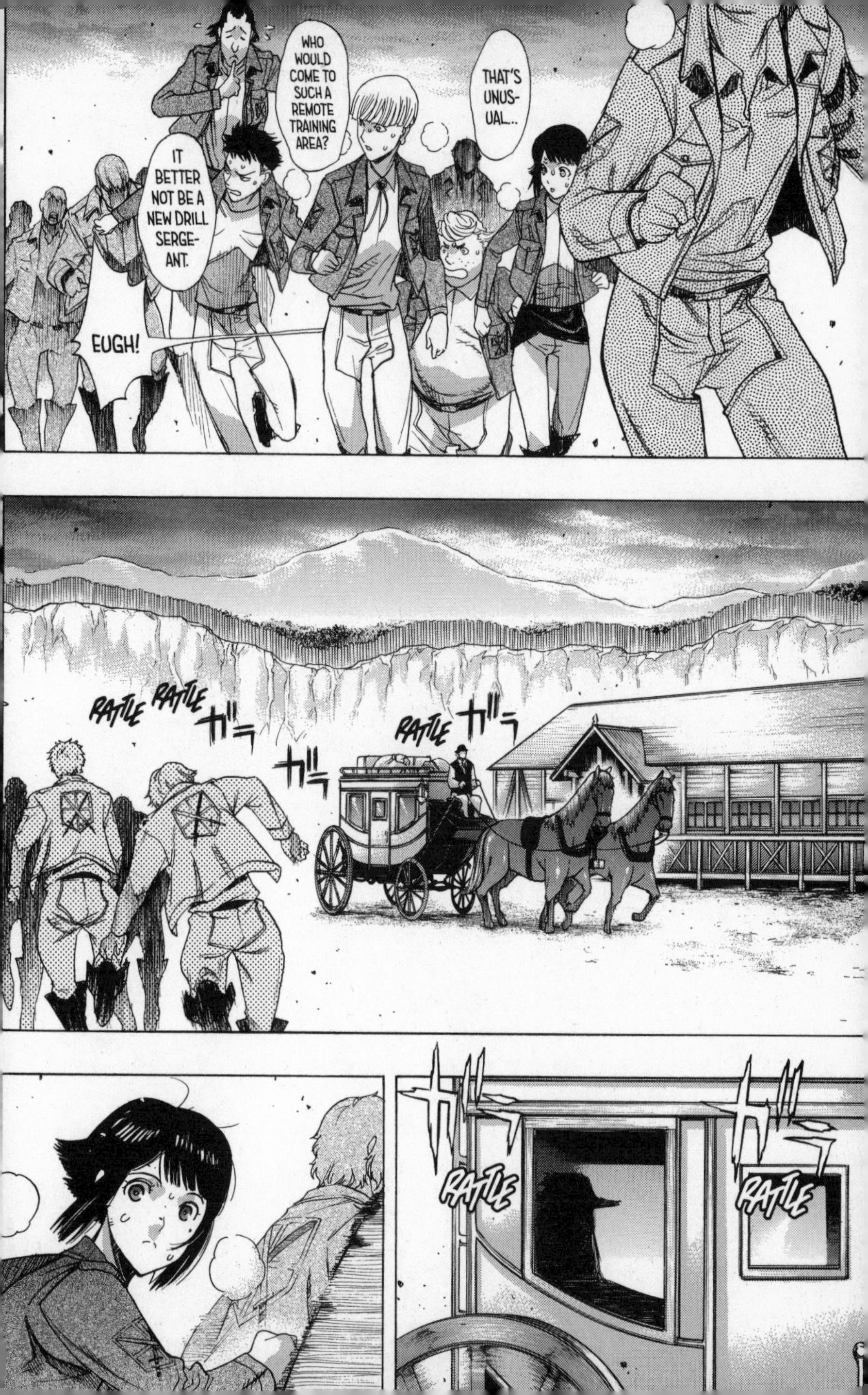
THAT'S UNUSUAL...
WHO WOULD COME TO SUCH A REMOTE TRAINING AREA?
IT BETTER NOT BE A NEW DRILL SERGEANT.
EUGH!
RATTLE
ガラ
ガラ
RATTLE RATTLE
ガラ
ガラ
RATTLE
ガラ
RATTLE

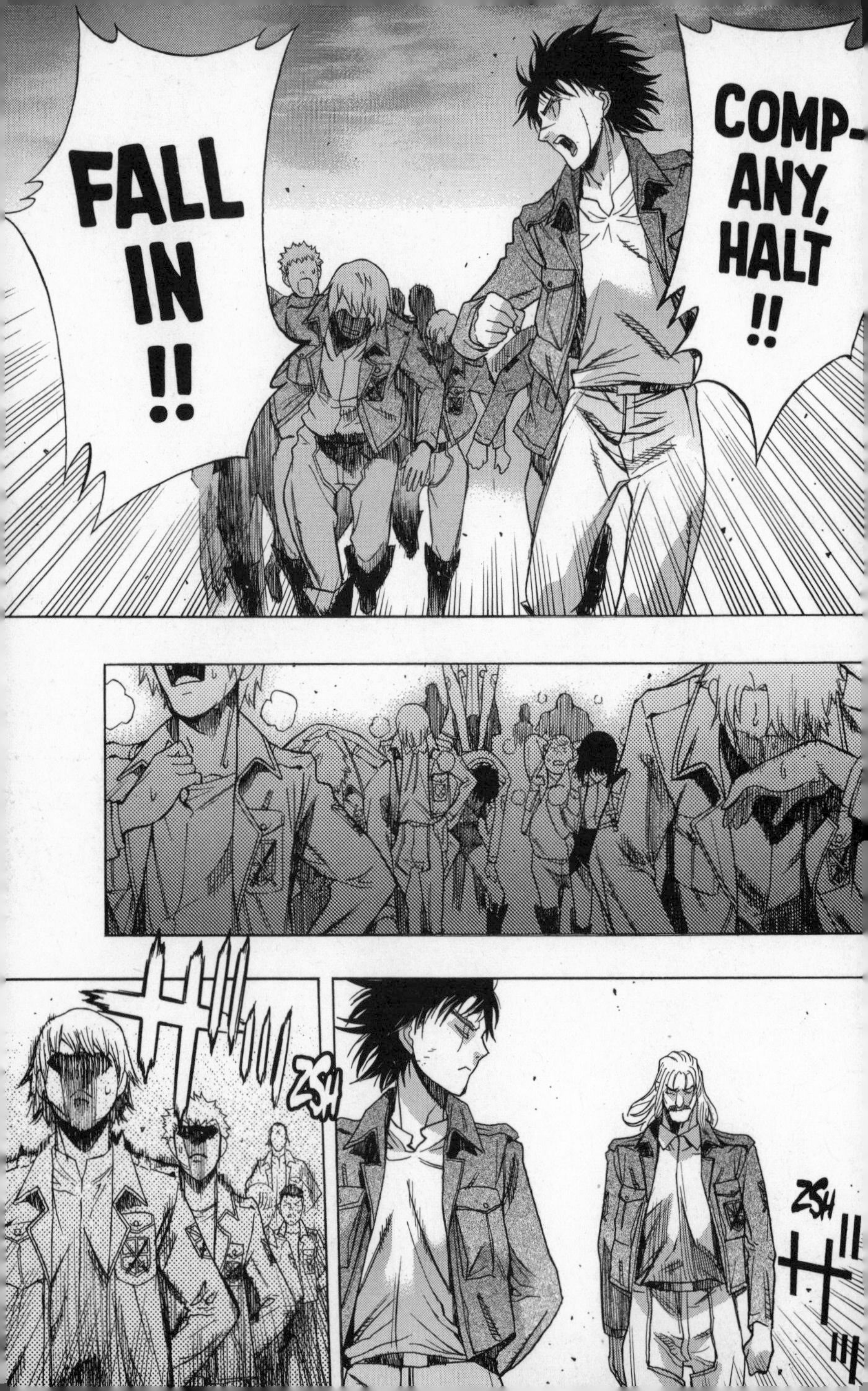
COMP-ANY, HALT!!
FALL IN!!
ZSH
ZSH

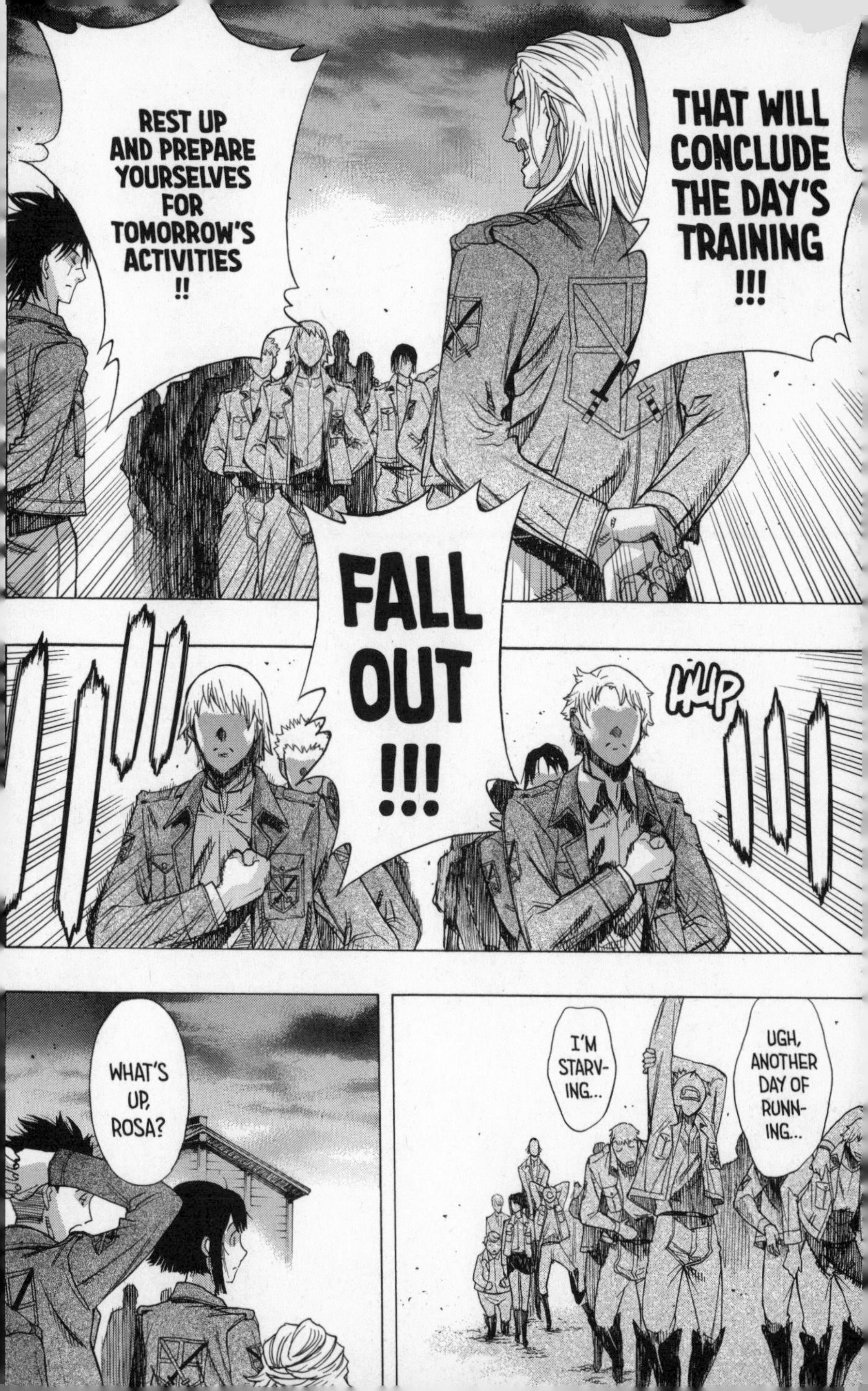
THAT WILL CONCLUDE THE DAY'S TRAINING !!!
REST UP AND PREPARE YOURSELVES FOR TOMORROW'S ACTIVITIES !!
FALL OUT !!!
HUP
UGH, ANOTHER DAY OF RUNN-ING...
I'M STARV-ING...
WHAT'S UP, ROSA?

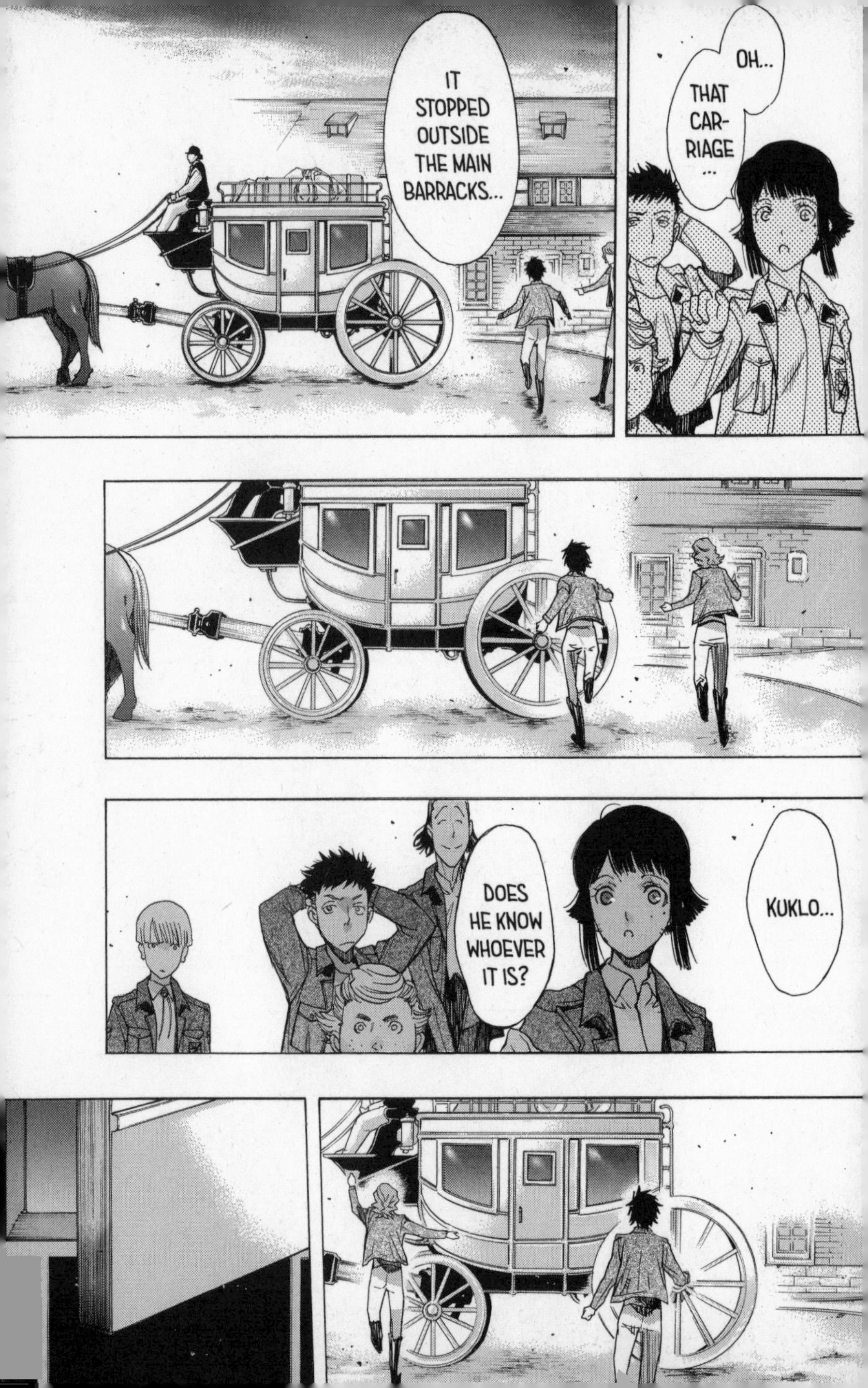
OH...
THAT CARRIAGE...
IT STOPPED OUTSIDE THE MAIN BARRACKS...
KUKLO...
DOES HE KNOW WHOEVER IT IS?

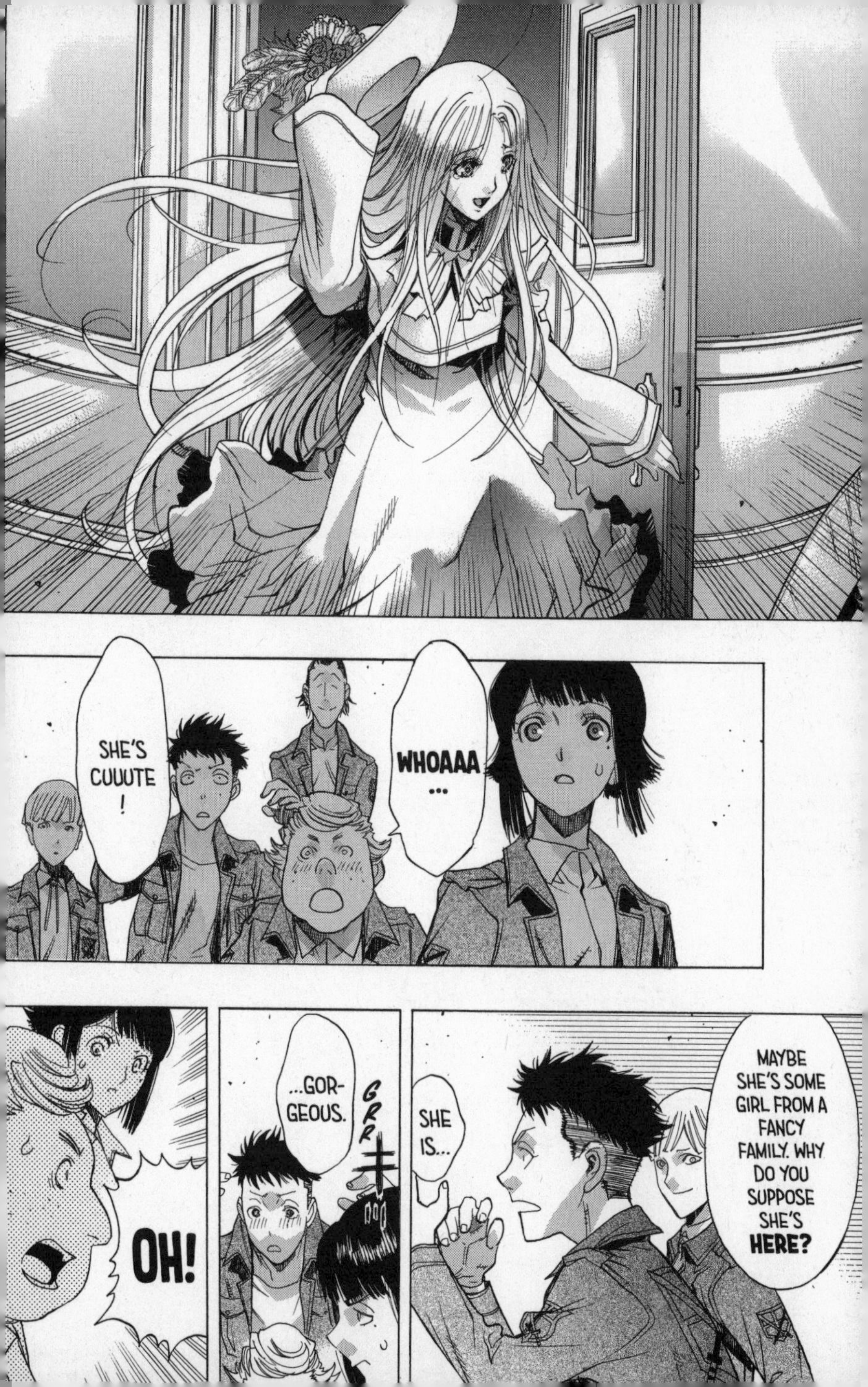
WHOAAA...
SHE'S CUUUTE!
MAYBE SHE'S SOME GIRL FROM A FANCY FAMILY. WHY DO YOU SUPPOSE SHE'S HERE?
SHE IS...
...GOR-GEOUS.
GRR
OH!

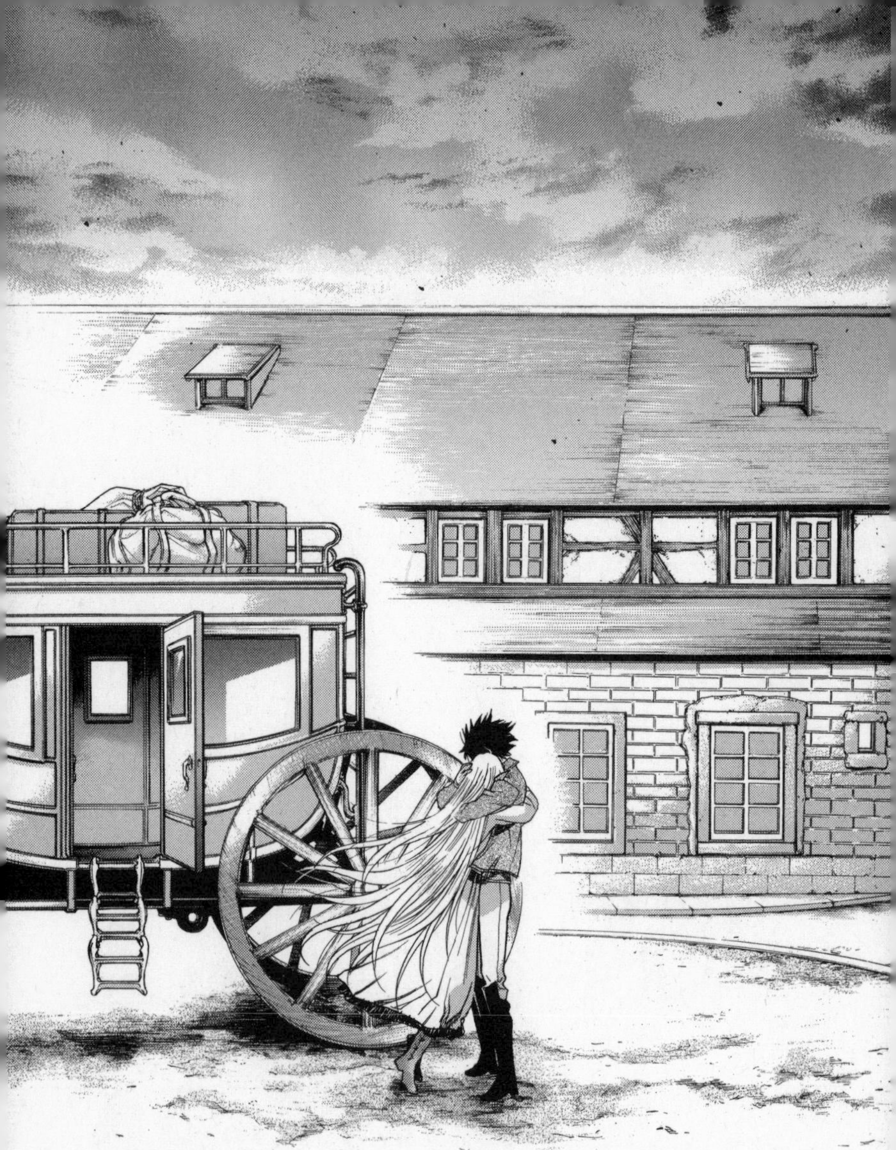

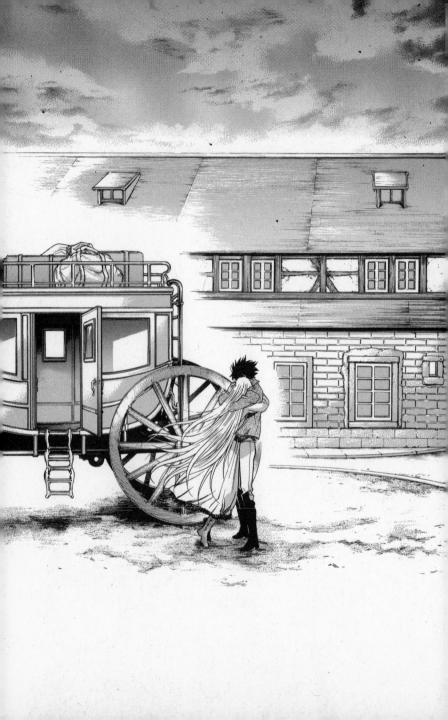

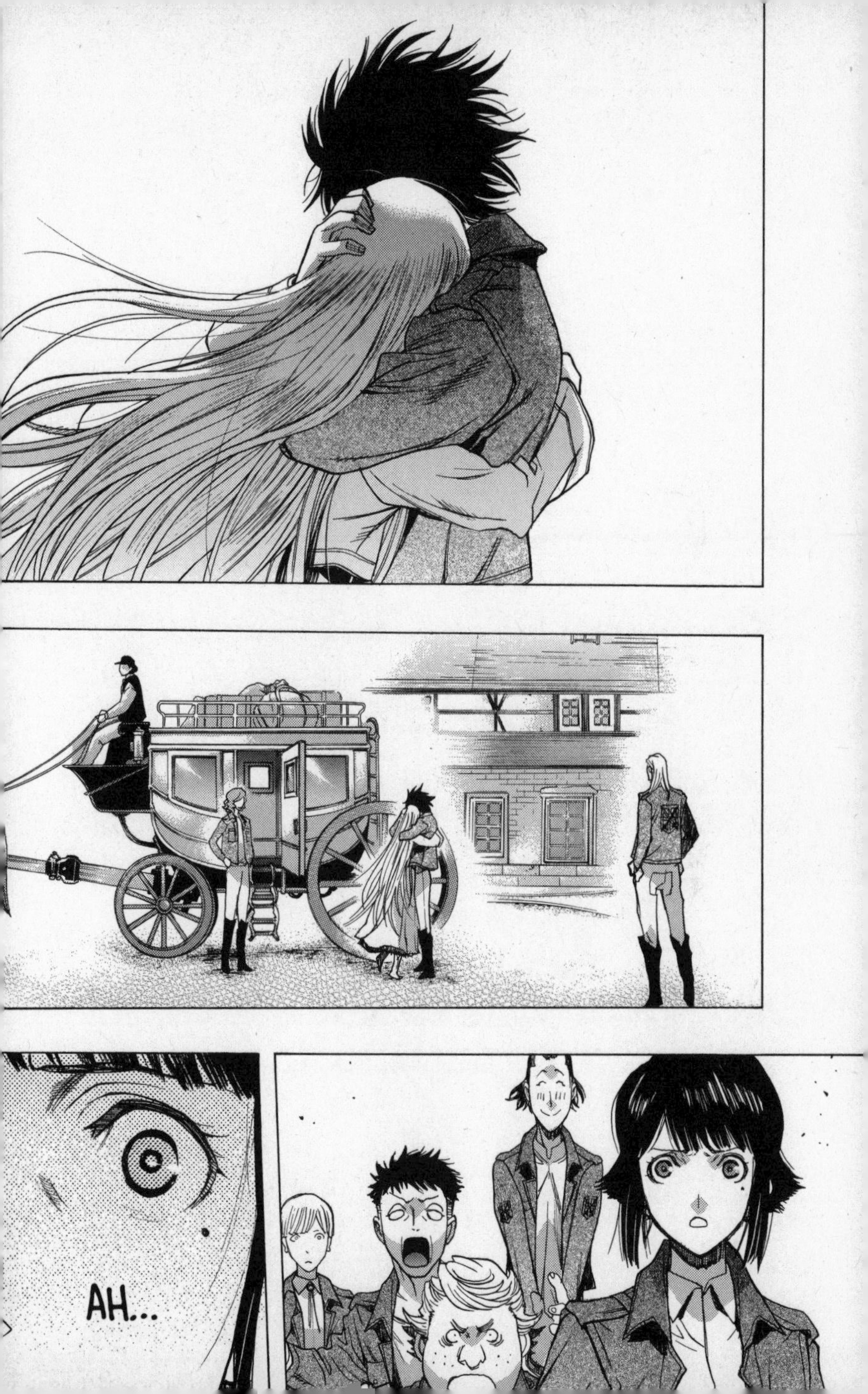
AH...

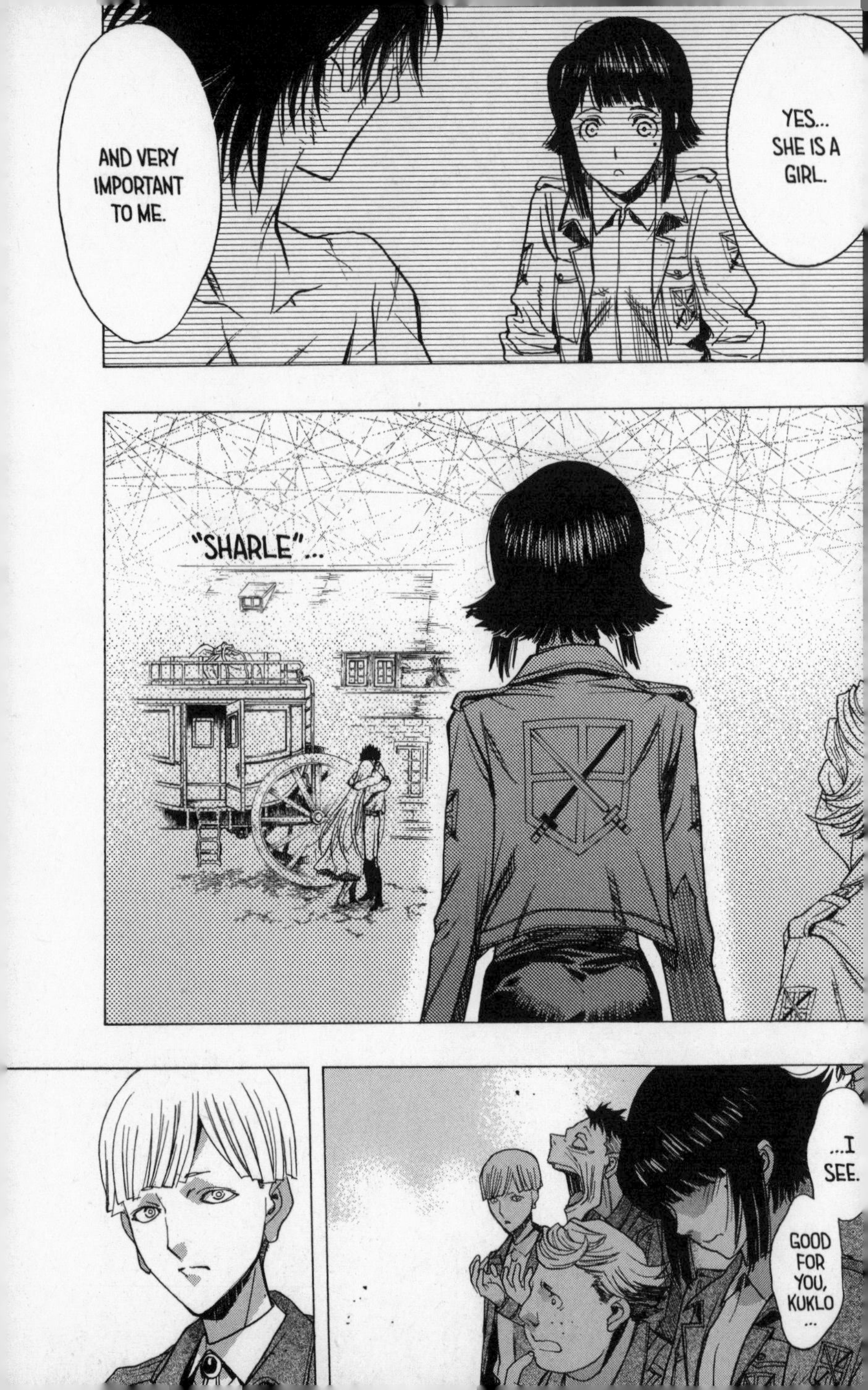
YES... SHE IS A GIRL.
AND VERY IMPORTANT TO ME.
"SHARLE"...
...I SEE.
GOOD FOR YOU, KUKLO ...

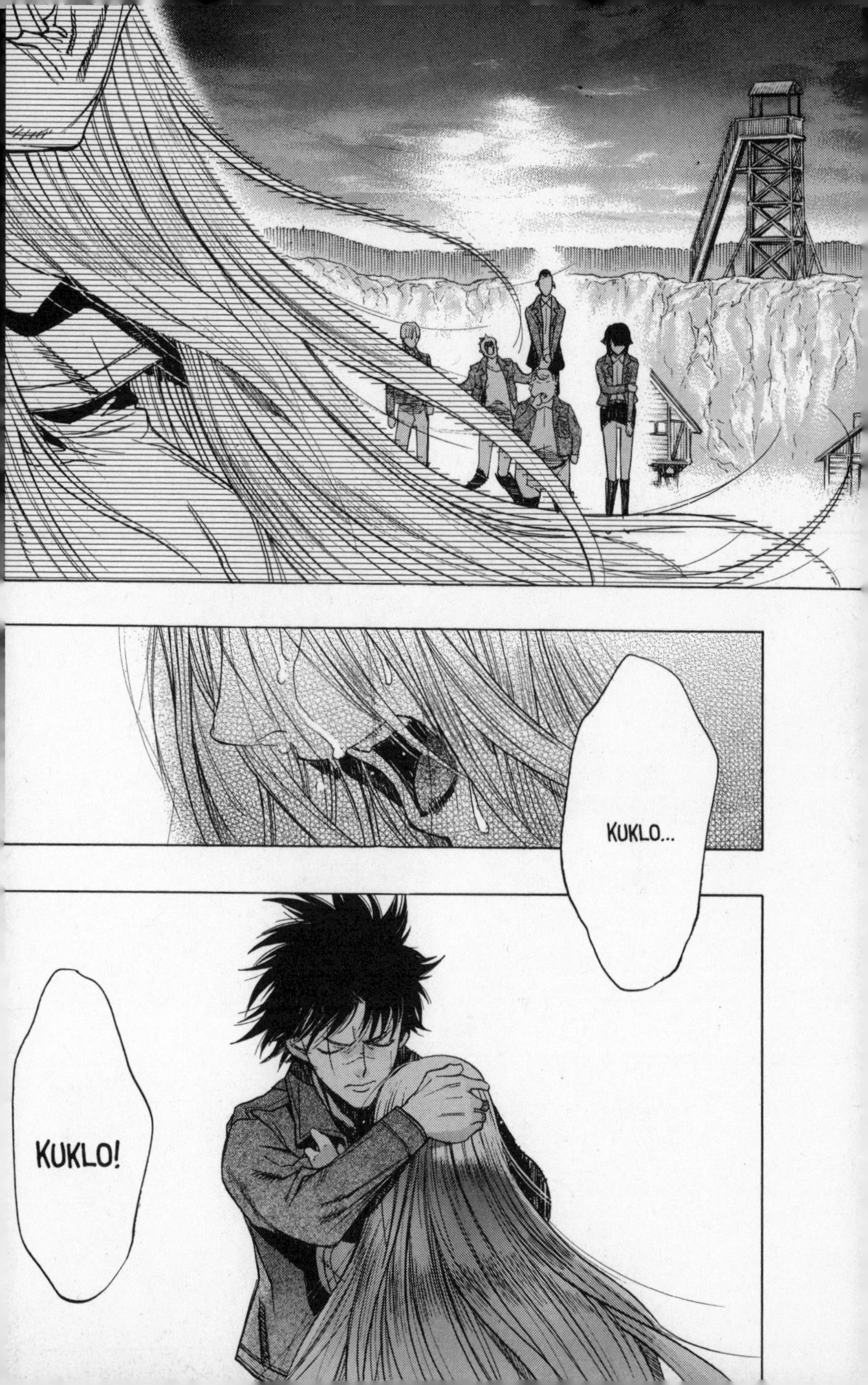
KUKLO...
KUKLO!

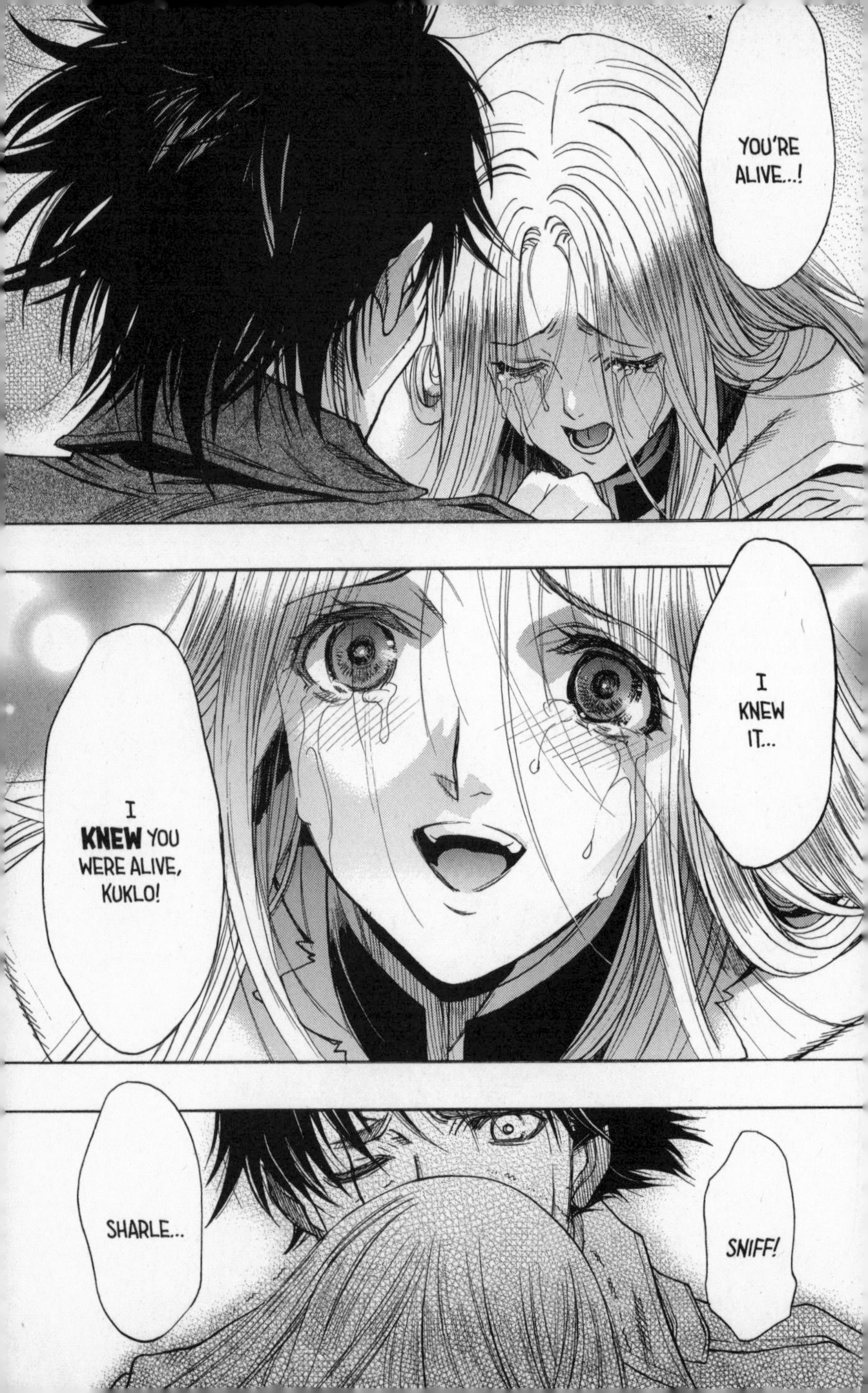
YOU'RE ALIVE...!
I KNEW IT...
I **KNEW** YOU WERE ALIVE, KUKLO!
SNIFF!
SHARLE...

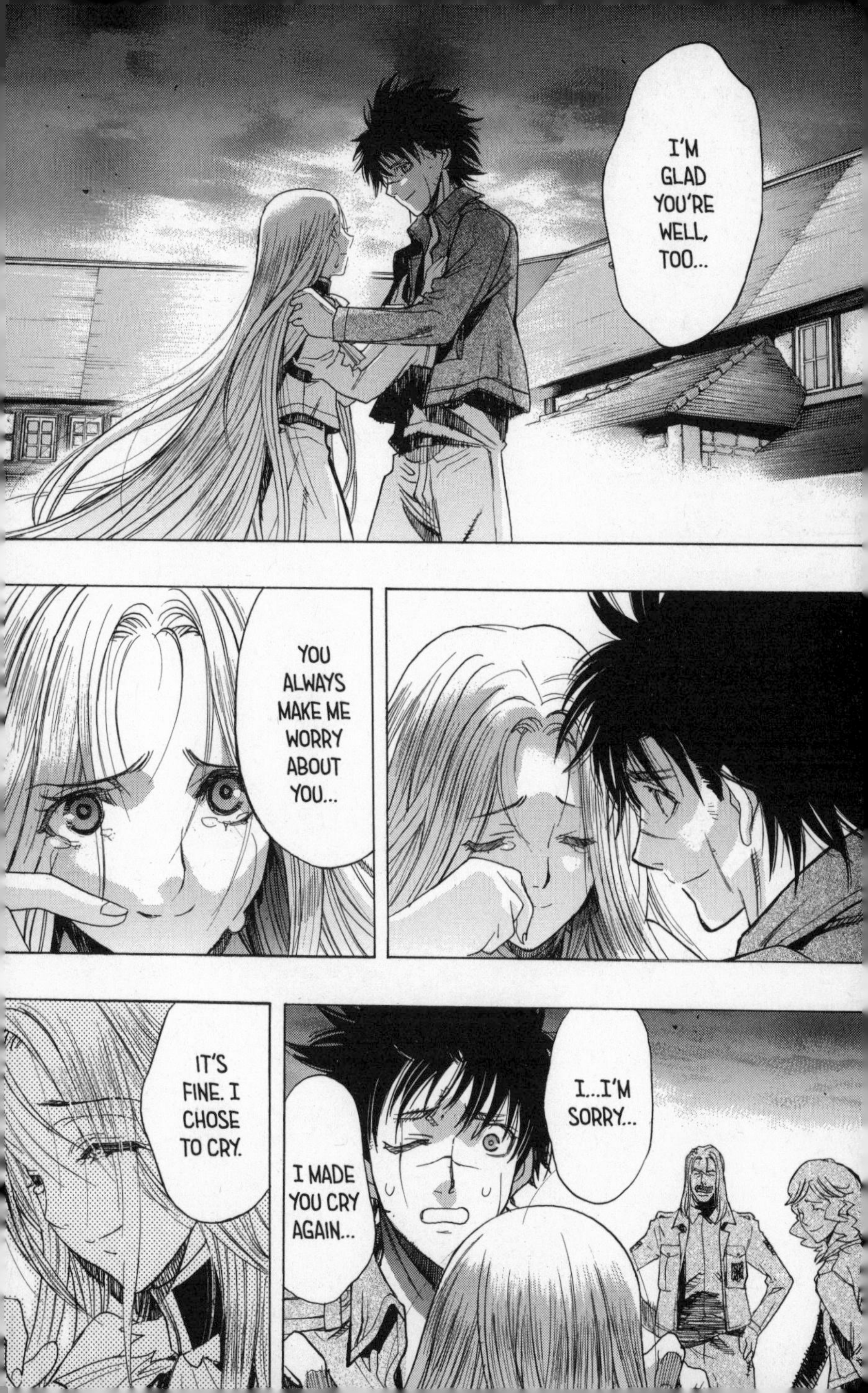
I'M GLAD YOU'RE WELL, TOO...
YOU ALWAYS MAKE ME WORRY ABOUT YOU...
I...I'M SORRY...
I MADE YOU CRY AGAIN...
IT'S FINE. I CHOSE TO CRY.

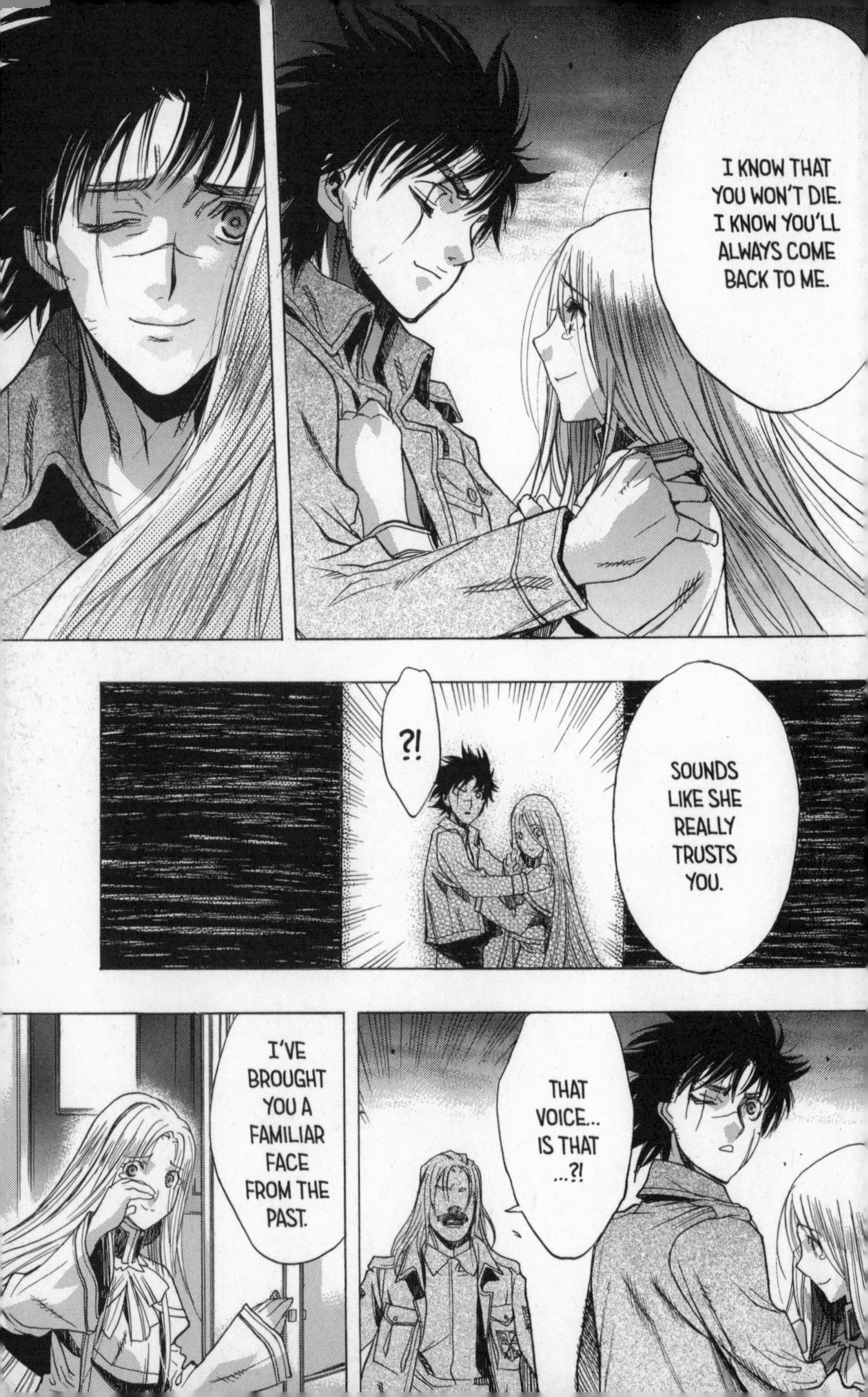
I KNOW THAT YOU WON'T DIE. I KNOW YOU'LL ALWAYS COME BACK TO ME.
SOUNDS LIKE SHE REALLY TRUSTS YOU.
?!
THAT VOICE... IS THAT ...?!
I'VE BROUGHT YOU A FAMILIAR FACE FROM THE PAST.

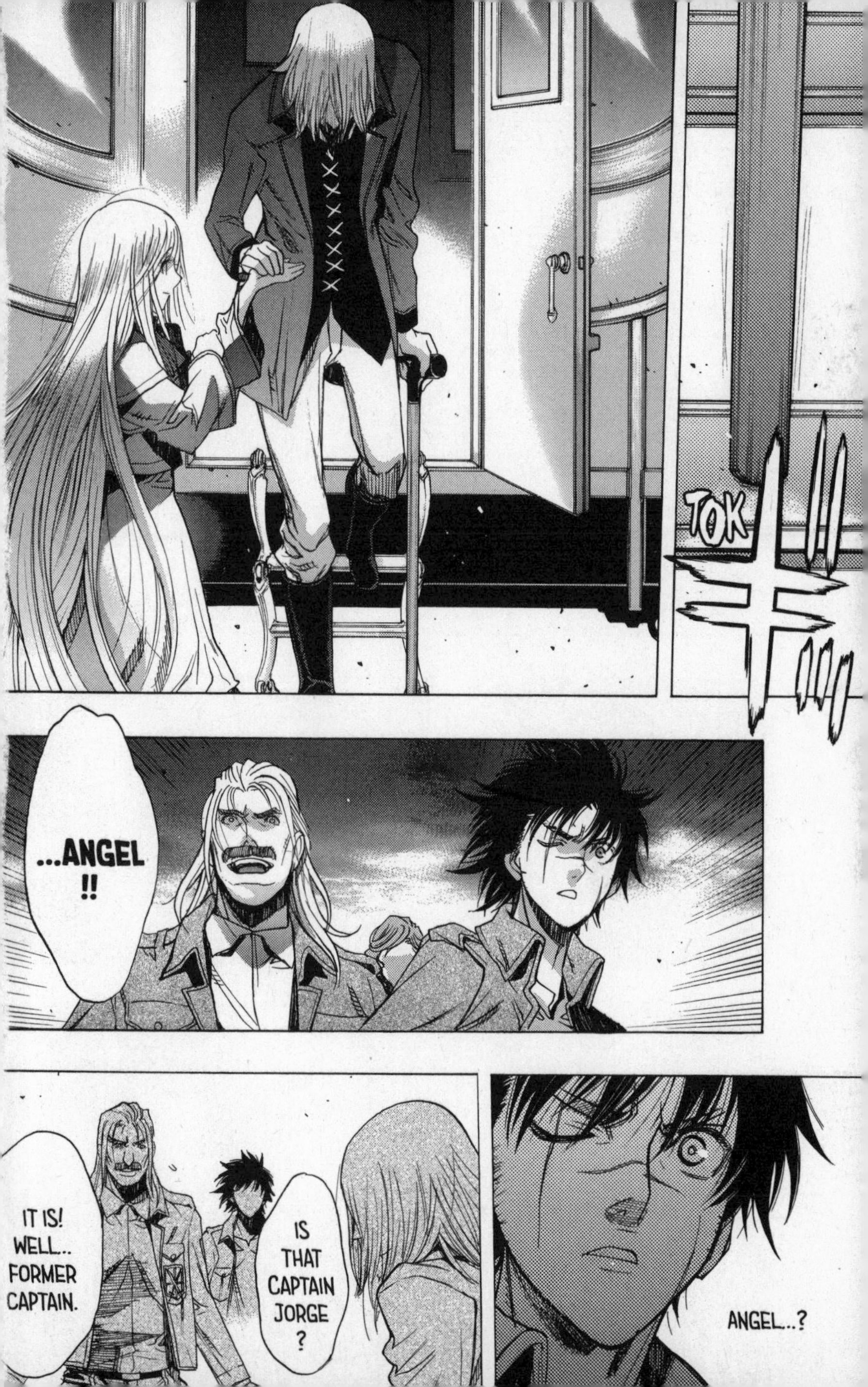
TOK
...ANGEL !!
ANGEL..?
IS THAT CAPTAIN JORGE ?
IT IS! WELL... FORMER CAPTAIN.

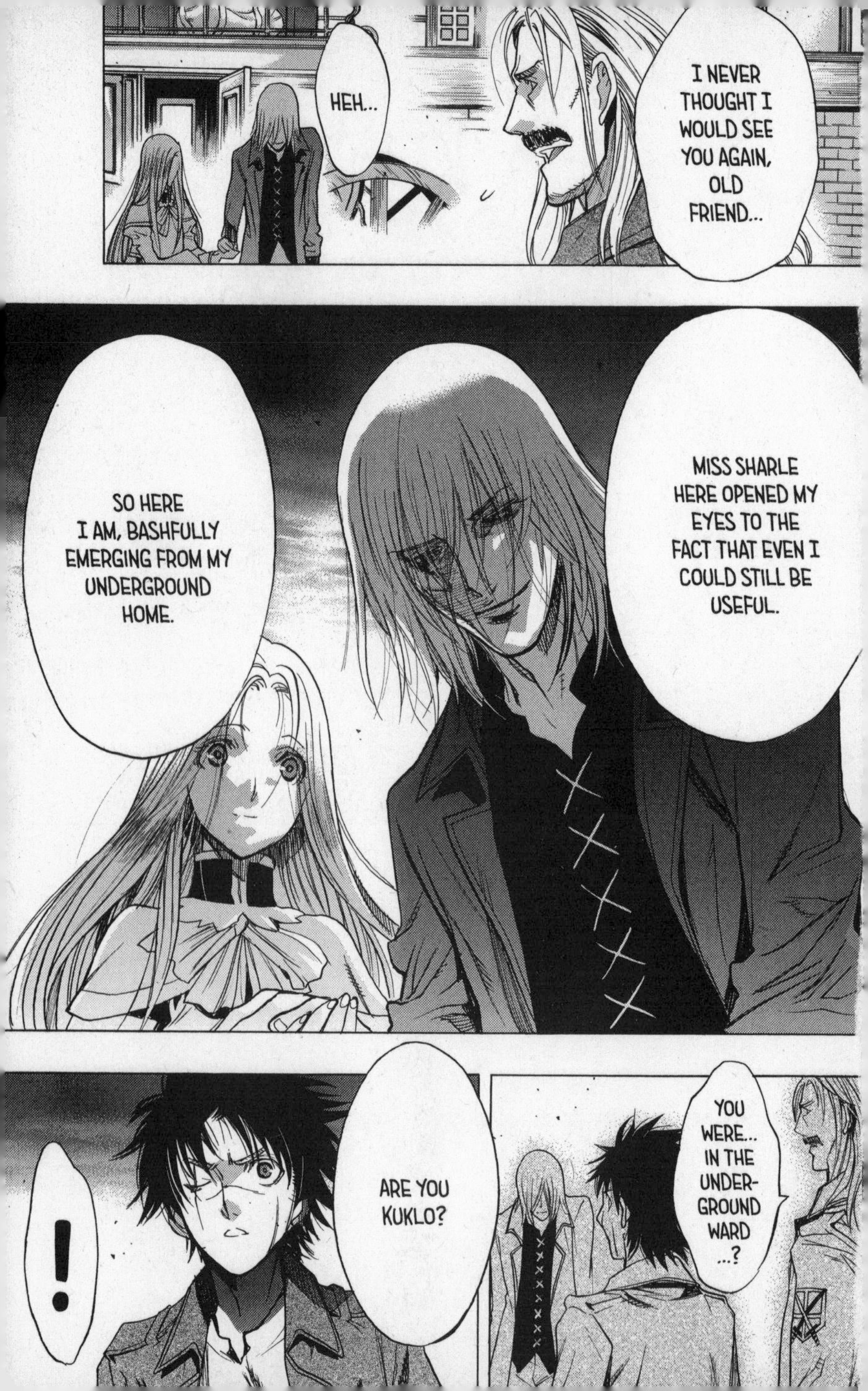
I NEVER THOUGHT I WOULD SEE YOU AGAIN, OLD FRIEND...
HEH...
MISS SHARLE HERE OPENED MY EYES TO THE FACT THAT EVEN I COULD STILL BE USEFUL.
SO HERE I AM, BASHFULLY EMERGING FROM MY UNDERGROUND HOME.
YOU WERE... IN THE UNDER-GROUND WARD ...?
ARE YOU KUKLO?
!

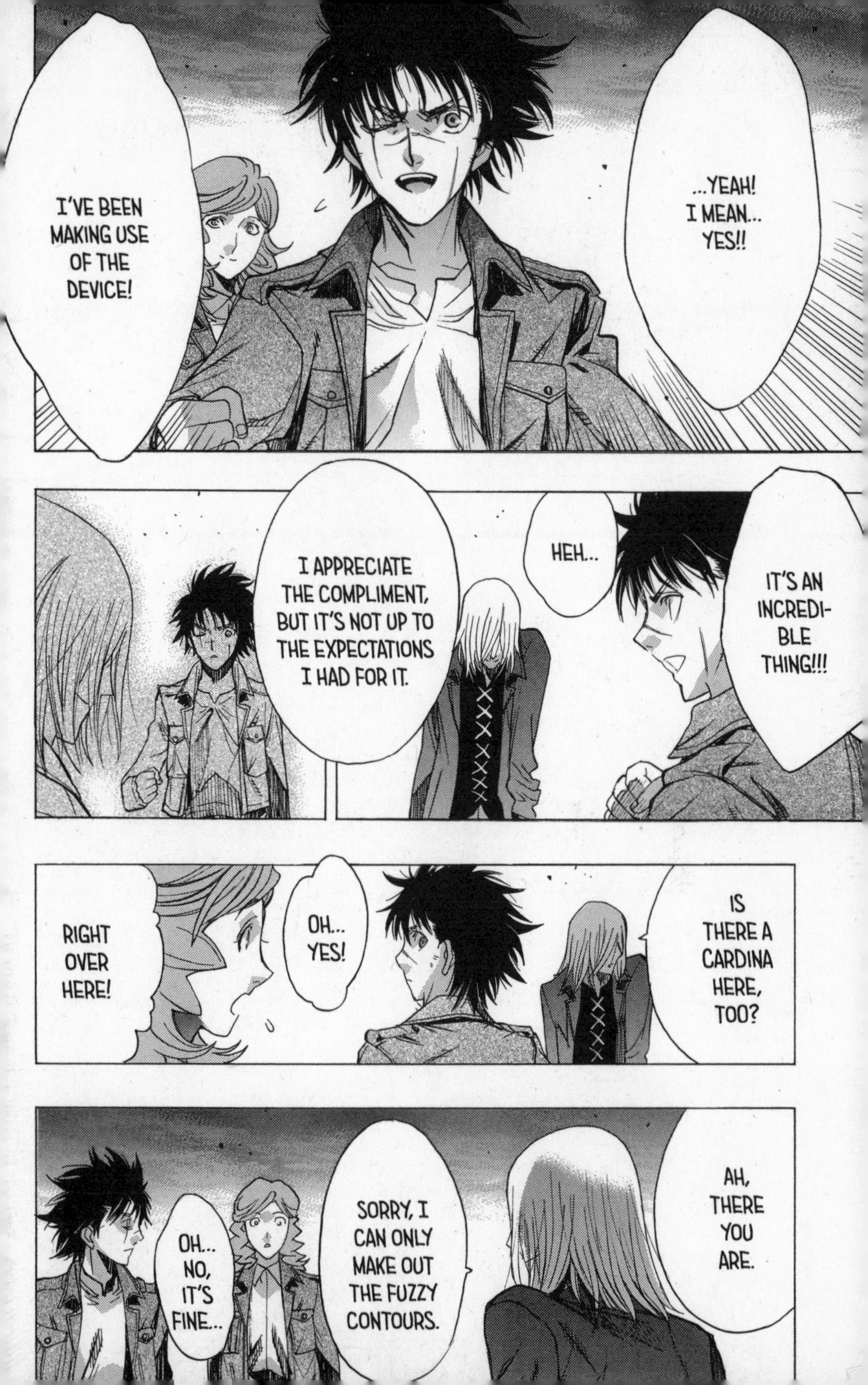
...YEAH! I MEAN... YES!!
I'VE BEEN MAKING USE OF THE DEVICE!
IT'S AN INCREDIBLE THING!!!
HEH...
I APPRECIATE THE COMPLIMENT, BUT IT'S NOT UP TO THE EXPECTATIONS I HAD FOR IT.
IS THERE A CARDINA HERE, TOO?
OH... YES!
RIGHT OVER HERE!
AH, THERE YOU ARE.
SORRY, I CAN ONLY MAKE OUT THE FUZZY CONTOURS.
OH... NO, IT'S FINE...

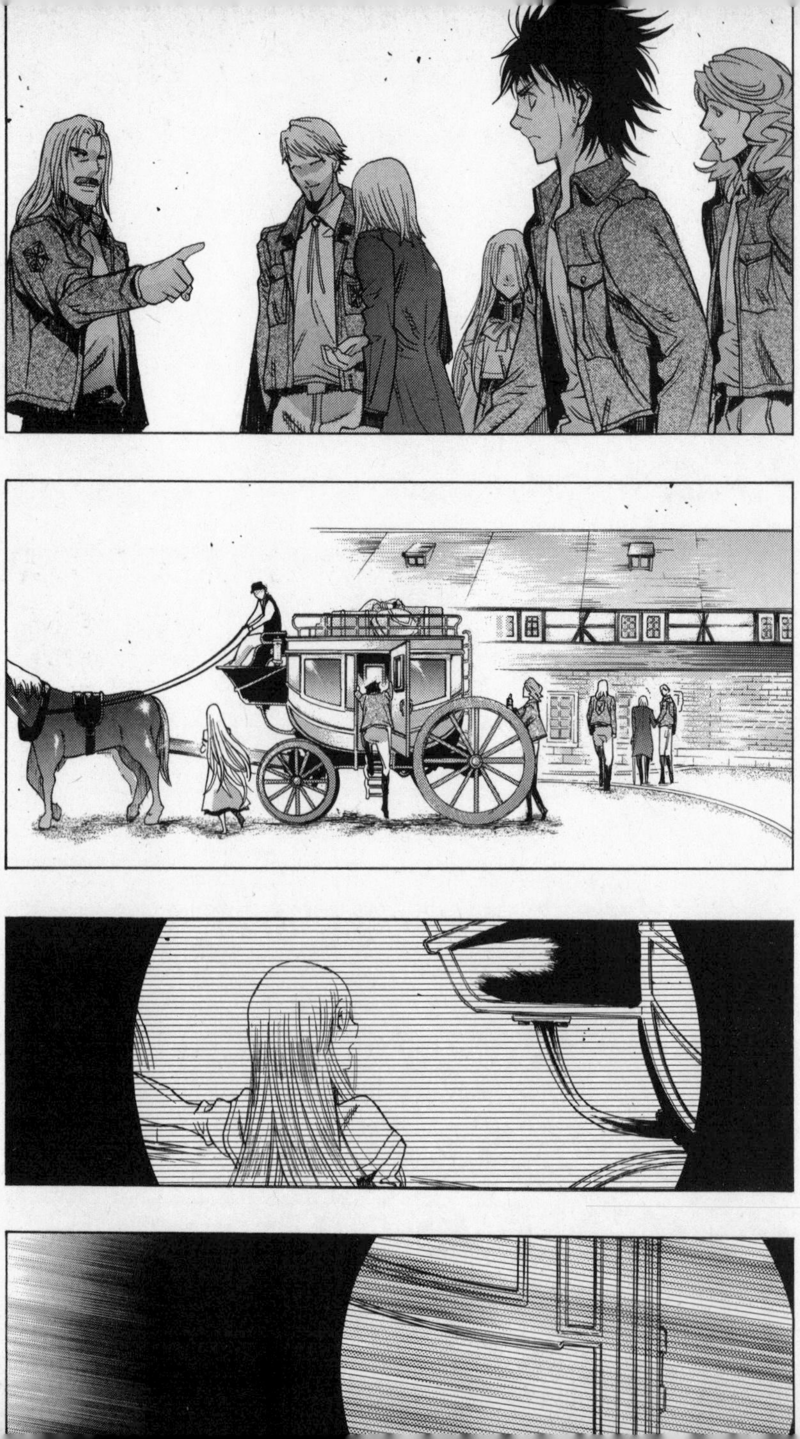

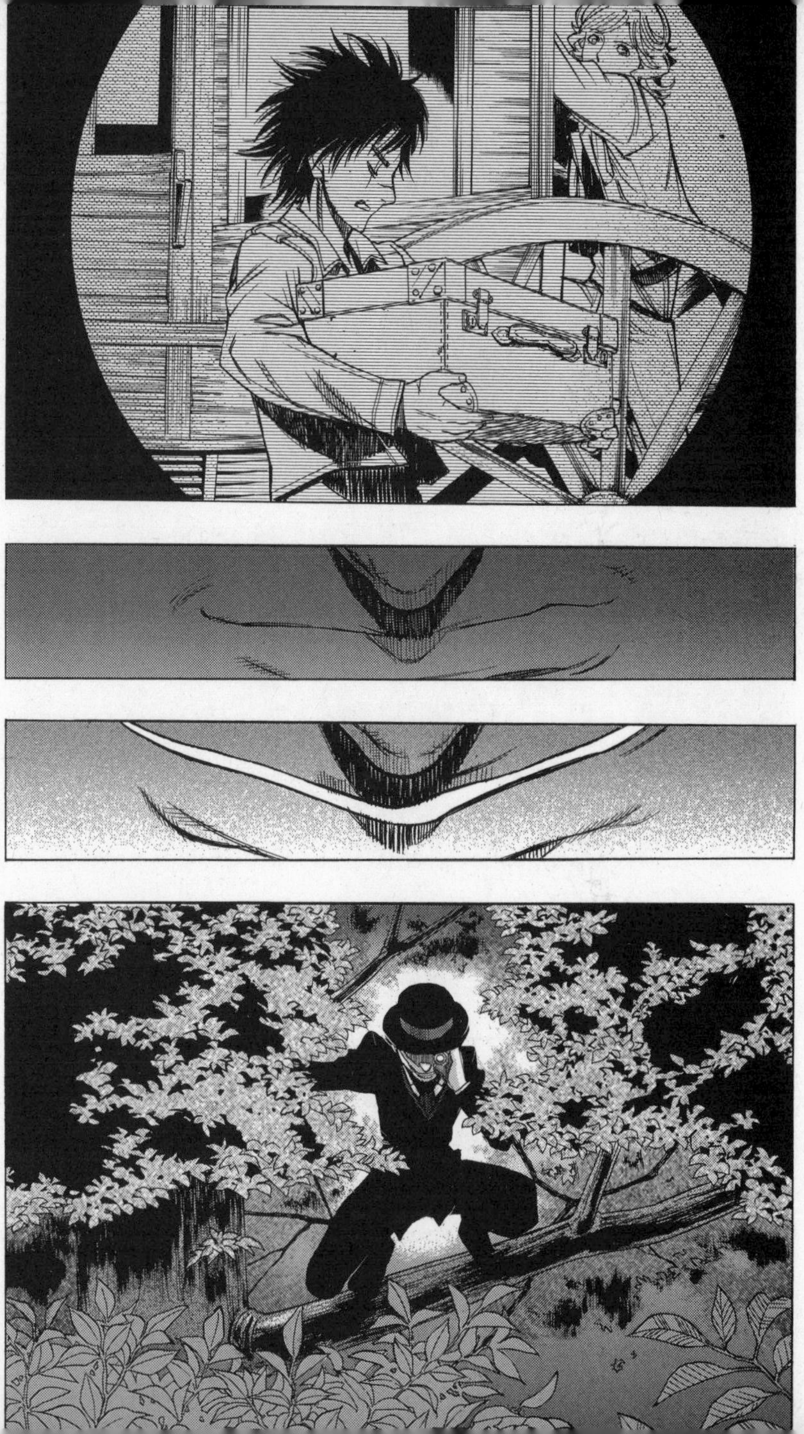

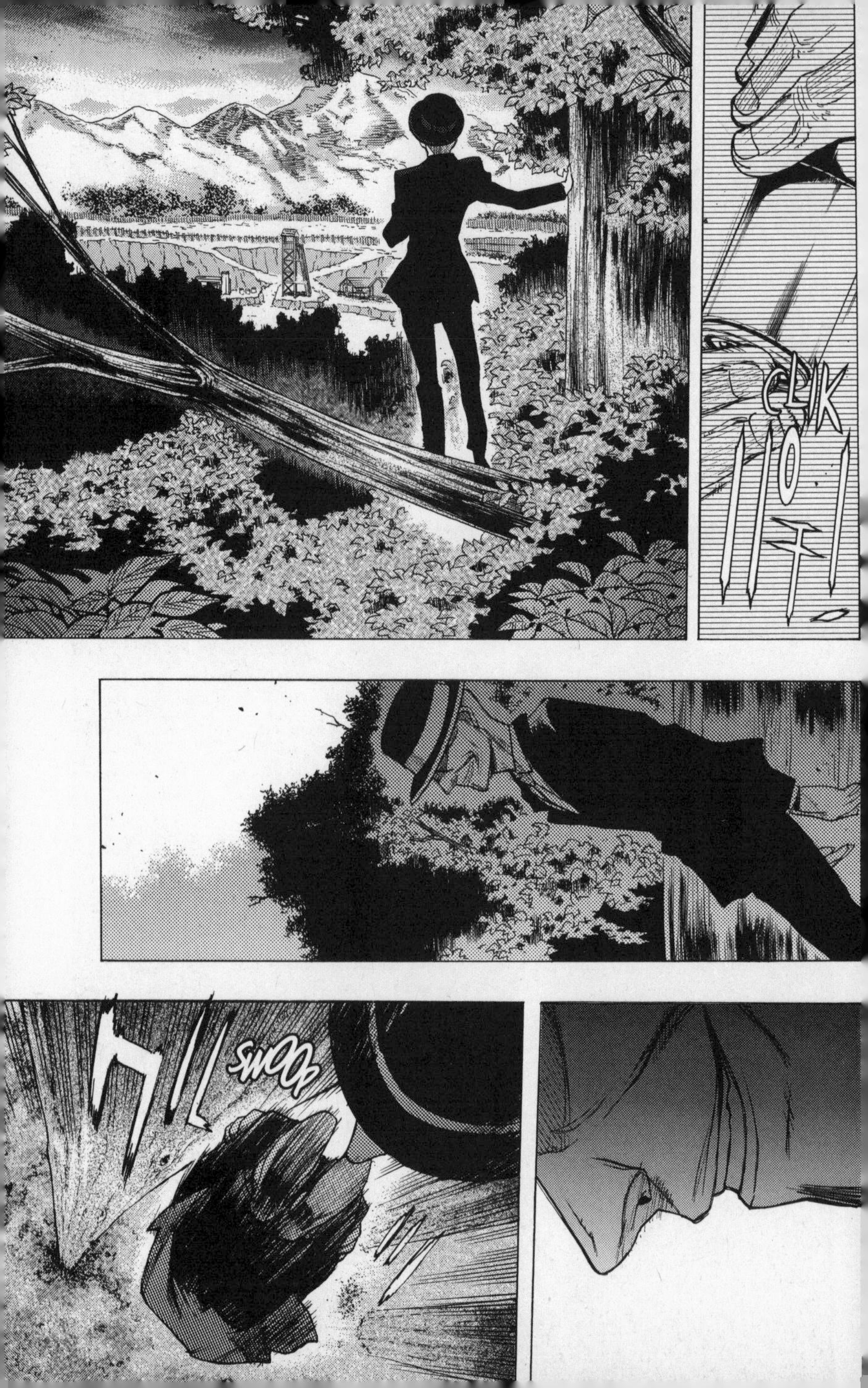
CLIK
SWOOP

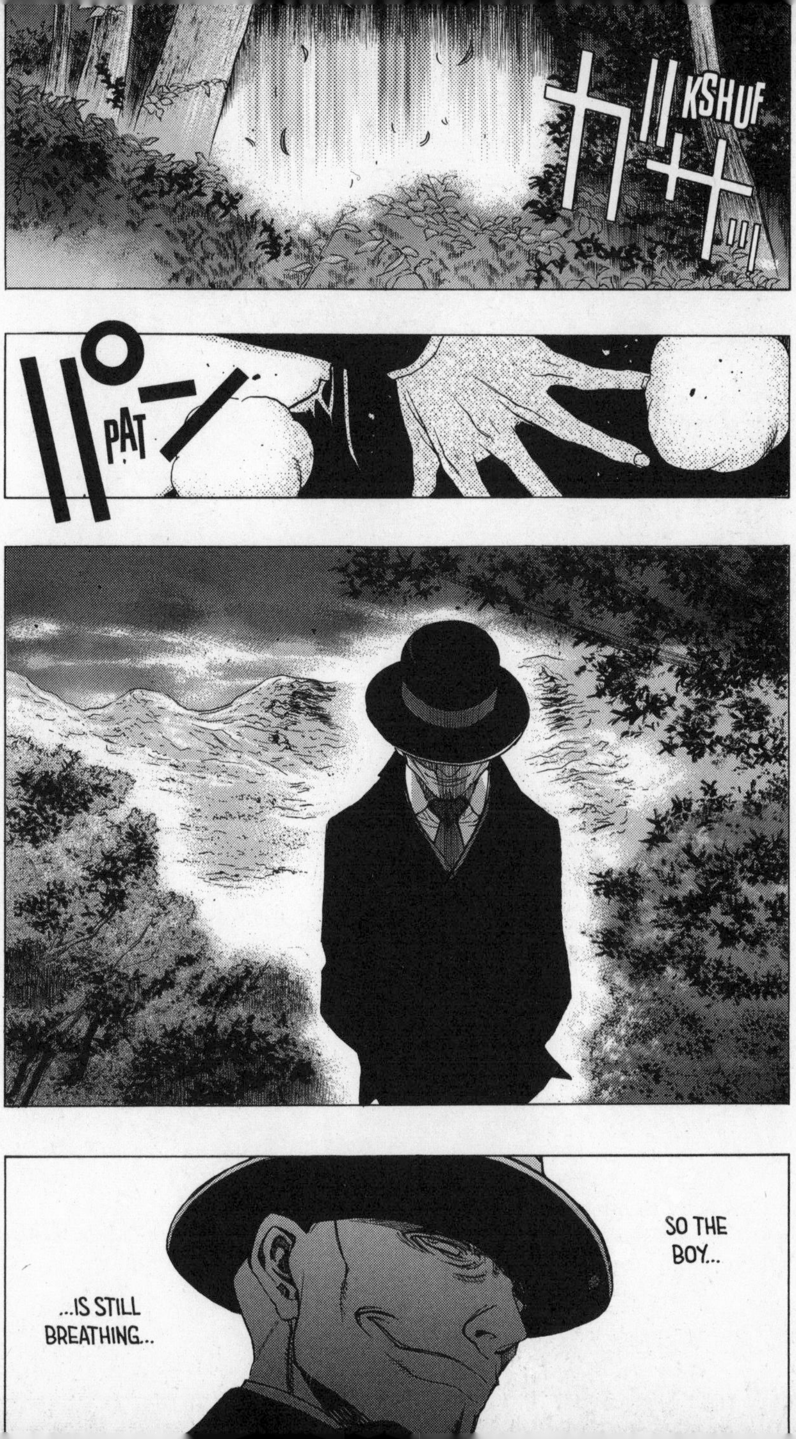
KSHUF
PAT
SO THE BOY...
...IS STILL BREATHING...

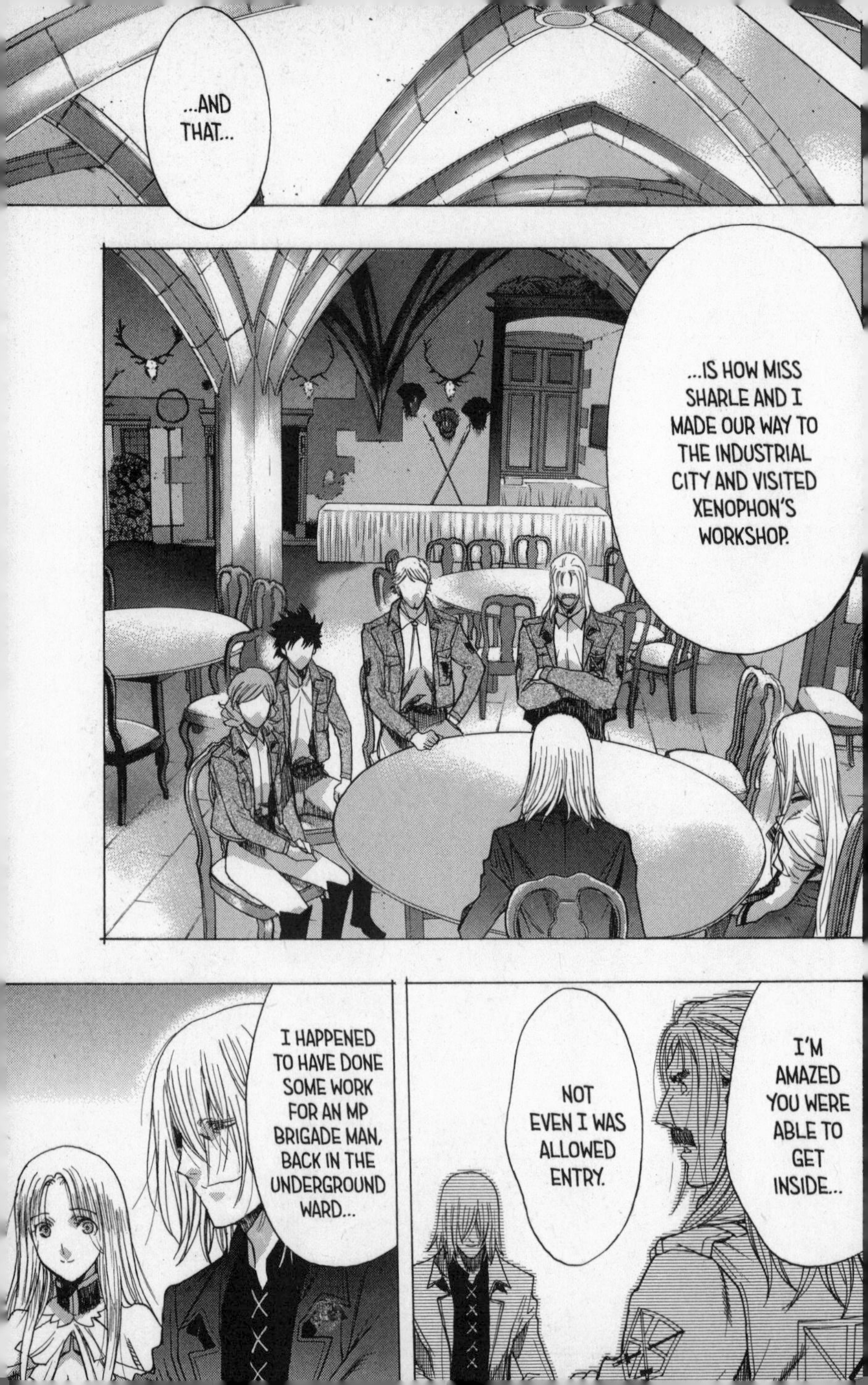
...AND THAT...
...IS HOW MISS SHARLE AND I MADE OUR WAY TO THE INDUSTRIAL CITY AND VISITED XENOPHON'S WORKSHOP.
I'M AMAZED YOU WERE ABLE TO GET INSIDE...
NOT EVEN I WAS ALLOWED ENTRY.
I HAPPENED TO HAVE DONE SOME WORK FOR AN MP BRIGADE MAN, BACK IN THE UNDERGROUND WARD...

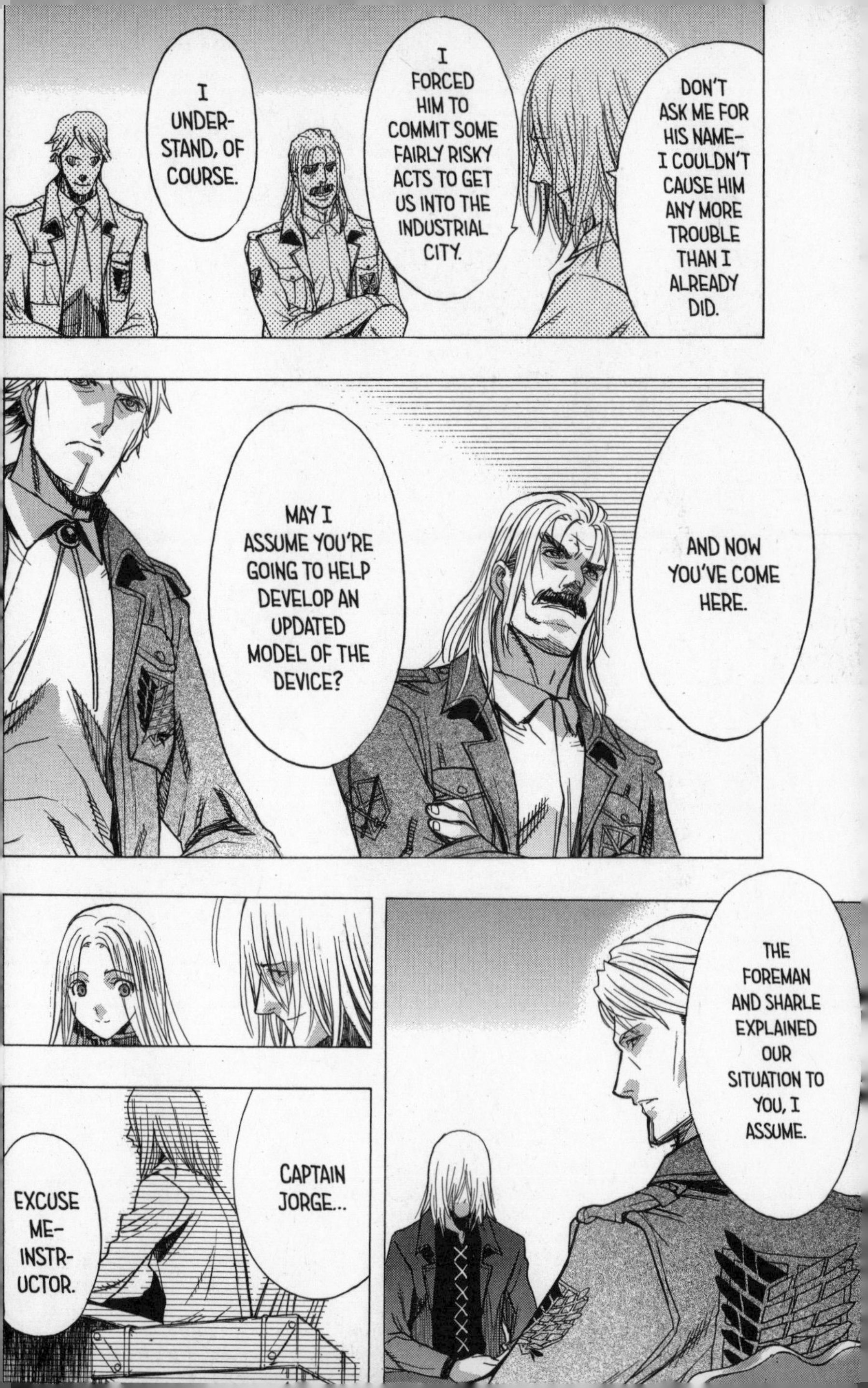
DON'T ASK ME FOR HIS NAME— I COULDN'T CAUSE HIM ANY MORE TROUBLE THAN I ALREADY DID.
I FORCED HIM TO COMMIT SOME FAIRLY RISKY ACTS TO GET US INTO THE INDUSTRIAL CITY.
I UNDER-STAND, OF COURSE.
AND NOW YOU'VE COME HERE.
MAY I ASSUME YOU'RE GOING TO HELP DEVELOP AN UPDATED MODEL OF THE DEVICE?
THE FOREMAN AND SHARLE EXPLAINED OUR SITUATION TO YOU, I ASSUME.
CAPTAIN JORGE...
EXCUSE ME— INSTR-UCTOR.

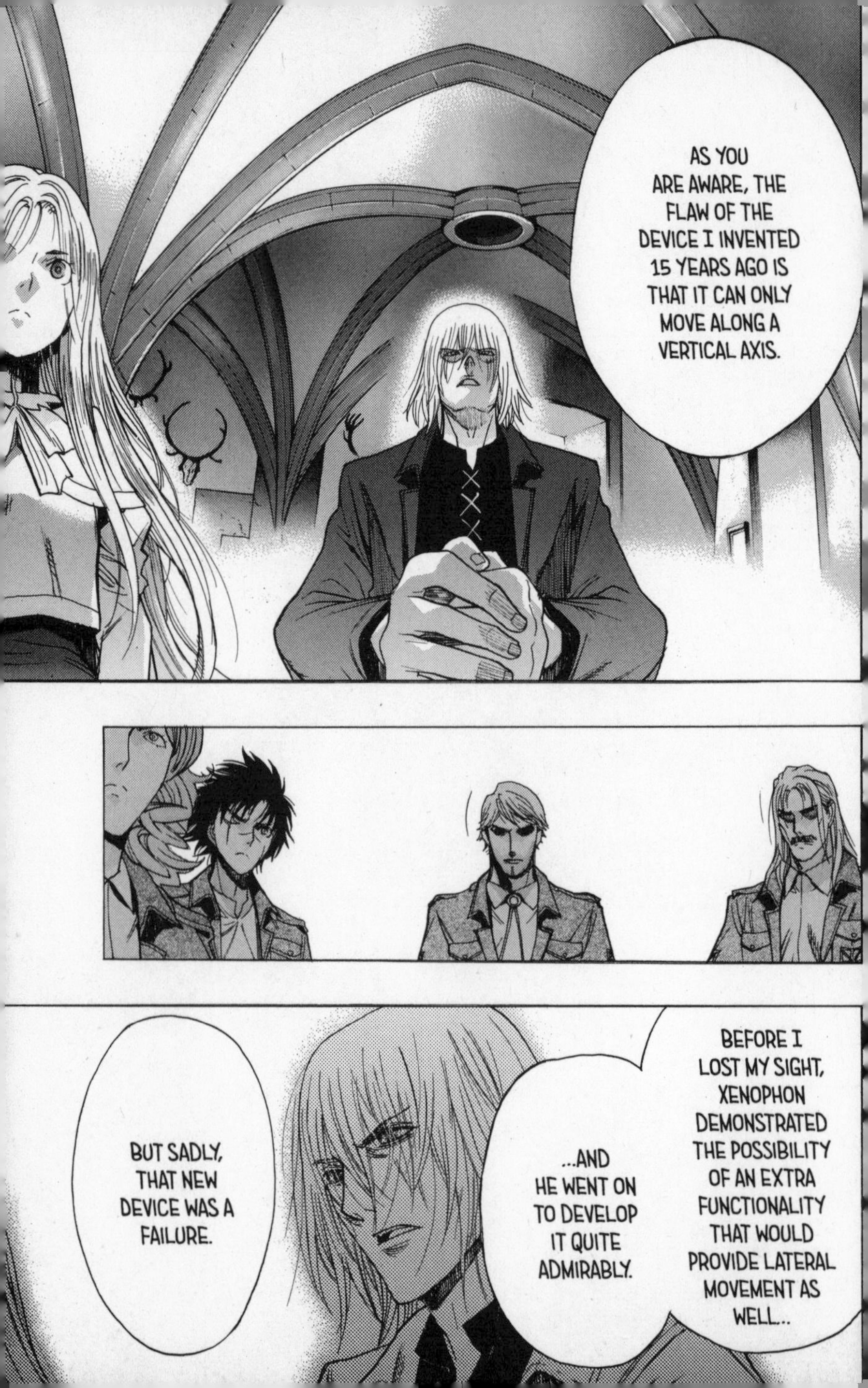
AS YOU ARE AWARE, THE FLAW OF THE DEVICE I INVENTED 15 YEARS AGO IS THAT IT CAN ONLY MOVE ALONG A VERTICAL AXIS.
BEFORE I LOST MY SIGHT, XENOPHON DEMONSTRATED THE POSSIBILITY OF AN EXTRA FUNCTIONALITY THAT WOULD PROVIDE LATERAL MOVEMENT AS WELL...
...AND HE WENT ON TO DEVELOP IT QUITE ADMIRABLY.
BUT SADLY, THAT NEW DEVICE WAS A FAILURE.

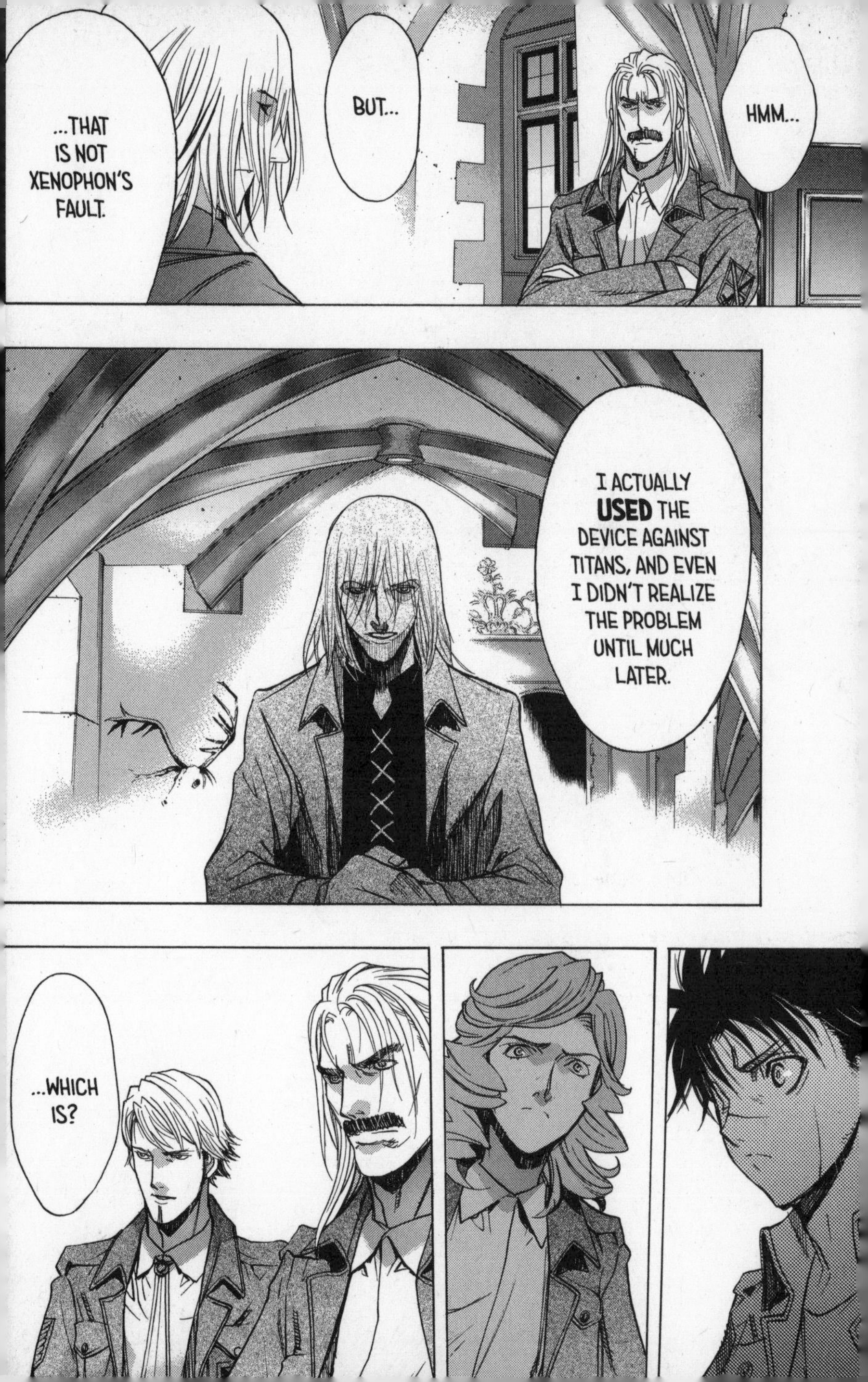
HMM...
BUT...
...THAT IS NOT XENOPHON'S FAULT.
I ACTUALLY **USED** THE DEVICE AGAINST TITANS, AND EVEN I DIDN'T REALIZE THE PROBLEM UNTIL MUCH LATER.
...WHICH IS?

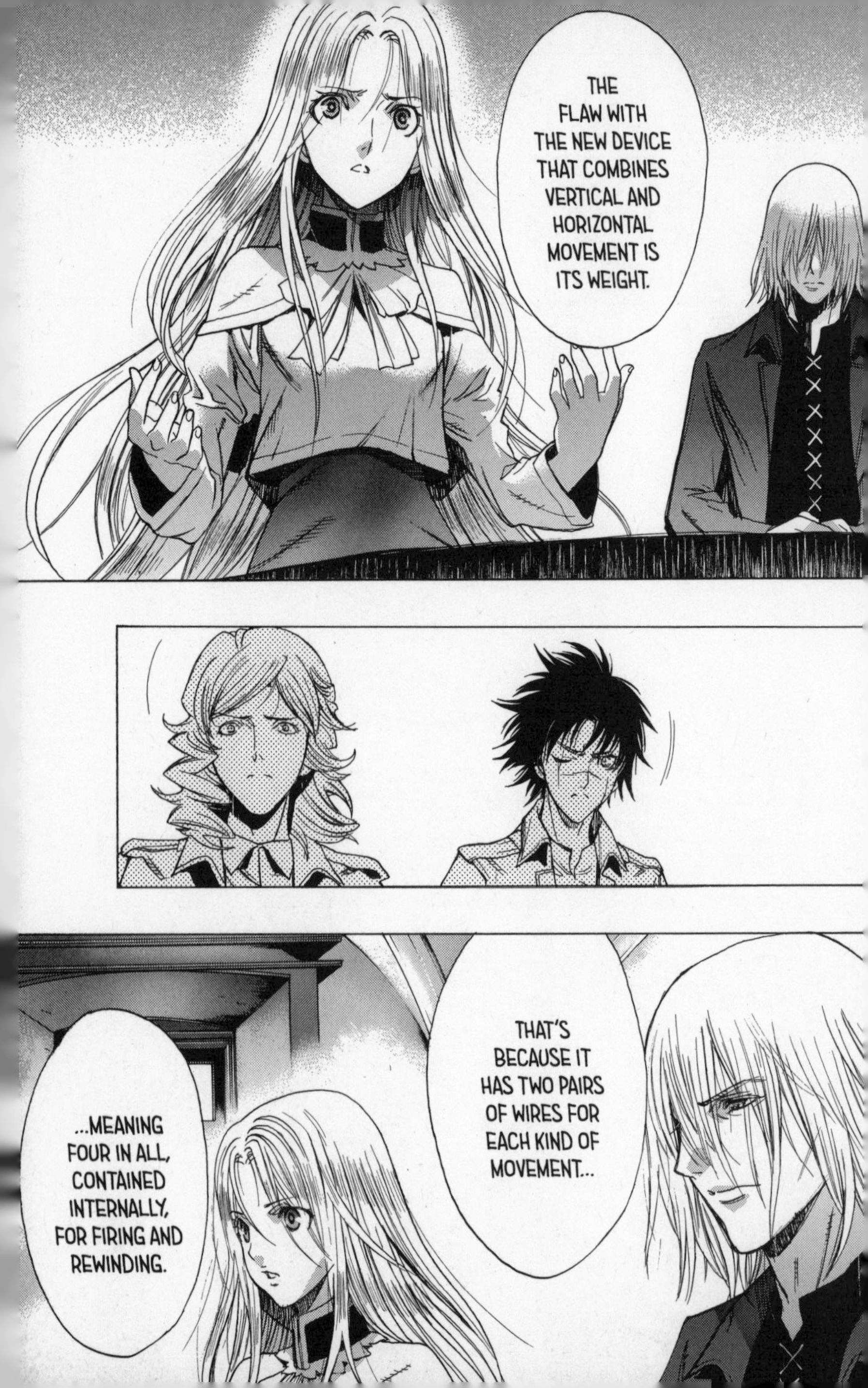
THE FLAW WITH THE NEW DEVICE THAT COMBINES VERTICAL AND HORIZONTAL MOVEMENT IS ITS WEIGHT.
THAT'S BECAUSE IT HAS TWO PAIRS OF WIRES FOR EACH KIND OF MOVEMENT...
...MEANING FOUR IN ALL, CONTAINED INTERNALLY, FOR FIRING AND REWINDING.

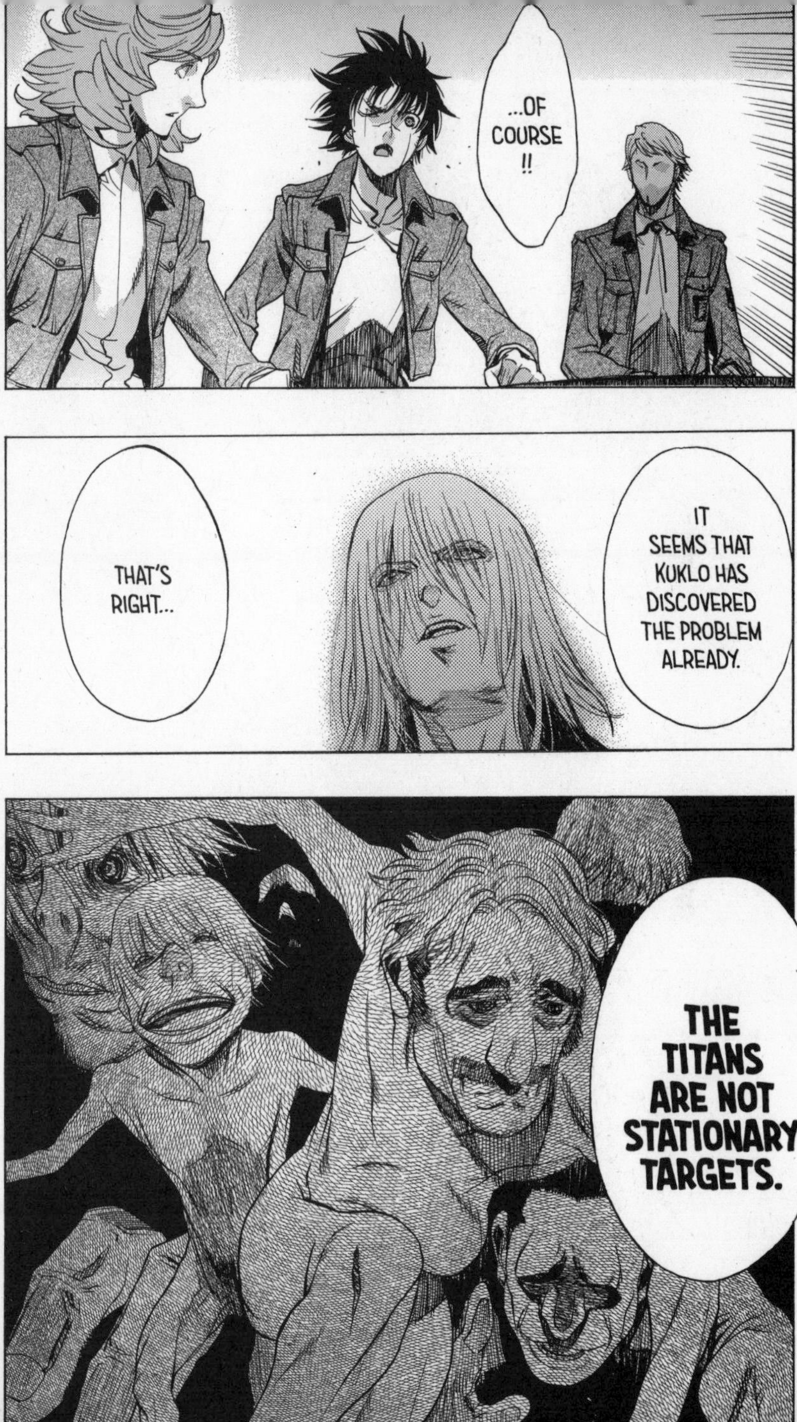
...OF COURSE !!
IT SEEMS THAT KUKLO HAS DISCOVERED THE PROBLEM ALREADY.
THAT'S RIGHT...
THE TITANS ARE NOT STATIONARY TARGETS.

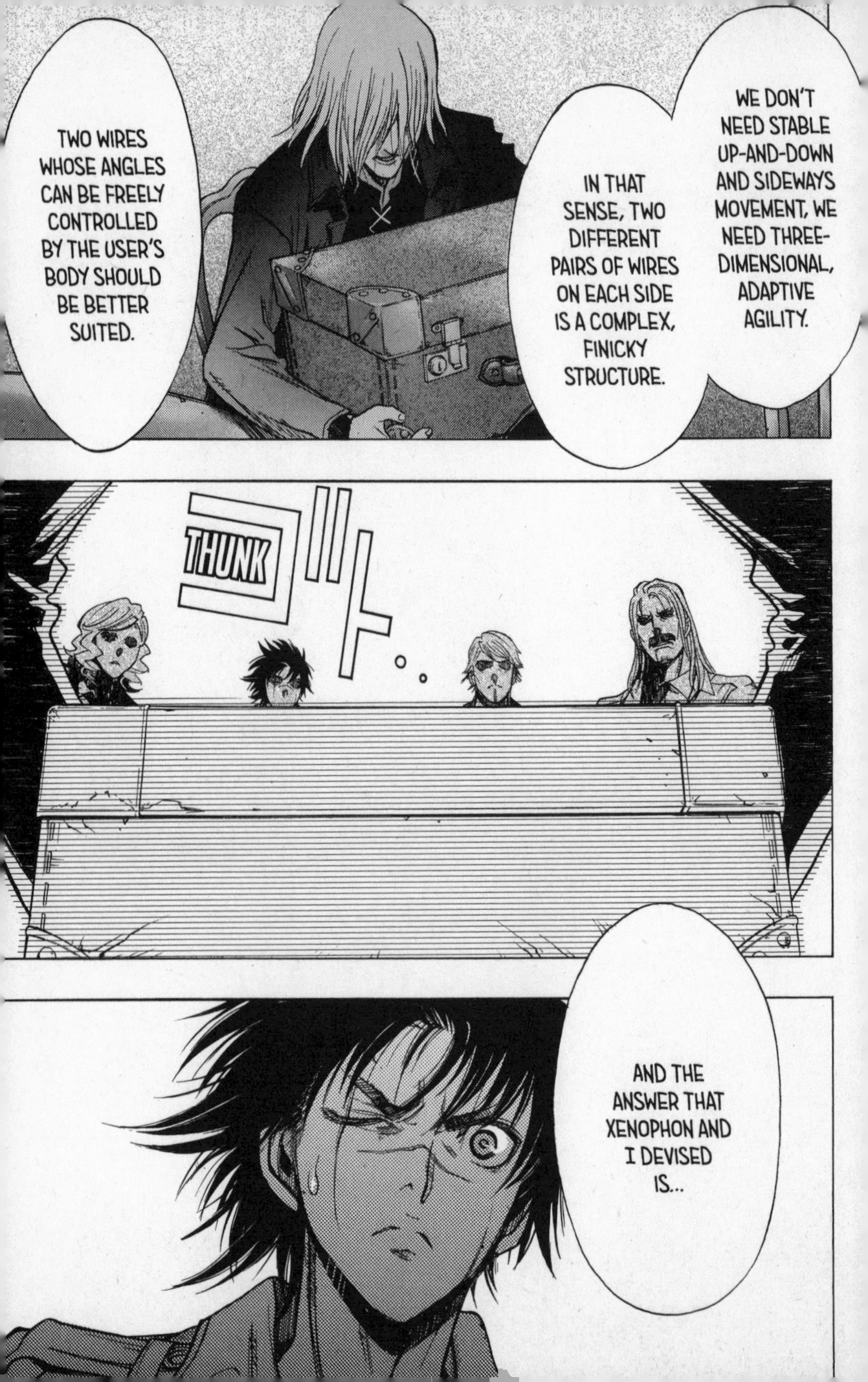
WE DON'T NEED STABLE UP-AND-DOWN AND SIDEWAYS MOVEMENT, WE NEED THREE-DIMENSIONAL, ADAPTIVE AGILITY.
IN THAT SENSE, TWO DIFFERENT PAIRS OF WIRES ON EACH SIDE IS A COMPLEX, FINICKY STRUCTURE.
TWO WIRES WHOSE ANGLES CAN BE FREELY CONTROLLED BY THE USER'S BODY SHOULD BE BETTER SUITED.
THUNK
AND THE ANSWER THAT XENOPHON AND I DEVISED IS...

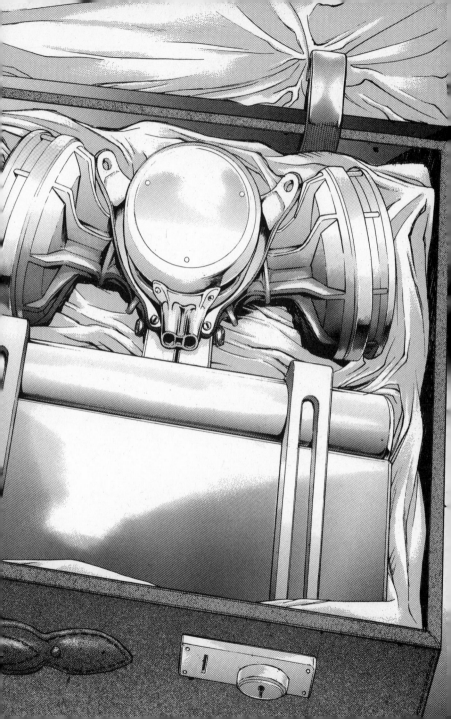

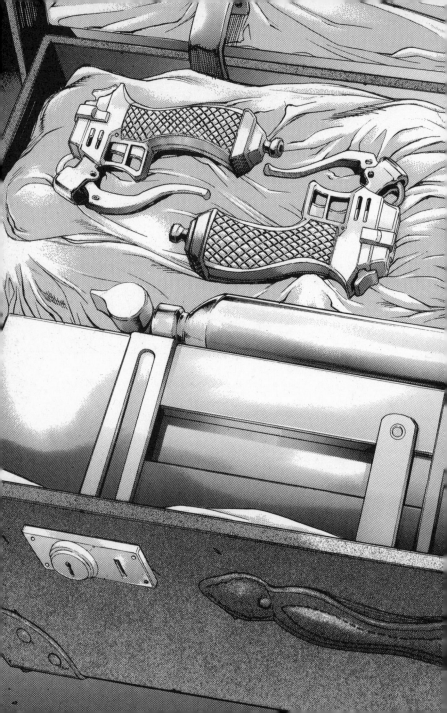

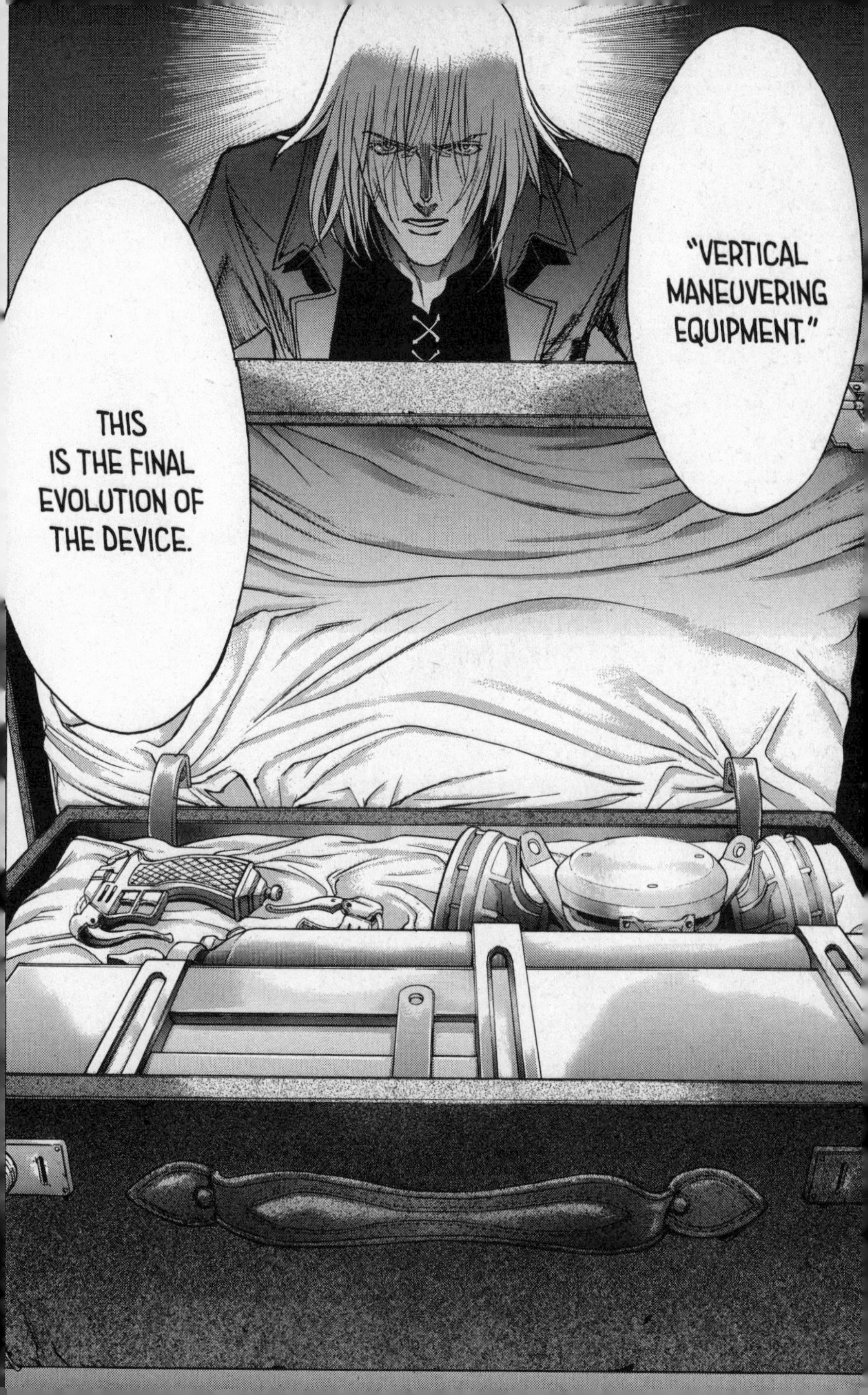
"VERTICAL MANEUVERING EQUIPMENT."
THIS IS THE FINAL EVOLUTION OF THE DEVICE.

ATTACK ON TITAN
BEFORE THE FALL

TO BE CONTINUED

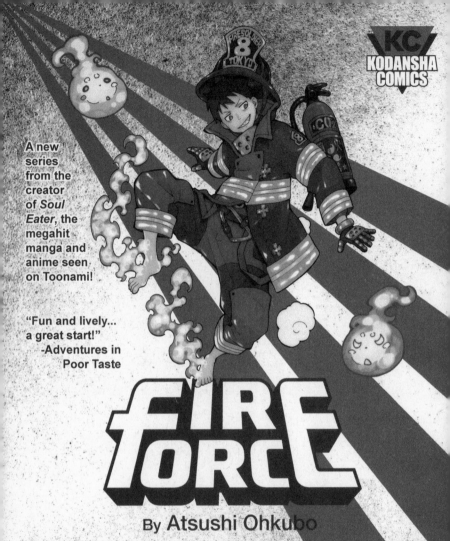

A new series from the creator of *Soul Eater*, the megahit manga and anime seen on Toonami!

"Fun and lively... a great start!"
-Adventures in Poor Taste

FIRE FORCE

By Atsushi Ohkubo

The city of Tokyo is plagued by a deadly phenomenon: spontaneous human combustion! Luckily, a special team is there to quench the inferno: The Fire Force! The fire soldiers at Special Fire Cathedral 8 are about to get a unique addition. Enter Shinra, a boy who possesses the power to run at the speed of a rocket, leaving behind the famous "devil's footprints" (and destroying his shoes in the process). Can Shinra and his colleagues discover the source of this strange epidemic before the city burns to ashes?

The Black Museum The Ghost and the Lady

By Kazuhiro Fujita

Deep in Scotland Yard in London sits an evidence room dedicated to the greatest mysteries of British history. In this "Black Museum" sits a misshapen hunk of lead—two bullets fused together—the key to a wartime encounter between Florence Nightingale, the mother of modern nursing, and a supernatural Man in Grey. This story is unknown to most scholars of history, but a special guest of the museum will tell the tale of *The Ghost and the Lady*...

Praise for Kazuhiro Fujita's *Ushio and Tora*

"A charming revival that combines a classic look with modern depth and pacing... **Essential viewing both for curmudgeons and new fans alike.**" — Anime News Network

"**GREAT!** The first episode of *Ushio and Tora* captures the essence of '90s anime." — IGN

HAPPINESS

——ハピネス——

By Shuzo Oshimi

From the creator of *The Flowers of Evil*

Nothing interesting is happening in Makoto Ozaki's first year of high school. HIs life is a series of quiet humiliations: low-grade bullies, unreliable friends, and the constant frustration of his adolescent lust. But one night, a pale, thin girl knocks him to the ground in an alley and offers him a choice.

Now everything is different. Daylight is searingly bright. Food tastes awful. And worse than anything is the terrible, consuming thirst...

Praise for Shuzo Oshimi's *The Flowers of Evil*

"A shockingly readable story that vividly—one might even say queasily—evokes the fear and confusion of discovering one's own sexuality. Recommended." —The Manga Critic

"A page-turning tale of sordid middle school blackmail." —Otaku USA Magazine

"A stunning new horror manga." —Third Eye Comics

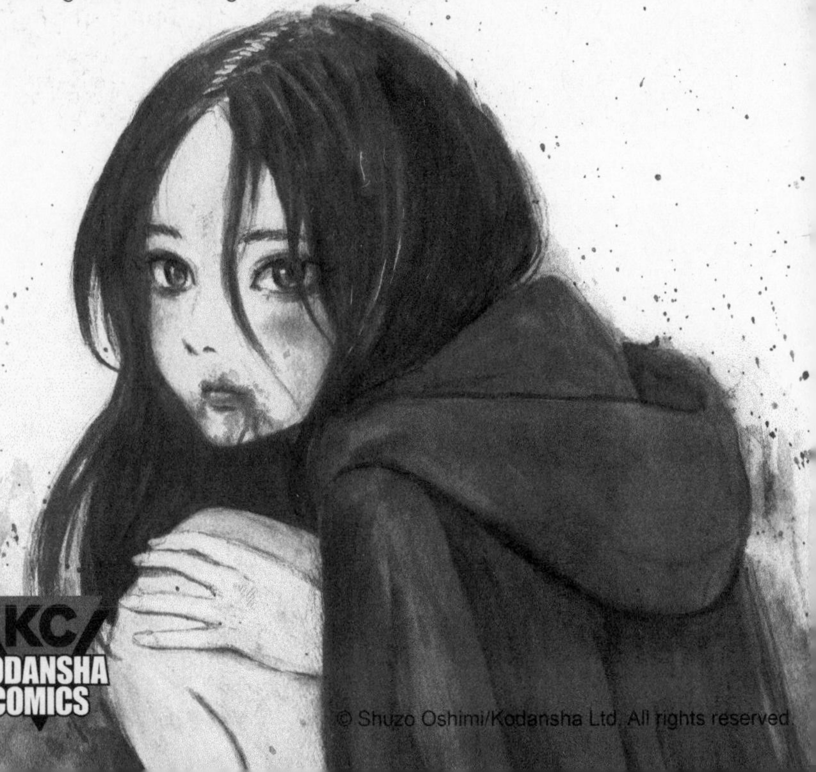

KC KODANSHA COMICS

KC KODANSHA COMICS

"I'm pleasantly surprised to find modern shojo using cross-dressing as a dramatic device to deliver social commentary... Recommended."

-Otaku USA Magazine

The prince in his dark days

By Hico Yamanaka

A drunkard for a father, a household of poverty... For 17-year-old Atsuko, misfortune is all she knows and believes in. Until one day, a chance encounter with Itaru-the wealthy heir of a huge corporation-changes everything. The two look identical, uncannily so. When Itaru curiously goes missing, Atsuko is roped into being his stand-in. There, in his shoes, Atsuko must parade like a prince in a palace. She encounters many new experiences, but at what cost...?

KC
KODANSHA
COMICS

Japan's most powerful spirit medium delves into the ghost world's greatest mysteries!

Story by Kyo Shirodaira, famed author of mystery fiction and creator of *Spiral*, *Blast of Tempest*, and *The Record of a Fallen Vampire*.

Both touched by spirits called yôkai, Kotoko and Kurô have gained unique superhuman powers. But to gain her powers Kotoko has given up an eye and a leg, and Kurô's personal life is in shambles. So when Kotoko suggests they team up to deal with renegades from the spirit world, Kurô doesn't have many other choices, but Kotoko might just have a few ulterior motives...

IN/SPECTRE

STORY BY KYO SHIRODAIRA
ART BY CHASHIBA KATASE

KC
KODANSHA
COMICS

New action series from Hiroyuki Takei, creator of the classic shonen franchise Shaman King!

In medieval Japan, a bell hanging on the collar is a sign that a cat has a master. Norachiyo's bell hangs from his katana sheath, but he is nonetheless a stray — a ronin. This one-eyed cat samurai travels across a dishonest world, cutting through pretense and deception with his blade.

STRAY CAT SAMURAI

By
Hiroyuki Takei

Based on the critically acclaimed classic horror manga

The first new *Parasyte* manga in over 20 years!

NEO PARASYTE f

BY ASUMIKO NAKAMURA, EMA TOYAMA, MIKI RINNO, LALAKO KOJIMA, KAORI YUKI, BANKO KUZE, YUUKI OBATA, KASHIO, YUI KUROE, ASIA WATANABE, MIKIMAKI, HIKARU SURUGA, HAJIME SHINJO, RENJURO KINDAICHI, AND YURI NARUSHIMA

A collection of chilling new *Parasyte* stories from Japan's top shojo artists!

Parasites: shape-shifting aliens whose only purpose is to assimilate with and consume the human race... but do these monsters have a different side? A parasite becomes a prince to save his romance-obsessed female host from a dangerous stalker. Another hosts a cooking show, in which the real monsters are revealed. These and 13 more stories, from some of the greatest shojo manga artists alive today, together make up a chilling, funny, and entertaining tribute to one of manga's horror classics!

"An emotional and artistic tour de force! We see incredible triumph, and crushing defeat... each panel [is] a thrill!"
—Anitay

"A journey that's instantly compelling."
—Anime News Network

WELCOME TO THE BALLROOM

By Tomo Takeuchi

Feckless high school student Tatara Fujita wants to be good at something—anything. Unfortunately, he's about as average as a slouchy teen can be. The local bullies know this, and make it a habit to hit him up for cash, but all that changes when the debonair Kaname Sengoku sends them packing. Sengoku's not the neighborhood watch, though. He's a professional ballroom dancer. And once Tatara Fujita gets pulled into the world of ballroom, his life will never be the same.

KC KODANSHA COMICS

The award-winning manga about what happens inside you!

"Far more entertaining than it ought to be... what kid doesn't want to think that every time they sneeze a torpedo shoots out their nose?"
—Anime News Network

Strep throat! Hay fever! Influenza! The world is a dangerous place for a red blood cell just trying to get her deliveries finished. Fortunately, she's not alone...she's got a whole human body's worth of cells ready to help out! The mysterious white blood cells, the buff and brash killer T cells, even the cute little platelets— everyone's got to come together if they want to keep you healthy!

Cells at Work!
はたらく細胞

By Akane Shimizu

Having lost his wife, high school teacher Kōhei Inuzuka is doing his best to raise his young daughter Tsumugi as a single father. He's pretty bad at cooking and doesn't have a huge appetite to begin with, but chance brings his little family together with one of his students, the lonely Kotori. The three of them are anything but comfortable in the kitchen, but the healing power of home cooking might just work on their grieving hearts.

"This season's number-one feel-good anime!" —Anime News Network

"A beautifully-drawn story about comfort food and family and grief. Recommended." —Otaku USA Magazine

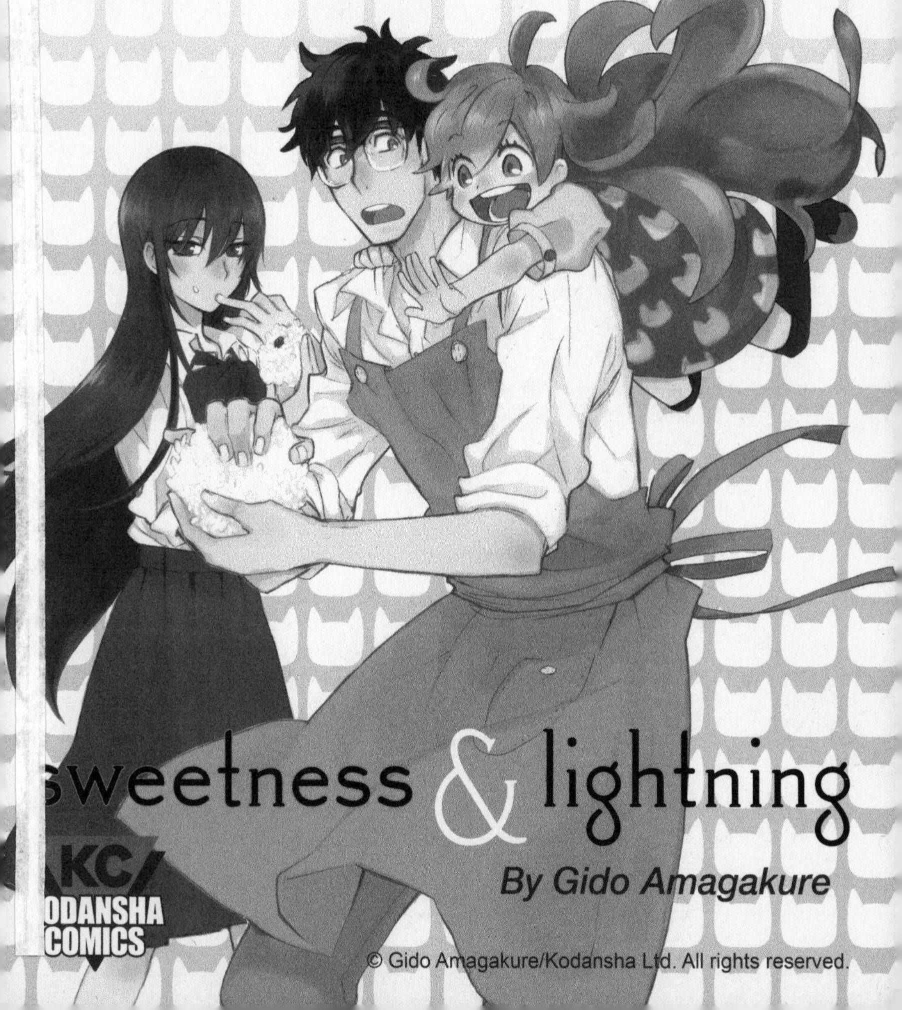
sweetness & lightning
By Gido Amagakure
KODANSHA COMICS

A Kodansha Comics Trade Paperback Original
Attack on Titan: Before the Fall volume 12 copyright © 2017 Hajime Isayama/
Ryo Suzukaze/Satoshi Shiki
English translation copyright © 2017 Hajime Isayama/Ryo Suzukaze/Satoshi Shiki

Published in the United States by Kodansha Comics, an imprint of
Kodansha USA Publishing, LLC, New York.

Publication rights for this English edition arranged through
Kodansha Ltd, Tokyo.

First published in Japan in 2017 by Kodansha Ltd., Tokyo
as *Shingeki no kyojin Before the fall*, volume 12.

ISBN 978-1-63236-383-1

Character designs by Thores Shibamoto
Original cover design by Takashi Shimoyama (Red Rooster)

Printed in the United States of America.

www.kodanshacomics.com

9 8 7 6 5 4 3 2 1
Translation: Stephen Paul
Lettering: Steve Wands
Editing: Lauren Scanlan
Kodansha Comics edition cover design by Phil Balsman

P9-BZG-546

You are going the *wrong way!*

Manga is a *completely* different type of reading experience.

To start at the *BEGINNING,*
go to the *END!*

That's right! Authentic manga is read the traditional Japanese way—from right to left, exactly the opposite of how American books are read. It's easy to follow: just go to the other end of the book, and read each page—and each panel—from the right side to the left side, starting at the top right. Now you're experiencing manga as it was meant to be.